Marian Apparitions, the Bible, and the Modern World

Marian Apparitions, the Bible, and the Modern World

Donal Anthony Foley

Jesus said to them, "Have you understood all this?" "Yes," they said. "Well then, every scribe who becomes a disciple of the kingdom of heaven is like a householder who brings out of his storeroom things both new and old." (Cf. Matt. 13:51–52)

GRACEWING

First published in 2002

Gracewing
2 Southern Avenue
Leominster
Herefordshire HR6 0QF

ISBN: 978-0-85244-313-2

Typesetting by Action Publishing Technology Ltd,
Gloucester, GL1 5SR

Contents

Acknowledgements

I would like to thank the following for their help in the preparation and production of this book: Timothy Tindal-Robertson for his advice and encouragement, and for reading and commenting on the text; Peter Grace for his proof-reading and grammatical skills; Leo Madigan for reading the text and for his helpful counsel; Martin Blake and Fergal Martin, for their work in the publication of the abridged CTS version of this book; Fr Peter Bristow, for reading the text and for his support, and John Beaumont and John Walsh for their encouragement.

I would also particularly like to thank Fr Louis Kondor, of the Postulation Center for the causes of Jacinta and Francisco Marto, in Fatima, for permission to quote extensively from Fatima in Lucia's own words, and also Fr John de Marchi, of the Consolata Fathers, also in Fatima, to similarly quote extensively from his book *Fatima from the Beginning*.

Concerning the more recent apparitions at Tre Fontane, I am grateful to Kyra Audley-Charles for her advice, and regarding L'Ile-Bouchard, to Paul Rhoads for permission to use his unpublished manuscript as the basis of my account of those apparitions.

Thanks also to Msgr. Arthur Calkins, and to Dr Sarah Boss for their help in suggesting useful books and resources, and the loan of particular books respectively. Similarly, thanks are due to the staff of the Marian Library/International Marian Research Institute at the University of Dayton, Ohio, for providing various resources, and to Professor John Saward for his advice and encouragement. And, of course, thanks to Fr Aidan Nichols for agreeing to write the foreword to this book, and to Fr Peter Fehlner for his commendation.

I would also like to thank all the persons associated with the various Marian shrines who took the trouble to reply to my letters and requests for material. In particular I am very grateful to the following for permission to use relevant images: Dr Cristino and his staff at the SESDI offices in Fatima; Brother Francis Mary Kavelage, of the Franciscan Friars of the Immaculate, for images relating to Guadalupe, Pompeii, and Tre Fontane; Pierre Bizet for his image relating to Rue du Bac; Anny de Deyn, of the International Secretariat, Banneux; and also Abbé Jacques Gilon, Rector of the Shrine at Beauraing, and the PRO MARIA organization, for the relevant permissions. Similarly, I am grateful to Père Louis de Pontbriand, Rector of the Shrine at La Salette; to Grace Mulqueen, of Knock Folk Museum in association with Knock Shrine; to Sr. Marie Hélène Olivereau, Archivist at Pontmain Shrine; and Père Pierre Afonso, of the parish church of St Gilles at L'Ile-Bouchard. Finally, thanks are also due to William Spendilow for permission to use his images of Fatima and Lourdes, and to Mike Daley for the cover image of Our Lady of Fatima. Special thanks to Roy Maddison for his photographic expertise.

It is not implied that any of the above, by virtue of their being included in this list of acknowledgements, necessarily agree with all the arguments and ideas being put forward in this book – nevertheless, I am grateful for all their help and support, as I am to all the other people who have assisted in any way in its production, including Jill Pinnock, for her editing skills, Judith Spittle for her help with the index, and the staff of Gracewing Publishers, particularly Tom Longford and Jo Ashworth. Thanks are also due to my mother and family.

I welcome comments and constructive criticism about this book and can be reached at:

info@theotokos.org.uk (www.theotokos.org.uk).

Illustrations

Foreword

Donal Foley has written a book with an extraordinary message. "Appearances" by the Blessed Virgin Mary to visionaries, often children, at what frequently became afterwards major centers of Marian cultus, are not to be considered—when creditworthy at all—theologically unimportant occurrences somewhere on the margins of Christian spirituality. The context for interpreting them aright is far different. For the Fathers of the Church—and many contemporary biblical scholars for that matter—the New Testament writers treated the symbolism of the Old Testament as "fulfilled" in the incarnation of the Word through Mary, the climax to which Jewish history was pointing. So likewise the Marian appearances of the early modern and modern periods constitute a divinely-originated exploitation of that same symbolism—but this time with a view to purifying and re-energizing the post-apostolic Church as founded on Jesus Christ.

Rather in the spirit of the early writings of the French lay philosopher and theologian Jacques Maritain, Foley sees the main lines of the history of Western culture since the sixteenth century as a progressive demolition of Christendom. Painting in broad strokes, like Henri Daniel-Rops and Christopher Dawson on whose work he draws, the student of overall historical trends will not satisfy the *historiens de métier*—and yet we *do* need some general picture of where, in 2002, we stand in human time. To correlate the general history of the modern West with a handful of visionary experiences will strike many as bizarre (especially when it be added that those experiences were chiefly enjoyed by simple nuns, semi-illiterates or those barely out of infancy). And yet the narratives and symbolic patterns of the Abrahamic, Mosaic, and Davidic dispensations were for Old Testament prophecy and apocalyptic a privileged key in the interpretation of world events. To the mind of the patristic Church that key was now supplied by Jesus Christ who in his Flesh-taking from Mary had brought the scattered pieces of the Old Testament mosaic into one. Perhaps the poor and simple, with their lack of excessive intellectual and material baggage, can see that more clearly.

When faced with approaches to the Marian apparitions of recent centuries, the choice of the present-day Catholic is likely to be an invidious one between skeptics and maximizers. The skeptics pooh-pooh the material as incredible. They forget that if there is a reality of grace—that is, of divine-human communication, then some commerce between humankind and the Word of God who became and remains human like them *only through Mary* can hardly be called implausible. By contrast, the *legenda* of the appearances (I use the word in the sense of a story told, not that of historical untruth) so fascinate the maximizers that their Christian imaginations can be all too easily hooked—and so rigidified—by them.

Donal Foley's study, by taking with full seriousness the possibility of—spectacular as well as humble—interventions of grace in the Church's life avoids the first pitfall. And by re-rooting these stories and their native imagery in biblical revelation as magisterially construed by the Fathers and the Liturgies of East and West, it also removes from them that theologically dislocated quality which afflicts them in much devotional writing. We see them related once again to the great biblical narrative of which they are (if we may accept his account) the derivative continuation.

I hope this book will make some readers look at the Marian appearance accounts with more sympathy and others reject "apparitionism"—the attempt to build a spirituality on such foundations alone. There is only one Gospel, the Gospel of Jesus Christ, to which all the Scriptures bear witness. But if Mary is the most eminent member of the Church that carries the Gospel, how can she lack all role in evangelism, the bearing of the Gospel to others? Christian history suggests how in charged and dramatic ways, albeit with the intimacy that belongs to personal witness, she continues to take the Word to other people, as once, on the hills of Palestine, she carried it to Elizabeth.

Aidan Nichols, OP

Preface

A few points need to be made to help the reader better to understand and appreciate this book.

- After looking at the apparitions of Our Lady of Guadalupe in Mexico, and how they relate to the Reformation period, there is a series of chapters detailing the historical consequences of the Reformation. These are not so much "Kings and Queens" history, though, but rather look at general historical trends, and are necessary if the reader is to understand the rationale for the major Marian apparitions of the nineteenth and twentieth centuries.
- Despite appearances, this book is not anti-Protestant. It is true that criticisms are made of historical Protestantism, and particularly of Luther, Calvin, and their immediate followers, but these criticisms do not apply to modern Protestants. No one can be held responsible for the actions of their spiritual forebears, actions which took place five centuries ago.
- It assumes the general Catholic position on the Bible, that it has been written under the inspiration of the God the Holy Spirit, and that thus, "without error" it teaches "that truth which God, for the sake of our salvation, wished to see confided to the Sacred Scriptures."[1] The Bible is thus seen as a truthful and accurate historical record.
- For reasons of space, it is impossible to discuss the biblical background to the teaching of the Church on Mary, and her role in pre-Reformation Church history, or that historical period itself in any depth.
- Criticisms of ideas, opinions or theories put forward by particular writers should not be taken as in any way questioning their good faith in these matters.
- Reference to particular works in the endnotes does not necessarily imply agreement with any interpretation found in such works.

Introduction

This book investigates the major Marian apparitions that have occurred during the last five centuries or so, and which the Catholic Church has decided to accept as authentic. It relates them to secular happenings, exploring the idea that they parallel important revolutionary events in modern Western history, such as the Reformation, the French and Russian Revolutions, and the rise of Nazism. It is argued that the major modern apparitions of the Mother of Jesus, as approved by the Catholic Church, and particularly those at Fatima, are not random or historically inconsequential events, but actually seem to follow a preordained plan. Thus they have a crucial importance if we are to understand the events of the last five hundred years, which have so shaped the modern world: their cumulative effect has been the development of the present immoral and unjust world-wide civilization, which has been aptly described by Pope John Paul II as a "culture of death."

In answer to the threat to God's plan for mankind, represented by aspects of these successive revolutions, Mary has repeatedly appeared and asked for repentance, a turning away from sin, if the most terrible disasters are to be avoided. As the spiritual Mother of mankind, she cannot stand idly by and watch humanity destroy itself through sin and selfishness. As the Pope said in his famous 1982 homily at Fatima:

> Can the Mother who, with all the force of the love that she fosters in the Holy Spirit, desires everyone's salvation, keep silence on what undermines the very bases of their salvation? No, she cannot. And so, while the message of Our Lady of Fatima is a motherly one, it is also strong and decisive. It sounds severe. It sounds like John the Baptist speaking on the banks of the Jordan. It invites to repentance. It gives a warning. It calls to prayer. It recommends the Rosary. The message is addressed to

every human being. The love of the Savior's Mother reaches every place touched by the work of salvation. Her care extends to every individual of our time, and to all the societies, nations and peoples. Societies menaced by apostasy, threatened by moral degradation. The collapse of morality involves the collapse of societies.[2]

In addition, this book also explores some intriguing typological affinities between the Marian apparitions and incidents found in the Bible. That is, it looks at the idea that each of the recognized apparitions has a biblical *type*, a symbolic representation, in the same way that many of the incidents in the Gospel accounts of Jesus have an Old Testament type to which they correspond. An example of this is the typological identification made between Abraham's son Isaac, who carried the wood for his own sacrificial fire on his back, and Christ, who carried the cross on his back to Calvary (Gen. 22:1–19; John 19:17). These typologies mainly concern biblical types of Mary, as identified by the Church Fathers, and are found throughout the Scriptures. Hence, it is argued that the Marian apparitions do seem to follow a definite pattern, laid down, apparently, in the Old Testament, and thus it appears that they have a greater significance for both the Church and the world than has generally been acknowledged. However, having said that, the historical and typological arguments put forward here are really secondary in relation to church approval. The primary need is to be guided by the Church in its acceptance of the major Marian apparitions.

For a variety of reasons, which are detailed below, there was a gradual decline in Christendom, the medieval Christian civilization, which culminated in the Reformation, the first great modern revolution. The Protestant Reformation represented a fateful weakening in the ideal and unity of Christendom, and one of the most serious effects of this was the secularization of western culture, which in turn led to the Enlightenment and the French Revolution. Since that time the world has been further convulsed by communism and two world wars, and we enter the twenty-first century in a state of increasing economic progress, but moral and cultural decline.[3]

The Marian apparitions generally seem to have happened as a sort of prelude (or response) to one of these particular revolutionary episodes. The first example of this is the series of apparitions of Our Lady of Guadalupe, which occurred in Mexico at the height of the Reformation, in 1531. This is also the case with the apparitions at the Rue du Bac, in 1830, which coincided with the revolution in Paris that year; similarly, the apparition at La Salette in 1846 happened just before the European revolutionary outbursts of 1848, and during that generally troubled era. The apparitions at Pontmain and Knock took place during the 1870s, a distressing time for the Church, with the *Kulturkampf* in Germany, a persecution of Catholics in that country, providing a repressive model for other European states. In the same way, the events at Fatima, in 1917, with their strong warning about Russia's future errors and the general spirit of godlessness spreading through the world, occurred just before the Russian Revolution. The apparitions at Banneux and Beauraing came in 1932–33, at the crucial time when neighboring Germany was turning towards Nazism. The apparitions at Tre Fontane, in Italy, and L'Ile Bouchard, in France, both in 1947, although not officially approved by the Church, do seem to be authentic, and were apparently in response to the threat from communism which both of these countries faced in the late 1940s. Even though there were no particular revolutionary events associated with Lourdes in 1858, it also appears to follow this pattern, in that the publication of Charles Darwin's *Origin of Species* in 1859, with its promotion of materialistic evolution, represents the real beginning of the modern atheistic intellectual revolution.

The above major apparitions, which are generally recognized as the most important of Mary's appearances during the modern era, have all enjoyed various degrees of church recognition. In most cases this has included episcopal sanction, liturgical grants, the building of a basilica and papal approval, as well as continuing large-scale pilgrimages.[4]

Thus while the Marian apparitions have their own innate spiritual importance, we can also see them as responses to particular revolutionary events and not just as disconnected incidents. It would be wrong, however, to pretend that the apparitions represent the *totality* of the heavenly response to these various revolutions. Rather they seem to have acted as catalysts in the work of renewing the Church, although to have their full effect they depended upon an adequate response from the faithful. Certainly in the case of France, for example, it is hard to deny that the nineteenth-century revival in the fortunes of the French Church was intimately linked to the major Marian apparitions that took place there, and particularly at Lourdes. The same can be said of Fatima and Portugal, where after the First World War the Church enjoyed an astonishing revival, and, to a lesser extent, this is also true of Beauraing and Banneux in Belgium. Knock, too, undoubtedly strengthened the faith of ordinary Catholics in Ireland. So in this pattern we can see the apparitions initiating and encouraging movements of spiritual reform.

One of the most striking things about the history of the Church, as outlined briefly below, is the way that often the actions of one outstanding saint in a particular era seem, from a human point of view, to be responsible for setting the Church on the right path. The early Church would have been very different without the missionary endeavours of St Paul, and, after the persecutions, St Athanasius (c.296–373), was crucial in saving it from devastation at the hands of heresy. Without the influence of St Benedict's monastic rule, written during the sixth century, Europe would have been very different after the collapse of the Roman Empire, and St Bernard (c.1090–1153), was another saint whose influence for good on Christendom was vast. The Reformation might well have happened earlier, and perhaps had more serious effects, without the work of Saints Francis and Dominic in the early thirteenth century; and similarly, in the pre-Reformation period, St Vincent Ferrer's preaching undoubtedly strengthened Catholicism in a large part of Europe, helping to prevent the Reformation, when it did happen, in the sixteenth century, from overwhelming the Church. And when the Protestant revolt had taken place, the great saints of the Catholic or Counter-Reformation, and particularly St Ignatius Loyola, as well as the Jesuit order he founded, were raised up to rebuild the Church.

But, as this book indicates, it is legitimate to regard the Protestant Reformation as a turning point, and since that time the influence of Catholicism on the world has been steadily waning. It is true that there have been great saints since the sixteenth century, such as St Vincent de Paul, but their field of action seems to have become more limited, in a world increasingly hostile to the truth. It seems that we are witnessing the advent of more "hidden" saints in recent centuries, and also of a great number of unknown martyrs, particularly in the twentieth century under Communism and Nazism. In fact we really have to go back to the nineteenth century, to men such as St John Vianney, the Curé d'Ars, or St John Bosco, to see anything like the phenomenon of the "miracle-working" saints of the Middle Ages, with Padre Pio being apparently one of the very few genuine exceptions to this.

What seems to have happened is that Mary, in her apparitions, has been playing a more important and "visible" role, as the influence of the Church generally, and thus of saintly figures in particular, has lessened. This has been especially the case in places such as Lourdes, which has been aptly described as a "miracle factory," although many other apparition sites have also been favored with miracles. In the light of this, we can see Mary's apparitions as part of a broader plan in which she has come down from heaven as a genuine Mother, in order to strengthen the Church. Her Son, Jesus Christ, will one day return to earth in the glorious splendor of his Second Coming, but we do not know when that will be, and so, as this book intends to demonstrate, for the time being we are still in the Age of Mary, and particularly the Age of Fatima.

There is also, too, the factor of the great "Marian" Popes from the time of Pius IX and the dogma of the Immaculate Conception, in 1854, and also Leo XIII, the Pope of the Rosary, and Pope St Pius X at the beginning of the twentieth century. Similarly, Benedict XV and Pius XI advocated Marian devotion, as did Pius XII, the Pope of the dogma of the Assumption (1950), and the "Pope" of Fatima itself, particularly since he was consecrated bishop on the very day of the first apparition, 13 May 1917. More recently, Paul VI both visited Fatima and issued impressive Marian teaching, such as the Apostolic Exhortation, *Marialis Cultus,* and, of course, we have John Paul II, the Marian Pope *par excellence,* whose devotion to Mary is apparent in everything he does. These popes have had an incalculable influence for good on the Church over the last century and a half.

Thus Marian devotion generally, and the Marian apparitions in particular, even though they have been largely ignored by the secular world, have had a profound, though often hidden, effect on the Church, and so indirectly on society as a whole. When the teachings of the Catholic Church, after immense sufferings and struggles, were implemented in Europe in the building up of Christendom, a morally-based, if humanly imperfect, civilization was created. It was the undermining of this structure during the Reformation, and its subsequent further weakening during the Enlightenment and the French Revolution, to say nothing of the attacks of modern secularism, which have led to the present amoral and irreligious state of world society. It is only when the teachings of Catholicism are again widely accepted and implemented that there will be any hope for genuine peace and progress in the world, that John Paul II's vision of a genuine "civilization of love" will replace the present spirit of corruption and godlessness. This is the essence of the appeal of Our Lady in the message of

Fatima, and underlines why this is the most important series of Marian apparitions of our times, and indeed why Pope John Paul II has entrusted the Third Millennium to her.

In sum, Mary's apparitions have played a large part in the major Catholic renewals of recent centuries, and if her message given at Fatima is heeded by enough people, then the Church can again experience a great renaissance. As Mary's specific requests during the Fatima apparitions make clear, this is not merely an option for mankind, but an absolute necessity if we are to have true peace in the world, and this is a theme that will be explored in the final section of this work.

It is hoped, too, that a further volume will be able to look at more recent alleged Marian apparitions, in the light of the problems facing both the Church and the world.

Meanwhile, the present work opens with the prelude to the dramatic intervention of Mary, as Our Lady of Guadalupe, in Mexico. She chose to make her first major appearance of modern times in the New World of the Americas, which, five centuries ago, were strange and exotic lands only recently discovered by European voyagers.

1

Guadalupe and the Conquest of Mexico

The Return of Quetzalcoatl

On Holy Thursday, 21 April 1519, a fleet of eleven caravels, containing just over six hundred men, anchored near a small island off the coast of the land we now call Mexico. Their leader was the Spaniard, Hernán Cortés, and they were about to begin an epic adventure that would see the conquest of the great, but bloody and cruel, Aztec empire—whose snow-topped mountains, behind which lay the capital Tenochtitlan, could clearly be seen in the distance. Their aim was conquest, both for personal glory and riches, and for the good of Spain and the Catholic Faith. When they were met by emissaries of Montezuma, the Aztec ruler, the magnitude of the task they had set themselves became clearer: the Aztec empire was highly organized, with millions of subjects and a strong warrior tradition, and would not succumb without a formidable struggle.

But in all this the Spaniards had a crucial psychological advantage: the Aztec traditions spoke of the return of Quetzalcoatl, a pale-faced Aztec god, who would one day reappear to claim leadership of the nation. His return was linked to his name year, 1-Reed in the Aztec calendar, a year which recurred only once every fifty-two years, and by one of those strange coincidences (or providences) of history, 1519 was such a year. This belief effectively paralyzed Montezuma and greatly facilitated the Spanish conquest, in that he thought he was facing not a man, but a returning god.[5]

In addition, Montezuma's sister, the Princess Papantzin, seems to have had a remarkable dream in 1509, one which exercised a singular influence over the emperor. She had become ill and fallen into a coma, and believing her to be dead the Aztecs had buried her. But she revived in the tomb and when released recounted the amazing dream she had just experienced. In it she was taken by a shining being, with a black cross on his forehead, to the shore of the ocean to see a number of ships with black crosses on their sails approaching. She was told that these were the future conquerors of the country, who would also bring knowledge of the true God.[6]

The next day, 22 April, Good Friday, Cortés and his men disembarked from their ships, with their black-crossed sails now hanging limp, heard Mass, and built a camp to install the horses and cannon, cargo which would prove crucial in securing their military advantage over the Aztecs. They also brought ashore some small wooden statues of the Virgin, and these too would play a very important part in subsequent events. It was Cortés's insistence that one of these statues, and an altar and a cross, be set up in the midst of the bloody temple of the Aztecs, and that human sacrifices should cease, that would precipitate the final conflict with the conquistadors.

Again fate favored the Spaniards, in that the Aztecs expected Quetzalcoatl to return on his personal name day, 9-Wind, and 22 April 1519 was such a day, and, equally amazingly, they expected him to wear black: as Cortés stepped ashore, he was wearing black in commemoration of the most somber day in the Christian calendar. On Easter Sunday, after sung High Mass, Cortés invited Montezuma's men aboard ship to dine. During the meal the Aztecs sprinkled human blood, fresh from the grisly sacrifices which were a feature of their religion, on the food. The horrified Spaniards spat it out, and again the forebodings of the Aztecs seemed to be confirmed: Quetzalcoatl, too, was known to be strongly opposed to human sacrifice. Montezuma's emissaries returned to their master and reported the awful news, that the strangers were clothed in iron and rode on deer as tall as the roof of a house, and that they had terrifying weapons which spat fire and destruction. Montezuma is said to have almost fainted with horror at this account, and become convinced that Quetzalcoatl had returned; indeed, all the evidence suggests that from this moment he felt that his empire was doomed, although that did not stop his subjects mounting a ferocious defense in the final battles for Mexico.[7]

Spain and the Conquest of Mexico

As detailed below, the first major modern apparition of Mary, after the initiation of the Reformation in Europe by Luther and his followers, took place near Mexico City in 1531. Thus it happened during the main phase of that momentous event, just as the initial stages of the Protestant revolt were being completed and the Catholic Reformation was beginning to take effect. This in itself was not just a reaction to Protestantism, but was a movement of reform within the Church that developed over a long period, although it is true to say that its most important developments occurred after the onset of the Protestant revolt. Since the apparitions of Our Lady of Guadalupe took place during the Reformation period, we can only really understand their full significance in relation to that historic event. Once this is done, it becomes clear that it is not far-fetched to regard Guadalupe as part of God's response to the break-up of Christendom, formalized by Martin Luther's revolt.

And indeed, it was just eighteen months before the arrival of the conquistadors in Mexico, on 31 October 1517, that Luther had nailed his famous ninety-five theses to the castle church door at Wittenberg, and sparked off that great religious, social, and political revolution. Now Cortés and his followers with their new and deadly weapons were hammering at a very different portal, the threshold of the Aztec empire, and their onslaught would open up a whole new world for the West.

As the Reformation progressed and took hold, Charles V's Spanish domains were well equipped with a crusading Catholic spirit for the work of both the Catholic Reformation in Europe, and the evangelization of the Americas. The momentous discovery, exploration, and exploitation of the New World, begun with Columbus in 1492, had further developed in the years leading up to the Reformation. The Church was mainly interested in the evangelization of the native peoples of the newly-discovered lands, and these were granted to the Spanish monarchs by the papacy, on condition that Christianity was effectively preached to the inhabitants. Regrettably, right from the beginning there was a clash between royal interests and those of the conquistadors and their followers. Although the monarchs wanted to exploit their new empire, they had a more benevolent approach than that of the conquerors and settlers, who were mainly concerned with riches and not too concerned about how the Indians were treated in the process.[8]

The Aztecs had quite an advanced civilization in terms of agriculture, art and architecture, as well as in scientific pursuits such as astronomy and mathematics, but they were also quite primitive in their beliefs, having an animistic approach to the world that made them backward-looking and fatalistic.[9] They called themselves the Mexica, and because of their warlike abilities they acted as mercenaries, although they were detested by other tribes for their immorality and enthusiasm for human sacrifice. Over time, they constructed the city of Tenochtitlan on an island in Lake Texcoco and gradually grew more powerful, extending their dominions through conquest in the first half of the fifteenth century. Captives taken in battle became sacrificial victims, and on one occasion at least twenty thousand had their hearts torn from their breasts while still alive; this took place during the ceremony of dedication for a new temple, built to honor their god Huitzilopochtli.

By the beginning of the sixteenth century, the Aztecs were in control of much of central and southern Mexico, but they had also made some quite bitter enemies, including the Tlaxcalan people, and this enmity was one of the reasons for their downfall when the Spaniards arrived. At the time of the conquest in 1519, the emperor Montezuma was absolute ruler, a religious but superstitious man who, as indicated above, believed in the old tradition that the god Quetzalcoatl would return to rule the country.[10]

Hernán Cortés had been commissioned by the Cuban governor, Velasquez, to explore the Mexican interior, so he was the man destined to be responsible for opening up Mexico to the influence of Christianity, and, thence, only twelve years later, in 1531, to the marvelous apparitions of Our Lady. Interestingly enough, Cortés was born only fifty miles away from the Marian shrine at Guadalupe in Spain, and he is known to have regarded Mary under this title as his special patron in his battles with the Aztecs.

Montezuma, unsure of himself, allowed the Spaniards to get closer and closer to his capital, as the foreigners gained allies amongst other tribes. Eventually the emperor, fearful of the wrath of the gods, greeted Cortés as the returning Quetzalcoatl, or his emissary, who had come to claim the throne.[11]

The Spaniards were welcomed to Tenochtitlan, the future Mexico City, by the Aztecs, but were only too well aware that, in effect, they were trapped, surrounded by thousands of hostile Indians. Fearful for the safety of his men and their mission, Cortés seized Montezuma as a hostage, and although he was well treated, some of the emperor's followers began to become increasingly angry with the Spaniards, particularly as Cortés demanded that human sacrifices cease and symbols of paganism be replaced with crosses and statues of Mary. Once he had conquered Mexico, he planned to bring in priests and religious to convert the Aztecs to Christianity *en masse*. Five priests had accompanied Cortés and his men, and his religious zeal in opposing pagan practices led even them to restrain him, as they felt he was jeopardizing the safety of the entire group.[12]

Cortés managed to enlarge his force by assimilating another group of Spaniards which had been sent by Governor Velasquez to stop him. A battle ensued in which they were repeatedly attacked by Aztec warriors, and during this struggle Montezuma was killed, struck down by a missile from his own side. Forced to retreat, the Spaniards were fortunate that their Tlaxcalan allies, and other natives, were still prepared to support them, for without this help they would have faced certain death. Cortés needed all of his considerable powers of persuasion to induce his men to return to take the city, in the knowledge that the Aztecs would now be ready for them and prove absolutely bitter and deadly foes. The city was besieged and finally taken during a ferocious battle that saw the defeat of the Aztec forces on 13 August 1521.[13] With fewer than a thousand men, and supported by his Indian allies, Cortés had subjugated a mighty military nation and gained control of a huge empire and millions of subjects.[14]

Guadalupe: the Apparitions at Tepeyac

Cortés's followers expected to receive rich booty from their crushing victory, but little gold was actually forthcoming, and so, to calm their anger, he distributed Indian towns to them; this practice, the *Encomienda* system, had been used before in other Spanish possessions in the Caribbean. In theory, it meant that the landowner looked after his Indian subjects and made sure they converted to Christianity, but in practice it made some Indians virtual slaves and subjected them to all sorts of abuse.[15] There was obviously some degree of bitterness amongst many Indians at what had happened to them, and this new system did not help matters. Among the Spaniards, the only people prepared to take the side of the Indians were the increasing number of churchmen arriving in Mexico, including, in 1527, the first bishop of Mexico City, Juan de Zumárraga. He bore the title "Protector of the Indians," but was still only bishop-elect at this stage, and was initially prevented from properly exercising his authority by corrupt officials, among whom was a judge, Nuno de Guzman. The bishop preached against the abuses being perpetrated against the Indians, but could really only work freely when Guzman, hoping to regain royal favor by fresh conquests, headed off for western Mexico in 1529.[16] In the meantime, Bishop Zumárraga administered his see wisely and helped to stabilize the rapidly growing Spanish colony in Mexico City.

Franciscans had been sent out as early as 1523, with Dominicans soon afterwards, and they began the work of Christianizing these vast new lands; but they faced many obstacles, from the need to learn new languages, to Indian attachment to the old ways, and, of course, resentment by the Spanish authorities at what they regarded as interference.[17] In addition, most of the Indians lived in small widely-dispersed villages, and many suspected the missionaries were just another part of the new regime that was designed to control and exploit them. Despite these disadvantages, the missionaries worked diligently, but even the most optimistic among them must have thought that the conversion of the natives would take an inordinately long time.[18]

There were some converts, however, and amongst these were a man and his wife who lived in the vicinity of Mexico City: they accepted the Faith, taking the names Juan Diego and Maria Lucia on their baptism in 1525. When Juan Diego's wife died in 1529, he moved to live with an older relative, an uncle, in a village nearer the capital. In order to be in time for Mass, he had to set off across the hills before dawn, and on Saturday, 9 December 1531 he journeyed to celebrate the feast of the Immaculate Conception of Mary, which in that era was held on that date, rather than on 8 December as today. Juan Diego had been instructed on the role and prerogatives of Mary by the Franciscan Friars of the convent at Tlatelolco, and no doubt he was able to appreciate the purity and holiness of Mary, and of Christianity, in comparison with the rather offensive and repellent nature of the Aztec religion.[19]

As he came close to the city, Juan Diego had to pass Tepeyac hill, where a pagan Aztec temple had formerly stood, and as he did so, he was surprised to hear the sound of extraordinarily beautiful music coming from the summit. He looked up in astonishment to see a white cloud streaming with rainbow-colored lights. Suddenly the music ceased, and he then heard an exquisite female voice calling to him, "Juanito, dearest Juan Diego," in his own Nahuatl language. He felt drawn towards this voice and climbed up the hill to be met by a Lady of surpassing beauty, enveloped in a dazzling light, a brilliance that illuminated the surroundings. This is the description given of Juan Diego's unexpected encounter in the words of the *Nican Mopohua,* an account probably written within ten to fifteen years of the apparitions:

He was filled with awe and admiration by her splendor. Her clothing was radiant like the sun; the crag on which her foot was resting was giving off rays of light, and looked like a bracelet of precious stones; even the earth glistened like the mist of a rainbow. The mesquite bushes, prickly pears, and the other lowly herbs and grasses which usually grow there seemed like emeralds, the foliage like fine turquoise, and the branches and thorns like shining gold.[20]

Juan Diego fell to his knees in reverence before this wonderful apparition, as the young Lady, who looked about fourteen, gently asked him where he was going. He told her he was going to Mass and she smiled in approval before continuing:

> Know, know for sure, my dearest, littlest, and youngest son, that I am the perfect and ever Virgin Holy Mary, Mother of the God of truth through Whom everything lives, the Lord of all things near us, the Lord of heaven and earth. I want very much to have a little house built here for me, in which I will show Him, I will exalt Him and make Him manifest. I will give Him to the people in all my personal love, in my compassion, in my help, in my protection: because I am truly your merciful Mother, yours and all the people who live united in this land and of all the other people of different ancestries, my lovers, who love me, those who seek me, those who trust in me. Here I will hear their weeping, their complaints and heal all their sorrows, hardships and sufferings. And to bring about what my compassionate and merciful concern is trying to achieve, you must go to the residence of the Bishop of Mexico and tell him that I sent you here to show him how strongly I wish him to build me a temple here on the plain; you will report to him exactly all you have seen, admired and what you have heard. Know for sure I will appreciate it very much, be grateful and will reward you. And you? You will deserve very much the reward I will give you for your fatigue, the work and trouble that my mission will cause you. Now my dearest son, you have heard my breath, my word; go now and put forth your best effort.[21]

In a state of wonderment, Juan Diego agreed to do what the Lady asked him, setting off for the city as day dawned. He must have been quite apprehensive at the thought of presenting himself before Bishop Zumárraga, but persevered with his commission and was told to wait by a servant. After an hour, he was summoned to meet the Spanish-speaking bishop, who questioned him through an interpreter. Juan Diego knelt before Zumárraga and told him what had happened and the words of the Lady; the bishop was impressed by the Mexican's humble and sincere demeanour, but said that he needed time to consider the matter, and with that Juan Diego was dismissed. He trudged back disappointedly towards Tepeyac hill and the route home, to find the Lady waiting for him. He recounted his meeting with the bishop and what he had said to him, before asking the "noble Lady" to entrust this mission to someone more important. She, though, just smiled and told him that she had specially chosen him to deliver her message, that he should return to the bishop and ask in her name for the erection of a *teocalli* or "temple," and that he should emphasize that she really was the Virgin Mary, the Mother of God.[22]

Encouraged and reassured, Juan Diego agreed to go and speak to the bishop the next day, which he did, after the Sunday morning Mass at Tlatelolco church. He was not treated so favorably by the bishop's servants on this occasion, though, and had to wait for several hours out on the cold wind-swept patio of the bishop's residence, before finally being admitted into his presence. Bishop Zumárraga, a kindly man, received him courteously, although he was probably surprised to see him again so soon. Juan Diego began to recount his story and the Lady's request, answering all the bishop's questions, again impressing him with his patent sincerity, although Zumárraga was understandably reluctant to build a chapel on such apparently slender testimony. He told the Indian that he would really need something more, such as a sign from heaven, and Juan Diego agreed to put this request to the Lady. With that he left the house, discreetly followed by two of the bishop's aides, who shadowed him to the vicinity of Tepeyac hill before losing sight of him. After a lengthy and fruitless search, they finally returned to the bishop, urging him to punish the Mexican for wasting their time. Zumárraga, however, decided to await the outcome of his request for a sign.

The Miraculous Image of Guadalupe

Meanwhile, Juan Diego had again met the beautiful Lady, enveloped in a luminous mist on the hilltop, and, after telling her what had happened, begged for a sign so that he would be believed. She spoke to reassure him, telling him that she would indeed give him a sign, and that she would wait for him at that spot.[23] Juan Diego returned to his village to find his uncle seriously ill with a fever, and so had to stay and nurse him all that night and the following day. By evening it was clear that the old man was dying, and he urged his nephew to go back to Mexico City and bring a priest who could administer the last sacraments. Juan Diego set off in the early hours, anxious about his uncle, but also somewhat embarrassed that he had not been able to keep his appointment with the Lady. In his worry and confusion he decided to try and avoid her by passing by on the other side of the hill, but she descended to meet him and asked him where he was going. He told her about his sick uncle and his important mission to fetch a priest, promising to deliver the expected sign the next day.

She spoke to assure Juan Diego that his uncle did not now need the last sacraments because he was no longer in danger of death:

> Am I not here, I, who am your Mother? Are you not under my shadow and protection? Am I not the source of your joy? Are you not in the hollow of my mantle, in the crossing of my arms? Do you need anything more? Let nothing else worry you, disturb you. Do not let your uncle's illness worry you, because he will not die now. You may be certain that he is already well.[24]

Juan Diego was overjoyed with this news, and immediately volunteered to take the promised sign to the bishop. The Lady told him to climb back to the top of the hill and gather flowers that he would find growing there and bring them back to her. He complied and must have been amazed, on that December morning, with the sight that greeted him on that cold hilltop: everywhere he found beautiful flowers, including roses, with an almost heavenly appearance, blooming completely out of season. He spread out his rough outer garment or *tilma*, made of *ayate* or cactus fibre, and scooped up the wonderful flowers before returning to the Lady and presenting them to her. She rearranged them with her own hands, saying to Juan Diego:

> My youngest and dearest son, these different kinds of flowers are the proof, the sign that you will take to the Bishop. ... I strictly order you not to unfold your *tilma* or reveal its contents until you are in his presence. You will relate to him everything very carefully ... so that my house of God which I requested will be made, will be built.[25]

Juan Diego hurried on towards the city, carrying his precious cargo with its beautiful fragrance. The bishop's servants were not pleased to see him and refused him entry, but eventually he was allowed into the bishop's presence. It happened that Bishop

Zumárraga was with some important people at this time, including the new governor of Mexico, and as Juan Diego once again described what had happened to him at Tepeyac he released the ends of the fabric and allowed the flowers to fall to the floor. All present must have been amazed at the unexpected sight, but they were in for a further surprise as they raised their eyes to the *tilma* still being held by Juan Diego; there in front of them they saw a beautiful and glorious image of Mary, just as she had been described by him, imprinted on the coarse fabric of his *tilma*. At the sight of this prodigy, they reverently sank to their knees; they were the first people to see the miraculous Image of Guadalupe, which has now been preserved in Mexico for over four and a half centuries.

At length Bishop Zumárraga rose, apologised to Juan Diego for having doubted his word, and invited him to stay, while the *tilma* was removed to the bishop's private oratory. News of the marvel quickly spread, and the next day the sacred Image of Mary was taken in procession to the cathedral. Later on, Juan Diego led the way to the site of the apparitions, while plans were made for the erection of a small chapel as a temporary measure. This site was to become doubly significant for the Indians, since it was the place where Tonantzin, the "mother of the gods," was traditionally worshipped.[26] Juan Diego then returned to his village with a guard of honor, to find that his uncle had recovered. He related to the older man all that had happened, and in turn was told by his uncle that it must have been the same beautiful Lady who had appeared and cured him. She had also told Juan Diego's uncle the name by which she wished to be known.

This information was later related to the bishop by an interpreter, who thought that the old man had been trying to say, "The Ever Virgin, Holy Mary of Guadalupe," although the interpreter was probably mistaken in this. Bishop Zumárraga was surprised because, as has been pointed out previously, Guadalupe was the name of an ancient Spanish shrine to Mary. Although it might have seemed inappropriate, this was the name eventually adopted for the shrine; it is more likely, however, that this represented the *phonetic* equivalent of what Juan Diego's uncle was trying to say.[27] It is not surprising that Bishop Zumárraga, a Franciscan, and the Spaniards with him, should have related the Image to the Guadalupe shrine in Spain, considering that the Franciscans were responsible for that shrine. In addition, there was also some similarity between the Image on the *tilma* and a statue of Mary, as the Immaculate Conception, at the Spanish shrine.[28] There have been a number of attempts to establish an exact rendering of the

Nahuatl word originally translated "Guadalupe," but the most likely answer is that it was the interpreter's attempt to render the Nahuatl title for Mary, *Coatlaxopeuh,* a word that means, "She who breaks, stamps or crushes the serpent."

This explanation makes perfect sense as a reference to the use of snake symbolism, which was so prevalent amongst the Aztecs, and so closely bound up with the worship of their main gods in their religion of human sacrifice. Snakes were the most frequently-portrayed animals in Aztec sculpture, which was the major medium of Aztec art. Quetzalcoatl, the feathered serpent deity, was one of their most important gods; he was seen as a creator and also as god of the wind, and of learning and knowledge. Other snake-gods included Mixcoatl, the "Cloud-serpent" deity, and two female gods, Cihuacoatl, "Serpent Woman," and Coatlicue, "Serpent Skirt", the mother of Huitzilopochtli, the sacrificial war god of the Aztecs at Tenochtitlan.[29] As Warren H. Carroll points out: "An almost universal symbol in Mexican religion was the serpent. Sacrifices were heralded by the prolonged beating of an immense drum, made of the skins of huge snakes, which could be heard two miles away. Nowhere else in human history has Satan so formalized and institutionalized his worship with so many of his own actual titles and symbols."[30] This is a significant point, given one of the themes of this book, that the various historical apparitions of Mary from Guadalupe onwards are paralleled by passages from the Old Testament. Thus at Guadalupe Mary, the "Woman of Genesis," the new Eve, crushed the head of the serpent-worshipping Aztec religion, and prepared the way for the worship of the one true God in Mexico.

Juan Diego himself lived on until 1548, and spent his time in charge of the little shrine which had been built to house the Image, explaining its significance to the many thousands of pilgrims who visited the site of the apparitions.[31]

Typology of Mary as the New Eve

The idea of seeing Mary as the new Eve was extremely popular with the early Christian writers, and we can trace its development from the second century. In his dialogue with Trypho the Jew, St Justin Martyr (*c.*100–*c.*165), writes:

> And since we find it written in the memoirs of the Apostles that He is the Son of God, and since we call Him by that same title,

we have understood that this is really He and that He proceeded before all creatures from the Father by His power ... and that He is born of the Virgin, in order that the disobedience caused by the serpent might be destroyed in the same manner in which it originated. For Eve, an undefiled virgin, conceived the word of the serpent, and brought forth disobedience and death. But the Virgin Mary, filled with faith and joy, ... gave birth to Him, concerning whom we have shown so many passages of Scripture were written, and by whom God destroys ... the serpent ...[32]

St Irenaeus (c.130–200), writing slightly later, held similar beliefs, as did Tertullian, and also St Cyril of Jerusalem (c.315–86), who wrote: "Through Eve, yet a virgin, came death; there was need that through a virgin, or rather from a virgin that life should appear, that as the serpent deceived the one, so Gabriel should bring good news to the other."[33]

St Athanasius, too, compared Mary with Eve:

Eve listened to the suggestion of the serpent and tribulations descended upon all. And you have inclined your ear to the supplications of Gabriel, and penitence flourished among the children of humankind. While Eve conversed with the serpent, the human race was affected by the venom of the serpent and tribulations came ... But Mary when she spoke with Gabriel about how she would come to bear, the lips of the entire human race were cleansed through penitence and justification. When Eve looked upon the tree with desire, lusts, voluptuousness, and impurity were multiplied upon the earth ... But Mary speaking with sweetness looked upon Gabriel, and modesty together with temperance, and purity flourished in virginity upon all humankind.[34]

Similarly, St Augustine (354–430), emphasized the contrast between Eve and Mary, and the way that the first woman had caused Adam to sin:

The first man, by persuasion of a virgin, fell; the Second Man, with consent of a Virgin, triumphed. By a woman the devil brought in death; by a woman the Lord brought in life. An evil angel of old seduced Eve, a good angel likewise encouraged Mary. Eve believed, so as to ruin her husband: Mary, so as to prepare her womb to be a habitation worthy of the Son of God, that Him whom she had as Lord, she might also have as Son ... From a woman was the beginning of sin, and on her account we all die; from a woman was the beginning of faith, and on her account are we repaired unto everlasting life.[35]

All of this was summed up by St Jerome (c.341–420): "But now that a virgin has conceived in the womb and has borne to us a child ... now the chain of the curse is broken. Death came through Eve, but life has come through Mary."[36]

Hence, it is appropriate that the first major modern apparition of Mary should find such an unmistakeable parallel in the opening chapters of the book of Genesis, the first book of the Bible. Not only does Guadalupe represent the first important appearance of Mary in the new era of world history which was begun by the Reformation, but it is also crucial in that it happened in the New World, in the realm of the serpent-worshipping Aztecs.

In Genesis we read of the creation in original perfection of the first man and woman, Adam and Eve, and their subsequent fall into sin after the temptation of Eve by the serpent (Gen. 3:1–15). This passage finishes with the "first Gospel," the *Protoevangelium*:

> The Lord God said to the serpent, "Because you have done this, cursed are you above all cattle, and above all wild animals; upon your belly you shall go, and dust you shall eat all the days of your life. I will put enmity between you and the woman, and between your seed and her seed; he shall bruise your head, and you shall bruise his heel."

This, then, was the promise of redemption, that the offspring of Eve would strike the head of the serpent, that is, do away with sin and death. Although the primary typological sense of this text is Messianic, in that it refers to Jesus, according to Catholic teaching it also includes Mary, and so it is more correct to regard Mary, rather than Eve, as "the Woman" in this passage. This is because, as a prophetic text, looking to the future, it cannot be applied to Eve, who was responsible for the first sin and did not see redemption in her own lifetime.[37]

It is important to consider the Protoevangelium at this juncture because of the way it can be linked to Mary's message to Juan Diego's uncle, concerning the title by which she wished to be known: Coatlaxopeuh, or "She who breaks, stamps or crushes the serpent." Mary has traditionally been identified with the "Woman" of Genesis who would "bruise" the head of the serpent. This biblical passage concludes with the following very interesting verse: "The man called his wife's name Eve, because she was the mother of all living," (Gen. 3:20). "Eve," in Hebrew *hawwah,* comes from the root *hayah*, "to live," and there is a clear correlation here with the content of Mary's message at Guadalupe. As indicated above, at her first meeting with Juan Diego, she had spoken of herself as "your merciful Mother, yours and all the people who live united in this land and of all the other people of different ancestries ..." This emphasis on Mary as the spiritual mother of not just the Aztecs, but of all mankind, parallels the idea found in Genesis that Eve received her name because she was the mother of all the living. As the new Eve, Mary's spiritual motherhood far transcends that of her original ancestor.

Another interesting factor to note is the connection between Tepeyac hill and its shrine to Tonantzin, the Aztec goddess whose name means "Our Mother." This usage caused early missionaries some misgivings, since they felt the Indians should have been referring to Mary as "Mother of God," rather than calling her Tonantzin, "Our Mother."[38] This tradition, though, only further emphasizes the connection between Genesis and Guadalupe, since it points to the way Eve's universal motherhood was superseded by Mary's universal spiritual motherhood. Likewise, the fact that the seer Juan Diego was a grown man, who had been married, something that is unusual with the modern approved apparitions, points to the role of Adam and Eve in Genesis, namely that they were adults. Perhaps even more surprising is the way that the situation of Mexico City itself, a city on an island in a lake, parallels the description of the earth following the creation. We are told in Genesis that on the third day of creation, the waters came together in a single mass, allowing the dry land to appear in their midst (Gen. 1:9–10); here we have land surrounded by water, just as in the case of Mexico City in the sixteenth century, although over time the lake was filled in.

The *Nican Mopohua* describes the moments before Juan Diego's initial encounter with Mary, when he heard heavenly singing:

> Dawn was breaking as he arrived at the foot of Tepeyac Hill. He heard singing from the crest of the hill, which sounded like the song of many birds. When at times their voices quieted, the hillside seemed to echo in response. Their singing, very soft and pleasant, surpassed that of the coyoltototl and tzinizcan and other fine songbirds. Juan Diego stopped to look and thought, "Could I be worthy of what I am hearing? Am I dreaming? Am I arising from sleep? Where am I? Perhaps it is the earthly paradise of flowers and corn, about which our ancestors spoke?"[39]

If we compare this account with those verses from the first chapter of Genesis, which describe the creation of the animals and birds, there seems to be an obvious correspondence between what Juan Diego experienced and the biblical account (cf. Gen. 1:20, 22). In passing it might also be noted, that the curse on the earth described in Genesis, that it would degenerate and produce "brambles and thistles," is neatly paralleled in reverse by the way Juan Diego went to the top of the hill and expected only to find such plants, but was rewarded by the out-of-season roses (Gen. 3:16–19). There are other elements of the Genesis account of the Fall that are also interesting from a Marian viewpoint. For example, we are told that God made "garments" for Adam and Eve once they had sinned (Gen. 3:21), a point that seems to parallel the fact that it was Juan Diego's *tilma*, an outer garment, that was the medium by which the message of Guadalupe, the Image, was passed on and preserved. This too was made by God. In fact, this is the only major Marian apparition where an article of clothing has been left as a historical artefact and given such prominence through its miraculous preservation down the centuries.

The final section of the biblical passage describes the expulsion of Adam and Eve from the garden of Eden:

> Then the Lord God said, "Behold, the man has become like one of us, knowing good and evil; and now, lest he put forth his hand and take also of the tree of life, and eat, and live for ever"— therefore the Lord God sent him forth from the garden of Eden, to till the ground from which he was taken. He drove out the man; and at the east of the garden of Eden he placed the cherubim, and a flaming sword which turned every way, to guard the way to the tree of life (Gen. 3:22–24).

Here there are two very interesting elements that recur in later passages, and which will be seen to have a definite Marian symbolism. The cherubim who guarded the way to the tree of life appear in the Bible as guardians of sacred places, beings who also assemble around God's throne, whereas angels, of whatever variety, are intermediaries or messengers. Subsequent chapters will make clear that cherubim or angels are present in a number of the biblical passages that typify particular Marian apparitions, and they are also connected with those apparitions themselves. The other interesting element is the tree of life, and although it appears infrequently in the Bible, only on two definite occasions, in fact, (Rev. 22:1–2,14), with a further allusion being made to it in Ezekiel (47:12), those appearances are very significant.

An early Guadalupe chronicler, Luis Becerra Tanco, writing in 1675, mentions both a spring of "bitter alum water" and a tree at the site of the fourth apparition. He describes how Juan Diego, following the Lady's instructions, went to the top of the hill to collect the roses he was to give to Bishop Zumárraga, then going on to make this comment: "considering the site, I judge that it is its ancient trunk which still exists there on the lower slope of the hill, towards the east, with the alum-water spring in front of it."[40] There is thus an interesting parallel here with the Genesis account that describes water flowing out of the earth to water it, and the tree of life in the garden of Eden (Gen. 2:4–9).

The early Christian writers did not just compare Mary with Eve, however, they also saw a typology in other aspects of the account given in Genesis. This idea is present in St Irenaeus's thought:

> And as Adam was first made from untilled soil and received his being from virgin earth (since God had not yet sent rain and man had not yet cultivated the ground) and was fashioned by the hand of God, that is by the Word of God, "by whom all things were made" ...; so he who existed as the Word restored in himself Adam, by his birth from Mary who was still a virgin, a birth befitting this restoration of Adam.[41]

St John Chrysostom (354–407), makes the following comparison between Mary and the garden of Eden: "Therefore he called it 'Eden' or 'virgin soil', because this virgin [the soil of paradise] was a type of that other Virgin. As the first soil produced for us the garden of paradise without any seed, so the Virgin gave birth to Christ for us without receiving any manly seed."[42] St Ephrem (c.306–73), also talks about Mary in this manner: "The virgin earth gave birth to that Adam, head of the earth; the Virgin today gave birth to [second] Adam, head of heaven."[43] Theodotus of Ancyra speaks of her too in this way: "O Virgin surpassing the Garden of Eden itself! For young plants of every kind were born in Eden, springing up from the virgin soil; yet this Virgin is better than that soil ... The Virgin became more glorious than paradise."[44]

The apparitions at Guadalupe acquire a deeper significance if we consider them in the light of the above passages from the Church Fathers: Mexico was, indeed, part of the new American continents which from a Western, Christian, point of view were "virginal" lands, although actually under the sway of paganism. Surely, then, it is not a coincidence that Mary, as the second Eve, should have appeared in the New World so recently discovered, as a sign of a new birth for mankind, even as the Reformation, like the sin of Adam, was beginning to run its harmful course, undermining the principles on which medieval Christian civilization had been so successfully founded, and allowing erroneous ideas to take root and flourish, principally through its rejection of the Catholic Church.[45]

Thus, these interesting typological points seem to indicate an affinity between episodes found in the book of Genesis and the Guadalupe apparitions, and this theme will be further explored in the accounts of the other major Marian apparitions.

Historical Accounts of Guadalupe

Unlike more modern apparitions, beginning with those to Catherine Labouré in 1830, most of the original documents relating to Guadalupe have not withstood the ravages of time; this has allowed criticism of the Mexican apparitions to surface periodically. But it is important to remember that the Image of Mary on Juan Diego's *tilma,* which was visited by John Paul II early in his pontificate, has been preserved for us as a miraculous sign to this day. This "relic" of the apparition was undoubtedly left to posterity for the precise purpose of showing that Guadalupe was not a myth or pious invention. In the early days of the conquest, there was quite a shortage of paper, and many early records were lost or destroyed, although, as in the case of the *first* copies of the Gospels, it is not essential to have original documents to support a particular belief, especially when the traditions surrounding an event such as Guadalupe are so strong. The Spanish documentary tradition concerning the apparitions dates from the seventeenth century, and this in turn is based on earlier writings; similarly, many sixteenth-century wills have been discovered which refer to Guadalupe, and contemporary historians also mention it.[46]

The three best-known accounts of the apparitions are those of Luis Lazo de Vega, Miguel Sánchez, and Luis Becerra Tanco, all of whom wrote in the mid-seventeenth century, basing their work on earlier accounts and oral traditions. The three Spanish accounts, like the Gospels, have slight differences of emphasis and wording, but agree on the essentials. Probably the earliest account, the *Nican Mopohua,* in the original Nahuatl language of the Indians, was made by the Aztec scholar Valeriano, a contemporary of both Bishop Zumárraga and Juan Diego.[47] Valeriano's document was considered a seventeenth-century forgery by some investigators, until the discovery of an independent document attesting to his existence; an analysis of the handwriting indicated that it was written between 1540 and 1580. An original, or very early, copy of the *Nican Mopohua* was recently rediscovered, indicating that we now have a contemporary account of the events at Tepeyac. Another sixteenth-century account, the *Primitive Relation*, probably written by the historian Juan de Tovar, used an earlier source, possibly that of Bishop Zumárraga's translator, Juan González.[48]

The bishop did not issue an official approval of the apparitions, possibly because of the tense situation in Mexico, where powerful interests were wary of anything that might be seen as favoring the Indians; there was also the danger of the miraculous Image being misrepresented and mixed up with pagan worship. In any event, by promoting the sanctuary at Tepeyac, Bishop Zumárraga gave tacit approval to the apparitions.[49] In 1556, twenty-five years after the events of 1531, there was an investigation by church authorities into what had happened. At the same time the Dominican who had replaced Zumárraga as bishop, Alonso de Montufar, implicitly defended the Image, preaching in its favor and authorizing the construction of a larger shrine for it in 1557. This would not have happened if he had any doubts about its origins. He also sent a copy of the Image to King Philip of Spain in 1570, and this is believed to have been on board Doria's ship at the Battle of Lepanto in 1571.[50]

Another investigation into the apparitions took place in 1666; existing documents and evidence were examined, and elderly people, who, as children, had heard of the events of 1531, testified under oath. Luis Becerra Tanco produced his chronicle for this enquiry, arguing that it was based on ancient Indian sources.[51] The loss of many original documents was noted with regret, a report was sent to the Vatican,[52] and it was in Rome that the most complete record of events at Guadalupe was kept. From the time of Pope Gregory XIII in 1575, privileges already granted to the shrine were extended, and this approval was continued by his successors. It thus seems clear that Rome had either recognized or conditionally recognized the validity of Guadalupe at a very early date.[53]

One document that has survived is an Aztec codex, illustrated with many drawings, known as the *Codex Tetlapalaco*, which is perhaps the oldest "book" in America, dating from the 1530s. In this codex, one of the drawings immediately below the Indian notation for the year 1532, thus indicating 1531, reveals under magnification the tiny figure of a woman with the same features as those found on the Image of Guadalupe. Hence, this constitutes contemporary supporting evidence for the reality of the apparitions.[54] A curious coincidence is that 1531 was also one of the years when Halley's comet made one of its periodic appearances, and this too is noted on the codex.[55] All important events were recorded in this pictorial way by the Aztecs, since they did not have a written language, although they were also able to record events by means of sung *cantares* and dances or *miotes*. At the investigation in 1666, Luis Becerra Tanco described how, as a boy, he had seen the Indians doing a circular dance on the feast of Our Lady of Guadalupe, while two old Indians would sing the *cantar* of the Virgin, a work that apparently described the events at Tepeyac.[56]

The preservation of the Image for over four hundred years is itself a miracle, especially given that, for a long time, it was exposed to the saline air and humidity of Mexico City, as well as the smoke and heat of candles and incense. The cactus fibres of a *tilma* generally disintegrate within twenty years, and many of the painted copies of the Image have deteriorated quite rapidly.[57] All these points indicate that the historical basis for belief in the apparitions of Guadalupe is firmly established, despite modern criticisms which have attempted to cast doubt on the origins of the shrine and the miraculous Image.

Modern Science and the Guadalupe Image

Recent scientific investigation of the Image has also brought some remarkable facts to light, especially regarding the reflections found in the right eye of the Virgin. These seem to follow the Purkinje–Sanson principle, which describes the way that the image of any object is reflected in the eye in three different places, due to the curvature of the cornea. Perhaps even more amazingly, the eye of the Image seems to behave like a human eye when examined with an opthalmoscope, rather than as a flat "painted" surface, and reflections of a human figure are found there. After working on computer-aided microscopic enlargements of the eyes of the Image, a researcher has claimed to have discovered at least four figures in the iris of the left eye, in a way that seems to exclude random patterning and coincidence; these may represent those present at the time of the production of the Image on the *tilma*.[58]

Jody Brant Smith and Dr Philip Callahan took infrared photographs of the Image in 1979, and also minutely examined its surface. They discovered that various painted additions, discernible in the photographs, had been made to the Image, but they had not affected its remarkable state of preservation and lack of cracking; old paintings are generally criss-crossed by hairline cracks as the paint slowly dries. Although the Image is made up of various pigments, it is not a "painting" in the ordinary sense of the word, since no brushstrokes are present. Smith and Callahan also observed the striking way that the Image seems to change size and coloring when viewed from various distances, a property caused by light diffraction, and similar to the iridescence seen on bird feathers and insect scales.[59] This is a natural phenomenon, though, and not something that can be effected by any human artist, and certainly not by a sixteenth-century forger. The infrared photographs also showed the absence of any "under sketch" beneath the Image, another indication that it was "not due to human hands."[60]

It is generally accepted, though, that the bottom third of the Image had been sized and painted over at some stage in the past, with elements, such as the cherub, the gold rays and trim, as well as the stars[61] on the mantle and the fleur-de-lis on the robe being added to. This was probably due to the bottom part of the Image being handled by pilgrims during the early years, and consequently wearing away. The infrared photographs confirmed this, since the later additions were opaque to the infrared, indicating the use of metallically-based paints which showed signs of deterioration. Earlier investigations, however, including one done by Dr Charles Wahlig in 1975, as well as the details of the Lepanto copy of the Image, indicate that the painted additions are overlays to original features, and not material additions.[62]

The turquoise blue of the Virgin's mantle ought to have faded by now, especially in a hot climate, if an ordinary blue pigment had been used, but, according to Callahan it is "of even density and not faded ... of unknown, semitransparent blue pigment ... bright enough to have been laid on last week." The rose-pink of the robe is even more transparent to the infrared than the blue, and still more inexplicable, since most pigments of this color are strongly opaque to the infrared. Even stranger, the white pigment found on the cheeks of the Image is unknown, and despite being quite thick, has not cracked, while the natural elements of the weave of the *tilma* seem to have been used very precisely to give the face extraordinary depth and life, when viewed from a distance. Callahan and Brant were able to conclude that, contrary to hostile reports, the bright colors of the mantle and robe were *not* due to over-painting during the course of the centuries; there are no signs of retouching on these areas, which, given their unfading brightness, is something of a mystery. There is no known sixteenth-century technology that could have produced the original portions of the Image, whether by stamping, dyeing or weaving.[63] Thus scientific studies of the Image establish very clearly that it cannot have been produced by natural means, and so uphold the Church's position on Guadalupe.

Michael P. Carroll, in his *The Cult of the Virgin Mary, Psychological Origins,* argues that the Guadalupe Image replaced an earlier statue sometime after 1575, but this is to ignore the clear evidence given above concerning the copy of the Image made in 1570. His theory, that the shrine at Tepeyac in Mexico arose as a deliberately fraudulent attempt to introduce a copy of the Guadalupe shrine in Spain, fails to take into account the existence of the Aztec codex mentioned above, with its copy of the Guadalupe Image, and implies that the whole business was concocted by the Church. Carroll is forced to put forward the weak conjecture that Juan Diego really saw a hallucination of his dead wife, or that he had taken hallucinogenic drugs. But there is no real evidence for any of this, and Carroll's discussion of the Image itself is particularly disappointing, since, although he mentions some of the scientific work that has been done on the *tilma*, work which clearly shows that it would never have survived this long if it were just an ordinary image, he fails to take any of this into account. This illustrates the major flaws in an approach where there is an unwillingness to consider all the evidence, and an excessive reliance on preconceived ideas.[64]

Guadalupe and Mexico

The consequences of the apparitions of Guadalupe were truly astounding. One of the early Franciscan Fathers, Toribio de Benavente, known as Motolinia or the "poor little one" by the Indians, claimed as early as 1537, only six years after Guadalupe, that nine million Indians had been baptized. The magnitude of this achievement becomes clear when it is realized that the evangelization of other Spanish and Portuguese possessions took centuries. This great surge in baptisms is itself testimony to the fact that *something* amazing happened in the early 1530s, and is indirect evidence in favor of the apparitions of Guadalupe.[65]

The symbolism of the sacred Image was very important for the Mexicans, since, although she was not dressed like an Aztec princess, they could see that she represented someone more powerful than their own divinities. She had described herself as the Mother of God, and was evidently greater than the sun and moon, which they adored, since these were behind and beneath her respectively. They also surmised that she was greater than the heavenly spirits, since the Angel beneath her feet was holding up her mantle. Therefore she was an all-powerful queen, and yet she was not a goddess, since her hands were folded together in supplication, which indicated that she was praying to One greater than she.[66] All of this helped in the process of conversion, and indicates for us the position of Mary as an intermediary who is open and sensitive to the needs and customs of all. In a more general sense, though, it can be said that Mary was appearing here as the "Immaculate Conception," since she appeared on the day on which the feast of the "Holy Conception of Mary" was celebrated at the time, December 9.

Thus, with this dramatic manifestation to Juan Diego, there began the series of apparitions that would culminate in her appearances to Bernadette at Lourdes, over three centuries later, where she would describe herself as the Immaculate Conception. By appearing at Tepeyac as the woman clothed with the sun, standing on the moon, one of the traditional iconographic representations of the Immaculate Conception, she was proclaiming in symbolic form the belief about her conception which the Church would define dogmatically in 1854.[67]

To the Spaniards, these mass conversions were a confirmation that God had specially chosen them to be the people to discover and evangelize the New World. In the minds of many, these new converts would make up for the losses to Protestantism in Europe, the most significant of which would prove to be England.[68] Nonetheless, the task of the missionaries, even with the help of Guadalupe, was still extremely difficult; this meant that many converts were not fully instructed, and retained an affection for the old Aztec gods, which, in practice, meant a religious syncretism, or mingling of beliefs and rituals.[69]

The people of Mexico still have an extraordinary affection for Our Lady of Guadalupe, and indeed it is the most visited Marian shrine in the world. Some writers maintain that this devotion has been one of the major factors in preserving Mexican Indians from the sort of cultural disintegration that has affected Indians in the rest of America.[70] To this day, the cult of Our Lady of Guadalupe has exerted a very powerful influence in Mexico. At the time of War of

Independence in 1810, Fr Hidalgo, the revolutionary leader, assumed the Image as the symbol of the revolution, while it was the Treaty of Guadalupe–Hidalgo which ended the American–Mexican war of 1846–48, a sign of the importance of the Image in the national consciousness. In 1945, Pope Pius XII gave further papal approval in describing the Image as one produced, "by brushes not of this earth"; and more recently the visit of Pope John Paul II to the shrine, in January 1979, shortly after his election in October 1978, celebrated the place of Our Lady of Guadalupe at the spiritual heart of Mexican religious life. On a return visit in 1990, the Pope beatified Juan Diego,[71] and he was canonized on 30 July 2002.

Guadalupe thus stands as the first in a great series of Marian apparitions in modern times, but in order really to understand why these interventions by Mary were so important, and how they relate to the Protestant Revolution and modern revolutionary events generally, we need to retrace our steps and look at the course of church history prior to this modern era, and the decline in Christendom that made the Reformation possible. After briefly considering these topics, the chapters which follow deal mainly with the historical situation from the time of the Reformation to the immediate aftermath of the French Revolution, and the beginnings of the Marian revival of the nineteenth century, a revival which began with the apparitions at the Rue du Bac in 1830. Thus these chapters are very important because it is difficult to understand the significance of the major Marian apparitions without an understanding of the historical background which made such divine interventions necessary.

2

Church History and the Protestant Revolution

Church History and the Growth of Christendom

The commandment that Jesus gave to his followers after his resurrection, that they should, "make disciples of all nations," (Matt. 28:19), would appear to have been asking the impossible. And yet the early Christians took Jesus at his word and proceeded to evangelize the pagan world, often in the face of the bitterest opposition. They managed not only to survive but to grow in numbers, pushed on by the incredible missionary energy of men such as St Paul. The result was that, after three centuries of savage persecutions, the Empire, under Constantine, was gradually converted to Christianity from the early fourth century onwards, culminating in the formation of Christendom, the medieval Catholic civilization which embraced Europe. It was by emphasizing spiritual matters and not by advocating political or social upheaval that Catholic teaching was able to change and renew Europe from within. This was not a question of revolution but of a genuine *reformation* of the whole of society, and it was a completely different process from the so-called Reformation of the sixteenth century, which actually brought about a complete upheaval that was indeed a *revolution*.[72]

Although the pagan Roman Empire did not succeed in its attempts to destroy Christianity, the conversion of Constantine did not remove the danger that the State would try to dominate the Church. The State here is understood in the sense of the powers governing society, whatever their nature. Constantine and many of his successors felt a need to control the Church, and this was a problem right down to the time of the Reformation, when, in effect, the ruling powers succeeded in largely destroying the power of Catholicism positively to influence European society. Since then, what remains of Christendom has come under ever-increasing pressure from the various anti-Christian forces operating in the world.

The early Christian centuries were also the period of the great Trinitarian debates, and controversies about God and the divine and human natures of Christ, debates in which Mary's place was not without importance. For example, her role as *Theotokos*, the "God-bearer" was brought out in the disputes involving the Arian heresy, which was a denial of Christ's divinity. This denial led on to a rejection of Mary's divine motherhood, and prompted St Athanasius, the Bishop of Alexandria, to describe her explicitly as *Theotokos*. Thus her role became important in upholding the orthodox teaching, that Jesus was both God and man. This role became more explicit after the Council of Ephesus in 431, when she was officially proclaimed as *Theotokos*, in the sense of "Mother of God," and churches were openly dedicated to her. Athanasius was one of the greatest saints in the history of the Church, constantly battling for the rights of orthodoxy against heresy and spending much of his life in exile.[73]

Arianism was really a sort of "proto-Reformation," in that it was an attempt to introduce in the fourth and fifth centuries the sort of changes that would eventually result from the Reformation over a thousand years later, that is, a domination of the Church by the State. At this time, though, the Church had only recently gone through the great persecutions, and was strong enough to fight off Arianism, in contrast to the position in the sixteenth century when Christendom was in decline.

St Ambrose (339–97), the Bishop of Milan, was an important figure in the defeat of Arianism, and also because of his insistence that the Emperor Theodosius should do penance before being readmitted to the sacraments, after he had ordered an unjustified massacre. Thus Ambrose established the very important position that even the Emperor was subject to the Church and not above it, a principle which helps to explain the spiritual authority of the Church in Europe right up until the time of the Reformation.[74]

The Roman Empire had allowed individuals few rights and little power in the face of an exalted State, an idea absorbed from the great Eastern Empires, with their "sacred" monarchies. This situation continued in the East, and so the Eastern Church always remained subservient to the State, although this was also partly due to the particular circumstances of the creation of Constantinople as a specifically Eastern Christian capital. This meant that Church and State in the East were closely united; in contrast Rome, and the West generally, were protected from too close a relationship with Constantinople and the emperors by means of distance. This, and the courage shown by leaders such as Ambrose, as well as the influence of men such as St Augustine of Hippo, meant that it was possible to fashion a new society in the West in which the spiritual authority of the Church was acknowledged, one where the ideals of freedom and social justice were recognized.[75]

Augustine was a supremely influential figure in this process, because he helped the Western Church to realize the importance of its role in the political and social fields, thus enabling it to act as the nucleus of European culture. One of his most famous works, the *City of God*, is a sustained argument about the opposition throughout history between those clinging to God and those defying him, as illustrated in the biblical account of mankind's origin and development, and the later vicissitudes of the Jewish people and the early Christian Church. The full title is *Concerning the City of God against the Pagans*. The crux of his argument is that this struggle will continue until the end of time, and although evil often seems to have the upper hand, in the end the good will be triumphant.

This "City of God" was represented by the early Church in its struggles with paganism, followed by the strife endured by Christians during the Dark Ages, before the glorious flowering of Christendom in the medieval era. All during this period, however, the "pagan city" was present as an evil undercurrent, one that eventually burst forth during the so-called Reformation. The last five hundred years have seen the eclipse of the Church by this worldly city, as revolution has followed revolution and mankind has increasingly turned away from God. As will be seen in the accounts of the Marian apparitions, however, God has given humanity a way forward and a pledge of eternal life, a promise that this reign of evil, which presently encompasses almost the entire world, will finally be destroyed and a period of true peace will commence for mankind.

The gradual collapse of the Roman Empire, a result both of internal moral decay and external invasions, left the Church as the only effective authority in Europe, with the Catholic bishops assuming important leadership roles in society. In fact, so bad was the desolation that it was necessary for the continent to be re-evangelized, and this was largely the work of Irish monks, who between the sixth and eleventh centuries worked as missionaries. The best of the classical civilizations was preserved by the Church, particularly through the work of the Benedictine Order, although the Irish also played an important part in this, as Europe descended into a state resembling chaos during the repeated invasions which took place during this period. St Benedict (c.480-c.550) is another example of those outstanding saints whose actions, like those of St Athanasius, have completely altered the course of history for the better. The papacy and the Benedictines were two of the most important social forces during the Dark Ages, and between them they saved Europe and made the rebuilding of civilization possible. Even so, the work of converting the barbarian invaders took centuries, and there was always the constant threat from new external enemies such as Islam, a threat which was only driven back at tremendous cost.[76]

Charlemagne (c.742–814) built up a great Frankish civilization, which covered most of the old Roman Empire, and he was seen as the temporal ruler, with the Pope as the spiritual ruler, of what was really the beginnings of Western Christendom. But this was to prove a false dawn, and fresh invasions saw tenth-century Europe once more in turmoil, with a widespread breakdown in order and culture as the continent was assailed from the north, east and south, by the Vikings, Magyars and Islamic forces respectively. The West survived because it was able to absorb and convert the pagan cultures of the North, and particularly the Vikings or Northmen, who, once civilized, helped to reanimate European society.[77]

Slowly Europe began to build itself up again; as trade and general prosperity grew, and influenced by factors such as the Crusades, the greatest period of Christendom, culminating in the thirteenth century, unfolded. This was also a time of great Marian devotion, with many shrines to Mary developing, a devotion particularly evident in the building of the great medieval cathedrals. These marvelous testimonials of living faith often took a century or more to complete, and were an expression of devotion to the Eucharist and of love for Mary, with a great many of them being dedicated to her. The medieval Church's influence extended to every part of religious and cultural life, and was evident in the great number of charitable institutions founded across Europe such as hospitals, orphanages and hospices for pilgrims, as well as in the growth of the universities.[78]

One of the most influential saints of the early part of this period was Bernard of Clairvaux (c.1090–1153), who has been regarded as the greatest figure of the twelfth century. He is credited with transforming religious life in Europe and saving the papacy from a dangerous schism, while also acting against heresy and launching a crusade. Under his leadership, the Cistercian order expanded rapidly and played a major part in building up medieval society through the diffusion of Christian culture. St Bernard was also important for his strong promotion of devotion to Mary, particularly his emphasis on her role as mediator between Christ and mankind.[79]

The spiritual authority of the Church, and particularly that of the popes, was widely acknowledged at this time, and indeed, Church and society were practically one in many respects. But as elements of Christendom grew richer, particularly the growing towns, but also sections of the Church itself, problems arose from the dangers of materialism and a weakening of spirituality. The appearance of St Francis of Assisi (1181–1226), who made poverty the cornerstone of his teaching, helped to bring about a return to the simplicity of the Gospel in Christendom as a whole. The Franciscans played an important role in keeping the Church in touch with the lives of ordinary people, and thus ensured that movements for reform were kept within it rather than pushed into opposition.[80]

St Dominic's life paralleled that of Francis, but his Dominican order was initially more concerned with the dangers involved in the heretical teachings of the Albigensians of southern France. Traditionally, Marian devotion has been seen as playing a part in the defeat of this heresy, since in response to it an early form of the rosary is said to have been preached with great success by Dominic. The ideas of the Albigensians were seen as a great threat by all Christendom, and if they had been allowed to prevail, they would undoubtedly have seriously affected Catholicism in Europe three centuries before the Reformation. It was about this time, too, that Mary appeared to St Simon Stock (d. 1265), the founder of the Carmelites in England, when at Aylesford in Kent she gave him the brown scapular and promised salvation to all who wore it with the proper dispositions.[81]

It is probably fair to say that, without the contribution of orders such as the Franciscans and Dominicans, the Church could have become increasingly remote in medieval urban society, and that the Reformation, or something very like it, might have happened much sooner and had even more serious effects.

The Decline of Christendom

Despite these good influences, however, serious problems continued to develop within medieval Christendom, particularly disputes between the papacy and the rulers of the Holy Roman Empire. In addition, the various states in Europe began to assert themselves more strongly, as the ideal of Christendom as a continent-wide realm weakened in the face of a growing sense of nationalism. Thus a process of decline set in during the thirteenth century, even as Christendom was at the height of its glory, a decline accelerated by the Black Death, which killed about twenty million people—a third of the population of Europe—in just a few years. Islam was still a threat to the south, and England and France were engaged on the Hundred Years War (1339–1453). It looked as though the French would be defeated in this long struggle, but France, the "eldest daughter" of the Church, that is, the pre-eminent Western Christian nation, was saved by the advent of Joan of Arc: Here is another example of God raising up a great saint in a very grave situation, in this case to save France from being drawn into Protestantism, something which would surely have happened if the country had been conquered by England and thus dominated by the English at the time of the Reformation.[82]

The pre-Reformation period also saw the role of the papacy called into question, particularly after the exile of the popes at Avignon for seventy years, while the Great Schism, (1378–1417), during which there were two and then three claimants to the papacy, caused a great deal of harm. However, even though the late medieval period saw Christendom declining, God nevertheless raised up powerful spiritual individuals who did all they could to halt this process. It was a time of fiery "apocalyptic" preachers, of whom the most notable was St Vincent Ferrer (1350–1419). He spent the last twenty years of his life preaching mainly, but not exclusively, in southern Europe, attracting vast crowds by his eloquence and reputation for sanctity. His mission was to exhort sinners to repentance and prepare them for the Last Judgment, a role which was later acknowledged by the Church in the papal bull of his canonization, which described him as "the Angel of the Apocalypse." His labours were incredibly successful, to the extent that it can certainly be argued that he seems to have converted a sufficient number of people to put off the Day of Judgment, which was apparently imminent, though conditional, at the time.[83] His task, along with other preachers, seems to have been to ensure that enough of Europe would remain faithful to Catholicism to prevent the Church from being overwhelmed by the Reformation. It is significant that no figures to compare with him emerged in northern Europe, in those countries which succumbed to Protestantism.

The north also had to face other problems in the appearance of religious reformers, such as Ockham and Wyclif in England, and Hus in Bohemia; their attacks on the Church prefigured those of later figures, such as Luther and Calvin. In addition, new humanistic ideas were coming to the fore and giving rise to a rebirth or *renaissance* of ancient culture in the West. The development of printing meant that these new ideas could be diffused ever more widely, further contributing to the intellectual ferment in pre-Reformation society. It was widely agreed that the Church was in need of reform, but no solid plan of action could be agreed on, and increasingly the popes became too involved in the Renaissance to be effective leaders of Christendom as a whole.[84]

This meant that, when it eventually happened, the Reformation was really more of a revolution, a radical change from the basic principles which had been instilled into society by the Church for fifteen hundred years, rather than a purging of harmful practices and a return to authentic Christianity. The Reformation was really the first successful stage in a revolution which has been going on for five centuries now, and which has seen the development of further profoundly influential episodes in the French and Russian Revolutions. This overall revolution, the revolution against the teaching of the Catholic Church, Christendom, and ultimately the truth revealed by God in Christ, came to its initial fruition in the Protestant Reformation, although it would really be more correct to describe it as the Protestant *Revolution,* like the two great revolutions which succeeded it. All of this makes it important to look at the reasons for the Reformation, and its course, as well as that of the two other major revolutions, because they tell us why the world is in such a serious state of moral and spiritual decay. The other main reason for looking at them is that it is difficult to understand the rationale for the various Marian apparitions, if they are not considered in the context of these revolutionary outbursts and their after effects.

Although it is useful to categorize these events in revolutionary terms, it is important to realize that they are only the most serious episodes in the history of mankind's revolt against God. The seeds of decay were already present when Christendom was at the height of its powers, particularly regarding corrupting influences within the Church. Later developments, such as secular humanism and the growth of capitalism, have become major factors in accelerating this process of spiritual and moral decline, and the move away from a God-centered to a more man-centered way of life.

However, in using the term "capitalism," it should be realized that this word has, to some extent, been linked, particularly by Marxist and Socialist writers, almost exclusively with the idea of the exploitation of workers. Although the economic system which can broadly be described as capitalism, that is, the control of trade and industry by private owners for profit, has often led in the past to abuses, it has also led, generally speaking, to much higher standards of living for many people. Capitalists contribute to economic activity and employment and, in this sense at least, benefit society. The problem is that it is difficult to avoid using the word, despite its negative connotations, and so the reader needs to be aware of these particular points. Likewise, the Renaissance and Humanism were responsible for a number of negative developments, but they also had positive aspects, particularly in the areas of philosophy and art, which must not be overlooked. As in all things it is a question of balance.

The various revolutions, then, represent the peaks of activity in what appears to be a steadily downward trend away from truth and goodness, although clearly God's grace is always at work in a hidden way, and he is able to bring good out of apparent evil. Nevertheless, it seems fair to say that these revolutions have been the major battles in a long-drawn-out war that has been going on for centuries now, a war that will go on until the end of time and the second coming of Christ.

It is important to keep in mind this long struggle between the claims of God upon man, as represented by the Church, and the claims of the world detached from God, as represented by the State, when reading this book, because it is the key to understanding how Europe, and indeed the world, have reached their present situation of moral decay.

The Protestant Revolution

At the time of the Reformation, in the early sixteenth century, the Church was still central in the lives of the people of Europe: the momentum of over a thousand years of Christianity was not to be lightly dissipated. The great majority still tended to keep to the faith of their ancestors in opposition to heretical teachings, and despite the many negative influences gaining ground. Preachers, such as St Vincent Ferrer, had initiated something of a revival in the fifteenth century, and church life, while far from perfect, did show definite signs of vitality. Regrettably, in some respects, there was a tendency to turn towards exterior forms of worship, with the abuse of relics and indulgences causing problems. There was also a hankering for superstitious practices, often combined with exaggerated devotion to the saints. All the upheavals of the preceding centuries, including the Avignon papacy, the great western schism and the Black Death, had a disturbing cumulative effect. Respect for authority, both religious and secular, was in decline, and this also affected morality, particularly sexual morality, as people followed the example of their leaders. Amongst the clergy, grave problems were caused by inadequate educational standards, priests cohabiting with women, and a lack of pastoral care for ordinary Christians. Some monasteries and religious orders had attempted to introduce reforms, but these were hampered by a lack of religious discipline and a tendency to accept unsuitable applicants. The low state of religious life in Germany[85] was graphically demonstrated by the large numbers of religious who apostatized, when given the chance by Luther's revolution.[86]

All this was taking place against a background of social, educational and technological change that unsettled people's minds and made them susceptible to the theories of those who offered simple solutions to very difficult and deep-seated problems. Germany in particular was in a state of ferment in the early sixteenth century, with a weak central government and antagonism between the different social classes. Humanistic ideas became a serious rival to the teachings of the Church, and humanist writers opposed her doctrines, as people began to lose sight of the central role of the papacy. In addition, the great wealth of the Church began to seem very tempting to those who wanted to get their hands on ecclesiastical lands. Similarly, heavy taxes and numerous alleged financial abuses, particularly in the area of indulgences, led to feelings of exasperation, especially when it seemed as though Rome and the Renaissance popes were unwilling to do anything much to remedy these problems.[87]

High levels of church taxation were thus undoubtedly a factor in preparing the way for the Protestant Reformation, and the Catholic historian Pierre Janelle argues that the point was finally reached, "where financial maladministration led to religious abuses properly speaking. The doctrinal contentions of the Reformers were, to a large extent, the translation into theological language of a protest against undue payments exacted from the laity."[88] Huge amounts of money were needed to run the Church, but the new and oppressive taxes introduced to deal with this, while causing much bad feeling, did not bring in as much as expected by the time those responsible for collecting the money had taken their own share. It is estimated that two-thirds of expected revenues never reached Rome at all, as various middle-men took their cut. This constant indebtedness of the papacy led to the inexcusable abuse of the sale of ecclesiastical offices, but, even so, the Renaissance popes were still obliged to obtain loans from the various banking houses to make up the shortfall. These bankers wanted some sort of security, and so they obtained permission to collect papal taxes locally; it was this type of conduct that led to the banking House of Fugger, at Augsburg, becoming involved in the promotion of the indulgence which led to Luther's protest in 1517.[89]

At that time Germany was not a unified centralized power, as France and England were under their kings; it existed instead as a conglomeration of four hundred states of various sizes, and this was a disorder that the weakened Holy Roman Empire was not able to overcome. Germany was thus in a state of confusion, waiting for someone to give it a sense of national consciousness, and it so happened that that person was to be Martin Luther. The secular rulers were aggrieved that a foreign power, the papacy, controlled the revenues of the German Church, a Church they saw as the main obstacle to a unified Germany. This resentment, coupled with the realization that they could solve many of their financial problems by appropriating the property of the Church, became the moving force behind the Reformation, which was really "a reformation of the medieval state at the expense of the Church." Luther's religious reformation was a parallel process that became bound up in these secular aspirations to form the mighty move-ment of revolt against the Catholic Church we know as the Reformation.[90]

The situation was particularly dangerous because of the way that the Church in Germany had effectively come under the control of the secular rulers of the small cities and states that made up the country. This tendency had developed during the confusion caused by the Conciliar theory, when the various popes were forced to make concessions that undermined the authority of the bishops; when the Reformation started in earnest, this practical domination of the Church by secular rulers proved crucial. If possession is nine points of the law, then the Church in Germany was *de facto* in the possession of the various princes before Luther had even said a word, and this factor proved to be a great determi-nant of the course of the Reformation. For when it came, the ordinary people were led to accept the change in religion, since it seemed only an extension of a system already in place.[91]

Although the situation in Germany was desperate, there were positive signs elsewhere, and particularly in Spain and Italy, where, in the case of the latter, the papacy was not seen as a remote and alien force, and where the Church was a genuine presence in everyday life. Spain was to become the bastion from which the Catholic counter-offensive would come, and by the late fifteenth century, with its new colonial possessions, it was developing into a world power. The Catholic faith of the people had been honed to an intense degree during the long reconquest of the country from its Muslim occupiers, only completed in 1492, which had welded all sections of society together. The Spanish monarchs, Isabella and Ferdinand, were deeply committed to the Faith, and had great control over the Spanish Church; as in Italy, the activities of the Inquisition had tended to remove those elements which would have caused trouble once the Reformation began. Likewise, the Church in Spain had gone through the sort of reform that was so sorely needed elsewhere, under the leadership of Cardinal Ximénes who founded the university at Alcala. He also supervised the publishing of a polyglot Bible in Hebrew, Greek and Latin, and worked for the educational and moral improvement of the clergy. All of this meant that Spain was able to play a crucial role in the Catholic or Counter-Reformation, which brought about the eventual spiritual renewal of the Catholic Church.[92]

Luther and the Reformation

Although there were points in favor of the Church in Germany, it was the victim of a sort of anticlerical spirit directed at Rome, a sign of growing German nationalism. There was also a cultural divide between Germany and southern Europe, which exacerbated the situation, and this social aspect of the Reformation cannot be ignored. Luther had an essentially medieval outlook and he was entirely opposed to the spirit of humanism and the Renaissance; emotionally he represented "the revolt of the awakening German national spirit." This was opposed to anything seen as too foreign, too intellectual, or too repressive, as in the case of asceticism.[93]

Martin Luther (1483–1546), in the years leading up to 1517 began to develop his own approach on predestination—the idea that God has already decided those to be saved or condemned—and also his notion that *faith alone* was capable of justifying men before God, thus making good works secondary, or even unnecessary.[94] He also placed the authority of the Bible over the supreme authority of the Church, and indeed, as time progressed, Luther's position became more thoroughly anti-Catholic until this element finally became its most distinguishing characteristic. However, the reality is that Luther's whole erroneous system was built on a few biblical texts taken out of context.[95]

At Wittenberg in 1517, Luther protested against the preaching of an indulgence, and his seed fell on to fertile ground; what began for him as really a theological protest rapidly developed into a social and political upheaval that can properly be termed a revolution. The ninety-five theses he had nailed to the church door were printed and circulated widely, causing much debate in the country, and his new ideas came to the attention of the authorities in Rome. Until at least 1519 it seems that Luther still wanted to remain part of the Church, but others, including Ulrich von Hutten, a German nationalist, saw him as a useful means of attaining their own ends, which went beyond religious reforms. Strengthened by such support, Luther grew bolder and more intemperate. The political situation favored him, because there was a lack of a sufficiently strong authority to bring him under control, while he also had the support of Frederick, the Elector of Saxony.[96]

Positions hardened and Germany divided into those for or against Luther, with support for him growing stronger; by 1520 there seemed to be no going back. He produced books putting forward his views, criticizing Rome and setting out an agenda for a future Council. He saw the Spirit guiding all Christians in the interpretation of the Scriptures, attacked church disciplinary rules and wanted to see more lay control over the Church. Meanwhile, in Rome his ideas were condemned as heretical, he was forbidden to teach, and he was urged to retract or be excommunicated. Luther rejected this ruling and produced a violent pamphlet in reply called *Against the Bull of Antichrist,* before burning the papal bull and so ensuring his excommunication in 1521. The Imperial Diet, or Assembly, then officially condemned Luther, but he was saved by the Elector of Saxony and hidden in a castle. Meanwhile, support for Luther's ideas continued to grow, and the political situation, which saw the emperor Charles V unable to intervene, also favored him.[97]

The common people, anxious for change, enthusiastically supported Luther, not realizing where it was all going to lead, and it is significant that many priests and religious abandoned their vocations at this stage, and even married. The situation became dangerous when mobs, responding to Luther's outbursts, started to attack church buildings, as extremists began to take over the uprising, a common element in many revolutions. Under their leader Thomas Munzer, the Anabaptists, who rejected infant baptism, in 1520, called for the complete destruction of the Roman Church; but Luther was still sufficiently in control of the situation to discourage such activities, at least for the time being.[98] Bohemia, already affected by the teaching of Jan Hus (c.1372–1415), for the most part rapidly succumbed to Lutheranism from 1520 onwards, allowing the nobility to get their hands on church property. Hungary, too, was affected by Lutheranism, and, perhaps surprisingly, given its subsequent history, Poland too showed initial signs of accepting Luther's ideas. Sweden under Gustavus Vasa also rejected Catholicism, essentially for political reasons, and by 1524 Sweden had a state church with Lutheranism imposed on the country; the other Scandinavian countries followed suit in the 1530s.[99] Poland's ultimate fidelity to Catholicism, however, would be symbolized in the following century by the defeat of an invading Swedish army at Czestochowa monastery. In 1665 Charles Gustave of Sweden and two thousand troops were defeated by a small force commanded by the Prior of the monastery, in what was seen as a miraculous victory. Czestochowa was and is the premier Marian shrine in the country, housing an icon of Mary attributed to St Luke—the Black Madonna.[100]

At this stage Luther's ideas were making rapid headway in northeastern Europe, but although France was affected to some extent, forceful action by Charles V in the Low Countries ended Protestant penetration there for the time being. In Spain and Italy, people were too much attached to Catholicism for heretical ideas to have any real impact, and likewise England was initially unreceptive to Luther's ideas; and certainly, at this stage, could anyone have foreseen that England, the Dowry of Mary, would embrace Protantism?[101]

Following the Peasants' War (1524–5), Luther found himself on the side of the princes, of authority, rather than that of the common man, and thus the religious movement he initiated now became definitely nationalist and political, as rulers realized what they had to gain by following, or rather using, Luther. Those gains were definitely of a material rather than a spiritual nature, since the princes used Lutheranism as an excuse to confiscate church possessions all over Germany. By now, Luther totally rejected any idea of the Church as a hierarchical body, seeing it rather as invisible and made up of baptized believers who accepted the Gospel, a position that in practice was often close to anarchy. The authority of the Pope and the Church was replaced by that of the State, whose rulers had a duty to impose the practice of Lutheranism on their people; rulers who had accepted Luther's ideas were quick to take control of such state churches in their domains. By 1530, Protestantism was firmly enough established, although it was already beginning to split into different parties, some of which were putting forward ideas totally alien to those of Luther. As a movement, it was really too strong to be destroyed by force, and was too intransigent to consider compromise, and so the decisive moment had been reached when it had to be accepted as a political and religious reality.[102]

The emperor Charles V realized this, and recognized that the problems with Luther had arisen because the Church had not carried out the necessary internal reforms. Nevertheless, he still had some hopes that a correction of abuses might eventually lead to a reconciliation between the two parties. But, following the breakdown of earlier talks at Augsburg, he decided on measures that would have led to the re-imposition of Catholicism in Protestant areas, to which, in February 1531, the Lutheran rulers responded by setting up the Schmalkaldic League. This was a Lutheran anti-imperial alliance centred on the Protestant areas of Germany and was a crucial step in the political consolidation of Protestantism.[103] Thus 1531 saw the moment when Luther's religious revolt became bound up with an accelerating political and social revolution, and, as we have seen, 1531 was also the year of the apparitions of Our Lady of Guadalupe.

3

Protestant Progress and Catholic Reform

The Consolidation of the Reformation

The breakdown in the unity of faith which Catholicism had given to Europe, and the progress made by Protestantism, meant that the new religion was now a threat to the Habsburgs, and that civil war at some stage within the Empire was inevitable. A long struggle now began between the forces of Charles V (1500–58), and the Protestant armies, one which saw an increase in the power of the German princes, as that of the emperor declined.[104] Finally, in 1555 a settlement known as the Peace of Augsburg was signed, which recognized the *status quo*, and accepted that each prince should decide upon his own religion and that of his subjects. Although this settlement is usually regarded as a victory for Protestantism, in fact the chief beneficiaries were the princes. It was religion that was the loser, as the spirit of genuine reform drained away, while Germany itself was left in a weakened, divided, condition for the next three hundred years, a chequered land of small states.[105]

By this stage, nearly forty years after Wittenberg, Luther's revolt had led to the creation of a series of separated churches and sovereign states, a system that would last with few changes until the French Revolution. Despite its almost overpoweringly religious overtones, the Reformation was essentially a struggle to resolve the conflict between the Church and the developing new states over who would have ultimate authority. Although the need for church reform was pressing, the bishops had become too closely bound to the state to be a source of reform. In Germany they had become secular rulers, while in France and England they were very much subject to the monarchy, and, in addition, many had neglected their spiritual duties. Similarly, the religious orders had also tended to decline in spiritual vitality, and, although in theory the papacy possessed the power to remedy these abuses, in the century prior to the Reformation the papacy had become corrupted through involvement in Italian politics. Its ability to act was also limited by the need to co-operate with the growing national powers.[106]

At this point it must have seemed to many that there was no way of stopping the steady advance of Protestantism in northern Europe, since all the advantages seemed to lie with the Reformers, as the revolutionary movement took on a momentum of its own and assumed more concrete social and political aspects. In addition, genuine reform of the Catholic Church was slow to take effect in the face of the Protestant offensive. The Council of Trent only began in 1545, and did not complete its work until 1563, while the Jesuit Order, founded in 1540 by St Ignatius Loyola, likewise took some time to become effective. It is important to emphasize, though, that the Catholic Reformation was *not* simply a reaction against the rise of Protestantism. It is true that the Protestant Reformation had the effect of greatly stimulating the Catholic reform, but it was not its primary cause. The Catholic reform movement was really another example of the work of *spiritual* reform undertaken by men such as St Bernard in the twelfth century, and St Francis and St Dominic in the thirteenth.[107] It was something which, given time, would have happened anyway. In a sense, then, it can be said that Luther's revolt had the effect of overshadowing and diverting energies away from the genuine reform movement, seriously undermining any chance of a true reform for the whole of Christendom.

The Reformation in England

Before and during Luther's revolt, the need for reform of the English Church was widely recognized, and humanists such as John Colet and Thomas More put forward various ideas for effecting reform, with some of these suggestions later being used, sadly, against the Catholic Church in England by those who sought to overthrow it. At that time there was a degree of resentment against the papacy, following all the problems of the great western schism, while the leader of the English Church, Cardinal Wolsey, was more of a politician than a churchman. Such a state of affairs pointed to future problems. From 1534 King Henry VIII enacted various measures to gain control of the English Church, including the Act of Supremacy, which demanded that he be recognized as its head, with full power to oversee religious affairs. This act effected the most complete usurpation of the Church's spiritual authority by any monarch since the beginning of the Reformation.[108]

Over the next four years, hundreds of monasteries were closed with little resistance and came into the hands of the Crown. Most of the properties and lands were sold at very low prices to supporters of the king to ensure their loyalty, and this in itself was enough to ensure that there could be no return to the *status quo* before Henry VIII's schism from Rome.[109] The crucial factor inherent in looting the Church's wealth was the denial of the authority of the Pope, the central principle of the Protestant position. The wealth of the monasteries could not be seized as long as their dependence on the papacy was acknowledged, and hence it was necessary to replace the juridical authority of the Catholic Church in England with a new state church which henceforth did not owe allegiance to the Pope.[110]

There was a great difference between the course of the Reformation as it unfolded in England and France, both of which had strong centralized monarchies, in comparison with Germany, whose lands were divided up among the princes. In neither of the former was there any great social or religious revolution leading to the destruction of the state church; instead the national Anglican and Gallican churches were created, and the monarch determined the religion of the people. Both countries were affected by Calvinism, France more acutely, but in neither case was it strong enough to prevail.[111]

Calvin and Protestantism

During the 1530s, John Calvin came to prominence, and he was destined to have an important role in consolidating Protestantism. He based himself in Geneva, where he began to implement his ideas, becoming the effective leader of the Protestant cause after Luther's death. Calvinism was essentially a modified and more extreme form of Lutheranism, and it too denied free will and believed in justification by faith without works; it held to an absolute predestination in which God had willed from eternity those who would be damned, as well as their sins. Like Luther, Calvin saw the Bible as central, rejecting the idea that the Church's Magisterium—which, however, is not above the Word of God, but serves it—was the authentic interpreter of Scripture.[112] He argued that the Holy Spirit provided an "inner testimony" to believers as to the Bible's authority and canonicity. Calvin worked hard to try and unify the various strands of Protestantism that had developed, although this proved impossible due to irreconcilable differences, especially on matters such as the Lord's Supper. The very nature of Protestantism, built as it was on the idea that religion was a personal matter between the believer and God, meant that such differences were inevitable. Nevertheless, Calvin's ideas were very influential and although his theology did not make much headway in Germany or England, or even France ultimately, in the long run it was more successful in parts of Switzerland and the Low Countries and particularly in Scotland, where his disciple, John Knox (1505–72), introduced Presbyterianism.[113]

It would be a mistake to imagine that Protestantism was an entirely negative phenomenon in religious or social terms, since it would never have attracted as much support as it did if that had been the case, but nevertheless, its overall effects were adverse, in that it led to an increased, but erroneous, emphasis on Scripture *alone* at the expense of the Church's Magisterium, along with an effective denial of free will, and eventually, to the secularization of European culture.

Catholic Reform, the Jesuits, and the Council of Trent

The Protestant Reformation thus brought about a rupture with ancient Christian traditions, whereas the Catholic Reformation was an authentic movement to *rediscover* the traditions of Christendom and all it stood for. It was not directed against Protestantism as such, but in its essence was rather a movement of spiritual reform. The various movements of reform within the Church were beginning to make an impact, but they were not very effective due to the poor leadership and bad example given by the hierarchy, and particularly by the Renaissance popes. The Church having grown too rich had become partly secularized, and thus calls for reform were continually frustrated. In the ensuing situation disputes between monarchs, the papacy, and those favouring Councils, were deadlocked—a state that was only broken by the Reformation, but in a way which had consequences completely opposed to the desires of those who sought for authentic reform.[114]

The desire for spiritual reform within the Church was a very broadly-based movement, and it is widely recognized that the main impetus came from two sources: the first was the Jesuits of

St Ignatius Loyola, whose *Spiritual Exercises,* a form of retreat notes, played an important part in the eventual success of the Catholic Revival, as did the educational work of the order. The other element was the wholehearted support of the papacy; and it was the papal backing for the Council of Trent, despite all sorts of obstacles, which assured its final success.[115]

On becoming Pope, Paul III (1534–49) quickly summed up the situation in Europe and realized that resolute action was necessary to combat its political and religious divisions, as well as the danger from Islam. With strenuous diplomacy, he managed to clear the way for the calling of a Council, choosing as cardinals men of integrity and ability to carry out the work of reform. The Pope still faced difficulties, however, in convening the Council, not least from those Protestants who wanted a Council on their own terms. It took nine years of hard work before it finally opened in December 1545, in the small city of Trent in the Tyrol. Initially there were few bishops in attendance, and its work was not to be completed for a further eighteen years.[116]

A tremendous amount was accomplished by the end of the final session, as Protestant teachings were censured and measures for reform introduced, with all of this work being subsequently disseminated, especially through the Catechism that was produced in 1566. In describing the results achieved at Trent, the Catholic historian, Henri Daniel-Rops, argues that it was the most important Council in the whole history of the Church, and played a crucial part in stabilizing Catholicism following the upheavals caused by the Reformation. In particular, he points to the fact that the Council's work was the fruit of centuries of effort and Christian tradition, in contrast to the doctrines of the Reformers, which had essentially sprung into being from but a few minds, and in a short time. Trent clarified the main areas of contention, namely, revelation and doctrine, the role of faith and works, grace and the sacraments, while the Council rejected the Protestant view that the Bible alone was sufficient to establish true Christianity. Trent pointed out that it was the role of the Church to guard and interpret the twin deposits of Scripture and Tradition, thus opposing the individualistic Protestant approach, which could, and unfortunately often did, lead people astray. The importance of Trent's dogmatic decrees lay in the fact that they ensured future stability and clearly taught what the Church believed, thus removing the uncertainty and confusion prevalent amongst Catholics in the period immediately following the Reformation.[117]

Trent, the Role of Mary, and the Battle of Lepanto

The Council had indirectly affirmed Mary's sinlessness in the following words, in the decree which stipulated the sinfulness of all human beings, apart from her, arguing for her preservation from all sin, even venial sin, by a special grace from God: "If anyone asserts that man, after he is once justified ... is able to avoid throughout his lifetime all, even venial sin, except by a special divine privilege, as the Church holds in regard to the Blessed Virgin, let him be anathema." This was to offset the negative approach taken towards Mary by the Reformers, who, because of their erroneous views on original sin, had rejected the principle of Mary's sinlessness. Their ideas that human nature was intrinsically corrupt, and that man was justified by faith alone, had led them to see Christ alone as sinless.[118] The Council also adopted a decree which reserved to the bishop concerned, and if necessary, to the pope, the task of recognizing the relics of saints, miracles, apparitions and other supernatural facts. Bishops were to take the advice of theologians and other "pious men" in assessing the truth about reported apparitions, and, in difficult cases, to obtain advice from higher authorities. This decree thus set out the way Marian apparitions would be investigated in future.[119]

The most difficult task of the Council was to ensure that its decrees were enforced, and it fell to Pope St Pius V (1566–72), to lead the way in securing this objective. He was a man of tremendous ability, iron determination and evident sanctity, who led by the personal example of an ascetic lifestyle, and who was determined to implement the decrees of Trent at all costs. He worked to establish order and discipline in the Church, ordering bishops back to their dioceses, while also launching a drive towards moral improvement, and particularly the elimination of simony and nepotism. His stance was widely supported in both Italy and Spain, and to a large extent he succeeded in his aims, in a drive to reinvigorate the Church that culminated in the crusade against Islam and the victory at Lepanto.

In 1571, Europe was threatened yet again by a Moslem invasion and Pius V decided to organize a crusade against a large fleet of over two hundred and fifty Turkish ships, which had gathered in the eastern Mediterranean. He managed to persuade the rulers of Spain, Venice and Genoa to support this project, and a Christian fleet of about the same size assembled under the leadership of Don John of Austria, the half-brother of the Spanish king, Philip II.[120] On 7 October 1571 the two fleets met at Lepanto, and the result was a crushing Christian victory, in which practically the entire enemy fleet was destroyed, with little loss for the Catholics. Lepanto was significant in that it was the first victory at sea over the Moslems, and although it did not immediately remove the threat from that quarter, it did indicate the decline of Turkish influence in Europe.[121]

It is noteworthy that Charles V of Spain had given a copy of the miraculous Image of Our Lady of Guadalupe to Prince Doria of Genoa, who, as an admiral, kept it in his cabin during the battle.[122] His squadron was cut off from the rest of the Christian fleet, and when the situation became desperate he is said to have knelt and prayed before the Image to save them from defeat; the tide of battle then began to turn in their favor and the destruction of the Turkish fleet led to the release of fifteen thousand Christian galley-slaves.[123]

The Pope is said to have had a vision of Mary during the battle itself, assuring him of victory; he was at work with his cardinals, when he suddenly opened a window and looked up to the sky, before asking those present to join him in thanksgiving to God for the great victory that had just been obtained.[124] Pius V did not hesitate to attribute this great victory to the prayers of rosary confraternities in Rome and elsewhere, and he ordered that Lepanto be commemorated annually. Initially known as the feast of "St Mary of Victory," this memorial eventually became the feast of "Our Lady of the Rosary," being extended to the whole Church in the eighteenth century.[125]

Nor was this the last time that it could be said that Christendom was saved from the threat posed by Islam: the crucial victory at Vienna by the Polish king, John III Sobieski, in 1683, is another example of the intercessory power of Our Lady of the Rosary. In fact, from this point on, the rosary assumed an ever more important place in the prayer life of the Church, a prayer recommended by numerous saints, including St Louis de Montfort, and one which Catholics have been encouraged to recite by practically all of the popes since the fifteenth century. Leo XIII, for example, between 1883 and 1898, issued no less than ten encyclicals devoted solely to the rosary, a measure of the importance he attached to it.[126] More recently, at Fatima, on each of the six occasions she appeared to the children, Mary asked them to say the rosary. As in the past the rosary saved civilization from external attack, so now it is the remedy given by Heaven to save us from the more insidious threat of a godless world.

The Catholic Reformation and Marian Apparitions

The course of the Reformation in France was much influenced by events in Switzerland, and particularly by Calvin's dictatorship in Geneva, which was a crucial support for the reforming movement in the country, while also providing a model for Protestant churches all over Europe. Unlike England, where the monarchy destroyed the Catholic Church and substituted Anglicanism, in France the throne supported Catholicism; but, despite this, the genius of Calvin meant that Protestantism was strong enough to offer determined resistance both to the government and to the majority of the people. Because of this, there was no possibility of some sort of "compromise" solution as in England, and the country was badly affected by the religious struggle that took place during the sixteenth century. Church and State were closely bound together, and this meant that it was in the interest of the king to support the Church against Protestantism, while he was, at the same time, opposed to the ideals of the Catholic Reformation which would have weakened his hold on the Church.[127]

By 1560, many conversions to Protestantism had taken place, particularly among the nobles, but also of numbers of common people, who had turned to the Bible for religious sustenance, to the extent that there was certainly a possibility of the country turning Protestant.[128] All this ensured that these religious wars only ended when the leader of the Protestant Huguenot party, Henry IV (1553–1610), converted to Catholicism on becoming king. Calvinism, however, continued to affect French life, and, paradoxically, influenced the development of the strong sense of religious scepticism within the country in the seventeenth and eighteenth centuries, which itself prepared the way for the French Revolution.

Spain was the most powerful European country during this period, its empire giving it a more international character than other states; and, as emperor, Charles V had taken seriously his responsibilities as the leader of the fight against both Protestantism and Islam. The Spanish Empire inherited by his son, Philip II (1527–98), was a world-wide affair, and, when animated by the ideals of Spanish Catholicism, became a very strong factor in the success of the Catholic Reformation.[129] The sixteenth century thus represented the height of Spanish power, a power expressed in an incredible dynamism, affecting both religious and secular life, which was particularly significant for the energizing effect it had on those governing the Church, primarily through the work of the Jesuits.[130]

Although Guadalupe was the most important of the "Counter-Reformation" apparitions, there were quite a number of other such incidents in the sixteenth and seventeenth centuries; but for the most part they are now forgotten. This is not to cast doubt on their authenticity but, for various reasons, they have not attracted a large following within the Church, or at least not one which has been maintained to the present day, unlike Guadalupe, which remains the most visited Marian shrine in the world, attracting up to fourteen million pilgrims annually in recent years. These apparitions seem to have acted as short-term measures to deal with the specific problems caused by the rise of Protestantism. That is, in areas either directly or indirectly affected by the Reformation, such as France, Italy, Spain and even Germany, they had the function of preventing the inroads of Protestantism. These include apparitions at Savona in Northern Italy in March and April 1536, and at Montallegro, again in Italy, in July 1557;[131] while other Marian shrines of this era can also be regarded as resulting from "local" small scale apparitions, for instance, the Spanish shrines at Reus, and Sant Aniol, both of which were connected with preexistent devotions.[132] France, though, was more directly affected by Calvinism and it seems that the apparitions at Vinay in 1649, and Le Laus in 1664, were a direct response to the threat this presented.[133] These French apparitions in particular, and other more minor ones, although they were important at the time, have not retained their importance into the modern era. As indicated, it seems that their main, although not exclusive, purpose was to assist the Church in its Counter-Reformation struggle with Protestantism.

4

The Reformation and Secularization

Britain Becomes Protestant

Following the death of Henry VIII in 1547, England gradually became more Protestant, especially as the nobility had no intention of handing back the ill-gotten gains they had acquired following the dissolution of the monasteries. By 1549, many aspects of the traditional faith were being changed, but slowly, so as not to arouse too much discontent; even so there were rebellions in Devon and Cornwall, which had a strong religious basis, against the imposition of the new beliefs. These, though, were bloodily suppressed and the Reformation in England progressed. Under Archbishop Cranmer, a new Prayer Book was issued in 1549, being revised in 1552, with anything that savored of Catholicism in churches being forbidden; altars were replaced by tables, and statues or paintings removed or covered up. The principles of Christ's real presence in the Eucharist, the Mass as a sacrifice, and the priesthood, were all rejected, with the main emphasis being placed on the pastor as the minister of the Word.[134]

When Mary Tudor became queen, she was determined to bring England back to Catholicism, and undo all the policies and laws passed by her immediate predecessors. But she was overzealous, and on her death in 1558, she left a legacy of bitterness, and indeed hatred, for Catholicism, which her Protestant successor, Elizabeth I (1533–1603), was well able to exploit during her long reign; this antagonism was set to last for a further three centuries. At this time Ireland was linked to England feudally, but Protestantism had made little headway there; an attempted rebellion in 1565, headed by the O'Neill clan, led to severe reprisals on Elizabeth's part, with bishops and priests being massacred and many religious houses being destroyed by marauding armies. A similar rebellion took place in northern England; this too was crushed, and these events, combined with her excommunication by Pope Pius V in 1570, who released her subjects from allegiance to her, led the queen to adopt extreme anti-Catholic measures. A climate of anti-Catholic hysteria was whipped up and Elizabeth allied herself with the Protestant powers of northern Europe, so that, when the Spanish Armada was destroyed in 1588, England's position as a fully Protestant power was firmly established.[135]

Elizabeth's government, under Lord Burghley, William Cecil, (1520–98), worked to establish a middle way, Anglicanism, between Calvinism and Catholicism, managing to retain control over those quite strong Puritan elements who would have done away with bishops altogether. It was Cecil who was responsible for many of the day-to-day decisions during Elizabeth's reign, sometimes even working against her; and so it was the "rabidly anti-Catholic" Cecil who was, more than anyone else, responsible for the success of the Protestant revolution in England.[136] Hilaire Belloc has described him as one of the greatest, but also one of the vilest men who ever lived.[137]

The defection of England from the Catholic faith was perhaps the most significant event of the Reformation, in that, without it, the revolt against the Church might well have been confined to mainland Europe and thus failed. The Catholic historian, Warren H. Carroll, points out that if Henry had remained faithful, allied to Catherine of Aragon, the best daughter of Isabella and Ferdinand, he could have worked with the Holy Roman Emperor Charles V to restore Christendom.[138] This failure was all the more tragic, given that America became a Protestant country because of England's rejection of Catholicism. If Spain, France, and England could have worked together in North and South America, a new "Catholic" hemisphere could have been created in the West. Perhaps much of the rivalry and dissension between the various European countries might have been avoided, and Christendom saved. It is possible to argue that if this had happened, then many of the evils besetting the modern world would never have occurred.

Thus by the end of Elizabeth's reign, in 1603, Anglicanism had become more solidly established; and indeed English Protestantism, unlike its continental counterparts, was not weakened by the civil wars and revolutions that occurred elsewhere, actually becoming stronger. This was an extremely important development because this English Protestant culture was destined to have a far-reaching influence on world events, especially with the growth of the British Empire, and particularly in the case of America, the country that would eventually lead the world.[139]

By now, Europe was split into two opposing religious camps, one Catholic and the other Protestant, with little immediate hope of reconciliation. Most of northern and eastern Europe, apart from Poland and Ireland, was solidly Protestant, while most of southern Europe was Catholic, with France having strong pockets of Calvinism. The old order of Christendom was being torn apart, and the old sense that people had of belonging to a brotherhood united by a common faith was being lost. Worse still, the situation had not stabilized, particularly in Germany, as the horror of the Thirty Years War was to show. The reign of James I (1603–25), Elizabeth's successor on the English throne, saw the failure of the Gunpowder Plot, an event that further poisoned public opinion against Catholicism, leading to renewed persecution and a further stripping of the rights of Catholics. By now, the Low Countries had split into a Catholic south and a Calvinist north, with Switzerland also divided between the two religions; in still mainly Catholic France the Edict of Nantes had, in April 1598, proclaimed toleration for Protestants.[140]

At a deeper level, too, a cultural division was opening up between the Catholic and Protestant parts of Europe, as the Reformation led to a deprecation of the ideals of celibacy, monasticism, and church authority generally, in northern Europe. As Protestant societies became more secular, religion changed from being the primary part of the social edifice into an increasingly private affair, with economic criteria becoming more important.[141] In particular, the Puritan spirit led to an accentuation of the masculine, as the influence of the Old Testament increasingly made itself felt in a patriarchal ideal, one that made the family the religious and social basis of society.[142] This meant that a new Protestant civilization was growing up which was private and domestic, as opposed to the previous Catholic spirit, which had been public and communal. But in one of those curious historical paradoxes, it was this same spirit of Puritanism which provided the impetus for the rise of industrialization in England. This is just one example of the way that the Reformation was perpetuated, not so much by a continued intellectual revolt against the Church, as by the development of a new culture hostile to the traditional order.[143]

The Secularization of Western Culture

In 1618, the Thirty Years War broke out between Catholics and Protestants in Germany, but just when it seemed as though the

Catholic imperial forces would triumph, the Protestant cause was saved by the intervention of the Swedish king Gustavus Adolphus (1594–1632). This resulted in the war being widened until practically the whole of Europe was involved; France supported Sweden against the Spanish imperial power; and so the situation was reached where the forces of two "Catholic" kings were engaged, proving that the fighting had ceased to be a purely religious matter. It was in "Catholic" France's interest to support the Protestant German states, on the principle that a weak and divided Germany was less dangerous than one that was part of the rival Habsburg Empire.[144] Germany was to remain in this fragmented state until the rise of Prussia in the nineteenth century.

The Thirty Years War dragged on, until a general state of weariness prevailed and all sides looked for an end to hostilities. Germany was completely prostrated, having lost something between a third and a half of its population, as life was reduced to subsistence level for those who remained. Thus the Treaties of Westphalia, which gave Catholics and Protestants equal political rights, were signed in 1648; these, however, were mainly concerned with the rights of princes rather than the common people, who were obliged in the main to accept the religion of their rulers. Even the right of internal religious reform was allowed to rulers, thus in effect making them secular popes in their own territories, in opposition to the enactments of the Council of Trent. Protestantism benefited from the treaties, but was unable to unite in a single church, while the papacy was excluded from the negotiations, a sign of its decreasing influence.[145] The main effect of the Thirty Years War was to increase the power of France, while lessening that of Germany and Spain, leading to the breakup of the Empire; thus it greatly influenced the course of European history in succeeding centuries.

Indeed Spain, the country that had recently been the greatest support to Catholicism, was about to enter a period of decline. Philip II's plan for a Spanish world empire, comprising Spain, the Empire, and the forces of the Catholic Reformation, was destroyed by the emergence of the Protestant alliance between England, Holland and French Calvinism, especially as the northern countries began to take control of the seas. This shift in the overall balance of power was not a good omen for the future of the Church, which had been very severely damaged by the Protestant revolution. But Protestantism, too, was harmed by the way it had been used politically and as a pretext for violence and war; and so the overall loser was the ideal of a united Christian Europe, and religion generally.[146]

The Catholic Church, following Trent, was able to develop a new spirit of reform and order, whereas the various Protestant churches lacked a unifying principle and so tended to move further apart. This meant that Catholicism was able to win back large parts of central and northern Europe, with the educational work of the Jesuits playing a major role in this. Nevertheless, the cultural divide that was developing in Europe as a whole was accentuated by the fact that Tridentine Catholicism was much influenced by Spanish and Italian ideas, and was thus more "Latin" than the previous northern European medieval Catholic culture. So besides the theological divide between Catholics and Protestants, there was also a developing *cultural* divide between north and south, and taken together they made reunion impossible in practice. The most serious consequence of this division of the previously common culture was that it facilitated the secularization of the West.[147]

Still, despite this division, and the secularization it caused, both parts of Europe still shared a common heritage of humanistic thought, and this allowed western culture to continue to develop in the sixteenth and seventeenth centuries. But by the eighteenth century, this relatively progressive culture was being replaced by Enlightenment thinking, with its damaging criticism of Christianity. The destructive effects of this rational approach would became clearer during the French Revolution and its aftermath.[148]

The principles of the Reformation, its rejection of the Church, the sacraments and good works, led to tremendous social and economic changes. The old medieval conception of a social order, based on its members working together for an essentially spiritual purpose, was destroyed, since, according to Reformation thinking, secular interests were completely opposed and antagonistic to the Gospel. As R. H. Tawney says: "In one sense, the distinction between the secular and religious life vanished. Monasticism was, so to speak, secularized; all men stood henceforward on the same footing with God; and that advance, *which contained the germ of all subsequent revolutions*, was so enormous that all else seems insignificant."[149]

The Reformers introduced a note of despondency into human thinking in contrast to the optimism of Renaissance writers; and their teaching, because it tended to build up a barrier between religion and ordinary life, was one of the main factors in this process of secularization, along with the Protestant rejection of monasticism.[150] Luther's doctrine of the total depravity of human nature, and his dualistic teaching on nature and grace, led to a split between the moral law and religion. As Christopher Dawson says: "The profound pessimism of Luther saw in Nature nothing but the kingdom of death and the Law of Nature as the law of wrath and punishment, and thus his extreme supernaturalism prepared the way for the secularization of the world and the abolition of objective standards."[151] Calvinism took this a stage further and, having destroyed monasticism where it triumphed, attempted to turn the secular world into a gigantic "monastery," to build a society that was both a Church and a State.[152]

This was possible because the Reformation had destroyed much of the medieval religious and artistic culture of northern Europe, with its rich liturgical tradition, replacing it with an intellectual approach based on the Bible and sermons, and by a move from a "community-based" to a more individualistic religion. Luther had promoted an iconoclastic movement against religious art, opposing its veneration; and this was taken literally in many of the areas affected by Protestantism; for example, in Holland, mobs descended on Catholic churches and smashed every work of art they could lay their hands on, thus destroying a priceless artistic heritage. The process was less chaotic in England, being sanctioned by the government, but, for all that, the results were just as devastating. Later on, in Protestant Europe, traditional religious drama and art were banned, thus leading to a progressive cleavage between Christian culture generally and the lives of the ordinary people.[153]

One of the curious things, though, about the "Puritan" ideal, taken up by the followers of Calvin in the English-speaking world, was the way that these groups evolved from being "theocratic dictatorships," that is, societies based solely on a narrow understanding of the Bible, eventually to become the first "liberal democracies." This was a movement from one end of the spectrum to the other, as the principle of individualism latent in early Protestantism came more to the fore.[154] The influence of Calvinism resulted in this individualism being applied particularly in the area of commerce, where the Puritan ideals of hard work and frugality gave the rising middle classes a religious justification for their new approach to life. Previously, society had functioned more as a whole, with tradition and heredity determining a person's role in life, but now a new order was created, which depended more on the enterprise of the individual. Paradoxically, although Calvinism rejected good works and man's ability to merit, it managed to influence strongly the introduction of a new economic system, capitalism, one based on individual activity. Puritanism was an important influence on the growth of capitalism in England, because as Dissenters, Puritans were excluded from state offices until 1828, and so tended to gravitate towards commerce and industry.[155]

In economic and social terms, Calvinism found its natural home amongst those involved in trade, industry, and the new commercial culture growing up in northern Europe. It took a new and different attitude to commerce, giving it a measure of respectability, whereas before it had been seen as dubious, if not insidious. Calvin had accepted the realities of the new economic society and the principle of charging interest, rejecting the teaching of the Bible and the Church Fathers on this as out of date. This was a tremendously important change, because it allied Calvinism with the financial systems of the future.[156]

It was argued that the sort of qualities demanded for economic success, such as frugality, diligence and sobriety, were not incompatible with the Christian virtues, and that they could be used to build up a new and spartan Christian order, in contrast to the alleged luxury and laxity of pre-Reformation Catholic society. Thus, almsgiving was rejected in favor of individual hard work and thrift, as the principle of "good works" was abandoned and Christians were encouraged to do business in a serious and "religious" way. This released the economic energies of the *bourgeoisie*, who felt that in making money they were doing the will of God, with the result that Calvinism introduced a new scale of moral and social values, a new approach that was part of the ongoing revolution instigated by the Reformation.[157]

But the counterpoint of the rise of the bourgeoisie was the growth of the *proletariat*, those without property and thus security of livelihood, who were increasingly at the mercy of the new capitalist employers. Such a group had existed in small numbers before the Reformation, but only in a few commercial centers; now, however, this dispossessed class grew in tandem with Protestantism, particularly in England, and even amongst agricultural workers. It was also increasingly present in the other Protestant countries beginning to industrialize.[158]

From a practical point of view, too, there were other reasons why the northern Protestant countries tended towards a more intense capitalistic development from the sixteenth century onwards. These included a general displacement of trade from the Mediterranean to the Atlantic following the discoveries of the new lands, but particularly in the case of England and Holland, because of their increasing monopoly of overseas markets, following the decline of Spain and Portugal. The northern countries turned henceforth towards more bourgeois forms of government, which allowed capitalism more scope, and generally they dominated more in economic matters, in contrast to the southern preoccupation with politics and aristocratic forms of government.[159]

Obviously, though, it would be wrong to say that the rise of the capitalist spirit in England, and Protestant countries generally, can be explained wholly as a perversion of religious ideals; clearly factors such as man's innate sinfulness and greed, as well as more positive elements, such as the need for any healthy society to develop, also played their part. But undoubtedly, the major factor was the breakdown in Christendom brought on by the Reformation, and thus, while Catholicism was opposed to secularization, Protestantism provided a seedbed for the new ideas. By destroying the old medieval social order and its symbols, often physically through iconoclastic attacks on churches and works of art, it created a vacuum, which allowed an individualistic "puritan" ethic to grow up amongst the bourgeoisie, one which was very supportive of capitalism. Thus the Protestant Reformation inexorably led to the secularization of Western culture.

The Decline of the Monarchy

In England, Cromwell's Puritan dictatorship had been followed by the restoration of the monarchy under Charles II (1660–85), who was forced by hostile public opinion to withdraw his attempt to ameliorate the condition of Catholics; the Popish Plot, fabricated by Titus Oates, led to renewed persecution for Catholics. This also had repercussions in Ireland and led to the martyrdom of Archbishop St Oliver Plunkett, the country's primate, in 1681. The king's brother succeeded him as James II (1685–88), and, despite his Catholicism, was initially accepted by the people, who had no wish to return to something like Cromwell's Commonwealth. But in his zeal to restore Catholicism, he upset many of his Protestant subjects and was forced to flee, as the Huguenot army of the Protestant William of Orange and his wife Mary landed in England to inaugurate the so-called Glorious Revolution of 1688. Under their rule (1689–1702), Catholicism was again proscribed, a policy continued under Queen Anne and George I.[160] The further weakening of the monarchy during this later period was symbolized by the placing of the German George on the English throne by the aristocracy: he never learnt English, and spent most of his life in Hanover.

The victory of William and Mary was a great triumph for the Protestant cause, since it united Puritans and Anglicans in a common Protestant front, and led to the struggle with France which gradually tipped the balance of power in favor of Protestantism in Europe. Louis XIV and Catholicism generally were seen as the enemies of "freedom of conscience," in their action against the Huguenots.[161] This Glorious Revolution, however, led to a reduction in the power of the monarchy and the rise of the middle classes, as the idea of "divine right" of kings, an idea also under attack in France, further lost its appeal, and a philosophical outlook embracing property, commerce, toleration, and political freedom, gained in importance. The old monarchical ideal in England was destroyed and replaced with rule by a privileged oligarchy of selfish individuals.

This new regime was controlled by a small number of powerful families, a union of landowners and business men, in a form of parliamentary rule under which the monarchy was subservient. This new form of government eventually transformed the whole social structure of English society, as the rights of property were given first place, and the traditional Christian attitude to the poor was abandoned. This attitude was based on Puritan individualism and new philosophical ideas that blamed poverty on the individual concerned and made selfishness a virtue, while regarding charity as self-indulgence, and money as the driving force of society. In England the overall effect of the Civil War, which took place in the mid seventeenth century, and the antagonism of religious extremists, was to create a desire for toleration, leaving out the Catholics, of course, who were still to be persecuted. This atmosphere of toleration was conducive to secularization, although England still remained a stronghold of "liberal" Protestantism. As the country became more powerful and prosperous, the idea grew that such a system represented the future everywhere.[162]

Thus the revolutionary movement begun at the Reformation, when the authority of the Church was replaced by that of monarchs, was now moving a step further, as rulers would in the future find themselves supplanted by "parliamentary" élites. England thus went through a process of "Enlightenment" during this period, but one that was much more moderate, and was to have much less bloody consequences than was the case with France.[163]

Meanwhile, Catholics were still undergoing persecution for their beliefs; the Irish again suffered when the abortive rebellion of 1688 led to defeat at the Battle of the Boyne, an event commemorated to this day by the Orangemen of Ulster. Under the subsequent peace treaty, Irish Catholics were promised freedom of religion, but persecution was quickly renewed, with heavy fines and punishments for any signs of allegiance to Catholicism. Further large amounts of land were confiscated and many cruel acts were committed, but despite all this, the Irish clung to their faith and hoped for a better future.[164] Likewise, strongly anti-Catholic laws were maintained in Scandinavia, while the condition of Catholics varied in Germany, depending on the attitude of the rulers of the particular states; generally, however, there was much hostility, particularly in Prussia, where Frederick I became king in 1688.

Catholicism, Capitalism and Secular Culture

Catholicism is essentially opposed to capitalism, at least in so far as it has developed in a historical sense, as a creed that puts economic motives above all others. This does not mean that, if the Reformation had not happened, there would have been no industrial or scientific developments, but that the Church would have ensured that these developments did not disrupt the social or moral fabric of society.[165] So the fact that capitalism began *before* the Reformation, and thus in a Catholic atmosphere, does not invalidate the idea that it only began to develop fully *after* that event. Those Catholics who acted, perhaps unwittingly, to advance capitalistic ideas through the Church's international financial activities, were really acting in opposition to true Catholic teaching. The rise of capitalistic ideals can be explained as a consequence of the decrease of faith in the years leading up to the Reformation in Christendom as a whole; that caused material factors to become increasingly important for people, as worldly standards predominated.[166]

Once the power of the Church was broken, the way was open for the capitalist spirit to permeate society, but for this to happen the institutions of the State unfavorable to capitalism also had to be removed or changed. The new "money power" wanted the freedom to decide its own ends, with the State as guarantor of this freedom, rather than as a force with its own particular pre-capitalist ideals. Progress towards "popular" parliamentary government, and thus towards a system more favorable to capitalism, was encouraged by the religious wars that followed the Reformation.

That was because such conflicts tended to divide rulers from their people in religious terms, leading to a situation where many would come to identify the State with its citizens, rather than with the monarch.[167] The religious wars thus had a very harmful effect on Christian culture and prepared the way for the future secularization of Europe; a trend was established that saw religion gradually pushed to the margins of social life and treated as something that concerned only the individual.[168]

This process was not accidental, but sprang from the basic tenets of Luther's thinking, his belief that religion was an internal ideal, an approach that meant that the secular world was no longer to be restrained in moral terms by spiritual ideals, as the authority of the Church was transferred to profane rulers.[169] That is not to say, though, that the early Reformers gave any particular support to capitalism; rather, they were almost universally opposed to it—apart from Calvin, who was prepared to allow usury—and tended to hark back to the sort of arguments used by the pre-Reformation scholastics. It was not so much what they particularly *said* about capitalism, however, that mattered, but their overall attitude which, by severing religion from the world, inevitably led to the world becoming more secular. The acceptance of usury in particular was a very powerful factor in the growth of capitalism and secularization, as is evident from the development of central banks in the northern Protestant countries by the eighteenth century, in contrast to the economically underdeveloped Catholic parts of Europe at the time.[170]

Holland has been described as the first "capitalist State," with her great wealth becoming increasingly dependent on financial activities. It was in her interest to attempt to remain neutral and encourage peace, as the best way of increasing trade, and to this end Holland promoted religious toleration, offering asylum to religious believers from all over Europe. That in itself was a powerful secularizing influence, since business interests and the profit motive would naturally tend to lessen the concern of traders as to the religion of their customers, and vice versa. Similarly, books and periodicals of all sorts were published in Holland, further stimulating the general sense of toleration, while also promoting the intellectual and monetary upheaval affecting European society. England took over Holland's role and eventually became itself the most powerful capitalist country, as the Calvinist ideology triumphed and power was transferred from southern Europe to the north.[171]

Protestantism did not act alone in this process, though, and was part of the general evolution of thought, exemplified by the Renaissance and humanism, which characterized the revolt against the medieval world. Still, it played a crucial part in all this, in that it legitimized capitalism by giving it a religious flavor, thus helping further to liberate man from a genuinely supernatural outlook, although the Reformers had no idea that this was where their ideas would lead.[172]

In contrast, the Catholic approach was expressed in the very artistically productive baroque culture that spread throughout the Catholic world in the seventeenth century. This represented a fusion of a revived medieval Catholic tradition and Renaissance humanism, but it was one based in the southern European countries, rather than the north, although it did have some influence there.[173] These two cultures were in conflict right up until the French Revolution, when the bourgeois mentality finally triumphed, with this struggle being played out in political and military terms in the conflict between Spain and the Protestant countries of the north.[174] In economic terms, there was a very great difference between the two cultures; whereas the southern Catholic culture was artistic, displaying its wealth in palaces, churches and monasteries, with little emphasis on industry or commerce, the Calvinist culture of the north produced a bourgeois capitalist society dominated by traders.[175] Thus the Reformation and the rise of capitalism in its modern form are inextricably linked, given that northern Protestant countries embraced the new ideas so enthusiastically, in contrast to the way they were resisted for so long in the south, where the Catholic spirit held sway.

The Intellectual Revolution

Despite the inroads made by the Renaissance, it was the Reformation itself which gave an added boost to the movement towards making man rather than God the center of things. By undermining the Church's religious authority and replacing it with the judgment of the individual, the Reformers unwittingly also undermined religious belief and prepared the way for irreligion. People were repeatedly told that the Catholic Church was in error, yet they could see for themselves that the Protestants were hopelessly divided, as the new religious authority they had set up, the Bible, was interpreted in a thousand different ways by those who claimed to be guided by the Spirit: a fact that led some people to question if there really were any universal truths at all.[176]

The unsettled period following the Reformation, then, was a time of growing irreligion, especially as it coincided with new inventions and discoveries, leading to a feeling in intellectual circles that soon there would be no need for God at all.[177]

Traditionally the Church had seen faith and reason as intimately linked, and certainly not contradictory, but the new thinking began to question the necessity of faith, seeing perhaps reason alone as sufficient. René Descartes, (1596–1650), was one thinker who was certainly not out to question the teaching of the Church, but his rationalist approach to philosophy, and his "method of doubt," were to lead to an intellectual revolt against previously-accepted ideas, such that doubt became a virtue. Even though he accepted God's existence as an essential part of his philosophy, this was to prove a very different God to that of traditional Christianity; Descartes' attempt to place the truths of faith outside and above his rational system was not accepted by many of the thinkers who followed him.[178]

By basing himself on the principles of "doubt" and "certainty," Descartes was constructing a subjective philosophy, since these are both subjective states of mind.[179] He was indirectly responsible for divorcing human reason from the experience and tradition of the centuries, thus preparing the way for a revolution in scientific thinking and a rejection of the inherited wisdom of the past as uncertain and erroneous, when contrasted with the new mathematical certainties. His separation of mind and matter likewise helped to promote materialism. Thus he was an important precursor of Enlightenment thought, particularly in the notion that it was possible for the individual to master his own mind, and thus nature.[180]

Such ideas were exploited during the eighteenth century, at the time of the Enlightenment, when an attempt was made to do away completely with religious ideals and replace them with a new culture based on reason. That attempt was largely successful and led to the further secularization of European society. In this respect, then, modern thinking owes far more to the Enlightenment than to either the Renaissance or Reformation, given that it largely results from the scientific revolution of the seventeenth and eighteenth centuries. This is because the revolution accomplished by the Enlightenment was far more thorough than that due to the Reformation. Although Protestantism had done away with the whole sacramental and priestly system of the Church, it had also retained many central aspects of Christian teaching. But the Enlightenment sought to do away with orthodox religious belief entirely, and so was a rejection of both Catholic and Protestant ideals alike.[181]

Overall, then, the main result of the Reformation was an increase in secularization, given that secular ideas were one of the few things which united Catholics and Protestants in Europe. The two sides had of necessity to coexist, and so there tended to be a greater emphasis on worldly matters. Gradually a secular atmosphere developed, as journalism and intellectual writing grew in the countries of northern Europe, particularly France, helping to create the secularized culture that dominated the intellectual circles of Europe in the eighteenth century.[182]

Europe after the Reformation

The general effect of the rise of the Protestant northern European countries was to tip the balance of power against those states that had given so much support to the Church, particularly in a missionary sense, including Spain, Portugal, and France. In the eighteenth century, Britain became a great colonial power at the expense of France, while Spain was in decline and the Calvinist Dutch were supplanting the Portuguese. This meant that the period of expansion for the Church that had opened up with the discovery of the New World was ending.[183]

The religious wars that resulted from the Reformation meant that Europe was in a state of upheaval until well into the seventeenth century, and it was only towards the end of that period that some sort of order and stability were established; this was particularly the case in the France of Louis XIV (1638–1715), where a centralized absolute monarchy developed. France became the leading country in Europe, admired for its economic life and its artistic and literary achievements. Catholicism had a privileged position in France, but one where it also often clashed with the absolutist royal state.[184]

During this period, too, Islam was still a threat to the West, with the Ottoman Empire penetrating deep into Eastern Europe; but despite appeals from Pope Innocent XI, Louis XIV refused to join a crusade against them, when Vienna was threatened by an army of two hundred and fifty thousand Muslims in 1683. It was left to the forces of the Polish king, John III Sobieski, to raise the siege and signal the beginning of the end of the Turkish threat to Europe.[185] That the Pope was able to rally the Christian forces in this way was a sign that the papacy still had a degree of spiritual authority, but its political role was steadily diminishing, although it was still treated with some deference by Catholic rulers. The secularization of international affairs meant that the papacy was progressively squeezed out of its ancient position as Christendom's arbiter. Increasingly, governments took decisions without reference to Christian principles or the Popes.[186]

Thus, as Europe began to settle down again after the upheavals caused by the Reformation, the Protestant parts of Europe, which comprised about two-thirds of Germany, most of Switzerland, England, Scotland, Scandinavia, parts of France, and the area around Hungary, moved into a closer anti-Catholic alliance, despite the considerable differences between Lutherans, Calvinists and Anglicans. The Protestant position was also strengthened by the increasing material prosperity of many of these countries, particularly England, which continued its prodigious growth during the seventeenth and eighteenth centuries, developing a powerful navy and the beginnings of its future industrial might. The leadership of Europe would pass from France to England, just as it had passed from Spain to France.[187]

5

Devotions to Jesus and Mary

Devotion to the Sacred Heart

At this point two popular devotions began to develop more fully in the life of the Church, those of Jesus' Sacred Heart and Mary's Immaculate Heart. But it would be an error to equate "popular" with "unimportant" or "merely pietistic" in regard to these devotions. The truth is that such inner devotions are crucial to the life of the Church, since without them everything can seem to be functioning, when actually the reality can be spiritual weakness if not decline. These two devotions, and particularly the devotion to the Sacred Heart, during this period acted as a spiritual antidote to the increasingly rationalistic temper of European society. They enabled the Church to combat the drift away from God, and for its members to grow spiritually and, when the time came, to be able to survive the ravages of the French Revolution. Then providentially, when, in the aftermath of the Revolution, the time came for rebuilding the Church, the devotion to Mary's Immaculate Heart, in conjunction with the nineteenth-century Marian apparitions, was able to contribute powerfully to the rebirth of Catholicism in France, and indeed Europe.

It was just after the apparitions at Le Laus, in 1664, when Jansenism, a Calvinist-influenced strain of teaching, was causing a "coldness" to enter into Catholic life in France, that the revelations to St Margaret Mary Alacoque, concerning devotion to the Sacred Heart of Jesus, were made. This was a devotion in which the heart symbolized Jesus' perfect love for mankind; it began to grow in importance in the eleventh and twelfth centuries and was later promoted by St Gertrude and St Bonaventure, amongst others. St Gertrude (d. 1302) is said to have had a vision of St John the Evangelist on his feast day, in which he told her that devotion to the Sacred Heart of Jesus was reserved for subsequent ages, when the world would need to be reminded of his infinite love. This devotion was very much a private affair until about the sixteenth century, when it came more into the mainstream of Christian practice, particularly under the influence of writers such as St Francis de Sales, and prominent Jesuits such as St Francis Borgia and St Peter Canisius. It was still essentially a private devotion, though, until St John Eudes worked to establish a feast day, which was first celebrated in 1670. This feast of the Sacred Heart gradually spread to other dioceses in France and eventually coalesced with the devotion that began as a result of the apparitions of Jesus to St Margaret Mary, in the small town of Paray-le-Monial in central France.[188] Earlier in the seventeenth century, France had been consecrated to Mary by Louis XIII, an example followed by a number of other nations, including Portugal.[189]

The first apparition took place on 27 December, the feast of St John the Evangelist, probably in 1673, while Margaret Mary was a nun in the Visitation convent at Paray-le-Monial. There is some uncertainty as to the precise dates of the apparitions, but not their content. She related what happened to Fr Claude de la Colombière, who was in charge of the Jesuit house in the town, describing how she had a vision of Jesus, during which she was given some idea of the greatness of his love for mankind. Jesus told her that he wanted her to tell the people of this love; and a similar theme was expressed during the second apparition, early in 1674, when Margaret Mary saw Jesus' Sacred Heart on a throne of flames, transparent as crystal, surrounded by a crown of thorns signifying the sins of mankind, with a cross above it. Again Jesus told her of his infinite love for mankind and his desire that he should be honored through the display of this image of his heart, with the promise that all who did so would be specially blessed.

The third apparition probably took place on 2 July 1674, while Margaret Mary was praying before the Blessed Sacrament exposed, that is, the host consecrated during Mass which had become the Body of Christ. She saw a vision of Jesus in glory, with his five wounds shining like suns; and he then showed her his heart on fire with love for mankind, a love that, sadly, was often ignored or treated with contempt. He asked her to make up for this coldness and ingratitude by receiving Holy Communion as often as she was allowed, and particularly on the first Friday of each month. This idea of making reparation for the sins of others is also prominent in the messages given by Mary to the children at Fatima in 1917. The fourth apparition, which probably took place on 16 June 1675, was the most important. Again it happened as Margaret Mary was praying before the Blessed Sacrament, when Jesus again showed her a representation of his heart, further complaining of the ingratitude and coldness of mankind towards him, and particularly when this was the case with those specially consecrated to him. To make up for this he asked that the first Friday after the feast of Corpus Christi, (Latin for the "Body of Christ"), should be dedicated as a feast in honor of his Sacred Heart, when people should receive Holy Communion in reparation.[190]

The "Great Promise," associated with this devotion applies to those who go to Communion on nine consecutive First Fridays: "I promise you, in the excess of the mercy of My Heart, that Its all-powerful love will grant to all those who shall receive Communion on the first Friday of nine consecutive months the grace of final repentance; they shall not die under My displeasure nor without receiving the Sacraments, My Divine Heart becoming their assured refuge at that last hour."[191]

Obviously, this last promise in particular is dependent on people adopting an interior attitude of love towards Jesus, and not abusing his goodness. This promise is really one of the grace of final repentance, that is, of dying in a state of grace, and so there is some similarity here to the promise attached to the brown scapular.[192] If somebody dies in this state, then, although they may have to spend time in purgatory, they will eventually get to heaven. To qualify for this tremendous grace, it is necessary to receive Holy Communion validly and worthily, that is, not being in a state of mortal sin, on the nine consecutive First Fridays as stated. In addition, the communicant must have the intention, at least implicitly, of making reparation to the Sacred Heart of Jesus for all the sinfulness and ingratitude of mankind.[193] This promise is paralleled by the one made to Lucia, that of the Five First Saturdays, following the apparitions at Fatima, a point which will be dealt with more fully later on.

This series of apparitions has been approved by the Church, which has vouched for their authenticity, as far as is possible. The writings of Margaret Mary, which included these revelations and her letters, were examined during the process of her beatification, and she would not have been canonized, that is, declared a saint, if they were not reliable. Likewise, various Popes have expressed their approval of these apparitions, with their essential content being included in the bull of canonization by Pope Benedict XV in 1920; while the feast of the Sacred Heart has been established in the Church calendar as requested.[194] This devotion, then, is important not only in itself, but also because it exemplifies a theme, that of the need for reparation for sin, which is very prominent in the various Marian apparitions which took place later; although it was, and has remained, central to the preaching of Christianity from the time of the Apostles onwards: "Repent, for the kingdom of heaven is at hand" (Matt. 3:2). The idea of making reparation, both for our own sins and, because of a common membership of the mystical body of Christ, for those of others, is only an extension of this basic Gospel message, a message that continues to be valid. As St Paul said: "Now I rejoice in my sufferings for your sake, and in my flesh I complete what is lacking in Christ's afflictions for the sake of his body, that is, the church ..." (Col. 1:24).

Devotion to the Sacred Heart has been renewed, in a slightly different form, nearer our own day in the Divine Mercy devotion promoted by St Faustina, a Polish sister who died in 1938, and was canonized by Pope John Paul II in April 2000. St Faustina and this devotion are dealt with in a later chapter.

Devotion to Mary's Immaculate Heart

Historically, devotion to the Heart of Mary grew up in parallel but at a lesser pitch than that of devotion to the Heart of Jesus, only starting to become more prominent during the time of St John Eudes. Even then, it was not until after the revelations concerning the "Miraculous Medal" made to Catherine Labouré in 1830, and the establishment of a society dedicated to the Immaculate Heart of Mary, at the Church of Our Lady of Victories in Paris in 1836, that this particular devotion became really well known. Both of these events are considered in more detail in subsequent chapters. Since then, devotion to the Immaculate Heart of Mary has gradually grown more widespread in the Church, particularly since the apparitions at Fatima, where there was an explicit manifestation of Mary's Immaculate Heart.

The main difference between these two devotions is that the one concerned with Jesus emphasizes his divine heart as being full of love for mankind, but with this love for the most part being ignored or rejected, while devotion to Mary's heart is essentially concerned with the love that *her* heart has for Jesus, for God. It is not an end in itself, and really the love of her heart is meant to be a model for the way we should love God. So, as in all things Marian, she leads us closer to God, rather than becoming an obstacle in our way.[195] Honoring Mary's Immaculate Heart is really just another way of honoring Mary as the person who was chosen to be the

Mother of God, recognizing her extraordinary holiness and the immense love she bestowed on Jesus as his mother, the person who was called to share in and cooperate in his redemptive sufferings. The whole aim of this devotion is to unite mankind to God through Mary's heart, and this process involves the ideas of *consecration* and *reparation*. A person is consecrated to Mary's Immaculate Heart as a way of being completely devoted to God. This involves a total gift of self, something only ultimately possible with reference to God; but because love and devotion shown to Mary are referred by her to God, it follows that acts of reparation for sin directed to her also apply to God, especially when we consider how closely united the hearts of Jesus and Mary were and are.[196]

St Louis de Montfort

The above principle of complete consecration to Mary was taken up and promoted by St Louis de Montfort (1673–1716), who flourished slightly later than St Margaret Mary; this belief had been gathering momentum in the Church over a period of centuries. He took the idea of "Holy Slavery" to Mary, as found amongst French spiritual writers, including St John Eudes, and developed it more fully. This idea of being Mary's "slave" had been present in the Church probably since the time of the earliest writers, so it was not an innovation, and seems to have been present throughout Europe even before the time of St Louis.[197] The notion of "slavery" sounds odd to modern ears, but all it really means is being in a *freely willed* state of total consecration, total abandonment, to the love and guidance of Mary, in the knowledge that it is the ideal way to draw closer to God. Similarly, the idea of consecration to Mary in the thought of St Louis, which can be misunderstood, really means consecrating oneself to Jesus *through* Mary, and is not an end in itself.[198]

St Louis spent most of his priestly life preaching and teaching in western France, basing his teaching on Mary on the principle that just as God had initiated the work of Redemption on the basis of her cooperation, so he would continue and finish that work by means of her: "It was through the blessed Virgin Mary that Jesus Christ came into the world, and it is also through her that he must reign in the world."[199] He also stressed Mary's role as spiritual mother of all Christians, basing himself on the fact of her divine maternity and her role in Redemption. He taught that, by means of her faith, trust, love, and holiness, she merited the status of "Co-Redemptrix," one that gives her rights over all mankind, since Jesus' death was sufficient to save all mankind. Since she is the spiritual mother of every human being, then we are her children in the order of grace, and just as children, especially when they are still in the womb or very small, are totally dependent on their mother, so we too are totally dependent on Mary as "Mediatrix" of all graces. This implies that we should be totally devoted to her, which is the essence of the "Holy slavery of love," although perhaps the idea of "spiritual childhood," as popularized through St Thérèse of Lisieux, is easier for the modern mind to understand and accept.

St Louis composed a formula of consecration to Mary which emphasized the idea of the individual making a total offering of self to God through Mary, arguing that this was really a renewal of the baptismal vows, in which the individual is completely consecrated to God. He insisted, however, that this consecration had to be carried over into daily life, as a lived spirit, if it was to be really effective. St Louis's major work, the *Treatise on True Devotion*, was hidden away and not found until 1842, when it providentially began to contribute to the resurgence of Marian ideas that took place from 1830 onwards. Another well-known work of his is *The Secret of the Rosary*, a small booklet which undoubtedly did a tremendous amount to promote this form of prayer. His work has been approved by a number of Popes, and he was finally canonized in 1947, thus indicating that the Church has found nothing objectionable in his ideas on the total consecration to Mary;[200] indeed recently the idea has been put forward that he should be declared a Doctor of the Church.

St Louis made a number of interesting prophecies concerning the future role of Mary in the Church and the world, including this statement in the *True Devotion*: "If ... as is certain, the knowledge and the kingdom of Jesus Christ must come into the world, it can only be as a necessary consequence of the knowledge and reign of Mary. She who first gave him to the world will establish his kingdom in the world." He argued that this was the case "because God has decided to begin and accomplish his greatest works through the Blessed Virgin ever since he created her, [and so] we can safely believe that he will not change his plan in the time to come, for he is God and therefore does not change in his thoughts or his way of acting."[201]

St Louis then went on to describe Mary's future role: "The salvation of the world began through Mary and through her it must be accomplished. Mary scarcely appeared in the first coming of Jesus

Christ so that men, as yet insufficiently instructed and enlightened concerning the person of her Son, might not wander from the truth by becoming too strongly attached to her." He argues that the reasons for hiding Mary's importance, that is, the danger of her being treated as a goddess by the early Church, no longer exist. This prophecy certainly seems to have been at least partially fulfilled in the nineteenth- and twentieth-century Marian apparitions and their aftermath, but St Louis apparently goes on to argue that an even more splendid Marian age is to come. He foresaw men and women who, in their true devotion to Mary, would prepare the way for Christ by living the message of the Gospel in simplicity and humility, and thus inaugurate a future great triumph for Christianity, but one also involving persecution and suffering for the Church.[202] This seems to agree with the prophecies made by St John Bosco in the nineteenth and by Mary herself at Fatima in the twentieth century, as will be made clear later on.

6

The Enlightenment

Rationalism and Secularization

In France, all the upheavals following the Reformation had their effect, and there was a reaction during the eighteenth century. For the time being, however, religion was still a major factor in the lives of ordinary people, and it was still the generally-accepted wisdom that the whole social order was based on Christianity. There were very few atheists or "freethinkers" at this stage, although they were influential and their power was growing. The French Church was the most important in Europe, holding much of the land in the country, with exclusive right to public worship and exemption from taxes. With time, these privileges provoked resentment and finally outright hostility, particularly regarding the worldly and luxurious lives led by many bishops, who came almost exclusively from the nobility. There was also a growing gulf between those bishops and ordinary priests, many of whom were very poor, and this meant that the Church was divided when the Revolution began in 1789.[203]

There were deeper reasons, however, for a new mood at the beginning of the eighteenth century: the process of questioning authority begun during the Renaissance and promoted during the Reformation was developing further, as some began to question the whole principle of the monarchy or of a hierarchical society. The theory of the divine right of kings was further weakened by the accession of both William of Orange in 1689 and George I in 1714, to the English throne, since it was clear they had become monarchs due to human machinations alone. These questions were given added impetus by the tremendous changes which were brought about by the growth of capitalism, the beginnings of industrialization, and the new scientific discoveries being made.[204] All these developments in turn prepared the ground for further upheavals in Europe.

Rationalist teachings were reaching a wider audience following the success of Descartes' approach, with his most influential follower being Baruch Spinoza (1632–77), the Dutch Jewish philosopher, who also pioneered a more critical, rational approach to the Bible. Spinoza took Descartes' ideas to their logical conclusion and argued that there was no essential difference between God and nature, both comprising one infinite substance, with the human mind as part of the divine intellect. This pantheistic approach ruled out free will, and the idea that God was a personal being, and that man had an immortal soul. He was particularly influential in nineteenth-century Germany, where so much of the prevalent destructive criticism of the Bible originated.[205]

At the same time, new scientific and mathematical discoveries were being made, which tended to give the impression that a completely rationalistic explanation of man and the universe was possible. All over Europe, scientific investigations were taking place, and the work of Isaac Newton (1642–1727), in particular, can be seen as a watershed in the process by which the concrete realities of the universe took precedence over supernatural and transcendent truths in men's minds. Despite the fact that most scientists, including Newton, were still believing Christians, religion increasingly came to be seen as less and less important. Science was seen as the road to knowledge and thus to power, the way to ensure man's material progress and future happiness.[206] Belief in the miraculous was regarded as superstition, and the whole idea of the supernatural was declared to be against reason; in short there was a move to reject the received wisdom of the past, which included the whole idea of God, and replace it with a new man-centered approach. All of this tended to increase the pace of secularization. This critical spirit can be traced in essence to the Renaissance, with its emphasis on the human rather than the divine, an emphasis that valued new inventions and discoveries, and one which encapsulated all the great themes that were to be exploited by the French Revolution, a century before that tremendous event.[207]

The great increase in travel and exploration also contributed to an increase in secular thought: whole new continents, civilizations and religions had been discovered, and so the centrality of Christianity was further questioned. China in particular was much admired by freethinkers for its well-developed political and cultural system, one that had apparently grown up without divine revelation and Western religion.[208] That these ideas were superficial and betrayed a lack of understanding of these foreign cultures did not stop them being very popular at the time. This study of other religions was part of the general growth in literature, much of it heterodox, centered on Holland in particular, and was one of the continuing effects of the spirit of the Reformation, a spirit that questioned all orthodoxies. [209]

Meanwhile, attempts by the various Protestant churches to present a more united front failed in the face of continued disagreements during the late seventeenth century. This was really due to the essential nature of Protestantism, which saw itself preserving the rights of conscience against external authority, a principle that ensured argument would continue and new groups come into being, as individuals refused to accept the authority of particular church leaders. It was a seemingly endless process of division and further division.[210]

Thus the rise of rationalistic thought meant that reason was increasingly exalted at the expense of faith, as the Bible began to come under intellectual attack. A new "scientific" approach hostile to Christianity was growing up, one which would come to fruition in the Enlightenment and the French Revolution, and this development represented another step further away from the recognition of God's presence in the world, a process begun, with quite different motives, at the Reformation.

Deism and Philosophy

This intellectual upheaval was not happening only in France: in England Deism, with its roots in the naturalism of the Italian Renaissance, began to develop at the expense of Anglicanism. It was a belief in a "supreme being" rather than in the Christian God of revelation. There were a number of varieties of Deism, with John Locke (1632–1704) and John Toland (1670–1722) being its best-known exponents; but generally it involved some degree of denial of the supernatural, seeing God as having initially created the world, but now having little further interest in it. Deism turned God into a remote figure, who did not require worship or demand adherence to particular dogmas, whilst it also rejected belief in future rewards or punishments. As such, it was a convenient halfway house between belief and atheism. Religion came to be seen by some as good only insofar as it could be used by governments to keep their citizens in order.

Philosophy had tended to split into two schools, those of the rationalists, such as Spinoza and Leibniz, who saw ideas coming from the human mind, and the empiricists, such as Hobbes, Locke, Berkeley and Hume, who saw ideas coming from sense experience. But both of these approaches were based on the Cartesian principle of immanence, that is, that we start with man rather than any transcendent principle outside of man, such as God. These trends have developed further in modern times, as humanism has been progressively secularized.[211]

In France, as the eighteenth century progressed, the effects of rationalism, scepticism and Deism began to make their mark on a larger section of society. It was not a particularly creative age, being dependent on seventeenth-century secular thinking, and was quite destructive of old traditions and standards; French thinkers took English ideas and gave them a Gallic tone, enabling a Europe-wide French-speaking intellectual culture, one allegedly based on human reason, to grow up. This culture aimed at overthrowing previous methods of thought and institutions, particularly those concerned with Christianity; it rejected the idea of original sin, proclaiming man's innate goodness, and was very much concerned with this life rather than the hereafter, in an attempt to construct a perfect society on earth.[212]

The great strides being made by science, particularly physics and chemistry, gave further impetus to the belief that humanity was on the threshold of a wonderful new age, one that would not be impeded by outdated religious dogmas. There was also quite a degree of political discontent, directed at a social system so unequally weighted in favor of the aristocracy and the rich; the Church, which was identified with the regime, could not escape such criticism. Overall, then, there was a philosophical spirit abroad that saw man as central and exalted human reason, and which attacked supernaturalism and morality, content with at most a Deist God, the Supreme Being, and a natural religion.[213]

Voltaire (1694–1778), was the most notorious anti-Christian writer of this period. He was very successful in infecting the intelligentsia with irreligious ideas and scepticism, and his attacks on Christianity were extremely harmful, preparing the ground, as they did, both for the French Revolution and nineteenth-century anti-clericalism. He also did much to introduce the Newtonian world view into French thought, thus giving the new ideas a scientific basis.[214] Jean-Jacques Rousseau (1712–78), was another highly influential writer whose basic idea was that man was naturally good and that most of the world's problems were due to society rather than the individual. His emotional approach represented something of a reaction against the cold, logical, rationalism of the age.

He maintained that, if all men were free and equal, then a new paradise could be created on earth; he was really advocating a new religion, one which would reject original sin and thus the need for redemption, while seeing the individual conscience as able to judge between good and evil, without the need for revelation of any sort. His most famous work, *The Social Contract*, (1762), with its emphasis on liberty and equality, was very important in shaping the thinking that led to the French Revolution, and his ideas remained influential well beyond that period.[215] He was responsible for reinterpreting Enlightenment thought, so as to make it accessible to the ordinary citizen; he changed it from an intellectual to a new, almost *religious*, belief, the new faith of *democracy*, an idea that gained its force from the impression that such a movement could truly change society. He summed up the hopeful eighteenth-century belief, that human nature could express itself most fully through better education and an improved environment.[216] His approach, however, was largely based on individualism and sentiment, and in this he was taking "the principles of individual conscience and justification by faith which lay at the heart of Protestantism," and applying them outside religion and theology, as the historian John Roberts argues.[217]

The main cultural focus of Enlightenment ideas, then, was in France, and it was the destructive attitudes found amongst French writers that helped to foment a great spiritual and cultural revolution, which, in the nature of things, eventually led to a *political* revolution too. Christopher Dawson argues that the Jacobin revolutionary party used Rousseau's ideas in the same way that communism used the theories of Karl Marx, with the later European revolutionary movement being a long-term development of all this, combining, at various times, elements from democracy, nationalism, socialism, and communism.[218] Thus these new literary and philosophical approaches greatly increased the intellectual unrest which was taking place in Europe. Christian ideals were being sidelined, as new revolutionary philosophies and deistic ideas grew in strength, preparing the way for the "cult of reason" and the French Revolution itself.

Freemasonry and the Enlightenment

During the seventeenth century a whole network of theosophical organizations and societies had developed across Europe, as the new ideas were discussed. Groups such as the Rosicrucians advocated esoteric "Gnostic" ideas mixed in with elements from Christianity, while naturalistic belief systems developed and flourished, based on the idea that only initiates had the key to real knowledge.[219] The philosophy underpinning the Enlightenment was in some respects a new religion, one that saw itself vanquishing beliefs based on ignorance and superstition, to be replaced by a new form of revelation based on reason, in a church made up of philosophers, intellectuals, Freemasons and *Illuminati*, the deist group founded by Adam Weishaupt (1748–1830). It was, though, also a revival of a very old, but false, religion, the gnosticism which affected the early Church, and of the medieval Cathars, under a new form. The secret principles of these Illuminati, who outwardly professed Christianity, but actually repudiated Christian ideals and practices, were merged with Freemasonry in the late eighteenth century. By this time the Masonic craft was widespread and very influential in France, thus helping to spread a spirit of impiety and revolt against the established order.[220]

Freemasonry in its modern form developed in the early eighteenth century in the England of Deism, before quickly spreading to the Continent. It absorbed the esoteric pantheist and materialist philosophy of the Rosicrucians, and its official beginnings are said to date from 1717, when the first Grand Master of the English Lodges was appointed. Interestingly this was exactly two hundred years after the start of Luther's Revolt in 1517, and, indeed, the original constitutions and arcane rituals of Freemasonry were drawn up by a Scottish Presbyterian Minister, James Anderson, and a Huguenot refugee, Jean Desaguliers. This shows the intimate relationship between Protestantism and the early propagation of Freemasonry.

Its influence can be gauged from the fact that Sir Robert Walpole (1676–1745), the British Prime Minister, was a Mason, as were many government officials. Masonic activities involved acceptance of a naturalistic religion, without the dogmas and rites of Christianity, and belief in a "Great Architect," the Deist "God," who did not interfere in human affairs. Freemasonry encouraged religious indifference and a cosmopolitan humanitarian attitude opposed to patriotism and one's duty to the State. It also provided a ready means of transmission for all the various anti-religious currents of thought circulating in educated society. Masonic ideals were held by a large number of those involved in publishing and journalism, and it seems that Freemasonry was bound up with the "radical" Enlightenment, representing the ritualistic side of the new "religion" of nature. In this sense the Enlightenment could be said to be similar to the Reformation, which also had a radical wing in the activities of the Anabaptists and other groups. These Enlightenment radicals went beyond those in the movement of ideas in eighteenth-century thinking who wanted to retain belief in God, or at least in some sort of distant deity. Their materialistic and republican ideas came more to the fore as the century progressed, having been previously expressed in a more hidden way.[221]

It is a disputed question as to whether there was an active "Freemasons" conspiracy against "throne and altar," but what is certain is that they represented a strong counterculture, which weakened the influence of Catholicism, and that Freemasonry was undoubtedly one of the agents responsible for fomenting revolutions, assassinations and religious persecution in succeeding years. One only has to instance Portugal at the time of the apparitions at Fatima for proof of that, and a similar pattern of activities occurred in many other countries. A characteristic of these secret societies was the way that their members were bound by fearsome oaths to their Masonic brethren. These oaths inculcated absolute obedience to Masonic superiors, becoming progressively more gruesome as the individual rose in the organization. The secretive nature of Freemasonry, where only an inner circle of initiates would really know its irreligious essence, explains why it could adopt a benevolent exterior, and why Freemasons of lower degree could accept its apparently harmless tenets.[222]

Perhaps it is better speak of an *ideological* movement than a conspiracy proper, when dealing with Freemasonry.[223] That is, although there may well have been an active conspiracy in the very highest levels of Masonry, as far as most of its members were concerned, they would have merely been involved in an *ideologically-motivated* anti-religious and anti-Catholic movement. Of course, they would not have used such terms or probably even been aware of them, but that is in effect what was happening. The advantage of allowing such ideological movements to grow is that they beautifully solve the problem of how to motivate individuals and groups to take actions that are basically unpleasant or immoral, that is through giving them a veneer of political, economic, or religious respectability.

Freemasonry itself seems to have had a "chameleon-like" ability to adapt to the particular circumstances of individual countries, whilst always advancing an anti-religious, and particularly anti-Catholic, liberal agenda. For this reason it has usually had more success in Protestant countries, where it has generally been able to proceed by peaceful means, in contrast to Catholic countries, where liberalism and Freemasonry have often resorted to violence. From the early eighteenth century onwards, then, Freemasonry could be accurately described as an animating spirit of liberalism. From a Catholic point of view, this is the only description that makes sense, given the repeated condemnations of Freemasonry by successive popes. From the time of Pope Clement XII onwards, (1730–40), practically all the popes directly condemned Freemasonry in the strongest possible language, invoking excommunication on those involved in it, a sentence that could only be revoked by the Pope himself, or at the point of death. The severity of these denunciations is practically unique in the history of the Church. It is inconceivable that those popes would have so consistently censured Freemasonry, given its obvious power and influence, unless it really was a great force for evil, and unless they were in full possession of the facts. To this end, they kept themselves well informed about Masonry, and, in addition, could often call on the testimony of those who had formerly been Masons but had returned to the Church.[224]

As has been indicated, these intellectual and political movements were so influential at the time, because Enlightenment thinkers generally thought that mankind was on the brink of a new cultural era. This view was particularly found amongst those revolutionaries and political theorists concerned with the immediate future, while later on it was especially present in nineteenth-century socialist thinking, which envisaged a completely transformed society.[225] The use of a term, such as "Enlightenment," implied a previous "dark age" under the sway of Christianity, one to be swept away by a new rationalistic era based on the first Greek enlightenment. Thus, Christian belief was the main object of Enlightenment criticism, which did a great deal to damage religious institutions and particularly the Catholic Church. Religion was to be replaced by reason, but, in practice, attempts to organize society without proper moral limits have failed, and instead immoral systems driven by erroneous ideology, such as Communism or Nazism, have come to power, with devastating results for mankind. Through its anticlerical and anti-Christian principles, the Enlightenment prepared the way for the present godless and immoral state of the world.[226]

In many respects, the French Revolution represented the violent fulfillment of these unduly hopeful Enlightenment aspirations; it destroyed the old regime, but not by means of reasoned arguments, as had been hoped. In the Terror and its other unsavory aspects, it was to demonstrate that doing away with the old religious and secular authorities would lead to anarchy rather than a new golden age. It was the culmination of the Age of Reason, a period during which both the Church and the papacy were at a very low ebb, but it was to be followed by a period of revival, when once more Christianity would be valued as a safeguard against the dangerous forces of revolution.

Wesley and Protestant Culture

England, however, was not affected by these revolutionary currents to the same extent, and the main reason for this seems to have been the growth of John Wesley's Methodism. Wesley, (1703–91), was instrumental in both creating a powerful missionary movement and imparting new life to Christianity in Britain, although, in his emphasis on "good works" it seems fair to say that he had really broken, in spirit, with "Reformation" Protestantism and moved back towards the "Catholic" mainstream. The importance of Methodism lies in the way it helped to rejuvenate Protestantism by its practical charitable approach, although it could not escape the fate of Protestant churches in general, that of subdivision into smaller bodies.[227] Louis Bouyer emphasizes Wesley's importance in describing him as "a Reformer of the Reformation" who, in his work with the de-Christianized poorer classes of Britain, helped to preserve the country from a complete decline into godless materialism.[228] Methodism was thus part of the reaction away from the approach of the earlier Reformers towards the poor and unfortunate, one which had been less than charitable; Luther had allied himself with the princes and condemned the peasants and Anabaptists, while Calvin had equated riches with "godliness," as had the Puritans in England.

Overall we can see here the triumph of Erasmus's humanistic Christianity based on moderation and reason, as opposed to the negative and contradictory approach of Luther and Calvin, based on subjectivism or literalism. Wesley represented a continuation of the tradition of Erasmus, and thus, according to Christopher Dawson, modern Protestantism, in its practical aspects, owes far more to the Dutch humanist than to the original Reformers. This is an important point and indicates that the eighteenth-century "evangelical" Christianity of groups such as the Methodists was really something new, a reaction against Enlightenment thought, and, as such, distinct from the spirit of the Protestant Reformation.[229]

But despite its positive points, Methodism was not ultimately able to prevent the Protestant world from becoming more secular. The modern world and a new type of society were being born in the Protestant countries of Europe and particularly in England, where a combination of ideas from Protestantism, capitalism and democracy came together, a combination that would eventually evolve into the modern parliamentary state, of which England was the first example. Modern capitalism and the Industrial Revolution began their seemingly irresistible rise, first in England and afterwards in America, which itself became the first great modern democracy. Clearly, the fact that this new form of society arose in Protestant countries suggests a strong link between Protestantism, capitalism, industrialization, and democracy.[230]

This development was possible because, during the sixteenth and seventeenth centuries, in England in particular, a new economically united society was formed, a full two centuries before France and two and a half centuries before Germany. This involved the secularization of economic, political, and social ideals, with religion being marginalized and many of its functions being assumed by the State. Before this period, social morality was widely regarded as the definite province of the Church, but by the middle of the seventeenth century economics had taken precedence over Christian traditions and ideals.[231] By the eighteenth century, economic liberalism, the notion that capitalism should have free reign, was growing in strength, as the parliamentary form of government developed in England; this was the system most suited to the growth of capitalism, since it was the form of government most easily controlled by rich oligarchies. Political theories were thus elaborated to rationalize the demands of the middle classes for a greater freedom to make money, with an emphasis on the rights of property and less interference by government.

Europe on the Brink of Revolution

For the Church, the years leading up to the French Revolution saw the power of the papacy in decline, ignored by the great powers in their political maneuverings and hard-pressed to impose spiritual discipline on an increasingly troubled Catholic world. This decline over a long period was partly due to the increasing influence of Catholic rulers in the papal elections, which tended to ensure that mediocre popes, who would upset no one, were elected. So while they were not particularly bad, of the eighteenth-century popes only Benedict XIV (1740–58) was outstanding, and the situation really demanded more than one great individual, if the intellectual assault on Christianity was to be met.[232]

The whole Christian concept of some sort of international moral order seemed to be draining away, leaving nothing but competing national interests desiring to control the Church and Christianity. The prevalent attitude of cynicism and respect for power alone was shown in the shameful partition of Poland at the end of the eighteenth century. The country had been growing steadily weaker over a long period and eventually it was split between Russia, Prussia, and Austria, disappearing from history for over a century.[233] The Prussian ruler, Frederick the Great, was to leave a terrible legacy in his masterminding of the growth in power of the Prussian State in the late eighteenth century. He organized Prussia for military conquest, and thus provided a pattern for other European states, and particularly Russia. Frederick was thus the remote father of the totalitarian State.[234]

Although France was materially prosperous in the latter half of the eighteenth century, its government was weak and royal power was declining, which, in turn, meant that it was unable to enforce the sort of reforms needed to avoid revolution. So social inequalities grew worse, the tax system and the economy went unreformed, and a revolutionary spirit continued to grow. This situation was not helped by the wealth of the Church and the privileged position of the bishops; all this meant that the Church was linked too closely in the public mind with the aristocratic regime.[235] There were also problems with the religious orders, and so the *general* picture was one of relative decline, although on paper the Church's position looked strong. It was wealthy and exempt from taxation, but behind this façade there were worrying signs, since secular thinking had made deep inroads.[236]

The Catholic Church still seemed to be an important power in Europe on the eve of the French Revolution, covering nearly two-thirds of the continent, even after the ravages of the Protestant Reformation: but it was a power in decline as nation-states grew ever stronger. Spain and Austria were still strongly Catholic, as was the area across Europe from Belgium thorough southern Germany to Hungary, and these areas, and Italy, were generally to prove faithful to Catholicism after the upheavals caused by the Revolution.[237]

The great revolutionary movement that developed during the

eighteenth century was not originally a democratic movement in the modern sense, since the initial goal of Enlightenment thought was to introduce a benevolent despotism in which the intellectuals would rule and the ordinary people obey. Only in the second half of the century did the democratic ideal come more to the fore, particularly during the American and French Revolutions.[238] The American Revolution was much influenced by the ideas of English thinkers and particularly Locke, and, in turn, the ideals it represented affected the French Revolution and the Enlightenment generally. Men such as Benjamin Franklin, Thomas Paine, and the third President of the United States, Thomas Jefferson, were all Deists; they helped to influence profoundly the creation of a new culture in America, where there was something of a religious vacuum in the period following the winning of Independence.

Although the Founding Fathers introduced freedom of worship in America, their attitude to religion was ambivalent. Without the efforts of Wesley and his collaborator, Whitefield, it is probable that American society would have been quite secular in the nineteenth century, instead of which it developed its predominantly Protestant and biblical ethos. Unlike the Old World, where a combination of industrialization, urbanization, and a rigid social structure led to an ever-increasing loss of belief amongst ordinary people, in America the Churches, and particularly the Catholic Church from the nineteenth century onwards, proved effective in maintaining a strong religious belief amongst a majority of citizens.[239]

The American Revolution had a genuinely democratic element, one realized in the *Declaration of Independence*, in its emphasis on the "sacred rights of mankind," but also as forcefully found in the writings of Thomas Paine (1737–1809). In his pamphlet *Common Sense* (1776), he laid down what was to become the revolutionary blueprint for the future, with its idea of political revolution as a universal process and the closely-allied ideal of a social millennium, one in which wrongs would be righted and humanity would enter a new golden age. It has been argued that Paine's ideas had their roots in the apocalyptic and revolutionary tendencies of groups such as the millenarian sects and the Anabaptists, and, when combined with the naturalism and rationalism of the Enlightenment, produced a new revolutionary belief.[240] The American Revolution, however, differed from the French Revolution in that it was essentially nonviolent. Similarly it was essentially a "conservative" movement, one concerned with protecting existing freedoms from the threat of over-powerful government,[241] rather than a violent outburst designed to overthrow the existing order.

7

The French Revolution

French Society before the Revolution

In the period just before the Revolution, then, the idea of a new naturalistic religion took root, one whose main tenets were a belief in progress and of the coming of a new age when a perfect society would be created. This new order was to be based on the ideals of democracy, equality, freedom, and universal brotherhood, and be driven by the new scientific discoveries.[242]

In the aftermath of the Reformation, Protestant thinkers, because of their renewed emphasis on the Bible, had absorbed Jewish and apocalyptic views of history, and over time a new rationalized theology developed which became allied with a secularized form of millenarianism, the belief in a thousand-year reign of Christ with his saints, expressing itself in the idea of *progress*. It is difficult to understand modern culture, particularly in its liberal form, without grasping the importance of this underlying idea of progress. In this sense "progress" might be defined as a contempt for the past, combined with a belief that some sort of "heaven on earth" can be created by man. Christopher Dawson describes the above process as "a new reformation, which attempted to rationalize and spiritualize religion in an even more complete and drastic way than the first Reformation had done, but which ended in emptying Christianity of all supernatural elements and interpreting history as the progressive development of an immanent principle."[243]

But when it came, far from being the precursor of a new and splendid rationalistic age, the French Revolution turned out to be the second great act of revolt against all that Christendom had stood for before the Reformation, and it proved to be a decisive act in the further disintegration of Catholic Europe. Clearly, just as in the case of the Reformation, there were many subsidiary events both leading up to and following the French Revolution that were of importance; but it seems sensible to concentrate on what happened in France, especially since the majority of the Marian apparitions that took place in the nineteenth century occurred there, and it was one of the great centers of the Catholic revival.

The success of the American Revolution in the early 1780s influenced European Enlightenment thought, giving it a political and revolutionary tendency, and in France calls for government reform, based on democratic ideals, began to grow. The Government itself had begun some religious and social reforms, but the main obstacle to change lay in the very centralized nature of control and organization in France. This was focused on the person of the king, Louis XVI, (1754–93), who lacked the will to enforce change against the opposition of the privileged classes. At a deeper level, though, the *ancien régime*, based on aristocracy and hierarchy, was incompatible with the new financial realities of the growth of a capitalist economy. The desires of the rising moneyed class were to prove too strong for the old traditions based on nobility, and the balance of power in the country shifted as this class began to demand a share in political power.[244]

French Freemasonry, under the leadership of the Duke of Orléans, played an important part in fomenting the new idealistic spirit of revolution that was growing in strength in the country, with one of its leading exponents being Lafayette. He had experienced the American Revolution at first hand, and his main interest was in promoting the "Rights of Man," an ideal that became the "creed" of the French Revolution. Men like Lafayette, and those who succeeded them, saw their struggle as part of a world-wide revolution to restore the original rights of mankind, which had been taken away by a combination of kings and priests. It was their *religious* zeal for this purpose that gave the French Revolution its driving force and made it such an important historical event. It seems that there is good evidence to suggest that many important figures in the period leading up to the French Revolution, including Voltaire, Rousseau, d'Alembert, and Frederick II of Prussia, were connected with Freemasonry and what amounts to an anti-Christian conspiracy. Likewise "a relatively large number of the leading revolutionists were members of Masonic lodges, trained by lodge life for their political career. Even the program of the Revolution expressed in the 'rights of man' was ... drawn from Masonic principles, and its device: 'Liberty, Equality, Fraternity' is the very device of Freemasonry."[245]

The question then becomes: was there an active conspiracy involving Freemasonry to promote the Enlightenment and ultimately the French Revolution? The modern secular view has tended to deny this, but that was not the opinion of some important writers of the time, who at least had the benefit of firsthand acquaintance with the events in question. The British politician, Edmund Burke, was to denounce the French Revolution in 1790, in his *Reflections on the Revolution in France*. This work followed that of a former Jesuit priest, the Abbé Barruel, who, in 1797, produced a history of "Jacobinism" to illustrate the essentially evil nature of both the Enlightenment and the French Revolution. This work was very influential in the nineteenth century, when a reaction against eighteenth-century political thinking took place. Barruel's thesis was that an active conspiracy of Freemasons and Illuminati had plotted to bring about the Revolution, and, although such ideas are frowned upon nowadays, there does seem to be a good degree of evidence to support his main points.[246]

The fact is that the French Revolution was something of a surprise when it did occur, since the traditional harbingers of revolution—war, famine and disease—were not present. For the most part, the ordinary people were content with their religious beliefs, and there was no organized political opposition. This point is all the more telling when the French Revolution is compared with the Communist Revolution in Russia in 1917, the only similarly important event in recent history, when all the usual factors such as war, disease and famine *were* present.[247] These points suggest that it is not fanciful to believe that there was a conspiracy of some sort behind the outbreak of the Revolution, that it was a movement plotted from above rather than a spontaneous outburst from below, even if it did get out of hand and take on a life of its own.

The Revolt against the "Ancien Régime"

The French Revolution thus began innocuously enough in May 1789, with a meeting of the Estates-General to deal with the financial problems facing the country. The initial concern was with the reform, rather than the overthrow, of Church and monarchy. This gathering comprised the "First Estate," the clergy, the "Second Estate," the nobility, and the "Third Estate," the bourgeoisie or middle class. It was this last group which was to assume control of the Revolution. By July a new constitution was formulated by the Estates-General, and this document was strongly influenced by the new philosophical ideas. Like the American Constitution of 1776, it spoke of the "Rights of Man," but without any real reference to God, and thus it was an essentially atheistic document that only helped to promote the continuing intellectual revolt.[248]

By October it was proposed that the Church's wealth be placed at "the disposal of the nation," to solve the continuing financial crisis in the country, and within a year it had lost every source of income. Church goods and properties were sold off, often very cheaply, and so, as at the time of the English Reformation, when Henry VIII sold off the monasteries, a powerful group of new landowners was created who had profited through the Revolution; they would have no desire to restore the Church to its former position. This weakened the old order and greatly strengthened the rising capitalistic and bourgeois forces, the investors, speculators, brokers, and moneylenders.[249]

At the same time, religious communities were split up, and a new Civil Constitution was put forward, which included a law framed in July 1790 to control the religious functions of bishops and priests, proposing that, in future, they be elected by the people and obliging them to swear an oath of loyalty to the State. Despite the danger, most of the clergy refused to take the oath, and the persecution it caused had the effect of making people realize what the Revolution really involved. When Pope Pius VI formally condemned the Civil Constitution in March 1792, it was the signal for a full-scale propaganda war against the Church. Despite that, most ordinary French Catholics refused to accept the artificial Constitutional Church, and since they were barred from using their own churches, began to live their faith in a clandestine manner.[250]

A new governing body, the *Legislative Assembly*, was formed in October 1791, and it proved much more hostile to the Church, proposing a bill further threatening those priests who refused the oath; but this was vetoed by the king, who still had that power at this stage. One of the most influential new groups to emerge at this time was based at the Jacobin club in Paris, which, by 1791, was affiliated to four hundred similar clubs throughout France, giving the liberal bourgeoisie Jacobins a strong power base. A rival club, the Cordeliers, included amongst its members revolutionary leaders such as Danton, Marat and Desmoulins. These clubs functioned as the conduits by which revolutionary decrees reached the people; they became the "churches" of the new religion, having absorbed the traditions of eighteenth-century Freemasonry. In reality, the "religion" of the Jacobins was to prove to be fanatically rigid and intolerant. It mimicked Christianity, in that had its own creed, the *Declaration of Rights*, while the *Social Contract* could be regarded as its Bible; but salvation for the Jacobins was a purely human affair, to be accomplished by the use of reason alone, one which had no place for the idea of Christian redemption.[251] Increasingly, the Revolution began to demand the "worship" of a new totalitarian civic religion, based on the principle of the citizen's duty to the State.[252]

Proposals for more severe laws against priests and religious were vetoed by the king, but an attack on the eastern frontiers by a Prussian force in July gave the revolutionaries, led by Danton, the excuse they needed to overthrow the monarchy and imprison the royal family. Immediately, persecution of the Church began, as a climate of fear and violence shook the country, especially when in September 1792 the military threat from Prussia intensified and panic overtook the revolutionary government. A terrible series of massacres now took place, in which over a thousand people, including about two hundred and fifty priests, were killed, but this was only a prelude to the dreadful "Reign of Terror" that was soon to come.[253] These deaths were not enough for Marat, who was reported to have stated that at least another forty thousand would have to die to ensure the success of the Revolution.[254] Once the revolutionary government was in power, it set about destroying the old political and social structure, by replacing the old provinces with newly-drawn departments, and particularly through attacks on the Church's position and privileges. This included assaults on Marian shrines and sanctuaries.

The revolutionaries, however, hesitated to kill the king despite enthusiastically adopting an anti-monarchical policy. Nevertheless, it was eventually realized that the downward spiral of revolution demanded the death of Louis, and so, although there was no evidence against him of any wrongdoing, he was put on trial in December 1792. Robespierre, another revolutionary leader, stated that, if Louis was innocent, then the Revolution was guilty, and it was this principle that led inexorably to the conviction and execution of the king in January 1793. This news was received badly in England, and soon afterwards the Revolutionary Convention declared war on Britain and the Netherlands, thus entering into a state of conflict with virtually all the major powers in Europe.[255] Robespierre and his associates saw the revolutionary struggle almost in religious terms, and were determined in their zeal to allow nothing to get in their way, as Christopher Dawson indicates: "To Robespierre, as to Thomas Paine and to William Blake, the

French Revolution was no mere political event, it was a crisis in world history which announced the birth of a new moral world and the regeneration of humanity."[256]

This course of events caused practically the whole of western France to rise up against the revolutionaries, and particularly the area known as the Vendée. The execution of the king caused deep distress to the royalist people of the west, and the news in March that conscription was to be introduced led the ordinary people to take up arms against the government's *Garde Nationale*. The rising quickly grew in strength and had some encouraging early victories, but it lacked adequate leadership and by the end of the year it was crushed with appalling cruelty. At one stage the Vendean army, under their leader Cathelineau, had nearly taken the city of Nantes, which would have opened the way to Paris and probably stopped the revolution in its tracks. However, it was not to be, and after Cathelineau was shot and fatally wounded, his army lost heart and withdrew; the opportunity for victory never arose again. The motivation of the insurgents was primarily religious, the defence of the Catholic faith, and, indeed, the Vendée was one of those areas evangelized by St Louis de Montfort earlier in the century.[257]

During the period from autumn 1793 to summer 1794, the Church faced the full fury of the revolutionaries, determined to do away with religion, faith and God; many priests perished during this period. What can only be described as a satanic atmosphere reigned, as evil was allowed to flourish freely, and many lost their lives to the guillotine, particularly once execution without trial was introduced. Attempts were made to do away with all references to Christianity, with a new calendar being introduced, while many churches were mutilated or destroyed, thus causing the destruction of a large part of the country's religious heritage, as had happened in England during the Reformation. The revolutionary government had by now become a totalitarian dictatorship, one that sought to control every aspect of people's lives. The nature of the Terror has led to its being regarded as one of the forerunners of socialism, in that those responsible saw it as a preparatory stage before a truly "democratic" regime could begin. In the same way, Communism was to see itself as preparing the way for a classless society.[258] All these measures, though, failed to destroy Catholicism and provoked stout resistance, even from many "constitutional" priests, who had initially supported the revolution but later realized their mistake. It is possible to see the sacrifices of those who suffered and died during this time as bearing fruit in the nineteenth-century revival of the Church in France.[259]

Robespierre had assumed effective power early in 1794 and intensified the Terror, but when the military situation improved in the summer, he was overthrown and himself executed. Robespierre's eventual method of "government" has been much imitated by dictators, and particularly Communist dictators, ever since: he ruled by periodically conducting purges of those who might oppose him, thus effectively frightening the rest into acquiescence. Eventually, however, the revolutionary leadership turned on him and he too had to face the guillotine. With his death, in July 1794, the Reign of Terror was effectively ended.[260]

In just four years, the revolutionary movement had gone from wanting to either limit or reduce the powers of the monarchy, to demanding full control of the government and the reduction of the king to a figurehead, then to sanctioning his execution, and eventually seeking to carry the revolution from France to the whole world. The parallel with the later ambitions of Soviet Communism, that of complete global domination, is striking, as is the similarity with the earlier Protestant attempt at supremacy in Europe.[261]

During the summer of 1794, there was a resurgence of Catholicism in the country, despite lingering persecution by revolutionaries, and the regime decided on a separation of Church and State early in 1795, thus ending the Constitutional Church, although anti-religious laws were still in being. The Church's position grew still stronger under the new government, the Directory, which came to power later in the year, as exiled priests returned and churches and chapels were reopened.[262]

One effect of the end of the Terror was the end of strict price controls, and this in turn led to an economic crisis, which completed the work of the Revolution by dissolving what remained of the old social and economic order, while giving rise to a new ruling class of individualistic and harsh entrepreneurs. Meanwhile, the last remnants of Jacobinism, under the leadership of Babeuf, became the forerunners of socialism in their attack on the right of private property as the root of social inequality. They attempted to enthuse the urban proletariat with the idea of class war, that the unfinished business of the Revolution lay in the resolution of the struggle between rich and poor, but by 1796 the ordinary people had lost all faith in revolutionary ideals, and so this came to nothing.[263]

The general situation for the Church then, because of the Revolution, was very serious, leading in France to persecution and the loss of its previously privileged position, while, in both Germany and Italy, Church property was secularized. All this meant that the

French Revolution was far more than a political revolution, and that it was really a more intense form of the Protestant Reformation, but a "reformation" that attempted to do away with Christianity altogether. Both Reformation and Revolution affected the whole of Europe, and both contained a mixture of the highest ideals and the lowest materialism. The most important factor in the French Revolution, though, was the way that "democratic ideals" became the new religion of the Revolution. This was the new faith of the revolutionaries, but it did not prove to be a benign faith, and only succeeded in unloosing violent and unpredictable forces on society, as the desire for power took over.[264]

Napoleon and the Church

A final bout of persecution broke out in France in 1797, and attempts were again made to destroy Christianity and introduce secular religions. To make matters worse, in a move that seemed to many to signal the end of the papacy, Pope Pius VI was seized and brought to France, where he later died. In 1799 Napoleon Bonaparte came to power in a *coup d'état,* and early in the next year a new Pope, Pius VII, was elected in Venice, as Napoleon completed a stunning victory over the Austrians at Marengo.[265]

Napoleon realized he needed the Church to restore order in France, having seen the resistance of many Catholics to the Revolution, and so accepted that it was better to try and work with the Church and the papacy than against it. This, in itself, was a tribute to the deep-rooted hold that Catholicism had on the French people, although he personally had no real sympathy for the Church and merely sought to use it for his own ends.[266]

By 1812 Napoleon had reached the height of his power, having won control of a large part of western Europe, either directly by means of members of his family, or through dependent states, over which he sought to impose his own ideas. Britain, though, was a formidable enemy, and once the French fleet was defeated at Trafalgar in 1805, and Napoleon had made his fateful decision to invade Russia in 1812, where he suffered a crushing defeat, the end was in sight.[267] It was Napoleon's misfortune to come up against, in England, the only great power that had resisted revolutionary ideas, mainly because it had not been so badly affected by Enlightenment thought; Methodism in particular had strengthened religion in the country. This meant that revolutionary political idealism was less influential than the principle of individual moral and religious conversion, as well as the practical business of the Industrial Revolution, which had originated in, and was rapidly developing in the country.[268]

Napoleon's defeat at Waterloo by Wellington's forces, in 1815, finally ended his ambitions; but without an alliance of the Protestants of Prussia and England, the Catholics of Europe, and the Eastern Orthodox under the Tsar, he might well have succeeded in his plan to control the Church, conquer Europe, and then form an empire embracing the rest of the world. It was not until this victory that the most dangerous elements of the French Revolutionary inheritance were finally brought to heel, and even then its true spirit of violence, anarchy and irreligion, proved very durable, being taken up in the twentieth century by the Russian Communists, the true heirs of the French Revolution in its darker and more sinister side.[269] This is evident in looking at the Jacobins and the way they anticipated more recent totalitarian regimes, particularly in their use of propaganda and violence, and also in their imposition of a uniform ideology and their opposition to any other form of political thought.[270]

The Results of the Revolution

In 1815, Britain, Prussia, Austria, and Russia formed an alliance to ensure that revolutionary ideas would not cause trouble in future, but there was still discontent in many parts of Europe. One of the main effects of the Congress of Vienna, finalized in the same year, was to weaken France seriously and undo all that Napoleon had worked for. Cardinal Consalvi, the papal diplomat, did a great deal to help rebuild the Church in Europe by negotiating concordats with various countries. This process was made more difficult by the tendency of governments to want to control the Church, as well as by their reluctance to give too much influence to the papacy. Despite their drawbacks, these agreements had the great virtue of being a public recognition of the central role of the popes in the life of the Church, and helped to avoid the danger of national churches developing. By recognizing the rights of governments, while accepting limitations on its own position, the papacy was distancing itself from those who wanted to see a complete return to the pre-Revolutionary system. The refusal to demand the return of all expropriated church property, for example, meant that she would be less wealthy, but more independent of governments, and so better fitted for the more spiritual role demanded in future.[271]

Napoleon accomplished some good in integrating elements of the Revolution into the new social and political order created during his reign, but, with the collapse of his empire, Europe had to cope with a situation resembling chaos after years of war and upheaval, and somehow create a new and stable social order. The problem was that Revolutionary ideas were a mixture of good and bad: ideals such as justice and liberty obviously had their place in any society, but other innovations were less welcome. The Revolution was not just a revolt against religion and the old social order; there was also a genuine "popular" element of opposition to over-powerful government, and of legitimate "national" feeling. These positive aspects, though, were not really recognized by the statesmen who constructed the new European order in 1815, and thus "revolutionary" national movements grew up without any legitimate way of expressing themselves, except by social upheaval. There were also true "revolutionaries," the liberals, who wanted to continue with the work of their predecessors, a work that included subjugating and, if possible, eliminating Christianity.[272]

In some respects the new situation for the Church was an improvement, because one of the hallmarks of the pre-Revolutionary era was that of state-controlled churches and a very weak papacy, whereas now the idea of concordats seemed to offer some hope of greater liberty in future. One of the unfortunate consequences of the defeat of Napoleon, however, given its future role, was the strengthening of Prussia, as it made substantial gains in the Rhineland. Still, the peace negotiated by the Austrian chancellor, Metternich, did give the Church a chance to recuperate, and this situation was to last substantially until 1848.[273]

Overall then, the French Revolution was more than just a political movement, being also a spiritual revolution, but one that ushered in a "religion" of humanity, one opposed to Christianity on many points. On a broader cultural level, one of its major consequences was the breaking down of some of the barriers that had existed since the Reformation between the Protestant and Catholic parts of Europe. This was very important for the Church, because it meant that the political obstacles that had existed to its religious mission were gradually removed, thus enabling it to re-establish its international position, just as its close allegiance with the older Catholic states was passing.[274]

One of the rather unexpected aftereffects of the French Revolution was a revival of religious ideals all over Europe, both in the strictly religious and also the philosophical and social spheres.

This revival of at least respect for religion was all the more surprising, given the colossal amount of material damage to religious buildings, and the confiscation of church property, that occurred during the Revolution. As it turned out, though, the persecution suffered by the Church during the revolution tended to strengthen religion. The quarter-century of upheaval from 1790 onwards tended to make many intelligent people lose faith in the principles of rationalism, and, in some cases, turn back towards religious belief.[275]

But, as in other times of religious revolution, there were more losses than gains, in that most of the French population were left in a state of confusion. The new secular culture being created was dominated by intellectuals and the working-classes of the cities, from whom socialism derived, and both were determined to carry on the "revolution," despite the Catholic beliefs of the majority.[276] The liberal groups who opposed both the Church and the re-instituted monarchy still hoped that, by eliminating the former, they could bring down the latter, and so they embarked on an anticlerical propaganda campaign which gradually succeeded in influencing popular opinion to regard the Church as the opponent of freedom. At the same time, throughout Europe there were outbursts of nationalism and liberalism, which proved a continuous threat to the monarchist system that generally supported the Church. In its turn, the Church had to face the problem of deciding whether to stay with the old system, which was losing ground, or try to come to terms with the new ideas. On all sides people were coming to realize that the very occurrence of the Revolution showed that future major changes in society could not be ruled out.[277]

Up to this point, then, we have been looking at the way the Reformation, despite its religious aspects, really amounted to a revolution which led to Christendom being divided into Catholic and Protestant areas. Although the Catholic Reformation was successful in winning back parts of Europe to the Faith, Protestantism was firmly established in the north, and particularly in England and Holland. As has been made clear, however, despite the fact that the apparitions of Our Lady in Mexico led to a vast expansion of the Church in the New World, which offset the losses to Protestantism in Europe, this revolution was really a turning point in Western history, and the sign of a new way of thinking and acting. This new revolutionary movement, in combination with the effects of capitalism, led to the secularization of Western culture, as religion in Europe was increasingly marginalized, with the result being the Enlightenment and the French Revolution. Although the Church was gravely weakened during this period, as we shall see, the nineteenth century would witness a resurgence of Catholicism, one due in no small part to Marian Apparitions, and particularly those in France, including Rue du Bac, La Salette, and Lourdes.

But religious principles would not have the field to themselves during this period, since secular philosophies and movements were also growing in strength. Even so, rationalistic principles such as "science" or "reason" would prove too narrow to encompass all the richness of human thought and being, and this gave the Romantic movement a chance to influence society. This movement concerned itself with ideas such as change, history, and evolution, as it sought to discern universal laws of development, thus providing fertile ground for the later theory of the biological evolution of mankind. Generally speaking, the eighteenth century had seen the whole universe in terms of Newton's idea of a complex, but essentially static, "machine," but one where mankind, by means of reason and science, and the principle of progress generally, could transform the world. This overall approach began to change, however, as the nineteenth century progressed, particularly through the work of men like Linnaeus and Buffon, who began to develop evolutionary thinking. The century was to be captivated by the idea of evolution, of change, the principle that the world and mankind were moving towards some perfect state, a position that contained elements from both rationalism and romanticism. These currents of thought explain why Darwin's theory of evolution was so well received in the years following the publication of his *Origin of Species* in 1859.[278]

8

Private Revelations, Typology, and the Church

The Nature of Private Revelations

Before examining the major Marian apparitions of the nineteenth century and their role in the history of this era, beginning in the next chapter with the events involving St Catherine Labouré at the Rue du Bac in 1830, we need to look briefly at the whole area of visions and apparitions, in order to put these events in context. Regarding the early Church, it is significant that, right from the beginning, just after the descent of the Holy Spirit at Pentecost on the assembled Apostles and Mary, as recounted in the Acts of the Apostles, we find talk of visions and portents prominent. Strengthened by the Spirit, Jesus' formerly timid followers began to preach boldly to the people from Jerusalem, who had gathered following the sound of the "great wind from heaven." This crowd was amazed to hear the Apostles preaching in their own languages, although some of them laughed at the whole business, thinking they were drunk. But St Peter stood up and rejected this idea, pointing out that it was still early in the morning and that what they were experiencing had been foretold by the prophet Joel long ago (Joel 2:28–32). He argued that this was an example of what was to happen during the "last days"—the messianic era when God would manifest his judgment of the world, which had now begun with the death and Resurrection of Jesus:

> And in the last days it shall be, God declares, that I will pour out my Spirit upon all flesh, and your sons and your daughters shall prophesy, and your young men shall see visions, and your old men shall dream dreams; yea, and on my menservants and my maidservants in those days I will pour out my Spirit; and they shall prophesy. And I will show wonders in the heaven above and signs on the earth beneath... (Acts 2:17–19).

This text is obviously significant, in the context of the various Marian apparitions, since it specifically mentions young people seeing visions, with portents in the sky above and signs on the earth below. The miracle of the sun at Fatima immediately comes to mind here, as does the youth of the three shepherd children; and similarly we have the many miraculous cures worked at Lourdes and other shrines. It seems legitimate, then, following Peter's approach, to regard the time before the "last days," the historical epoch beginning with Christianity, as a period when we might well expect manifestations of the supernatural, at least on occasion. This text seems to say that individuals will see visions, and heavenly and earthly signs, throughout the life of the Church, but particularly as history reaches its grand climax.

At this stage it is appropriate to define more exactly what is meant by visions or apparitions, so as to have a better understanding of what they involve. For the purposes of this book, the basic difference between a "vision" and an "apparition," in Catholic terms, is as follows: in a vision God produces a concept or image without there necessarily being anything external to the viewer, whereas, in an apparition, God apparently causes something external to the viewer to be perceived through the senses, which act normally, even if the "seer" is in an ecstatic state.[279]

Broadly speaking, it is probably accurate to say that, in the history of the Church, *visions* have been granted to saints and other holy people who have advanced some way in spiritual terms. That is because they have reached the stage where God can act more directly on the soul, and so produce visions and ecstasies of a more interior nature.[280] The approved Marian *apparitions,* on the other hand, seem to be of a more "exterior" nature, and have often been experienced by those who can be regarded as spiritual "novices." This distinction between "visions" and "apparitions" has been followed in this book, although some writers see apparitions as special cases of visions. To avoid confusion, however, it seems best to keep them separate, especially since one of the aims of this volume is to *describe* rather than analyze these events, given that such an analysis is difficult and not crucial to the arguments presented here.[281]

Fr Karl Rahner in his book *Visions and Prophecies* seems to want to categorize most visions or apparitions, including the Marian apparitions, as "imaginative," that is, as the "interior" type of visions usually granted to the saints. But even he admits that this hypothesis runs into trouble when we consider apparitions seen by more than one person, and which are apparently perceived in the normal way. Evidence from those who have experienced apparitions themselves, such as St Catherine Labouré and St Bernadette, strongly suggests they really did see Mary with their bodily eyes, rather than in an "imaginary" interior fashion. Fr Rahner himself cites the following two sayings of the above saints, but seems to imagine they made a "false judgment." After the apparitions at Lourdes, Bernadette exclaimed, "I saw her with my own eyes," while Catherine Labouré spoke to another sister, who doubted the bodily reality of the apparitions, in the following manner, "My child, the Sister who saw the Blessed Virgin, saw her in flesh and blood."

We also have, for example, as has already been indicated, the part of the Guadalupe account where Mary *with her own hands* rearranged the flowers in Juan Diego's *tilma*: obviously "imaginary" visions do not do such things. When this testimony is added to the report of Catherine Labouré, which is dealt with further on, that she put her hands on Mary's lap and looked into her eyes, it would seem that we are definitely not dealing with purely imaginative visions. This is the view of the Marian writer Fr Frederick M. Jelly, OP, on this point: "The accounts of the Marian apparitions, such as those at Lourdes and Fatima, ... indicate that the visionaries perceived something corporeal and physical. The imaginative type may apply in certain cases, but a purely intellectual apparition appears unlikely. The senses usually occupy a significant role in Marian apparitions."[282]

Fr Rahner also deals with an experiment conducted by the writer Carlos Staehlin on six youths aged between fifteen and eighteen, who were told to imagine that a battle between medieval warriors was going on above a tree. Two apparently saw or heard nothing, two saw the battle and the last two both saw and heard it, with their reports apparently agreeing.[283] This point is taken up by Hilda Graef in her *Mary: A History Of Doctrine and Devotion*, as a possible psychological explanation for Marian apparitions. She feels that the results of Staehlin's experiment can be applied to apparitions such as those at La Salette, Fatima and Beauraing, and mean that there is some justification for those who want to doubt the authenticity of these church-approved apparitions, or at least reserve judgment until their psychological background is more fully investigated.[284]

But Staehlin's experiment and the approved Marian apparitions are totally different. He deliberately encouraged the youths to fantasize in what could have been a psychologically dangerous

manner, to say nothing of inviting a possible diabolical intervention; whereas, in dealing with genuine apparitions, the children
involved really did claim to see something supernatural. As such,
Staehlin's experiment tells us very little, even if there was some
agreement between the children involved, and it was actually a
dangerous and foolish thing to do. Comparisons with experiments
with Ouija boards, and all the hazards involved in such matters,
come to mind.

With the more "exterior" Marian apparitions, it seems that the
main dangers are illusion and hallucination. It would be a case of
illusion if someone thought that a physical object was acting in an
apparition-like manner, as in the case of those who think they have
seen statues of Mary moving. Some of the people of Knock, in
1879, initially thought that the apparition of Mary they could see
by the church was a collection of new statues ordered by the parish
priest and left outside. This was the natural initial conclusion to
come to, but it was incorrect, because one of those present tried to
kiss one of these supposed statues and found nothing there.
Hallucinations, on the other hand, are usually due to some disorder of the brain, either organic or drug-induced, which leads to
the production of images that can be regarded as having different
levels of "reality" for the individual. "Hallucinations" may also
possibly have a diabolical origin.

A true vision or apparition, then, comes from God, but a hallucination comes from the individual's own imagination, or is caused
by some bodily or mental disorder, or, more seriously, comes from
the devil. So while a highly suggestible and unbalanced individual
might be subject to some sort of hallucination, usually there are
clear signs to indicate this: that is, moral defects are also present.
The seers of the approved Marian apparitions have generally been
regarded as very levelheaded, and thus unlikely to be subject to
hallucinations. Similarly, there are good textual accounts of these
apparitions, indicating that they do not contradict church teaching
or dogma, another positive point regarding their authenticity,
although the Church itself has not rushed into proclaiming their
truthfulness, but has taken time to evaluate all the evidence.[285]

In most of the Marian apparitions, we are dealing with simple
people or children, who, although not advanced spiritually, were
usually uncorrupted by the world, and so able to see things hidden
from other people. This was the case with Pontmain in 1871, where
the apparition of Mary in the sky was seen only by young children,
who were not in ecstasy, while the adults present saw nothing.

Knock is the exception to this, in that most of those who went to the church on 21 August 1879 and saw the apparition were adults, albeit undoubtedly simple and unsophisticated country people with a childlike faith. Although Juan Diego, the seer of Guadalupe, was an adult, he had only been baptized a few years previously and so was, in spiritual terms, a child.

On the surface, it might seem that the testimony of adults would be more trustworthy than that of children, but in reality, in relation to the Marian apparitions, the witness of children is actually far more likely to be truthful and reliable. This is because the "ignorant" children who saw Mary had the advantage of not having a mind cluttered with years of reading and worldly knowledge. Their minds were fresh, capable of receiving the message of Our Lady and passing it on without adulteration, unlike most adults, who would find it very difficult to avoid embellishment. Their accounts were thus simple and direct, with the simplicity and directness possessed only by a child or one with a childlike attitude.[286]

The question also arises as to how certain we can be that an apparition really comes from God. In the Old Testament period, prophets such as Elijah appeared and claimed to speak in the name of God, apparently proving this by miraculous signs accepted by the people. These signs were necessary because of the presence of false prophets, and so a process of discernment was needed. Likewise, Christ proved that he was divine by performing miracles. This is the view of the French spiritual writer, Poulain, on how much credibility we should give to revelations and visions generally, and, by extension, this also applies to Marian apparitions:

> When a miracle is performed, and it is stated that it is worked with this intention, [as a sign] or when circumstances show this to be the case, it is an undeniable proof of the divine nature of the revelation. A prophecy fulfilled will be the equivalent of a miracle, if it was couched in definite language and could not have been the result of chance or a conjecture of the Devil.[287]

The miraculous healings at Lourdes seem to fulfil that criteria, while at Fatima there was both a fulfilled prophecy and a miraculous sign in the foretelling and actual occurrence of the "miracle of the sun." This indicates that these Marian apparitions really did come from God, and so we can be *morally certain* they are worthy of belief.

Regarding the Marian apparitions dealt with in this book, from the time of Guadalupe onwards, they have been chosen on the basis that they involve Mary visually appearing and giving a definite message, either spoken or in some symbolic form, to a seer or seers. In addition, elements such as episcopal approval and the development of a relatively extensive cult, as well as wider ecclesiastical and papal approval, have all been taken as indicating the genuineness of particular apparitions. In practice, this comes down to the nine major Marian apparitions of the modern era, between Guadalupe in 1531 and Beauraing and Banneux in the 1930s. The others are Rue du Bac in 1830; La Salette in 1846; Lourdes in 1858; Pontmain in 1871; Knock in 1879; Fatima in 1917, plus two or three others. This means that not every possibly authentic Marian "event" has been included here, because, in some cases, the people involved did not *see* Mary in the way that seers involved in the major recognized apparitions saw her, or such apparitions simply have not made a big enough impact on the Church.

Church Approval of Marian Apparitions

The various Marian apparitions are classed as "private" revelations, in that the *public* revelation of the Church was completed during Apostolic times, and is now closed. All that the Church has done since then is to develop and clarify those public truths, and Catholics are *bound* to believe them as truths of the Faith. Private revelations, though, including the approved Marian apparitions, are given to an individual or group for their own good or that of others; Catholics are not obliged to believe in them, and they do not add to the sum total of public revelation,[288] as the *Catechism of the Catholic Church* (67) makes clear:

> Throughout the ages, there have been so-called "private" revelations, some of which have been recognized by the authority of the Church. They do not belong, however, to the deposit of faith. It is not their role to improve or complete Christ's definitive Revelation, but to help live more fully by it in a certain period of history. Guided by the Magisterium of the Church, the *sensus fidelium* knows how to discern and welcome in these revelations whatever constitutes an authentic call of Christ or his saints to the Church.

There is always the danger of illusion or deception in visions or apparitions, and that is why the Church, in the person of the local bishop initially, has always been reluctant to accept them without a great deal of scrutiny. In approving particular private revelations, the Church is only proposing them for assent on the basis that they require an act of human faith, based on human testimony. The classic view on this matter was expressed by Pope Benedict XIV (1675–1758), as follows: "Although an assent of Catholic faith may not and can not be given to revelations thus approved, still, an assent of human faith, made according to the rules of prudence is due them; for, according to these rules such revelations are probable and worthy of pious credence."[289]

It could be remarked in passing, though, that Pope Benedict wrote in the period before the major modern Marian apparitions, and there has been some development in thinking since then. That is particularly so if we recognize the particular nature of the messages received and transmitted by the various more recent Marian seers, which seem to be a special case of "private" revelation, since they form a series which has been of great importance in strengthening the Church in modern times. They certainly differ from the various "private" revelations to individual saints, which might have been concerned with, for example, the foundation of a religious order.

As Fr William Most states, "Some private revelations of our own times, such as those at Fatima, are directed to all Christians, not only to one individual; still they are technically called private, to distinguish them from that revelation which closed with the death of St John."[290] Thus we have to distinguish between those revelations made to individuals, for their own good, and those meant for the whole Church. Fatima and Lourdes certainly seem to fall into the latter category, and, given the miraculous events surrounding them, it can be argued that they represent an authentic divine call to the Church.[291]

The fact that these apparitions seem, from a secular historical point of view, to have been of "almost negligible importance," is not the crucial point; the same could be said for Israel, which also made little impression on history; yet, in moral terms, our whole civilization is built on that foundation. In the same way, the Marian apparitions have a significance that goes far beyond their surface importance as a reiteration of the Gospel message of prayer and repentance. They can also be seen as the first presentiments of the certain fact that Christ will come again at the Last Day. Mary was an intimate part of Christ's first coming, and similarly, she has an important role in preparing the way for his second advent, principally, it would seem, by means of her apparitions.[292]

The decision as to the authenticity of an apparition rests in the first place with the local bishop, who is the "Pope" of his own diocese. If, after sufficient study, there is solid evidence to support the apparition, in terms of the facts surrounding it and the activities of the seer or seers, and also regarding such matters as miraculous healings, then the bishop is empowered to issue some form of edict declaring the authenticity of a particular apparition. Such a statement is not, of course, infallible, and no one is absolutely *obliged* to believe in that particular apparition, but the position of the bishop as the spiritual ruler of the diocese means that his decision should be respected. The two extremes to be avoided are excessive credulity, which believes every report of an apparition, and excessive scepticism, which holds apparitions almost in contempt.

Over time, the papacy may grant special privileges to particular shrines, and those are a sign of further approval by the Church as a whole.[293] One such liturgical sign is the granting of a feast day, as, for example, that of Our Lady of Lourdes on 11 February. In recent times, popes such as Paul VI and John Paul II have visited a number of Marian shrines, thus giving them the highest possible level of approval. These are the elements, then, that we have to bear in mind, when considering the authenticity of the Marian apparitions of the nineteenth and twentieth centuries, which will be dealt with in succeeding chapters, and, as will be realized, they were also present in the apparitions of Our Lady of Guadalupe in Mexico in 1531. There Bishop Zumárraga conducted an inquiry into Juan Diego's claims, one that was unusually speedy, given the miraculous production of the image of Mary on the *tilma*, and due to the reports of cures which he could verify for himself. The same general principles guided the approach taken by those investigating the apparitions at Vinay and Le Laus, amongst others, in the seventeenth century.

In sum then, the Church has consistently taken a very cautious attitude towards Marian apparitions, with only a very small minority of such reported events being accepted. Episcopal approval is the first step in such acceptance, but other factors such as general church approval, expressed in the building of a basilica, for example, or a papal visit, are also necessary if an apparition is to be fully acknowledged.

Biblical Typology and Mary

One of the important themes of this book is an examination of the links between the major Marian apparitions and important revolutionary events in world history since the time of the Reformation. But the idea that there are typological parallels between aspects of these apparitions and biblical passages, a principle supported by the Church Fathers, also forms a significant theme. Thus, this will now be explored.

The Church Fathers and early writers identified many different types and prophecies concerning Mary in the Old Testament, and, broadly speaking, we can divide them into a number of classes, comprising persons, themes, prophecies, and objects. For instance, Mary has been compared with such biblical women as Sarah, the wife of Abraham, or Judith the savior of the city of Bethulia, while the themes of her motherhood, in comparison with that of Eve, or her intercessory power, have also been developed by some of the early writers.[294] An example of a prophecy associated with Mary is that found in Isaiah, which describes the coming of the virgin with child, (Isa. 7:14); while some of the objects that have been interpreted as types of Mary include the burning bush seen by Moses, and the Eastern gate of the Temple as seen in vision by the prophet Ezekiel.

For the Fathers, Scripture had two senses, or levels of meaning, the literal and the spiritual. In this they were influenced by Jewish rabbinical methods and by the realization that much of the Old Testament was difficult to comprehend, unless it had a deeper spiritual meaning. This spiritual meaning was divided into typological and allegorical senses, although the Fathers did not always carefully distinguish between these two approaches. Regrettably, this is still the case to some extent today; and at times, depending on the writer, typology is sharply differentiated from allegory, while at other times it is regarded as a part of the broad allegorical sense.

For the Fathers, a type was an historical biblical event, but one which also had a deeper significance, a meaning which was determined by the tradition of the Church. This Christian typology was essentially something new, particularly in its emphasis on Christ as the one who had fulfilled the Scriptures. The point about types being part of a tradition is important because it underlines the principle that the Fathers were not innovators; rather they were concerned to pass on and deepen a tradition which they had themselves received. Allegory, however, was something different, because in its use the historical sense was generally avoided and tradition played no controlling part; thus the Fathers could be quite imaginative in using it.[295]

The French theologian, Jean Daniélou, comments on the way that the main body of biblical typology is concerned with the way

that aspects of the Old Testament have a Christological significance in that they act as genuine types of Christ, and are thus
fulfilled in the New Testament. He contrasts this with the more
allegorical approach of writers, such as Philo, a Hellenistic Jewish
writer from Alexandria in Egypt, who lived around the time of
Christ, which strays from the literal meaning of the text and intro-
duces foreign elements. He also argues that typology and prophecy
are organically related, such that "prophecy is the typological interpretation of history."[296]

Fr Stefano Manelli points out that the traditional teaching of the
Church, also encompassing its liturgy and art, indicates that the
Marian typology adopted by the Fathers is more than mere accom-
modation, and that its use in the liturgy in particular indicates the
guidance of the Holy Spirit. He criticizes those modern writers who
have discarded this rich heritage of Marian symbolism, arguing
that this position equates biblical exegesis with philology. That is,
it reduces it to the level of a mere study of language, to an ornate
linguistic analysis which does not grasp the real meaning of the
Marian types found in the Old Testament. Because it does not
acknowledge the Faith of the Church, such an approach has lost
touch with ultimate reality and is thus false.[297]

This was not the attitude of Pope Pius IX, (1792–1878), who, in
his dogmatic bull on the Immaculate Conception, *Ineffabilis Deus,*
promulgated in 1854, discussed with approval such Marian symbols
as the virgin earth, Jacob's ladder, and the burning bush. Fr
Manelli also points to the use of other Marian symbols, such as the
Ark of the Covenant in the present-day liturgy, for the feast of the
Assumption on 15 August, and the recurrence of such symbols of
Mary as the Rod of Aaron, and Gideon's fleece, in the tradition,
liturgy, and sacred art of the Church.[298] This approach is also
found in more recent Church documents. Vatican II's *Lumen
Gentium* reiterates the teaching about Mary as the new Eve, as
found in the works of Saints Irenaeus, Epiphanius and Jerome
(56), and goes on to say that Mary is "the new Eve, who put her
absolute trust not in the ancient serpent but in God's messenger"
(63). The *Catechism of the Catholic Church* backs this teaching up
(411, 494), and also describes her in the following way: "In Mary,
the Holy Spirit *manifests* the Son of the Father, now become the
Son of the Virgin. She is the burning bush of the definitive theo-
phany" (724).[299]

Examples of the liturgical use of types are found in the Divine
Office. The following antiphon occurs in the first Evening Prayer
of the Solemnity of Mary, Mother of God, on 1 January: "Moses saw

the thornbush which was on fire yet was not burnt up. In it we see a sign of your virginity which all must honor; Mother of God, pray for us." Similarly, amongst the intercessions for the feast of the Annunciation, 25 March, we find: "The new Eve was obedient to your divine Word—Give us the grace to submit to your holy will: Holy Mother of God, intercede for us." The same theme is found in an antiphon for Evening Prayer I of the feast of the Assumption, 15 August: "The gates of paradise were closed to all men because of Eve, but they have been opened again through the Virgin Mary, alleluia."

The above types of Mary, then, have not lost their value or meaning, and as such it is legitimate to see them as divinely-intended comparisons developed under the guidance of the Holy Spirit, and not as examples of mere "piety."

Henri de Lubac, however, in discussing allegory, apparently criticizes[300] aspects of "typology," but on examination it seems that what he is really criticizing is typology as a method of "exegesis" rather than as a method of "writing." That is, as a method concerned with, for example, finding similarities between the names of Old and New Testament characters and thus seeing an "exegetical" typological link between them. In this he is probably justified, in that the links found by such an approach can be very tenuous. This contrasts with finding connections in a straightforward way, such as seeing Elijah as the forerunner of John the Baptist, a typology explored in the New Testament (e.g. Matt. 11:14), on the basis of the actions or attributes of both. De Lubac's criticism is not applicable to the typological principles explored in this book, since these are concerned with an objective comparison between biblical events and the Marian apparitions, that is between one set of historical, or at least "prophetic," events and another.

Given this, and given that there is no consensus amongst theologians as to the exact dividing line between typology and allegory, it does not seem unreasonable to pursue the idea that the Old Testament Marian types are divinely-intended. The crucial question then, however, is whether this approach can be extended and whether these Marian types can be seen as prophetically foreshadowing the modern Marian apparitions. That is, is there a parallel to the way that Old Testament events acted as types for Christ in the New Testament? It would certainly seem "unnatural" to draw an artificial dividing-line between biblical times and the present "time of the Church." The two are surely organically linked. We find written prophecies in the Old Testament, so why not "typical" prophecies too?

Recalling Jean Daniélou's words that "prophecy is the typological interpretation of history," we can certainly say that prophecy and typology are very closely linked. Anyone who is familiar with the Bible will realize that many of the prophecies found in the Old Testament still await fulfilment. This is particularly the case with the restoration of Israel, and what might broadly be termed "the end of the world." In fact, it is difficult to open parts of the Old Testament *without* coming across such material, such is its abundance. Of course, the modern mentality rejects the idea that scriptural prophecies still await fulfillment, but anyone who takes the teaching of the Church seriously, and indeed the principle that the Bible itself is the inerrant Word of God, will realize that such an approach is wrong.

Thus we have a situation where the *written* prophecies of the Old Testament, in the main, await fulfillment, and thus there is a clear link between biblical and ecclesiastical history. That fact, though, that certain biblical prophecies have not been fulfilled, does not indicate that Christ's salvific work is in any sense incomplete or inadequate, but rather that its consequences have yet to be worked out in history. In the case of typology, it is being argued here that there is also a link between the *typical* scriptural "prophecies" concerning Mary in the Old Testament, and the Marian apparitions of the modern age. But it has to be remembered that whereas those Old Testament prophecies which have been fulfilled by Christ in his first coming are organically linked to the *public* revelation given to the Church, the link proposed above is concerned only with the theme of *private* revelations.

In theological terms, the Church accepts the principle of the development of dogma, that is, that ideas innate in Scripture and Tradition come to fruition only at the particular moment in history when they are really needed by the Church, as the dogmas of the Immaculate Conception and Assumption demonstrate. Thus it is quite possible that the Marian types of the Old Testament are linked to the modern Marian apparitions, and that is what the appropriate sections of this book seek to demonstrate.

Mary as the Ark of the Covenant

But we can go further than this, and say that the typological approach discussed in this work follows the general pattern found in the fulfillment of a particular Marian type, that of the New Testament account of the Visitation of Mary to her cousin

Elizabeth just after the Annunciation (Luke 1:39–56). There is quite an interesting parallel between Elizabeth's sense of unworthiness in the presence of Mary and her child, and King David's feelings in the presence of the Ark of the Covenant, as indicated in the Old Testament. David was the greatest king of Israel, and, having defeated the Philistines in battle, decided to transport the Ark to Jerusalem, which he had recently made his capital, thus giving it a religious as well as a political significance. The Ark of the Covenant was the chest, overlaid inside and out with gold, which was constructed on Moses' orders to hold the two tablets of the Law that he had received from God on Mount Sinai. Moses also had a mercy-seat of pure gold constructed and placed on top of the Ark to act as God's "throne"; this was where God was to meet Moses and instruct him (Ex. 25:10–22).

For the Israelites, then, the Ark was the place where God's presence was particularly manifested. Previously it had fallen into the hands of the Philistines, but after they were afflicted with tumors, they returned it with a guilt-offering of gold (1 Sam. 4–7:1). Now, as David was escorting the Ark in a new cart drawn by oxen, all the people rejoiced and danced in a great procession. When they reached a certain point, however, one of those accompanying the Ark, Uzzah, reached out his hand to steady it, and, for violating its holiness by touching it, was struck down by the Lord and died (2 Sam. 6:9–11). The text then continues:

> And David was afraid of the Lord that day; and he said, "How can the ark of the Lord come to me?" So David was not willing to take the ark of the Lord into the city of David; but David took it aside to the house of Obed-edom the Gittite. And the ark of the Lord remained in the house of Obed-edom the Gittite three months; and the Lord blessed Obed-edom and all his household.

Compare this with the account of the Visitation:

> In those days Mary arose and went with haste into the hill country, to a city of Judah, and she entered the house of Zechariah and greeted Elizabeth. And when Elizabeth heard the greeting of Mary, the babe leaped in her womb; and Elizabeth was filled with the Holy Spirit and she exclaimed with a loud cry, "Blessed are you among women, and blessed is the fruit of your womb! And why is this granted me, that the mother of my Lord should come to me? For behold, when the voice of your greeting came to my ears, the babe in my womb leaped for joy ..." And

Mary remained with her about three months, and returned to her home (Luke 1:39–44, 56).

The significance of this is in the comparison between Elizabeth and David, in the similar sense of awe and unworthiness they both felt in the presence of a clear manifestation of God's holiness. For David, it was the Ark which "embodied" the presence of the Lord, the God of the Israelites, whereas for Elizabeth it was Mary who carried within herself the child who was God, and who was also the fulfillment of all the promises made to the Jewish people. Mary, like the Ark, had traveled up towards the Judean hills, and both David and John the Baptist "leaped for joy" before God (2 Sam. 6:12,16). The other intriguing parallel between Mary and the Ark is that, just as the Ark remained at the house of Obed-edom for three months and was a blessing for his whole household, so also Mary remained with Elizabeth for three months before going home (Luke 1:56). That Luke uses the word "about" to describe this three-month period means that we should understand these events as historical, and not as symbolical, or an invention. Undoubtedly, too, the presence of Mary, and the divine child within her womb, was a blessing on the household of Elizabeth and Zechariah.[301]

What St Luke was doing here, then, was pointing out how the Marian typology of this episode involving the Ark of the Covenant was fulfilled in Mary's Visitation to Elizabeth. That is, a true historical event provided the fulfillment of a prophetic Old Testament Marian type. The examples that follow in this book take this application a step further, pursuing the idea that other Marian types are fulfilled in the modern approved Marian apparitions.

9

Catherine Labouré and the Miraculous Medal

Catherine Labouré before the Apparitions

The first major "modern" approved apparition of Mary took place in Paris, to a young religious sister called Catherine Labouré in 1830, nearly three hundred years after the apparitions at Guadalupe in Mexico in 1531. Catherine, then known as Zoe, was born into a poor farming family in Burgundy in 1806, where her early life was hard and not without sadness, her mother dying at the early age of forty-two. From this point on, she regarded Mary as her mother, and this helps us to understand how she could have such a desire to see Mary, that this was her constant prayer, a prayer which, without presumption, she had every expectation would be realized one day.

When her eldest sister decided to become a nun with the Daughters of Charity, Catherine persuaded her father that she was able to take charge of running the household, a very heavy burden for a young girl. She usually found time to attend Mass at the local church in Moutiers, involving a journey on foot of over two miles each way at daybreak. She made her First Communion there in 1818 at the age of twelve, and seems to have decided to devote herself to God from an early age. Her sister Tonine maintained in later years that Catherine had become "entirely mystic" from that moment, absolutely determined to put the things of God first, regardless of cost. She fasted on Fridays and Saturdays and withdrew to the local chapel to pray whenever possible, kneeling on the stone floor even during the depths of winter, a practice which resulted in her knees becoming arthritic as she grew older. She had a very poor education, even though her father had spent some time in the seminary, and it almost seems as though God wanted someone who was as uncontaminated and childlike as possible to be the person to herald the modern Marian age.[302]

Just before she was eighteen, she had an unusual dream which confirmed for her the future direction of her life. She saw herself praying in the local chapel as an old priest celebrated Mass. When he had finished, he beckoned her nearer, but she turned away in fright, only to find that the dream continued. She was now at the bed of a sick person with the old priest. He spoke to her: "You do well to visit the sick, my child. You flee from me now, but one day you will be glad to come to me. God has plans for you; do not forget it." On waking she realized that her vocation lay in serving the sick and suffering, but she had to wait until she was twenty-two before her younger sister could replace her on the farm. After staying in Paris, she went to live in Châtillon-sur-Seine, a town that happened to have a house of the Daughters of Charity. During a visit there, she saw a picture of an old priest on the wall of the parlor and realized it was the same man she had seen in her dream. On asking about this she was told that it was a picture of the founder of the order, St Vincent de Paul. Eventually her father, who had been against her vocation, was persuaded that he should give his permission for Catherine to enter the order, and she began her postulancy early in 1830. Later on, in April, she moved to the mother house of the Daughters of Charity, the convent in the Rue du Bac in Paris, to begin her period of formation.

The Rue du Bac was not far away from the Vincentian church where the relics of St Vincent de Paul had recently been translated, and the sisters and novices, including Catherine, often went there to pray. On three successive evenings, when she returned to the Rue du Bac, she saw a vision of the heart of St Vincent, in the chapel, just over a shrine containing a bone from his right arm. The first two visions concerned the community, but the last saw the heart take on a dark red color, which Catherine interiorly understood meant sadness and suffering both for herself and France, in that a change of government was imminent. On Trinity Sunday, 6 June 1830, Catherine had a vision of Christ, as a King, during the Gospel of the Mass; suddenly all his kingly ornaments fell to the ground and she felt herself plunged into spiritual gloom, a sign that the change of government, which would involve Charles X's losing his throne, was getting closer. She told her confessor, Fr Aladel, about these visions, but he did not take her seriously and told her put such things out of her mind.[303]

The First Apparition – July 1830

18 July was the eve of the feast of St Vincent and that night Catherine went to sleep in the dormitory with the other young novices. In all simplicity, she continued to pray for the grace of seeing Mary and hoped that this would now be granted through the intercession of St Vincent, particularly following the visions of his heart. She seems to have had an intuition that this would really happen: "I went to bed thinking ... that, that very night, I would see my Blessed Mother. I had been wanting to see her for so long." Before going to sleep, she swallowed a little piece of a surplice that had belonged to St Vincent, confident that he would intercede, that she would indeed see the Blessed Virgin that very night. She later told Fr Aladel that she was awoken at about half-past eleven by someone calling her name; looking in the direction of the voice, she drew the curtain aside to see a child of about four or five, dressed in white, saying to her: "Get up promptly and come to the chapel. The Blessed Virgin is waiting for you." Catherine followed him, worried they would be discovered, but the child reassured her and she was amazed to see lights blazing everywhere as they made their way to the chapel; she followed the child to the sanctuary, and knelt by the chair used to give conferences to the Sisters.[304]

They waited for several minutes and then the child suddenly spoke, saying: "Here is the Blessed Virgin," as Catherine heard a sound like the rustling of a silk dress and saw a Lady descending the altar steps and seating herself on the director's chair. A doubt held her back, but the child told her twice that this really was the Blessed Virgin, the second time imperatively, with a strong man's voice. She then threw herself at Mary's feet, put her hands on her lap and looked up into her eyes; she was later to describe that moment as the sweetest of her life. Mary then spoke, telling her that God wished to charge her with a mission, that she would have trials to bear and many difficulties to overcome, but that she would always have an inner certainty as to what she should do. She was told to tell everything she saw and heard to her confessor. With a look of grief on her face, Mary continued: "There will be bad times to come. Misfortunes will come crashing down on France. The throne will be toppled. The whole world will be turned upside-down by misfortunes of all kinds [...] But come to the foot of this altar. There, graces will be poured out on all those, small, or great, who ask for them with confidence and fervor. Graces will be poured out especially on those who ask for them."

After detailing faults in the community life of both the

Vincentian Fathers and Sisters, Mary reassured Catherine that the community as a whole would be enlarged and enjoy peace. This prediction was fulfilled in 1850 when two communities, the Sisters of Charity, founded by Elizabeth-Ann Seton, the first canonized saint from the United States, and the Sisters of Charity of Austria, entered the Vincentian family.

Mary then returned to the theme of the sorrows coming to France and the whole world, but told her not to be afraid, since she would always be protected and granted many graces. A moment would come when everything would seem lost, but she should continue to have confidence since God was with her. Other communities and individuals, though, would have to suffer. Mary continued with tears in her eyes: "There will be victims [...] There will be victims among the clergy of Paris; Monsignor the Archbishop will die [...] My child, the cross will be held in contempt. It will be thrown to the ground. Blood will flow. Our Saviour's side will be opened anew. The streets will run with blood. Monsignor the Archbishop will be stripped of his vestments ..." At this point, according to Catherine's account, Mary's tears prevented her from continuing properly; she could only conclude: "My child, the whole world will be plunged into gloom."

Catherine wondered in her own mind when all this would happen and immediately understood interiorly: *forty years*. She was also told about the new Association to be founded, the Children of Mary, of the way May would become a special Marian month, and of how devotion to the Sacred Heart would greatly increase.[305] Catherine then asked Mary some private questions, which were answered, before the Blessed Virgin faded from her gaze, leaving her to return with the child to the dormitory. Once she was back in bed, the child, who Catherine now understood was her guardian angel, also vanished, just as the clock struck two; she then realized she had been with Mary for over two hours.[306]

She repeated all she was told to Fr Aladel, but perhaps naturally he was somewhat sceptical. This scepticism quickly vanished, however, when just over a week later, on 27 July 1830, Mary's prophecies were fulfilled as the revolution began in Paris, and opposition to Charles X's absolutist rule grew. His government was under attack from both left and right, following the decision to rule with the support of the army alone, in defiance of public opinion. At the same time it suspended freedom of the press and modified electoral law, so as to prevent the liberal middle classes from voting. This attempt to turn back the clock ended in disaster, and after a few days Charles X was overthrown, with the Church, unhappily, implicated in his downfall, as bishops, priests, and religious were imprisoned, ill-treated, and in some cases killed. Churches were desecrated and the cross was trampled underfoot as foretold. Mgr de Quélen, the archbishop, only just managed to escape the mob, although the Vincentian community were spared persecution. Fr Aladel was forced to accept that the things Catherine had spoken about had come true, despite the fact that, isolated in the convent, she could have had no idea of outside political events.

Revolutionary upheavals had also occurred in Belgium, Poland and Ireland, while in Italy and Spain liberal movements grew in strength. The situation in France, though, was particularly alarming, since the revolution there was targeted at the Church in particular. Pope Pius VIII tried to make the best of the situation by recognizing the new government and monarch, Louis Philippe, Charles's cousin, a realistic and far-sighted approach.[307]

Catholics in England and, indeed, the whole British Empire had been encouraged by the Emancipation Act of 1829, which had restored the majority of their civil and religious rights. The situation for Irish Catholics likewise improved to an extent, as some of the worst of the penal laws were repealed. This had come about because of the long campaign of nonviolent agitation conducted by Daniel O' Connell, and was a notable achievement. This episode was a good example of the beneficial effects that could be obtained through a proper application of the ideals of liberalism and nationalism. Such ideals were widespread in Europe, and showed more clearly the dilemma facing the Church, that of how to absorb the best of the new ideas without sacrificing principles. In countries such as Belgium, Poland or Ireland, should the Church support those Catholics who wanted to ally themselves with liberal elements in the struggle for freedom, or should the traditional order be upheld?[308]

Second and Third Apparitions

Later in the same year, on Saturday 27 November, Catherine was in the chapel at 5:30 in the evening for the community meditation, when she heard the same rustling of silk. She then saw a radiant apparition of Mary in the sanctuary, standing on a globe: "I perceived the Blessed Virgin [...] standing, dressed in white, medium height, her face so beautiful that it would be impossible for me to tell of her beauty."[309]

Mary wore a white silk dress with a white veil that fell to her feet, and in her hands held a golden ball; her lips moved silently in prayer as she turned her eyes to heaven, with the attitude of somebody making an offering. Catherine noticed rings on her fingers with precious stones which glittered and flashed with light. Mary looked at her, and although Catherine did not see her lips move, she heard an inner voice: "The ball which you see represents the whole world, especially France, and each person in particular. These rays symbolize the graces I shed upon those who ask for them. The gems from which rays do not fall are the graces for which souls forget to ask."[310]

The principle that Mary is the "Mediatrix" between God and man has been developing during the course of Church history,[311] and involves the idea that while Jesus is the sole mediator Mary plays a subordinate role in the distribution of graces, a point expressed very well in the imagery of the Rue du Bac apparitions. Mary's part in the distribution of graces is based on her role in the acquisition of those same graces, that is, she is the Mother of the Redeemer, and the person most closely associated with Jesus in his Passion and death.

This is a point made particularly with regard to Rue du Bac by St Maximilian Kolbe, writing in 1938, a few years before his martyrdom in Auschwitz during the Second World War. He was deeply impressed by these apparitions, and also by Lourdes, because he saw them as *factual* proof of Mary's mediation: "In 1830 the Most Blessed Virgin appeared to Sister Catherine Labouré. From the account given by this novice we learn the purpose of Mary's appearing: she wished to affirm her Immaculate Conception and her extraordinary power with God."[312]

In Catherine's own written account, she explains how she came to understand "how pleasing it was to pray to the Blessed Virgin and how generous she was towards those who pray to her; what graces she granted to those who ask them of her, what joy she felt in granting those graces."[313]

Catherine experienced the end of the second apparition in something of an ecstatic state, as the golden ball vanished, and then the third apparition began. Mary stretched out her arms in a compassionate gesture, and from her fingers rays of light fell upon the globe at her feet. An oval frame then formed around her with golden lettering that read: *O Mary, conceived without sin, pray for us who have recourse to thee.* She again heard the voice speaking: "Have a Medal struck after this model. All who wear it will receive great graces; they should wear it around the neck. Graces will abound for persons who wear it with confidence." The whole apparition then revolved and Catherine saw a large "M" surmounted by a bar and cross, with two hearts beneath it, one crowned with thorns, the other pierced with a sword, all encircled by twelve stars; this indicated the design for the reverse of the medal. This tableau then vanished, as Catherine gradually returned to normality.

These second and third apparitions express very clearly the idea of Mary as "Mediatrix," which, although it has not been solemnly defined by the Church, does appear to be well founded. The golden ball that Catherine saw in Mary's hands can also be seen as symbolic of an orb and thus of her Queenship. Despite the fact that the things she had spoken about earlier in the year had come true, Fr Aladel was reluctant to proceed with the making and distributing of the medal; in fact, the apparition of the medal probably occurred at least another five times, and each time Catherine had to approach him and insist he take her seriously. It was only in 1832 that he began to act, submitting the design of the medal to an engraver. He came to realize that the idea that a young, illiterate novice could have made up such things was unlikely; she was usually so unimaginative, and, additionally, her prophecies had been fulfilled. Still his position was difficult, particularly as she insisted on her identity being kept hidden, a secret she was to keep for the next forty-six years until shortly before her death, despite many attempts to discover her identity.[314]

In 1831, Catherine moved to the Hospice d'Enghien for elderly men, at Reuilly, also in Paris, where Fr Aladel was the regular confessor, and so he could keep in touch with her. Satisfied now as to Catherine's character and honesty, Fr Aladel consulted with a fellow priest, Fr Etienne, and in January 1832, they both went to see Archbishop de Quélen, with Fr Aladel telling him the whole story. After asking many questions, he was satisfied that the medal represented nothing contrary to Church teaching and gave his permission for it to be struck, although the first batch of 1,500 was not ready until June, when Catherine told her confessor: "Now it must be propagated." This happened very quickly, and the archbishop was given a rapid idea of the medal's efficacy when he took one with him on a visit to an excommunicated former bishop, who had sided with Napoleon; he was gratified and impressed by his deathbed repentance in the most unpromising of circumstances. Word of the new medal spread very quickly, with widespread reports of miracles of grace and nature.[315]

The situation reached such a stage, that in 1833, Archbishop de Quélen decided on a report into the results of the propagation of the "Medal of the Immaculate Conception," which by now was known simply as the "Miraculous Medal." This favorable report led to a proper canonical inquiry, which met in February 1836 to interview witnesses, including Catherine. But she was determined to remain hidden, despite Fr Aladel's insistence, and the inquiry reached its conclusions without her direct assistance. It concluded that she was of good character, that her apparitions were to be accepted as reliable, and, most importantly, that the Medal was supernaturally inspired and responsible for genuine miracles.

With hindsight, we can see that Catherine was wise to preserve her anonymity, given the problems that the status of "visionary" would cause later seers: both Mélanie and Maximin, the children who saw Mary at La Salette, and Bernadette at Lourdes, were worn down by constant questioning and attempts to make them divulge their "secrets."[316] By that year, too, the original engravers, Vachette, had produced several million medals, and eleven other Paris engravers were working hard to meet a growing demand.[317] The Medal had become an icon for the poor, a sign of Mary's presence and concern, and it was an important factor in re-rooting the people in the Catholic religious tradition upset by the Revolution and its consequences.[318] The fact that the inquiry had been so thorough and positive meant that the way was clear for approval of the Medal by Rome, which also allowed Archbishop de Quélen to propagate devotion to the Immaculate Conception with enthusiasm within his own diocese.

Catherine was now thirty and had settled down into the routine of looking after the old men at the hospice, obediently doing all the tasks involved in such a difficult life, continuing in this for the next forty years, something that is almost a sign of sanctity in itself. She also told Fr Aladel that the Blessed Virgin wished him to establish a religious society for young people, mainly girls, the Confraternity of the Children of Mary, and this came into existence in 1838, spreading rapidly thereafter. Similarly, a book about the apparitions by Fr Aladel was very successful, going through many editions. In 1841, at her confessor's request, she wrote out a complete account of what she had experienced, while also reminding him that Mary had requested a statue be made representing her offering the globe of the world to God. This request was to cause Catherine endless anxiety, and the statue was not finally completed until after her death, although there was no hint of this distress discernible in the way she carried out her duties.[319]

Jacob's Ladder and the Church Fathers

The early Christian writers saw the mysterious ladder, which was seen in a dream by the Patriarch Jacob, as a *type* of Mary. This section will develop the idea that there is an apparent connection between the apparitions associated with the Miraculous Medal, and events in the lives of both Jacob and his son Joseph, as recounted in the book of Genesis. This idea might seem a little strange at first sight, so it is necessary to look at some of the early Christian writings, as well as the biblical account, in some detail.

St John Damascene (*c.*657–*c.*749), compared Mary with Jacob's ladder in this fashion: "That man [Jacob] contemplated heaven joined to earth by the two ends of a ladder and saw angels going up and down upon it ... So you have assumed the role of a mediatrix, having become the ladder by which God comes down to us, ... Thus [O Mary] you have reunited what had been divided."[320]

Elsewhere he says: "Today [Christ] ... built himself a living ladder, whose base is planted on the earth and whose tip reaches heaven. God rests upon it. Jacob saw a figure of it. God, unchanged, came down on it. ... He was made manifest on the earth and lived among Men."[321] A sermon attributed to the sixth-century writer, St Anastasius of Antioch, describes Mary as "the ladder stretched towards heaven, the gate of paradise, the entry into incorruption, the union and harmony of men with God." St Theodore of Studion (*c.*759–826), made a similar comparison, and this idea is also found in the *Akathistos* hymn.[322] Those quotes from some of the early Christian writers, then, show that the idea of comparing Mary to the *heavenly ladder*, that is, the ladder of Jacob, was known and understood in the early Church.

Jacob was the grandson of Abraham, the father of the Jewish people, and both he and his father Isaac were privileged with experiencing visions (using the word in its biblical sense) of the Lord. God had appeared to Isaac during a time of famine to reassure and encourage him, telling him not to go down to Egypt, but to remain where he was, so as to receive the blessing promised to his father Abraham (Gen. 26:2–6). Later on, the Lord appeared to him by night, when he was staying in Beersheba, to reassure him and promise him numerous offspring (Gen. 26:24). We are told that, in response, Isaac built an altar in that place. In both these "theophanies," Isaac is assured that God is with him, and in the second, he is told not to be afraid; while likewise, both were concerned with the welfare of his descendants. In this there is a similarity to the

Annunciation made to Mary by the Angel Gabriel, where matching themes are found (Luke 1:28-33).

These theophanies then form the backdrop to the incident involving Jacob. Although he was not the first-born son, he managed to obtain his father's blessing and thus assume the premier position. But this left his usurped brother Esau in a rage and determined to kill him. When their mother Rebecca found out, she sent him to her brother Laban, who lived in Haran. On the way, he had a mysterious encounter with God. "And he came to a certain place, and stayed there that night, because the sun had set. Taking one of the stones of the place, he put it under his head and lay down in that place to sleep. And he dreamed that there was a ladder set up on the earth, and the top of it reached to heaven; and behold, the angels of God were ascending and descending on it!" (Gen. 28:11-12).

Like his father Isaac, and like Mary, Jacob is assured that God is with him and that his descendants, and indeed the whole earth, will receive blessings through him. For the early Christian writers, however, the more intimate connection with Mary was in the ladder that reached from earth to heaven, which Jacob saw in his dream. The symbolism of this ladder involves our recognizing that Mary, with her human nature, belonged to the earth, but through her divine motherhood was intimately associated with heaven. Thus, she was able to act as a link, a "mediatrix" between heaven and earth, with the angels explained as symbolizing the way that the prayers of mankind were carried to God by her, while in return all graces and blessings from heaven came down to earth through her.[323]

Catherine Labouré and Jacob's Ladder

At first sight, it might seem difficult to see a connection between the apparitions at the convent in the Rue du Bac chapel and Jacob's dream, but there are several points of interest to note. The first apparition to Catherine took place at night, just as in the case of Jacob. He was asleep and saw the ladder with the angels ascending and descending in his dream, and she was wakened from sleep by an *angel* and led to the chapel to meet the Blessed Virgin. Catherine vividly described the sweetness of these moments for her: "There, a period of time passed, the sweetest of my life. It would be impossible for me to say what I experienced."[324] Similarly, Jacob was taken up with feelings of awe and joy: "Then Jacob woke from his sleep and said, 'Surely the Lord is in this place; and I did not know it.' And he was afraid, and said, 'How awesome is this place! This is none other than the house of God, and this is the gate of heaven'" (Gen. 28:16–17).

Just as Jacob was given a mission, that of being faithful to God's promises, so that the chosen people should grow and flourish, Catherine too received a mission, that of building up the life of the Church through the apostolate of the Miraculous Medal. Jacob was told that all the earth would receive a blessing through him and his descendants, and so also Mary promised Catherine that all who came to her with faith would receive a blessing: "But come to the foot of this altar. There, graces will be poured out on all those, small or great, who ask for them with confidence and fervor."[325] When Jacob awoke, he took the stone he used for a pillow and anointed it as a sign of God's presence. He called the place *Bethel*, which literally means *House of God*, and of course, most unusually, the apparitions to Catherine took place in the Rue du Bac Chapel, that is in the "house of God," with the first one actually happening next to the altar.

The second apparition, which took place on 27 November 1830, developed the idea of the blessings for all mankind obtainable through the intercession of Mary. As we have seen, Catherine described the events of that evening, when she saw Mary standing on a ball and holding a globe, representing the world, in her hands. Her eyes were turned towards heaven, and rings on Mary's fingers were giving out various rays of light, corresponding to the graces poured out on those who asked for them.

If we look at the other direct encounters which Jacob had with God, including the mysterious encounter with God in the form of a "man" who wrestled with him, and another meeting at Bethel (Gen. 31:3, 32:23–32, 35:1–15), it does not appear that they really relate very well to this second apparition to Catherine; they are essentially recapitulations of previous events. It would seem that something more is necessary to do justice to the full meaning of the second apparition at the Rue du Bac, particularly as the second vision at Bethel makes no mention of the blessings all mankind would receive, as did the first. In the light of this the following interpretation is an attempt to find a more exact correlation between the biblical text and the message of the second apparition to Catherine. This seems to be justified, too, on typological grounds, because over four months separate the first from the second and third apparitions—a period which is appreciably longer than the whole duration of some other Marian apparitions.

Joseph in Egypt and Mary's Mediation

The following events all took place during Jacob's lifetime and so it seems reasonable to include them as part of this interpretation. Jacob's favorite son was Joseph, the only child of Rachel, but this love for him made his other brothers jealous. This situation was not helped when Joseph had two dreams, which seemed to foretell they would all be subservient to him (Gen. 37:5–11). The brothers were looking after their father's flocks, when the opportunity came to get rid of Joseph by selling him to passing traders; they did this, and then pretended that Joseph had been killed by a wild animal. He was taken to Egypt, where he was sold as a slave to one of Pharaoh's officials, Potiphar; but because God was with him, his abilities led the Egyptian to put him in charge of his household.

Joseph fell into disfavor, however, and was thrown into the royal prison, but again God was with him and everything went well, as he was entrusted with running the internal affairs of the prison. He interpreted the dreams of two of Pharaoh's officials imprisoned with him, correctly prophesying that one would be freed and the other executed. The one who was freed, however, forgot all about Joseph, until Pharaoh had a couple of unusual dreams that no one could interpret. The official remembered the way Joseph had correctly interpreted his dream, and so he was summoned to see Pharaoh. Joseph told the Egyptian king that the two dreams, in which he successively saw seven lean cows eating seven fat cows on the banks of the river Nile, and then seven scanty ears of grain swallowing seven fat ears of grain, were a revelation of what God was about to do. They indicated that there would be seven years of great plenty, followed by seven years of severe famine, which would affect the whole known world, and that this would happen very soon. Joseph recommended that Pharaoh should appoint someone as governor, with responsibility for collecting a grain tax and storing it for the coming famine. Pharaoh and his advisors approved of this, and he made Joseph governor of Egypt and second only to himself, dressing him in fine linen and putting a gold chain around his neck. During the seven years of plenty, Joseph supervised the collection of grain throughout Egypt, and then, when the famine arrived, he was able to feed the people (Gen. 41:37–49; 53–57).

This famine forced Joseph's brothers, who were living in Canaan, to travel to Egypt to get grain. They met Joseph in his exalted position but did not recognize him, until eventually, after several journeys back and forth to Canaan at his orders, he, as

Governor of Egypt, revealed himself to them (Gen. 45:3–8). He then told them to fetch his father, Jacob, and their families, and come down to Egypt to escape the famine. This they did and the Israelites settled in the region of Goshen, where they prospered. Jacob, whose other name was Israel, made Joseph swear that he would take his body back to Canaan for burial, and Joseph agreed to this (Gen. 47:29–31). After Jacob died Joseph arranged for doctors to embalm his father, a process taking forty days. Following the period of mourning, Jacob was buried with his ancestors in Abraham's tomb at Machpelah, near Mamre in Canaan (Gen. 25:7–10). Joseph and the others then returned to Egypt, where he died at an advanced age, but not before making the Israelites promise they would likewise return his embalmed body to Canaan, when, as a people, they eventually left Egypt.

If we compare Joseph's role as Governor of Egypt during the famine with the traditional idea of Mary as Mediatrix of all graces, then some interesting points emerge. As indicated, the actual title of the Miraculous Medal is the Medal of the Immaculate Conception, although in reality the content of the second apparition, when the design of the medal was shown to Catherine, shows that the main stress should be placed on the idea of all graces being obtained through Mary. The make-up of the medal is also interesting for its scriptural allusions and the way that it harmonizes with elements found in the story of Joseph. The message in golden words around the frame said, "O Mary conceived without sin, pray for us who have recourse to thee," and there seems to be some connection here with the dependence of the Egyptians on Joseph to save them from famine, that is, that he played an important role as an *intermediary*.

The design of the reverse of the medal, with its letter "M" surmounted by a cross and crossbar beneath it, with two hearts, one encircled by a crown of thorns and the other pierced by a sword, obviously points to the Passion of Christ and the closeness of Mary to him in our redemption. This joining of the two hearts on the design of the medal provides a definite link between the hearts of Jesus and Mary. The image of the small heart on the left, surrounded by a crown of thorns is also reminiscent of the vision of Jesus' Sacred Heart, as seen by St Margaret Mary at Paray-le-Monial.

The twelve stars on the medal have a deep significance too. In the book of Revelation, St John the Evangelist was shown a mysterious vision of a woman: "And a great portent appeared in heaven, a woman clothed with the sun, with the moon under her feet, and on her head a crown of twelve stars" (Rev. 12:1). The rest of this difficult passage, describing the woman as pregnant and in labor, while under threat from the huge red dragon, Satan, has been traditionally interpreted as a reference both to Mary and to the Church (Rev. 12:2–6).[326] The crown of twelve stars corresponds to the twelve stars on the Miraculous Medal, but there is also a connection with the two dreams Joseph had before he went to Egypt. In the first, Joseph dreamt that, while he and his family were binding sheaves of wheat, his sheaf rose and stood upright, while his family's sheaves came and bowed down to it. In the second dream, the sun, moon and eleven stars came and bowed down to him; his family rightly understood the elements from this dream as representing their future subordination under Joseph, a point that upset them (Gen. 37:5–11).

The same elements then, sun, moon and stars, are present in this passage and the previous one from the book of Revelation, indicating a link between them, and so, by implication, there is also a typological link between the story of Jacob and Joseph and the apparitions of Mary to Catherine. Joseph was made second in the kingdom to Pharaoh, and similarly, Mary is the human being who is second only to Christ, the God-man. Pharaoh took the ring from his hand and put it on Joseph: Catherine saw rings on Mary's fingers giving out rays of light, which symbolized the graces which would be poured out on those who asked for them. Pharaoh put a gold chain around Joseph's neck and, of course, the Miraculous Medal is meant to be worn on a *chain* around the neck. This is unusual because other sacramentals worn around the neck, such as the brown scapular, are made of cloth and are *not* meant to be used with a chain. The only other actual instance of someone in the Bible having a gold chain put around their neck involves the prophet Daniel, who like Joseph was rewarded for his interpretative abilities (Dan. 5:29). There is a mention of chain around a neck in Ezekiel, but this is in an allegorical description of Jerusalem (Ezek. 16:11). Pharaoh gave total control over Egypt's affairs into the hands of Joseph, and in a similar way Mary has been visualized as having a subordinate role, under Christ of course, in the distribution of God's spiritual blessings to mankind, that is, that she acts as "Mediatrix." But again, this has to be understood as not implying that Mary is in any way independent of Christ— everything she does is done in complete dependence on him.

Joseph gathered in all the grain of Egypt, storing it until the time of famine, when it was redistributed; and, likewise, Mary offers up the prayers and sacrifices of those who pray to her, while also acting as their spiritual mother. People came to Egypt from all over the known world to get grain—they were literally in Joseph's hands, while Mary held a globe in her hands to symbolize her mediating role, under Christ, in the order of grace. There is also an allusion to Pharaoh's words to the Egyptians when they appealed for food: "Go to Joseph and do whatever he tells you," in the advice Mary gave to the servants at the wedding feast at Cana, "Do whatever he tells you" (John 2:5). This again indicates that it is not completely fanciful to link the account of Joseph in Egypt and Mary's role as Mediatrix at Rue du Bac.

Finally regarding both Jacob and Joseph, there is also a connection between them and Catherine Labouré in the manner of their deaths, and particularly in the preservation of their bodies. As has been indicated above, both Jacob and Joseph died in Egypt and were embalmed as a way of preserving their bodies, before being buried in the land of Canaan, where, in Jacob's case, he had originally encountered God. When the Israelites left Egypt under Moses, they took Joseph's bones with them (Ex. 13:19) and these were finally buried at Shechem in the time of Joshua (Josh. 24:32). Catherine's body was exhumed in 1933 and brought back to the place of her apparitions, the convent at the Rue du Bac, where it was found to be incorrupt, and it is still preserved there to the right of the main altar.

Our Lady of Victories – 1836

The church of *Notre-Dame des Victoires*, or "Our Lady of Victories," had reached quite a low ebb by the 1830s, having been originally built in 1629 as an act of thanksgiving for favors received by King Louis XIII, and dedicated to the Blessed Virgin. The church suffered degradation during the time of the French revolution and its aftermath, ending up as a stock exchange, before reverting to its former use in 1809, but with very few parishioners.[327] The parish priest, Charles Desgenettes, after arriving in 1832, found himself battling against general religious indifference and even hostility; he felt his own unworthiness was to blame, and even asked the archbishop to remove him, but this request was refused. He continued to pray for his parishioners, however, and eventually his prayers were answered. He was saying Mass on 3 December 1836 when he was assailed by unusually persistent distracting thoughts which caused him to pray for relief. Almost immediately, in the center of his being, he heard a voice telling him to consecrate his parish to the Holy and Immaculate Heart of Mary. At the same moment his sense of distress and distraction vanished and he felt a great calm. In the sacristy afterwards he felt the return of the distractions, but immediately he again heard the voice making the same request for consecration."[328]

Abbé Desgenettes recognized the seemingly supernatural aspect of what had happened; an inward impulse urged him to act, and so on arriving home he drew up the statutes for an association in honor of Mary's Immaculate Heart for the conversion of sinners. These statutes were accepted by the archbishop of Paris within a week, and so began the work of the famous Confraternity of Our Lady of Victories, an association that was to have a world-wide influence,[329] becoming a global Arch-confraternity at the insistence of the Pope. With this impetus the association grew rapidly and succeeded in promoting the idea of intercession through the Immaculate Heart of Mary. It also popularized the idea of Marian consecration.[330] The importance of this movement, and that of the Miraculous Medal, is that they form the background to the various more public apparitions of Mary in France in the later years of the nineteenth century. This means that apparitions such as those at La Salette, Lourdes, and Pontmain should be seen in the context of a general revival in Catholicism, with a particular emphasis on devotion to Mary.

As the Arch-confraternity of Our Lady of Victories was growing, and ten years after the events connected with the Miraculous Medal, another series of "private" apparitions took place at the Sisters of Charity house at the Rue du Bac. Mary appeared revealing her Immaculate Heart to a novice called Justine Bisqueyburu during a retreat in January 1840, wearing a long white dress with a blue mantle. In her hand she held her Immaculate Heart pierced with a sword and surrounded with flames, with this apparition being repeated several more times during the retreat, and later on the major feasts of Mary. During the apparition of 8 September 1840, Our Lady's birthday, an extra detail was added as Justine saw her holding a scapular of green cloth in her left hand. On one side there was a representation of Mary as she had appeared in the apparitions previously, and on the reverse: "a heart all burning with rays more brilliant than the sun and as transparent as crystal; this heart, surmounted by a cross, was pierced with a sword, and around it were the words: 'Immaculate Heart of Mary, pray for us now and at the hour of our death.'" Sister Justine told Fr Aladel what had happened, but just as with Catherine Labouré he was reluctant to get involved in the production of this new green scapular; it was only in 1846 that official approval came for its use.[331]

The Miraculous Medal and Alphonse Ratisbonne

The conversion of the wealthy Jewish banker and lawyer Alphonse Ratisbonne, in 1842, was a significant event in making the Miraculous Medal more widely known. At the age of twenty-eight he seemed to have the world at this feet, but he also had a violent aversion to Catholicism, particularly as his elder brother had been converted and had become a Catholic priest. In the months leading up to his forthcoming marriage, he had decided to leave his home in Strasbourg and spend the winter in southern Europe, intending to avoid Catholic Rome at all costs. But because of a delay, and his restlessness, he managed to end up in the Eternal City after all, where he met an old friend, Gustave Bussières, who was accompanied by his brother, Baron Bussières, a fervent Catholic. Rome, though, did not impress Ratisbonne and he even got into an argument with the Baron, during which he was challenged to wear a Miraculous Medal and recite the prayer to Mary, the *Memorare*; if he really believed that Catholicism was just superstition then it could not do any harm. To avoid giving offence Ratisbonne agreed to this, even making his own copy of the Memorare.[332] This was the beginning of his conversion, since a few nights later he had a strange vision of a plain cross, which made him very uneasy. Meanwhile Bussières had spoken with a friend of his, the elderly ex-diplomat, Comte de la Ferronnays, who promised to pray for Ratisbonne. The Count went to the basilica of St Mary Major to do just that, but sadly, shortly after returning home, he had a heart attack and died.

Ratisbonne was making arrangements to leave Rome, somewhat worried about his strange vision, when he again met the Baron and agreed to accompany him to the church of S. Andrea delle Fratte where arrangements were being made for the funeral of De la Ferronnays. Ratisbonne decided to go in and look around rather than wait outside, and immediately saw a menacing great black dog which suddenly disappeared, as he realized that a very bright light was coming from a side chapel. He looked up and saw that it was the Virgin Mary just as she is represented on the Miraculous Medal, but her face was so bright that he could look no higher than her hands. He heard no voice but understood interiorly, as the vision vanished leaving him converted and a completely new man. The Baron found him kneeling and a little later Ratisbonne asked for a priest so that he could be baptized.

After a period of instruction with the Jesuits he was received into the Church, in a ceremony that was something of a sensation, given his former position. Because he moved in important diplomatic and financial circles, including that of the banking family, the Rothschilds, Ratisbonne's conversion and the role of the Miraculous Medal in it became very widely known in Europe, and led to an official enquiry into the Medal in Rome. This concluded that his conversion was due to the intercession of Mary, thus implicitly approving the Medal. Ratisbonne became a Jesuit priest but after ten years joined his brother, who had founded a society for the evangelization of the Jews, the Congregation of Our Lady of Sion, spending more than thirty years in Palestine working amongst his former co-religionists.[333]

10

La Salette and the 1848 Revolution

The Church, Industrialization, and New Philosophies

A new Pope, Gregory XVI, was elected in February 1831, and, like his predecessor Pius VIII, soon faced many difficulties, particularly from Italian nationalism; Europe was very unsettled during this period, a situation that culminated in the further revolutionary upheavals of 1848. The Industrial Revolution, which had begun to gather pace around the time of the French Revolution, was changing European society very rapidly, as capitalism and the use of factory machinery both developed further. Migrants from the countryside began to work in the factories, creating a growing class of people, the industrial proletariat, who had no real connection with the old social order and thus were open to socialist propaganda. The new machinery was usually beyond the economic grasp of all but the rich, and this led to a further concentration of wealth in the hands of the few, with more and more people becoming "wage-slaves." New economic theories were developed by writers such as Adam Smith (1723–90), who favored the removal of all restrictions on trade as the best way of increasing productivity and prosperity, even though individuals might suffer in the short term. This soon developed into the principle that the most profitable investment should always be sought, even if this involved immoral or dubious holdings.[334]

Utilitarianism, the philosophy developed by the English writer Jeremy Bentham (1748–1832), similarly became popular as the nineteenth century progressed. It was an attempt to order society on purely rational grounds, without reference to either God or the natural law, and was concerned with what was socially useful, based on the principle that all men sought to avoid pain and procure pleasure. Bentham wanted to introduce laws that would supposedly bring the greatest happiness to the greatest number of people, even if this meant going against previous principles based on applying divine or natural law to society as a whole. As in the case of Rousseau, though, this utilitarian approach could, and did, lead to the rights of the individual being trampled upon; but this has not prevented its being widely adopted as the measure by which laws are formulated and society ordered. This secular utilitarianism developed out of the "religious" utilitarianism of Puritanism, despite the fact that Bentham was a follower of Enlightenment thought; and it has been one of the major factors in the development of our harsh modern culture.[335]

Another important thinker was Thomas Malthus (1766–1834), a clergyman and economist, who produced his *Essay on the Principles of Population* in 1798. This set out the notion that poverty and hardship were unavoidable, since population growth always tended to increase much more quickly than food supply. Therefore, given that people were reluctant to abstain from sexual activity, it was "natural" that population should be kept down by war, epidemics, and famine, and thus any attempts to eradicate poverty were doomed to failure. Not surprisingly, these supposedly "scientific" notions were congenial to those making large profits out of the burgeoning Industrial Revolution, while treating their workers abysmally. Subsequent history has shown that Malthus's pessimistic prophecies of disaster have not come true, since human ingenuity has found ways of dramatically increasing food supplies; but he was very influential at the time.[336]

David Ricardo (1772–1823), the son of a Jewish merchant from Holland, was an early *laissez-faire* economist who also, like Malthus, had a rather harsh view of the way ordinary people should be treated. He argued that all commodities, including labor, had a "natural price," and that even if this fell below subsistence level it should be adhered to. He saw the society of his day, with all its economic problems and widespread distress, as the inevitable state of things. Ricardo saw three competing groups in society, workers, capitalists, and landowners, as having such conflicting interests that it was impossible to conceive of their successfully cooperating; this element of class conflict was later taken up and expanded by Karl Marx. The importance of thinkers like Malthus and Ricardo lay in the fact that influential members of society really believed what they said, and used their arguments to oppose programs of charitable relief and factory legislation.[337]

Britain was the leading industrial nation in the early part of the nineteenth century and it was *laissez-faire* thinking like this that formed the basic economic ideology at the time. It was based on the principles of free trade, free competition, and employers and employees freely negotiating wage levels, with the State acting to protect these principles. In practice this meant that rich capitalists, who could easily export their capital overseas if necessary, were in a position of absolute dominance. They were prepared, in most cases, to offer only work of long hours at the lowest possible wages, knowing that it was either that or starvation for the worker. Proponents of this thinking intended to produce a society made up of two sections, a small property-owning group of capitalists and the great mass of the people who were expected to work for a subsistence wage. It was argued that if wages rose, or indeed if anything was allowed to interfere with the "free market," then capital and industry would go elsewhere and ordinary workers would end up unemployed, and so far worse off, as the economy collapsed. This inhuman policy, which ensured that people lived and worked in the most appalling conditions, was the logical outcome of the capitalist mindset that had been building up for centuries.

What was worse was that its advocates sought to show that this state of affairs was due to immutable laws that were part of the natural order. Eventually this approach would have led to all-out class war as the gap between rich and poor became intolerable, but this situation was avoided because, in practice, measures were taken to lessen the harshness of the system, for example, the factory acts and other social legislation, and also because ordinary workers began to organize trade unions to defend themselves.[338] As in the case of those proved wrong in thinking that the abolition of slavery would be an intolerable economic burden, so also *laissez-faire* thinkers were proved wrong. Employment conditions were gradually improved, workers were eventually treated like human beings and the financial sky did not fall. Behind this massive industrial and economic expansion was the growing power of finance capitalism, as exemplified by the large banking houses including Ricardo, Barings and Rothschilds. Christopher Hollis points out that the name of Rothschild is found everywhere behind the scenes of nineteenth-century history, behind the deeds of figures such as Disraeli, Bismarck, Napoleon III, Cavour and others, as one of the main sources of finance, particularly for war.[339]

Thus the first part of the nineteenth century saw the further development of ideologies and practices hostile to traditional Christian thinking, whether in terms of utilitarianism, "eugenic" Malthusianism, *laissez-faire* economics, finance capitalism, or in the injustices facing working people in an expanding industrial revolution.

The Church, then, faced the difficult task of coming to terms with all this upheaval and change, but Pope Gregory XVI was by nature a conservative and thus unwilling to make concessions to the new ideas, especially as he faced continuous discontent in the Papal States; all this led him to adopt rather heavy-handed policies. During this period the French Church began to turn increasingly towards the papacy as a source of support, as the Gallican spirit was replaced by ultramontanism, a spirit that looked to Rome and the popes, "beyond the mountains."[340] Towards the end of the Pope's reign, although he had suffered setbacks and disappointments, he could at least take some comfort in the fact that the Church was better organized than before, that the religious orders were reviving, and that the foreign missions were expanding greatly. The future for Europe in a political sense did not look so promising, however, with the French government still opposed to reform, despite many signs of discontent among the workers. Elsewhere liberalism and nationalism were continuing to make progress, and regrettably the situation in the Papal States continued to deteriorate up until the time of the Pope's death in June 1846.[341] His successor, Pope Pius IX, was elected with the expectation that he would be somewhat liberal in contrast to the conservative Gregory, but few could have realized the importance of his pontificate which was to last thirty-two years, the longest so far in the history of the Church. His reign was to witness the temporal eclipse, but the spiritual rise of the papacy, as the millstone of the Papal States was eventually removed and the Church was finally able to concentrate on more religious matters. Pius IX decided to try and utilize those aspects of modernity that were not a threat to the Church rather than to condemn everything, and in this sense he was initially a liberal. He quickly became popular by adopting a freer approach to affairs in the Papal States; this gave many the impression that he was prepared to break with the "conservative" past and take the Church in a new direction, although this was not the way the situation ultimately developed.[342]

La Salette Apparition – September 1846

The small town of Corps near Grenoble in south-eastern France was very far removed from the Paris convent of Catherine Labouré, both geographically and spiritually. It was a poor place, whose inhabitants were mostly indifferent to religion, and the two children privileged to see Mary near the small village of La Salette,

Maximin and Mélanie, shared in this general poverty. Maximin Giraud was eleven years old in 1846 but was unable to read or write, and knew virtually nothing of religious matters; he had barely managed to learn the *Our Father* or *Hail Mary*. Mélanie Mathieu (or Calvat) was fourteen and had looked after the cows of neighboring farmers from an early age; like Maximin she was virtually without education.[343]

On Thursday 17 September 1846, Mélanie was working for Baptiste Pra who lived in the hamlet of Ablandins. She was looking after his cattle in the high pasture, when for the first time she met young Maximin; he was working for another farmer as a replacement for his usual cowherd, who was ill. They were not acquainted prior to this since they lived at opposite ends of Corps, and Mélanie was nearly four years older than Maximin, although the boy knew the Pra family, since his sister had formerly worked for them. The next day the two children pastured their respective herds together, and on Saturday 19 September they again rose early and drove their cows ahead of them, with Maximin's employer, Pierre Selme, coming on behind. The morning passed without incident as the children sat on the grass watching the cows, until, at the sound of the midday Angelus bell of La Salette church, a couple of miles away down in the valley, Selme told Maximin to water the animals. Mélanie joined him and after seeing to the animals they went on to a spring surrounded by stones a few yards away where they sat down to eat their lunch of bread and cheese. After this they moved a little further down the mountain to rest near another spring, again encircled by stones, but dry at the end of the long hot summer. It was a beautiful warm autumn day with a clear blue sky, and after their very early start they decided to lie down nearby.[344] It is worth noting that Selme, in his formal deposition concerning the events at La Salette, made it clear that he was certain that no one had approached the children on the mountain or spoken to them prior to the apparition.[345]

It was unusual for either to sleep during the day, and Mélanie was the first to wake with a start after about an hour. Her first thought was for the cows, but after she and Maximin had found they were all there, she returned to the spring to fetch her satchel. There she was met by an astonishing sight. She could see a dazzling globe of light on the stones of the dry spring, near where they had recently been resting and called to Maximin in fright. Both children shaded their eyes from the glare of the globe as it grew bigger and began to open, revealing a seated woman with her head in her hands. She then stood up and spoke to them: "Come, my children.

Do not be afraid. I am here to tell you great news." Her voice reassured them and they ran towards her, close enough to see all the details of her appearance. They later described her as very tall and beautiful, wearing a long white, pearl-studded, sleeved dress, and a white shawl, with some sort of tiara or crown on her head. Hanging from her neck was a large crucifix adorned with a small hammer and pincers, with a brilliantly shining figure of Christ on it. The whole effect was as if she was made of light and indeed the children could see through her, although neither she nor they cast a shadow.[346]

The Message of the Lady

Mélanie could look at the face of the Lady but her radiance was too much for Maximin, although he could hear her words; both remarked that she was in tears the whole time she spoke to them:

> If my people do not obey, I shall be compelled to loose my Son's arm. It is so heavy I can no longer restrain it. How long have I suffered for you! If my son is not to abandon you, I am obliged to entreat Him without ceasing. But you take no heed of that. No matter how well you pray in the future, no matter how well you act, you will never be able to make up to me what I have endured on your behalf. I have given you six days to work. The seventh I have reserved for myself, yet no one will give it to me. This is what causes the weight of my Son's arm to be so crushing. The cart drivers cannot swear without bringing in my Son's name. These are the two things which make my son's arm so heavy.[347]

The Lady then went on to speak about the coming punishments for these sins of Sabbath-breaking and blasphemy, including crop blights and famine, at one point switching from French, which the children did not understand very well, to the local patois. Then she spoke to Maximin alone, imparting a secret to him which Mélanie could not hear, before turning to her to give a secret that Maximin likewise could not hear. Presently she again spoke to both saying that if the people were converted, then the fields would produce self-sown potatoes and the stones become wheat. She then asked a significant question: "Do you say your prayers well, my children?" They replied that they hardly prayed, and she told them they should say at least their morning and night prayers, before continuing: "Only a few rather old women go to Mass in the summer. Everyone else works every Sunday all summer long. And in the winter, when they don't know what else to do, they go to Mass only to scoff at religion. During Lent, they go to the butcher shops like dogs."[348]

She then asked the children if they had ever seen spoiled wheat and when both replied that they had not, the Lady reminded Maximin that he had once seen it when on a visit to a nearby hamlet with his father; he then remembered that what she had said was true. Finally the Lady spoke to them in French: "Well, my children, you will make this known to all my people," before moving forward between them. She went on a few yards and then re-emphasized her message to them without turning around: "Now, my children, be sure to make this known to all my people." She continued to move away from them up the slope, hovering over the ground, and then stopping near the summit she turned towards the southeast, towards Italy and Rome, no longer crying now, but with a look of great sadness. Then she began to disappear into a light similar to that which had initially encircled her, and in a few moments she was gone, and the globe of light then dissolved into the autumn sunshine.

It was only at this point that they fully realized that the Lady was more than an ordinary human being, and they began to wonder if she was some great saint. This conviction was strengthened, when on returning to pick up their belongings, they realized that Maximin's dog Loulou was still asleep and had not barked at the Lady; this would certainly have happened had she been an ordinary person. The children spoke to each other about the Lady and realized that both had been given a secret that was not to be revealed. They continued to talk as they drove their cattle homewards, little realizing that the moment they spoke about what had happened their lives would be completely transformed.[349]

Mélanie and Maximin separated at the village as dusk fell, and the boy went to Pierre Selme's cottage, where, on being questioned, he expressed surprise that Selme had not seen what had happened, since he too had been on the mountain; Maximin recounted how he and Mélanie had seen a beautiful Lady who had spoken with them for a long time. He repeated her message, and Selme, somewhat surprised at the serious tone of Maximin, usually the most lively of boys, made no comment. The youngster then ran off towards home calling at the house of Mélanie's employer, Baptiste Pra, where, on meeting the man's mother, he immediately said to her: "Didn't you see a beautiful Lady, all on fire, float above the valley?" The old woman asked which Lady, and Maximin described the glittering woman who had spoken to him and

Mélanie. He then went inside to recount what had happened to the Pra family, who listened to him in silence, struck by the solemn way that he spoke. When he finished the old grandmother expressed her belief that the Lady must have been the Blessed Virgin, since she was the only one who had power over her Son.

Mélanie was still in the cowshed, and she was told to come in and say what she had seen, and while Pierre Selme arrived to consult with his neighbor over Maximin's story, the boy slipped away. Baptiste Pra rebuked her for not speaking sooner, but she said she had intended to tell them once her work was finished. Mélanie then told her version of what had happened, and again there was surprise, not just at the things she said but also at her whole manner, which had been transformed; usually she was shy and a little abrupt, but now she seemed more gentle, yet confident and fluent. The grandmother spoke up and rebuked her son for working on Sundays, but he retorted that he couldn't be expected to believe that the Blessed Virgin had appeared to a girl who didn't say her prayers. Nevertheless, he decided not to work the following day, and proposed that both children should the next morning, Sunday, tell the local priest, M. Perrin, what had happened.[350]

Mélanie and Maximin told their story before Mass, and the priest in his excitement and emotion repeated it to his meager congregation as his homily. The mayor of La Salette-Fallavaux, M. Peytard, and the council were informed and soon the news was well known. He decided to investigate; and so on that same evening he called to see Mélanie and heard her story, threatening her with jail if she was lying, and even trying to bribe her with twenty francs, a very large sum at the time, to say nothing more. The Mayor questioned her for three hours but was unable to shake her insistence, and left impressed by what she had said, as was Baptiste Pra, who, once he had gone, called in Pierre Selme and another neighbor to record Mélanie's experience in writing. As she dictated, Baptiste Pra wrote her words down and the other two men checked this and signed it jointly, thus giving us the most important basic text of the apparition, written only a day after the event.

The mayor went to see Maximin the next day and questioned him, as he had Mélanie, but despite the same tactics the boy maintained his story, something that M. Peytard found all the more impressive since by now he was aware of Maximin's reputation for carelessness and his tendency to tell lies. The boy's father became the subject of mockery and he in turn took it out on Maximin, but this did nothing to affect his steadfastness. A few days later the Mayor led a little party, including the children, up the mountain and they showed him the place of the apparition and indicated what had happened. Shortly after this they again went up the mountain, this time with M. Mélin, the parish priest of Corps, his sacristan, and other witnesses, where the children faced more questions. Although this priest was favorably impressed by their demeanor, he decided to act as prudently as possible. He informed the aged bishop of Grenoble, Mgr de Bruillard, of events, telling him that despite everything the children were clinging to their story, and the latter told his priests not to mention the matter in their sermons. The two children were kept apart for the next few months, and so did not have the opportunity of collaborating and "enhancing" their accounts.[351]

Aftermath of the Apparition

The bishop set up two commissions to study the matter, one made up of cathedral clergy and the other of professors from the seminary. Their initial report came in December, and while favorable towards the children, cautioned that extreme care was needed in the matter, and that it was best to wait before giving any definitive ruling as to the truth or falsity of events at La Salette. To further the investigation, two of the seminary professors interviewed both of the children the following summer, while also collecting evidence on the miraculous cures apparently resulting from the use of spring water from the place of the apparition. Once the two professors had reported, another commission, headed by the bishop, again considered the whole matter, once more questioning the children separately and also looking at the reported healings, so that by the final session a majority of the commission accepted the truth of the apparition. The bishop then allowed his clergy to accompany pilgrimages to La Salette and authorized the production of a book on the apparition. It was not until four years later, however, in 1851, that he publicly declared his acceptance of the children's apparition, in an episcopal letter read out in the churches of Grenoble diocese, which contained the following points:

> We judge that the apparition of the Blessed Virgin to two shepherds, on September 19, 1846, on a mountain in the Alpine chain, situated in the parish of La Salette, of the archpresbytery of Corps, bears all the characteristics of truth and that the faithful have grounds for believing it indubitable and certain; ...

Wherefore, to show our heartfelt gratitude to God and to the glorious Virgin Mary, we authorise the devotion of Our Lady of La Salette.[352]

Archbishop William Ullathorne of Birmingham went to La Salette in May 1854, nearly eight years after the event, and was able to verify for himself that there had been a failure of the potato crop in the autumn of 1846, leading to widespread hunger in the mountain areas. He was of the opinion that the warnings given at La Salette were one of the major reasons for a general religious revival in the south of France, especially with regard to keeping Sunday holy and eliminating blasphemy. The fact that not every prophecy made by Mary was fulfilled can be explained on the basis that those prophecies were *conditional* on the people repenting and being converted.

The archbishop also explained a point that had caused some commentators problems, when Mary said the following words to the children, as part of her message: "I have given you six days in which to work. I have reserved the seventh for myself and yet you do not wish to let me have it." Objections were made on the grounds that only God could make such a statement, but in reality it is a paraphrase of a passage from the book of Leviticus concerning the commandments: "Six days shall work be done; but on the seventh day is a sabbath of solemn rest, a holy convocation; you shall do no work; it is a sabbath to the Lord in all your dwellings" (Lev. 23:3). Ullathorne argued that Mary was speaking as the prophets of the Old Testament had done, directly in the name of God, in the first person, and not in the sense that any of the commandments referred directly to her. This is significant in the light of the connection that will be made further on between La Salette and Moses' act of giving the Law to the Israelites.[353]

After the apparition Mélanie and Maximin became the center of attention, and were placed at a local convent, where, in the light of their intellectual slowness, they received a reasonable degree of education. Both made their First Communion only in the May of 1848, nearly two years after the apparition. According to all accounts they were totally incompatible and indeed awkward personalities, who neither shunned nor clung to each other; their only common point was the apparition itself. Early in 1847, the Abbé Lagier, a priest who was a native of Corps, came to stay in the town, and took the opportunity to question the children thoroughly. Although they talked willingly and at length about the details of the apparition, despite all his efforts he could not prise the secrets they had been given from either of them. He tried every possible approach but in the end had to admit defeat, surprised and somewhat perturbed by their assurance.[354] In June 1848 another important witness, the Abbé Dupanloup, who was to become bishop of Orléans the following year, interviewed Mélanie and Maximin. He was not impressed by either of them initially, and yet despite that, he was forced to come to a contrary conclusion:

> Every time they were led—however unexpectedly—to speak of the apparition, an instantaneous change came over them. It was strange and profound. At once, they became serious and simple, and took on an air of dignity and one of great reverence for what they said. Those who listened to them were seized with a kind of religious fear of their words and also with respect for them ...[355]

The Curé d'Ars, the Pope, and the Secrets

During this period St John Vianney, the Curé d'Ars, was probably the most famous priest in France, known for his extremely mortified life and for spending anything up to sixteen or seventeen hours daily in the confessional, coping with an ever-increasing flood of pilgrims seeking his advice. It is perhaps possible to see him as a sort of precursor of Mary, in that part of his task seems to have been to prepare the French people for the various Marian apparitions during the rest of the nineteenth century.[356] He must have been responsible for helping thousands to discover their true vocation, and thereby making an immeasurable contribution to the rebuilding of the Catholic Church in France. And, in view of her position as the "eldest daughter" of the Church, and the number of approved Marian apparitions which took place there during the nineteenth century, France's influence tended in turn to affect the whole Catholic world.

It was an incident involving the Curé d'Ars and Maximin, however, which put La Salette under something of a cloud for a number of years. Ars, like La Salette, was in south-eastern France, although in a different diocese, and the Curé was aware of the apparition by the summer of 1847, privately favoring it, but, following his bishop's example, not publicly endorsing it. His assistant priest, however, a M. Raymond, a rather truculent character, had met Maximin at La Salette and formed an unfavorable opinion both of him and the apparition. Maximin had been asked to stay in the diocese of Grenoble by the bishop, but he was desperate to get away from La Salette and was brought to Ars accompanied by a priest and a group of men with political interests. Ostensibly they were on their way to Lyons, where Maximin would continue his education, and the stop at Ars was designed to allow the boy to ask the holy priest about his vocation. Maximin's new friends were supporters of a man who was claiming to be the son of Louis XVI, the French king who had been executed by the revolutionaries in 1793; but in reality this son, Louis XVII, whose fate is uncertain, probably died in prison as a young boy. The men who were with Maximin perhaps thought that his secret might concern the heir to the French throne. Thus there were mixed motives behind this journey, and it may well be that the Curé d'Ars somehow realized this.

When Maximin arrived at Ars, the Abbé Raymond roughly accosted him, and in the argument that ensued the boy gave the unfortunate impression that he had not actually seen the Blessed Virgin, and this report was carried to the Curé that evening. Next morning Maximin himself met the old priest, they talked for some time, and he certainly seems to have told the Curé that he had indeed seen nothing. But as subsequent events were to show, this was probably mainly due to his being angry and upset at the time of their encounter.[357]

What seems to have happened is that Maximin, annoyed at the way he had been treated by M. Raymond, and seeing the Curé as another probable tormentor, told the priest, in a fit of pique, that he had seen nothing, then became afraid to own up to this later. Given the fact that he was still only fifteen, as well as the ordeal of relentless questioning he had been through, it is perhaps not surprising that he finally broke down and acted so irresponsibly. Although this incident did damage the reputation of La Salette to some extent, eventually the Curé d'Ars recovered his certainty about the shrine, following a request for a sign from God, which was apparently forthcoming.[358] He was visited by Archbishop Ullathorne of Birmingham in May 1854, who has left this description of what happened as he was explaining to the Curé the need for prayers for English Catholics, who were suffering so much:

> ... suddenly he interrupted me by opening those eyes—cast into shadow by their depth, when listening or reflecting—and streaming their full light upon me in a manner I can never forget, he said, in a voice as firm and full of confidence as though he were making an act of faith ... "I believe that the Church in England will recover her ancient splendour." I am

sure he firmly believes this, from whatever source he has derived the impression.[359]

The incident at Ars also led to the children's secrets being communicated to Pope Pius IX, although neither of them were prepared to reveal these easily. Part of the content of Mélanie's secret, which indicated that it specifically concerned the papacy, had earlier become apparent during the questioning of the children. Mélanie was asked if she was worried at the thought of the Pope publishing her secret once he knew it. She replied that it would then be his affair, but intimated that the secret concerned the Pope. This seemed to be confirmed in a later interview: when asked about the Pope's reaction to her secret, she replied, "a Pope ought to love to suffer."[360] There seems to be a similarity here with events at Fatima in 1917, where Mary said that "the Holy Father would have much to suffer." Jacinta, one of the seers, also had a vision of the residence of a future pope being surrounded by an angry mob and attacked.

Maximin wrote his secret rapidly, and after the bishop had read it to ensure that it was worth conveying to the Pontiff, it was sealed in an envelope. Mélanie wrote for an hour, without pause, filling three pages of narrow-lined paper, and then placed her secret in an envelope without reading it. She then said she was mistaken in a minor point so it was agreed that she should rewrite the secret, and again she wrote rapidly, only pausing to ask a few questions. She wanted to know the exact meaning of "infallibly" and the spelling of "soiled" (*souillée*), and "Antichrist" (*antéchrist*). Mélanie was then taken to the bishop, who read the secret alone in his room, before emerging disquieted and in tears. This version was then sealed and taken, together with Maximin's, by two priests, Fathers Rousselot and Gerin, from Bishop Bruillard to Rome, where they had a private audience with the Pope.

Pius IX unsealed the messages in their presence, reading Maximin's first and remarking on its frankness and simplicity. Mélanie's secret was apparently more serious, since the two men saw the Pope's expression change as he read it. Finally he spoke: "I will have to reread these letters more at my leisure. There are scourges threatening France, but Germany, Italy, the whole of Europe are guilty and deserve punishment. I have less to fear from outright godlessness than from indifference and human respect. The Church is not called militant without cause and here you see its leader."

Some time later, the Pope was asked if the secrets could be

revealed, and his reply was: "So you want to know the secrets of La Salette? Well, here they are: unless you repent you will all perish." This has been understood to imply that the secrets, like the Gospels, are essentially calls to repentance: the above details are all that is publicly and definitely known about the messages given to the children, although an unreliable version of Mélanie's secret was later published.[361]

Criticism of La Salette and the Children

Even though the Pope was in possession of the children's secrets, and Bishop Bruillard had approved of La Salette, with Pius IX's implicit support, hostility towards the apparition from some quarters did not diminish. Sadly, two of the most prominent voices in the attempt to discredit the testimony of Mélanie and Maximin were priests. One of these, the Abbé Déléon, had been reprimanded by the bishop for a scandalous relationship with a woman, and in revenge, in 1852, produced a book called *La Salette: the Valley of Lies*, full of false allegations about the apparition. The other priest, the Abbé Cartellier, produced and distributed to the French bishops an equally outrageous book, but eventually agreed to recant, although at the time of his death in 1865 he was apparently working on another book hostile to La Salette. Déléon meanwhile, undeterred, produced another critical and deceitful book, implying that the children had only seen an ordinary woman; these allegations had a disturbing influence on La Salette and caused a great deal of doubt and uncertainty within the Church.[362]

Those who doubted La Salette tended to point to the rather unhappy adult lives of Mélanie and Maximin as further evidence for the falsity of the apparition; but later events have no real bearing on the truth of La Salette, since the public "mission" of the children was over once the bishop issued his statement. Maximin led an unsettled life after the apparition, being unsure as to his vocation, and, on one occasion, getting involved in an unsavory business deal. He continued to defend La Salette from further attacks, however, still firmly attesting to his continued belief in the apparition up until his death in 1875.

Mélanie's later life was equally turbulent, with her failing in an attempt to become a nun, partly because the apparition and subsequent events had tended to go to her head. Regrettably, she was not shielded from the sort of adulation reserved for "visionaries," and began to claim that she was the recipient of further visions and revelations, which increasingly took on an apocalyptic tone. She published a book claiming that it contained the full text of the secret, and this caused a great deal of trouble for the Church in France, to the extent that it was eventually placed on the "index" of forbidden books. Periods in the latter part of her life were unsettled and she died in 1904.[363]

Unlike Lourdes, which, in Catholic circles at least, has enjoyed a large measure of respect and prestige, La Salette has continued to come in for criticism from some writers. Hilda Graef objects to the concentration on sins such as Sabbath-breaking and blasphemy in the message of La Salette; she describes these as being concerned only with "mere superficial religious observance and lack of charity." She believes that more stress should have been put on "social" sins. But sins such as blasphemy and Sabbath-breaking are central to the Ten Commandments, and as such are very important. The commandments represent the whole basis of Christian morality, and if they are kept a civilization will be truly Christian. To attack "social" sins without worrying about the commandments is to attack the symptoms rather than the cause of the problem.[364] Graef's conclusions on La Salette betray the weakness of her position in its exaltation of private judgment above that of the Church: "That both miracles and conversions are believed to take place at La Salette is no cogent proof of the authenticity of the original apparitions [sic]. God answers the trusting prayers of the faithful in many places which, through these very prayers and, of course, the sanctuaries built on their site, acquire a holiness of their own, regardless of their origin."[365]

Although there is some truth in Graef's contention, God is a God of truth and holiness and it would go against his nature to support a false apparition with *genuine* miracles, i.e. supernatural interventions on the physical plane. It is true that, according to Catholic teaching, the devil may be able to simulate miraculous healings, but these are not true miracles: if Graef was right then it would be very difficult to distinguish between true and false apparitions, and for the Church to give an authoritative ruling on them. Her position implicitly argues that episcopal commissions have a questionable value, since their judgments in the past have, to a degree, depended on miraculous cures as an important point of evidence. If such cures could happen at true and false apparition sites, then clearly we have no way of telling them apart. The point about conversions is less clear-cut, because it is conceivable that someone might be "converted" at a false apparition site, in that

God could use the opportunity to grant a grace of conversion, in the sense of pointing the individual in the right direction. So although there are elements of truth in Graef's position, her overall criticism of La Salette, as an apparition recognized by the Church, is inadequate.

La Salette and Moses on Mount Sinai

There seems to be an intriguing typological connection between Moses and the events at La Salette. In chapter 19 of the book of Exodus we are told that, after leaving Egypt, the Israelites were pursued by Pharaoh's forces, but managed to escape finally when the Egyptian army was destroyed as the waters of the Red Sea returned to cover them. Moses led the people through the desert, but had continually to put up with their complaining and back-sliding. After three months they reached Mount Sinai, and it was there that God promised to make a covenant with them, his specially chosen people. The Israelites prepared themselves for this, and then God descended on to the mountain in great majesty and splendor, amidst thunder and lightning. Only Moses and Aaron were allowed to go up to him, with the people forbidden to follow on pain of death. The Ten Commandments were then delivered to Moses, the first one being concerned with the prohibition of other gods, with the second and third as follows:

> You shall not take the name of the Lord your God in vain; for the Lord will not hold him guiltless who takes his name in vain. Remember the sabbath day, to keep it holy. Six days you shall labor and do all your work; but the seventh day is a sabbath to the Lord your God; in it you shall not do any work ..." (Ex. 20:7–10).

The first significant point here is the way the basic message given to the children at La Salette is so concerned with these second and third commandments. Mary particularly pointed to the desecration of the Sabbath and the taking of the name of Jesus in vain, as the two things that made the arm of her Son so heavy. Similarly, the fact that both events took place on a high mountain indicates a possible connection between the events of Exodus and La Salette. When the children first saw Mary she was sitting on a stone in tears, and this seemingly incidental point is very significant. Moses is the only person described as sitting on a stone in the Old Testament, an incident which occurred in the wilderness, after the Israelites complained to Moses of being thirsty; this led God to provide water miraculously through Moses' striking the rock with his staff. After this the Amalekites attacked the Israelites at Rephidim, and it was only after Moses had sat on a stone, with Aaron and Hur beneath his arms, holding them up, that Joshua's forces were able to defeat the Amalekites (Ex. 17:1–13).

Here we have all the elements present in the apparition, with the water from the rock symbolizing both the tears of Mary and the water that was to come from the spring at La Salette. It is also worth noting that, in the additional account of this incident given in Numbers, the branch used to strike the rock was Aaron's branch, the same one which sprouted with blossoms and almonds, whose Marian symbolism will be discussed further on (Num. 17:1–11;[366] 20:7–11). The stone that Moses sat on prefigures the one sat upon by Mary, and there is also a Christological significance in the fact that Aaron and Hur held Moses' arms up, such that he assumed the shape of a cross. Moreover, in the New Testament there is the account of the Angel sitting on the stone that closed Jesus' tomb, which implies a further typological connection with the Crucifixion and Resurrection (Matt. 28:2).

What is even more important, though, is the reason *why* they held Moses' hands up; it was because they were growing *too heavy*, and this is precisely the complaint that Mary made to the children: "If my people will not submit, I shall be compelled to let go the arm of my Son. It is so *heavy* and so powerful that I can no longer sustain it." So a phrase which looks clumsy and theologically inaccurate at first sight, and has been criticized as such, turns out to be extremely significant and full of meaning.

It seems that, at La Salette, Mary was far more ornately dressed than during many of her other apparitions, particularly with respect to the stunning royal diadem on her head; the dazzling nature of her appearance made it difficult for the children to even look at her. They were also somewhat hampered in their description by a restricted vocabulary. Nevertheless, despite this, the main points are clear, and further investigation of these features indicates that Mary's clothing during this apparition strongly suggests elements of the dress of the Jewish high priest, originally Aaron, Moses' brother. This is a point which will be discussed more fully in the chapter on the apparition at Pontmain, but it seems to be the case that the *description* of the sanctuary and the high priest (Ex. 25—31), as given by God to Moses on the mountain, provides the biblical typology for Mary's appearance at La Salette in 1846; while the actual *construction* of the sanctuary and the institution of the priesthood

(Ex. 35—40), provide the typology for Mary's appearance and actions at Pontmain, twenty-five years later in 1871. This seems to explain the similarities between both apparitions.

Certainly the fact that Mary was wearing a large cross, next to which a hammer and pincers hung in the air, symbols of expiation and sacrifice, seems to link with the idea of priesthood and of Jesus as the new high priest (Heb. 9). In particular, it could represent the breastplate of judgement worn by the high priest. Similarly, the "apron" worn by Mary is reminiscent of the *ephod* of the high priest, while Exodus tells us that Aaron was to wear two chains of twisted gold with attached golden settings around his neck (Ex. 28:13–14): Mary's "shawl" was edged with multicolored roses, and she had two golden chains around her neck, one of which supported the crucifix. She also wore a crown or tiara with a garland of roses around it, and in the same way the high priest was to wear a turban with a golden flower on it, a symbol of his consecration to God (Ex. 28:36–38). This description of the building of the sanctuary and the clothing of its ministers was given to Moses *when he was on the mountain* (Ex. 25—31). In other words it ties in directly with God's act of giving the Law to Moses.

Deuteronomy details the reiteration of the Law by Moses to the Israelites, once they had come near the Promised Land, and it also sets out a series of blessings and curses which are very similar to Mary's words to the children. Thus there are parallels between the message of Mary at La Salette and the teaching of Moses. The children saw her crying and making the complaint that she was able to intercede for the people only with the greatest difficulty, as her Son's arm was so heavy: in other words, punishment was impending unless people changed their lives. Likewise Moses is presented as the great mediator, who saved the people on a number of occasions when God threatened to destroy them for their hard-heartedness and ingratitude (cf. Deut. 9:7–29).

Mary then told the children about the prevalence of Sabbath-desecration and blasphemy, and how these two faults in particular merited a chastisement; this can clearly be related to the importance of keeping the commandments, as set out by Moses (Deut. 5:1–22). She then went on to talk about the way that crops would be spoiled, and famine would come, unless people repented and began to pray and sanctify Sunday by attending Mass. Thus she summarized the need to obey the commandments of the Church. We can compare this with the series of blessings and curses which Moses outlined for the people, depending on whether or not they were faithful to the covenant and kept the commandments. It is noticeable that the blessings emphasize the fruitfulness, both of the people and of their livestock and land: "Blessed shall you be in the city, and blessed shall you be in the field. Blessed shall be the fruit of your body, and the fruit of your ground, and the fruit of your beasts, the increase of your cattle, and the young of your flock. Blessed shall be your basket and your kneading-trough" (Deut. 28:3–5).

But the list of curses for not keeping the commandments was considerably longer than the list of the blessings!

> Cursed shall you be in the city, and cursed shall you be in the field. Cursed shall be your basket and your kneading-trough. Cursed shall be the fruit of your body, and the fruit of your ground, the increase of your cattle, and the young of your flock. ... The Lord will make the pestilence cling to you until he has consumed you off the land which you are entering to take possession of it. The Lord will smite you with consumption, and with fever, inflammation, and fiery heat, and with drought, and with blasting, and with mildew; they shall pursue you until you perish. ...You shall carry much seed into the field, and shall gather little in; for the locust shall consume it. You shall plant vineyards and dress them, but you shall neither drink of the wine nor gather the grapes; for the worm shall eat them. You shall have olive trees throughout all your territory, but you shall not anoint yourself with the oil, for your olives shall drop off (Deut. 28:16–18, 21–22, 38–40).

It is striking how similar these words are to those of the warning given by Mary to Mélanie and Maximin, and it suggests that the secrets given to the children were of a very serious nature:

> If the harvest is spoilt, it is only because of you. Last year, I showed you this in the potato crop, but you took no notice. On the contrary, when you saw the spoilt potatoes, you swore, using the name of my Son. The potatoes will go on rotting and, by Christmas this year, there will be none. ... If you have wheat, do not sow it, for pests will devour all that you do sow, and any of it that ripens will fall to dust when it is threshed. A great famine will come. Before it comes, little children under seven will be seized with a palsy and will die in the arms of those carrying them. The rest of the people will suffer their penance through the famine. The nuts will be grub-ridden and the grapes will rot.

Mary departed from the children, moving up the mountain and pausing just before the top, for half a minute or so, gazing towards the south-east, in the direction of Italy and Rome,[367] but also in the direction of Israel. Moses, too, ascended Mount Nebo and looked down upon the promised land, but was not allowed by God to enter it (Deut. 34:1–4). Even the death of Moses is similar, in traditional terms, to that of Mary, in that when he died at the age of 120, "his eye was undimmed, and his vigour unimpaired," (Deut. 34:5–8), just as in church tradition Mary did not suffer from the usual effects of aging. Likewise, just as no one ever found the grave of Moses, so also no trace or relic of Mary's body has ever been found, supporting the belief that she has been assumed into heaven body and soul.

The Revolution of 1848 and its Results

The potato blight of 1846 affected the whole of Europe, and, coupled with a poor grain harvest and an industrial and financial crisis, led to the worst depression of the century. This in turn led to widespread unemployment and a growth of unrest in many areas. The year 1848 saw the outbreak of a crisis that profoundly shocked Europe, a much more serious affair than the events of 1830. Troubles began in some of the Italian states, and by late February Paris was embroiled in disputes centering on calls for electoral reform from the middle classes, as well as workers' grievances at the economic situation and unemployment. The often appalling living and working conditions of ordinary people, combined with an apparent lack of concern on the part of employers, contributed to growing frustration and discontent. This was true of other parts of Europe also, but in France the situation became so serious that Louis Philippe was forced to abdicate.[368]

The new republican government initially sought to work with the Church, recognizing, like Napoleon, that it was an essential stabilizing influence in society, but new socialist ideas started to cause trouble, as the threat of a split between the proletariat and most Catholics became evident. Social conditions for factory workers were deplorable, but the country was still mainly rural, and socialist ideas on "equality" were seen as dangerous innovations by most people, who did not want a repeat of the events of half a century earlier. The government acted to quell the growing unrest, and this led to savage street fighting in Paris at the end of June 1848. The death of the Archbishop of Paris on the barricades, as he sought to intercede to end the fighting, caused a great shock in Catholic circles, and pushed the Church towards the side of the authorities and against liberalism; it was feared that the Revolution had again reared its head. Rationalism, nationalism and above all socialism were blamed for the disorders, despite the workers' legitimate grievances, and all three were duly stigmatized. Most Catholics then found themselves obliged to support a reactionary government, and, as in the past, this too-closely-knit association was to cause many problems, especially as it tended to cut the Church off from ordinary working people. There were also upheavals in Hungary, Austria, Germany and Italy, but there was no general revolution, and conservative governments were returned to power in most parts of Europe by 1849.[369]

As the nineteenth century progressed it became increasingly clear that the social question, that is, how the various classes were to work together for the common good, and also how those at the bottom of the ladder should be better treated, was becoming ever more important. The middle class, those involved in business and the professions, continued to grow in influence and power, and were primarily concerned to protect themselves from working-class discontent and to increase their wealth. As has been indicated, compared to rural workers, those in the towns, including children, had a much lower standard of living, having to work long hours for low wages. Matters were made worse by the prevailing mentality of economic liberalism, which held that nothing should interfere with "market forces." Conditions were thus ripe for the further development of socialist ideas, in the belief that they would produce a more equitable society.[370]

The reality was that the capitalist spirit had gradually emerged supreme in the centuries since the Reformation, and was now reaching an inhuman climax. The drive to maximize profits and keep costs, including wages, as low as possible, was achieved by exploiting the workers to the absolute limit of their endurance, through a combination of extremely low wages and very long hours. Where possible employers would use child and female labor, even in heavy industries such as mining, in order to lower costs still further. In overseas colonies, this drive to realize the absolute minimum cost had led to the widespread use of slavery, although the slave trade had been abolished in Britain in 1807, and slavery itself was abolished throughout the Empire in 1833. This gross exploitation only ended when employers realized that, by investing in more powerful machinery, they could produce more in a few hours than many workmen could produce in a day, a move which was also prompted by fear of an increasingly disaffected workforce.[371]

The problem for the Church lay in how best to help those suffering under the worst effects of unbridled capitalism, while rejecting those aspects of socialism, and even more so of Communism, that would undoubtedly lead to even worse evils. Given their situation, socialist ideas were very attractive to ordinary working people, and although many Catholic writers condemned incipient socialism, what was really needed was a social theory founded on Christian ideals and some means of implementing it, so as to improve the condition of the industrial proletariat. Earlier in the century, one of the most powerful influences on Catholic thought and action in this area had come from the work of Frédéric Ozanam, the founder, in 1833, of the Society of St Vincent de Paul, who certainly did a tremendous amount to raise public awareness of the problems facing the poor. The old idea of charitable assistance alone, however, began to appear inadequate as the century progressed, and increasingly demands were being made for major reforms, provided they would not involve revolutionary upheaval or compromise Church teaching.[372]

Meanwhile Pius IX found himself in an awkward situation as both ruler of the Church and head of the Papal States. Although he could see the advantages in Italian reunification for the country as a whole, his position as pontiff meant that he had to think of the spiritual good of the whole Church. It was argued, too, at the time, that the papacy still needed temporal estates to safeguard its independence. He was given conflicting advice, with some urging him to throw in his lot with the nationalists and others to appeal for help from Austria. Fearful for his safety, owing to the unsettled situation in Italy, he left Rome for Gaeta, while his secretary of state, Cardinal Antonelli, urged a policy of harshness towards the revolutionary movements in the Papal States, and particularly in Rome. An appeal was made to Austria, France, and Spain to intervene to restore papal rule, and eventually a French force took Rome in July 1848, allowing the Pope to rule with French backing. This whole episode greatly shook Pius, and from this point on any liberal ideas he may have had vanished, as he began to understand that the best way he could serve the Church, and society, was to strengthen its role in the areas of dogma and discipline.[373]

11

The Immaculate Conception and Lourdes

The Dogma of the Immaculate Conception

The apparitions of Mary to Catherine Labouré and the rapid spread of the Miraculous Medal meant that the Marian movement as a whole was growing at this time; Pius IX, who had a great devotion to Mary, made it publicly known that he intended to appeal to her to intercede for the Church in its troubles. As detailed above, he was also personally acquainted with the events at La Salette, which had his implicit support, and he intended to proclaim the dogma of Mary's Immaculate Conception to emphasize the importance of her role in the Church. With this in mind, in February 1849 he asked the Catholic bishops of the world for their views on the Immaculate Conception, which was already a solidly-held belief within the Church, but not a dogma. Over ninety per cent of the 603 who responded were in favor of the doctrinal definition, and so, after theological clarification, on 8 December 1854, the Pope promulgated the bull *Ineffabilis Deus,* which declared that belief in Mary's Immaculate Conception was now an article of faith for Catholics. This was the beginning of a century of greatly increased devotion to Mary within the Church, culminating in Pope Pius XII's dogmatic declaration in 1950 that Mary had been assumed into heaven.[374]

The proclamation of this dogma by Pius IX, that Mary from the first moment of her existence was free from original sin and its effects, is intimately connected with the events at Lourdes in 1858, only four years later. It is also interesting to compare how this dogma is related to the biblical account of Gideon's fleece, a well known biblical type of Mary, as found in the book of Judges. Gideon appeared at a time when the Israelites were being oppressed by the Midianites as a punishment for their worship of false gods (Judg. 2), and was told by God that he had been chosen to deliver his people from oppression (Judg. 6:1–32). The similarities between the encounter between Gideon and "the Angel of the Lord," and the Annunciation to Mary by the Angel Gabriel, are fairly well established; there is general agreement that there is a connection between the two.[375]

Gideon, though, was not certain if God was really with him and so wanted a sign. He placed a wool fleece on the ground; if the fleece was wet with dew but the ground was dry he would accept that God had chosen him. The next day Gideon found the fleece wet and the ground dry; but he was still not sure, and so he asked God to reverse the sign and make the fleece dry and the ground wet. On awaking he found God had done just that, and so he accepted God's call (Judg. 6:36–40).

Some of the early Christian writers, including St Proclus of Constantinople, who described her as the "loom" of the Incarnation, linked this incident with the fleece to Mary: "The holy Mary has called us together, that undefiled treasure of virginity, ... the most pure fleece of heavenly rain (Judg. 6:37), from which the Shepherd clothed the sheep ... She is the awe-inspiring loom of the Incarnation ..."[376]

As a type of Mary, Gideon's fleece can be regarded as a very appropriate symbol of her Immaculate Conception—the idea that she was free from original sin, in contrast to the rest of humanity, who, according to Catholic teaching, must be baptized if they are to be freed from this condition. So just as the fleece became wet while the floor remained dry, Mary was filled with grace, while everyone else was deprived of it through original sin; similarly, while the fleece was dry and the ground wet, Mary alone was preserved from the sin that affected the rest of the world. Hence, the story of Gideon and the fleece can be seen as a prophetic biblical type of the proclamation of the dogma of the Immaculate Conception. This assertion is strengthened when the events at Lourdes in 1858, which will be dealt with shortly, are taken into account. Gideon's fleece, however, does not fit the "chronological" sequence of types of Mary which prefigure the various apparitions, and it seems best to regard it as a "general" type of the Immaculate Conception, especially as this idea was present, at least implicitly, in much nineteenth-century Marian thought. This also explains why Moses can figure as a type in both the account of La Salette and, as will be seen, in the story of Lourdes. All this emphasizes the hidden, but intimate, link between these two apparitions, and with Rue du Bac which preceded them.

Problems for the Church

One of Pius IX's major achievements was to continue the work of transforming the Church that took place during the nineteenth century, and particularly the process of centralization which increased the power of the papacy. At the beginning of the century the popes had been very much hemmed in by the power of various national churches, but by the end of the nineteenth century the papacy's position at the heart of the Church was unquestioned. Pius IX appointed cardinals and bishops of true merit, men he could trust, and set about internationalizing the college of cardinals, thus giving the leadership of the Church a more world-wide basis. This strengthening of the papacy was accompanied by a general renewal of Christian life and society as the century progressed, and was particularly evident in a great expansion of the missions.[377]

But that did not mean that attacks on the Church subsided, or that liberal groups ceased to try and undermine her influence. Although concordats were signed with many countries, some of which were very favorable to the Church, as in the cases of Austria and Spain, it often happened in areas such as education and marriage that these achievements could be fairly short-lived. Catholics suffered at the hands of radicals in Switzerland and also in the kingdom of Piedmont, where the politician Cavour suppressed most religious orders and appropriated the proceeds, and where the question of Italian unity tended to become associated with anticlerical and anti-religious attitudes. A similar procedure was adopted in Portugal, and there were disputes over education between Catholics and liberals in Belgium. Germany was a cause for concern because of the desire for the unification of its small states, and the worry over whether this would be achieved by Catholic Austria or Protestant Prussia, both of which were vying to create a Germanic empire. Lamentably for Europe and the world, Prussia was victorious, and so a militaristic regime took control of Germany. This led in its turn to Bismarck's *Kulturkampf*, or "Struggle for civilization," the persecution waged against the Catholic Church later in the century. The emergence of a Germany dominated by Prussia completed the process by which the balance of power in Europe was tipped in favor of Protestantism.[378]

In France the immediate result of the 1848 revolution was to place Prince Louis Napoleon at the head of the new regime, and after four years he was able to consolidate his position, becoming

Emperor Napoleon III. The state was declared to be secular, but the Church was recognized as having a position of honor and certain rights. Although the leaders of the government were unbelievers, they wanted to work with the Church to promote good order, and to this end, the people were allowed to practise their faith in relative freedom. Still, as far as anticlerical writers and activists were concerned, Catholicism was the enemy of the common man, since it was associated in their eyes with those who exploited the workers. Meanwhile unrest in the Papal States was growing ever worse; Pope Pius IX's experiences in 1848 had made him unwilling to countenance reform, even as calls for Italian unity grew ever louder. Although it is probably fair to say that the papal states were somewhat backward in political and economic terms, Pius IX was very well aware that if he handed over the papal territories it would signal the start of secularization and a general persecution of the Church, and he was not prepared to accept that.[379]

Bernadette and Lourdes – 1858

The apparitions at Lourdes took place only four years after the proclamation of the dogma of the Immaculate Conception, and, given their nature, it is only natural to see a strong link between the two; indeed they are practically one event. It seems, though, that while Gideon's fleece is particularly appropriate as a symbol of the Immaculate Conception as a dogma, the events at Lourdes are probably better symbolized by some further incidents from Moses' life. The fact that the apparitions at Lourdes came only twelve years after those at La Salette also tends to suggest a connection with Moses. Lourdes, like the earlier shrine, is also an out-of-the-way place, nestling in the foothills of the Pyrenees.

Bernadette Soubirous, the seer of Lourdes, was born into a very poor family in January 1844; her father François was an impoverished miller, and her mother Louise a young and inexperienced woman of only nineteen. Initially they lived at the Boly mill, but for various reasons the business began to go downhill, and eventually, in 1856, they ended up in a back room of the former jail, the *Cachot*, a place so unhealthy that no one else was prepared to live there. By now there were four children, including Bernadette, and the whole family had to live in this one damp and dark room, having descended about as far as was possible down the social scale. These poor living conditions meant that Bernadette became quite a sickly child, prone and used to suffering, particularly from asthma, as well as the aftereffects of a cholera epidemic which retarded her growth, not to mention the effects of a poor diet. She received very little education, and at the time of the apparitions could neither read nor write, although she was certainly not backward.[380]

Thursday, 11 February 1858, was a cold damp day, and it was decided that Bernadette should accompany her sister and a friend to fetch firewood, although Louise Soubirous was initially unwilling because Bernadette had a cold. At about eleven o'clock the children made their way to the forest, eventually finding themselves near the rocky outcrop of Massabielle, about half a mile outside the town. The bottom of the rock face was naturally shaped into an arch from which a cave ran backwards, and to the right, about fourteen feet up, there was a small niche where a wild rose-bush was growing. The other two girls left Bernadette, and went to get more sticks on the other side of the canal or mill stream; she was unwilling to follow them because it would have meant taking her shoes and socks off and wading through the icy water. She had just resolved to join them, though, and had removed a stocking, when to her surprise she heard the noise of wind all around her, despite the fact that it was a calm day and the leaves of nearby trees were not moving. The wind stopped and she resumed her task; again she heard the noise and looked towards the cave entrance, to see the rosebush moving gently.

Standing above it she could see a beautiful young girl surrounded by a brilliant light and a golden cloud, extending her arms towards her and smiling. Instinctively Bernadette took out her rosary beads, but found herself unable to raise her hand to make the sign of the cross. Only when the beautiful girl had, in the most solemn manner, blessed herself with her own rosary, could Bernadette imitate her, and when she had finished praying the rosary, the apparition beckoned to her. Bernadette did not move, and the girl smiled at her before retreating into the niche, when the golden light that surrounded her disappeared. She later described how she had seen a young girl of about her own age and height, clothed in a brilliant and unearthly white robe, with a blue girdle around her waist and a white veil on her head. A rosary with a gold cross hung from one arm, her hands were joined at her breast in an attitude of prayer, and her whole bearing gave an impression of holiness, grace, majesty, and tenderness. She later said: "She is so beautiful that when you have seen her once, you would wish to die in order to see her again."[381]

Bernadette's companions returned to find her kneeling, and she crossed the canal barefoot to join them, saying as she did, to their surprise, that she found the water quite warm. On the way home she told her sister what she had seen, and she in turn told their mother, who, worried that it would only mean more trouble for the family, punished both of her daughters. On reflection, however, knowing that Bernadette was an honest girl, and worried that she might have indeed seen something which was of an evil nature, she made her daughter promise not to return to the grotto. The next day, 12 February, Bernadette did indeed feel drawn to the grotto, but her mother told her to get on with her work, and so that was the end of the matter. On the following day, Saturday, 13 February, she went to confession to one of the assistant priests, Fr Pomian, telling him that she had seen "something white, in the shape of a Lady." He listened to her story and was particularly struck by her mentioning the "gust of wind," a phrase that immediately reminded him of the "gust of wind" mentioned in chapter 2 of Acts, the sign of the Holy Spirit descending on Mary and the Apostles. He asked permission to speak of what she said to Fr Peyramale, the parish priest at Lourdes, and Bernadette agreed, surprised at his deference. Fr Peyramale's comment was that they must wait and see.[382]

The news of what had happened, however, began to spread, and on Sunday, 14 February, Bernadette, in the company of some young girls from Lourdes, went once again to the grotto with the reluctant permission of her parents, taking some holy water as a form of exorcism in case it was an evil spirit. Just before the end of the first decade of the rosary, Bernadette again saw the girl motioning her to come nearer, and she later recounted that the apparition bowed and moved forward, bending over and smiling at her, as the young girl fell into an ecstasy. Her friends became worried and shook her without any effect, and she only recovered properly when she was carried to the nearby Savy mill by the mill-owner, Antoine Nicolau. He was astonished both at finding such a small girl so heavy, and at the way she continued to seem to "see" something as he took her back, to be collected by her mother.[383]

Two well-to-do ladies of Lourdes, Jeanne-Marie Milhet and Antoinette Peyret, persuaded Louise Soubirous that an early-morning visit to the grotto was needed to check on the truth of what her daughter had claimed to see; and so on the following Thursday, 18 February, they all went to the grotto after six o'clock Mass. One of them thought that the apparition must be that of a deceased girl who had been president of the local group of the

"Children of Mary," coming to ask for prayers, and so had brought pen and paper to record any message given. Again Bernadette saw the beautiful young girl in the niche in the rock, but when she offered her the pen and paper and asked her to write down what she wanted, with a smile the apparition spoke for the first time saying: "It is not necessary." She then went on to extend this invitation to Bernadette: "Would you have the graciousness to come here for fifteen days?" She replied that she would, provided her parents agreed, and then, as if to emphasize that the future would hold more sorrow than joy for her, the Lady said before disappearing: "I do not promise you happiness in this world, but in the next." Bernadette had not recognized the apparition as the deceased Lourdes girl, and as they returned to the town, Madame Milhet remarked, "And what if it was the Holy Virgin?"[384]

More Apparitions and the Miraculous Spring

On Friday, 19 February, Bernadette went to the grotto after attending six o'clock Mass and entered into a state of ecstasy with about eight people present.[385] The next day, Saturday, 20 February, the crowd was about thirty strong, and the Lady taught Bernadette a secret prayer that she was not to reveal, and which she was to say daily for the rest of her life. On Sunday, 21 February, when about a hundred people were present, the Lady again spoke, giving Bernadette her mission: "Pray for sinners," while looking out over the spectators with sadness. Fr Peyramale had meanwhile told his fellow priests not to go to the grotto, in case of deceit, and his prudence was later supported by the bishop of Tarbes, Mgr Laurence.[386]

But the growing crowds at the grotto were causing the civil authorities to become alarmed, and it was decided that Bernadette should be unmasked as a false visionary. She was interviewed that Sunday evening by the local police commissioner, Dominique Jacomet. This interview was attended by two other witnesses, Jean-Baptiste Estrade, an excise tax officer, and his sister; Jacomet considered it was his duty to force Bernadette to confess that the whole business was an imposture. He was impressed by her simplicity and sincerity, but felt that someone must be manipulating her behind the scenes, while he was disconcerted at her use of the word *aquerò*, to describe the apparition: Bernadette denied that she had ever said she had seen the "Holy Virgin." In fact, she had refused to say who she thought the beautiful girl was, initially calling her "that person," *aquerò*, or "the little girl," *damisèle*. Eventually it was pointed out that a more respectful way of referring to her was needed, and so she began to describe her as "the Lady." The fact that she used these expressions suggests that she was not putting on a "pious" show, but was rather trying to express, as best she could, the totally unfamiliar world she was entering.[387] Jacomet failed to shake her assurance or trap her in self-contradictions; becoming exasperated, he eventually threatened her with jail unless she agreed not to go to the grotto. At that moment Bernadette's father arrived on the scene, and was forced to promise that he would restrain his daughter from further visits.[388]

The following day, Monday, 22 February, Bernadette was sent to school, but at midday on her way back after lunch, as she herself testified, she was unable to go in any direction except that of the grotto. Once there, however, she experienced no apparition, and perhaps this was meant to test her faith, and further discipline her in accepting suffering and disappointment. Her parents decided not to prevent her from going in future, and on the following day, Tuesday, 23 February, she again saw the beautiful Lady, in the presence of a crowd of about one hundred and fifty. This time she was entrusted with three secrets which she was forbidden to divulge to anyone—a commission which, on her deathbed, she declared she had carried out. Unlike those entrusted to the children of La Salette, the secrets given to Bernadette were apparently not concerned with France or the world, but personal to her, although she had to face much questioning from the curious about them.[389] The next day the crowd had doubled to about three hundred as Bernadette went forward on her knees and put her face to the ground. She explained later that the Lady had told her to kiss the ground as a penance for sinners.

Thursday, 25 February, again saw a crowd of more than three hundred present, and the discovery that was to make Lourdes famous, that of the miraculous spring in the grotto. Bernadette was part way through her rosary when she began to move about on her knees towards the back of the cave, seemingly following instructions, as the crowd tried to understand what was going on. They were surprised and then disgusted to see her begin to scratch at the ground and drink some dirty water she found there, before rubbing her face with it. Some of the onlookers expressed the view that she must have gone mad, and this opinion was strengthened when she knelt again to eat the leaves of a nearby plant. Bernadette repeated the words of the apparition just loudly enough to be heard, with a heart-rending look of sadness on her face and tears in her eyes: "Penance! Penance! Penance!" Significantly, these are the same words said by the angel in the third part of the secret of Fatima, as revealed recently. This point is discussed in a later chapter.

Even her relatives were put out at her behavior, but later that day Bernadette explained that the Lady had directed her to "Go and drink at the spring and wash yourself in it." As they had all seen, she had followed those instructions and found the trickle of spring water in the cave; she was also told to eat some leaves from a green herb she had found there. At the time neither Bernadette nor anyone else could explain what all this meant, and it was only later, when the miraculous effects of the water became known, that things became clearer. That evening Bernadette was called before the Imperial Prosecutor, Jacques Dutour; but, as in the case of Jacomet, his interrogation was not a success, and he could not dissuade her from returning to the grotto, even with the threat of imprisonment.[390]

Bernadette returned again on the following day, 26 February, but the Lady did not appear, and the crowd who had come to watch saw her go home in tears. It was noticed, however, that water was trickling from the place where she had scratched, and that this flow was growing greater with time.[391] On Saturday, 27 February, Bernadette had to carry out another humiliating request, when she was told once more to "kiss the ground as a penance for sinners." The Lady also said to her, "You will tell the priests to have a chapel built here." This was to prove a difficult task, since it meant confronting the parish priest, Fr Peyramale, a formidable and, to her, a somewhat frightening man, but who was also regarded as intelligent and charitable. Although he was favorably impressed by reports of the happenings at the grotto and of Bernadette's demeanor before Dutour and Jacomet, Fr Peyramale realized that he would have to act with apparent aloofness, and even harshness towards the girl, if he was not to compromise the position of the Church. She presented herself before him and delivered her message, but he told her that he needed to know who this Lady was and see some sort of sign, such as the rosebush blooming, before he could agree to having a chapel built.

During the apparition on the next morning, Sunday, 28 February, when over a thousand people were present, Bernadette put Fr Peyramale's points to the Lady, but only received a smile in answer. She was questioned again later that day, this time by a magistrate; but again she was not put out by his threats to imprison her, and in the end she was released, since nothing tangible could be held against her. The authorities were worried at the prospect of a religious movement out of their control taking root in the country, and made every effort to destroy her credibility, initially claiming that the whole thing was nonsense. When this failed and the crowds only grew greater, they then said that it was all due to fraud; finally, when no evidence for trickery was forthcoming, they said that Bernadette was mentally unstable, and that it was necessary to use force to restrain the spectators and preserve public order. Thus the very thoroughness with which the authorities dealt with Bernadette is a striking testimony to the plausibility of the apparitions.[392]

Meanwhile some workmen had dug a basin for the water which came from the spring, as talk about cures began to grow. These included cases such as that of Louis Bouriette, a man who had been blinded in an accident but had now recovered his sight, as well as a young child who was cured of some form of consumptive wasting disease, after being placed in the spring water.[393] These particular cures were submitted to the episcopal commission and declared miraculous in 1862. By the end of the year it had become necessary to establish a medical commission to deal with an increasing number of cures, and this work was carried on by the Lourdes Medical Bureau from 1884.[394] Thomas Kselman, in his *Miracles and Prophecies in Nineteenth-Century France,* a historical and sociological approach to French apparitions in particular, describes the work of this bureau as an "attempt" to be scientific. The reality is that it represented a far more objective scientific approach than that adopted by those who ruled out the possibility of miracles before even looking at the evidence. The same can be said for those who, when presented with incontrovertible proof of the miraculous, refused to accept it. This is an attitude which continues to this day.[395]

One of the most famous cures connected with Lourdes was that of Pierre de Rudder in 1875. His leg had been crushed by a falling tree in 1867, causing an open fracture that refused to heal, which led several doctors to advise amputation. He refused this option and instead decided to go on a pilgrimage to Oostacker in Belgium, where a replica of the Lourdes grotto had been built. On arriving at the grotto, his bones began to knit together in a matter of minutes so that he was able to leave without crutches or any wounds. His doctors were unable to explain his cure and he lived for a further twenty-three years; after his death the bones of both legs were exhumed as further evidence of the miraculously-healed fractures. In 1908 the Bishop of Bruges declared that his healing was a miracle, and this is one of more than sixty cures officially recognized by the Church since 1858.[396] Most of these cures have taken place either in the baths or during the Blessed Sacrament procession, but they probably represent only a small fraction of the many physical cures that have taken place at Lourdes, to say nothing of the spiritual conversions.

On Monday, 1 March, Bernadette saw the Lady before a crowd of about fifteen hundred and on the next day, before a similar crowd, she was given another message for Fr Peyramale: the request for a chapel was repeated and she was also to ask him that people should come to the grotto in procession. The priest, however, said that he would do nothing until he knew the Lady's name, and Bernadette faced more disappointment the following morning, March 3, when she went to the grotto, around which more than three thousand people had gathered, but saw no apparition. Later that day, though, she felt the inner call and returned to see her beautiful Lady, who explained to Bernadette that she had not seen her that morning because "there were people here who wanted to see your face in my presence, and they were unworthy of it. They spent the night at the Grotto and profaned it." This theme of sinfulness interfering with the course of the apparitions was repeated at the time of the "miracle of the sun" at Fatima in 1917, which would apparently have been much greater if the children had not been abducted on 13 August. Again Bernadette went to the presbytery, but was told by the priest that the Lady would have to supply the money if she wanted a chapel.

The next day, Thursday, March 4, was the last day of the promised fortnight, and a great crowd, estimated at up to twenty thousand, thronged the area surrounding the grotto, in the expectation of some great sign. At eleven o'clock the previous night and at five in the morning the police commissioner had carefully inspected the grotto to ensure that no deception was possible. The Prefect, Baron Massy, had ordered the authorities to ensure that order was kept; but there was no great disturbance as Bernadette saw her beautiful Lady and the people of Lourdes gazed on her transfigured features. Nothing spectacular happened, though, and Bernadette again had to confront Fr Peyramale, who, after listening to her carefully, again insisted that the Lady would have to reveal her name before anything could be done about a chapel or processions.[397]

"I am the Immaculate Conception"

The fortnight was over and Bernadette felt no inner call to return to the grotto, although it was already becoming a shrine with a growing number of visitors who left flowers and lit candles.[398] Early on 25 March, the feast of the Annunciation, she again felt the inner summons and made her way to the grotto, where the beautiful Lady was already waiting for her. Bernadette spoke from the depth of her heart, and seems to have had an intuition that the time had come for the Lady to reveal her identity. As she moved towards her from the niche into the grotto, Bernadette also moved closer and asked her name. The Lady bowed and smiled but said nothing, so Bernadette asked a second and a third time, to be given the same response. She persisted and asked again, and now the Lady extended her arms to assume the position shown on the Miraculous Medal before rejoining them at the breast, looking up to heaven and saying in patois, before disappearing, *Que soy era Immaculada Concepciou*, or "I am the Immaculate Conception."[399]

Bernadette hurried off toward the presbytery, repeating the Lady's strange words, so as not to forget them, since the phrase used by the Lady was a puzzle to her. Although she was familiar with the phrase, "O Mary conceived without sin, pray for us who have recourse to thee," since it was an invocation recited at her family's evening prayers, it seems that Bernadette was unaware of its true significance. This point is confirmed by the first draft of a letter she later sent to Pope Pius IX, when she was a religious, referring to his proclamation of the dogma of the Immaculate Conception in 1854, followed four years later by Mary's self declaration. In this letter Bernadette says, "*I did not know what that meant. I had not even heard the word.* Later, after thinking it over, I ... [said] to myself: 'The holy Virgin is nice. One could say that she came to confirm the word of our Holy Father.'"[400]

Fr Peyramale greeted her a little harshly, but was dumbfounded when Bernadette burst out with the words "I am the Immaculate Conception." He then realized that the Lady had indeed answered his request for her name. Controlling the emotion he felt, the priest asked if she knew what the words meant and when she replied that she did not, he sent her off telling her he would investigate the matter further. But if Bernadette did not know what the phrase meant, the people of Lourdes were not slow to realize the significance of the name the Lady had given herself.[401] Bernadette only realized its importance that evening, when it was explained to her by Estrade, and at last she could be really sure that she had seen the Blessed Virgin.[402] Although the message of Lourdes was now complete, Bernadette again saw Mary on the Wednesday after Easter, 7 April, remaining in an ecstasy for about three-quarters of an hour.

An attempt had been made in late March to have Bernadette consigned to hospital on the grounds of mental instability. A tendentious report, written by local doctors, was drawn up, and although admitting there was nothing wrong with her mentally, it concluded by alleging that she *might* have been the victim of hallucinations. But this plan was thwarted by Fr Peyramale, who told the Prefect that the police would have to step over his body to take Bernadette away. The next step in the campaign of harassment, in early May, was to declare the grotto an illegal place of worship, and when this failed to prevent people coming, it was closed on 8 June and the spring water declared insanitary. Fr Peyramale was barely able to restrain his enraged parishioners, and even so the barriers put up by the authorities were knocked down four times. Despite the opposition, however, larger crowds, including influential people, were coming to Lourdes. When the governess of Emperor Napoleon III's children arrived and reported on the harassment pilgrims faced, it was not long before an order came from the emperor that official opposition to Lourdes must cease, and that the barriers preventing access to the grotto should be removed.[403]

But opposition came from more than one quarter. A series of false apparitions, generally involving other young girls from Lourdes and the surrounding villages, began in early February and lasted for some time. These caused quite a lot of confusion at first, with even Fr Peyramale unsure what to do. But their false nature began to become apparent when the activities of these spurious copycat visionaries began to become ridiculous and bizarre, in contrast to the grace and dignity exhibited by Bernadette, so that eventually they had the opposite effect and tended to strengthen her testimony.[404]

Bernadette was able to receive her first Holy Communion on the feast of Corpus Christi; and, significantly, she saw Mary for the last time from outside the grotto, on 16 July, the feast of Our Lady of Mount Carmel, in a wordless apparition which she described thus: "I saw neither the boards or the [river] Gave. It seemed to me that I was in the grotto, no more distant than the other times. I saw only the Holy Virgin."[405]

Bishop Laurence set up a Canonical Commission of Inquiry into the apparitions and their cause on 28 July. The members of this body first interviewed Bernadette in mid-November; they were impressed by her testimony and by the evidence for a growing number of cures due to the miraculous spring. They met again two years later, and once more Bernadette's testimony was convincing, especially her re-enactment of the Lady's actions when she had declared herself the Immaculate Conception, which the bishop in particular found very moving. It was not until January 1862, nearly four years after the apparitions, that the bishop delivered his verdict on Lourdes in a pastoral letter, a verdict that silenced those hostile to Bernadette.[406] After discussing apparitions in general and the events at Massabielle in particular, he commented on how Bernadette's testimony had been strengthened by the miraculous healings and conversions that had taken place at Lourdes, before concluding with this article, the first of three:

> We adjudge that the Immaculate Mary, Mother of God, really appeared to Bernadette Soubirous on February 11th, 1858, and subsequent days, eighteen times in all, in the Grotto of Massabielle, near the town of Lourdes: that this apparition possesses all the marks of truth, and that the faithful are justified in believing it certain. We humbly submit our judgement to the judgement of the Supreme Pontiff to whom is committed the Government of the whole Church.[407]

Bernadette's later years were increasingly marked by sufferings, due to asthma and a tubercular condition that caused her to cough blood; she received the last rites on a number of occasions, and even described her "job" as being sick. A tumor on her knee was particularly painful and her general condition meant she was often confined to bed for long periods. Her knee caused her terrible pain; it would often take an hour to change her position in bed, and she spent whole nights without sleep. This was the way she lived out the hard saying she had heard from Mary: "I do not promise to make you happy in this world but in the next."[408] Bernadette died on 16 April 1879 at the age of thirty-five, at the convent in Nevers, but moves to canonize her did not begin until 1908; and in the following year her body was exhumed and found to be incorrupt although slightly emaciated. Her cause progressed and she was eventually beatified in 1925, when her body was moved to a shrine in the convent chapel. It can still be seen there today, completely lifelike apart from a thin covering of wax on face and hands. She was finally canonized in December 1933, becoming St Bernadette.[409] As in the case of St Catherine Labouré, however, she was made a saint not because she was privileged to see apparitions of Mary, but because of her simplicity, humility, and total acceptance of suffering, all of which had transformed her into a true image of Christ.

Biblical Typology, Bernadette, and Lourdes

There seems to be an interesting correlation between events involving Moses and Lourdes, in particular his encounter with the burning bush, but also on later occasions. We can examine this by seeing how the early Christian writers saw Mary as a type of this burning bush. Amongst others, Chrysippus, Hesychius, and Cyril of Alexandria, identified Mary in this manner, while Proclus described her as the "living bush that was not burned by the fire of the divine birth."[410] Severus of Antioch spoke of the burning bush as "the union of God the Word with the flesh, or the indwelling in the holy Virgin, so that it should appear, if but feebly, how the human flesh had borne the proximity and indwelling which no one approaches without being absorbed, consumed or perishing."[411]

St Gregory of Nyssa (c.330–c.395), in a Christmas homily, saw the burning bush as representative of Mary's virginity:

> It seems to me that already the great Moses had known of this mystery by means of that illumination in which God appeared to him, when he saw the bush burning without being consumed. . . . That is what in fact was prefigured in the burning bush; . . . the mystery in the Virgin was fully manifested. As on the mountain the burning bush was not consumed, so the Virgin brought forth a child and did so without stain.[412]

The connection between what happened at Lourdes and Moses' encounter with the burning bush becomes clearer when the salient features of this episode are recalled. Moses saw the bush burning but not consumed, and was told to take off his shoes because he was standing on holy ground. God then gave him his mission of leading the Israelites out of Egypt, before revealing the divine name, describing himself as "I AM WHO I AM" (Ex. 3:1–15).

In a published sermon, Mgr Ronald Knox indicates some points of contact between Bernadette and Moses; both were alone when they encountered the supernatural, and both events took place in mountainous country. Bernadette was working as a shepherdess at the time, and we read of Moses looking after the flocks of Jethro when he saw the burning bush and the Lord spoke to him from it. The bush Moses saw blazed and was not consumed, while

Bernadette saw Mary over a *rosebush* in a blaze of light. Moses was told to take off his sandals because he was standing on holy ground, while Bernadette had just taken off one of her stockings when she first saw Mary, and she, like him, was initially frightened.

Moses returned to that mountain when he had led the Israelites, as a great people, out of Egypt, although when he spoke with the Lord on the mountain, the vision of God was reserved for him alone. The people saw the thunder and lightning around the summit but did not hear the voice of God, while at Lourdes, the crowds saw the ecstatic face of Bernadette reflecting the heavenly beauty reserved only for her: they did not hear Mary speak. The Israelites were forbidden from going near the mountain (Ex. 19:12), and likewise the spectators at Lourdes were eventually prevented from approaching the grotto by barricades. Mgr Knox compares the Ten Commandments, with the ten words spoken by Mary during the various apparitions. He concludes that it is legitimate to regard Lourdes as a modern Sinai, with Bernadette taking the place of Moses in leading the people away from the bondage of sin, rather than from slavery in Egypt.[413]

Further themes from the life of Moses also seem to typify events at Lourdes. When Moses asked if he could see God's glory, he was told to stand on a rock and was then put in a "cleft of the rock" until God had passed by, only being allowed to see his back (Ex. 33:18–23). Mary too appeared in a niche or cleft in the rock of Massabielle. This is the only biblical passage where such an idea occurs with respect to a real individual, as a reference to a small "grotto-like hole" rather than a cave or larger opening. Another possible point of comparison, too, lies in the fact that the grotto of Massabielle lay some distance outside Lourdes, just as the "tent of meeting," where God came down as a pillar of cloud to speak with Moses "face to face," lay some distance outside the Israelite camp (Ex. 33:7–11). The pillar of cloud is a Marian symbol in itself, and Bernadette, too, spoke to Mary face to face. When Moses came down from the mountain, his face was shining (Ex. 34:29–35), and one of the things that convinced onlookers that Bernadette really had seen Mary was the heavenly look on her face during the apparitions.[414]

Moses struck the rock following God's instructions and water flowed from it, bringing relief to the Israelites (Ex. 17:1–7; Num. 20:1–11), while Mary told Bernadette where to find a spring of water, which was to become a source of both spiritual and physical healing for many. The instruction to Bernadette, that she should eat some leaves from a plant near the place where she discovered the spring, has been a puzzle for many. One possible explanation may lie in the fact that God appeared to Moses in a *bush*, in other words in something which expresses plant life and growth; another explanation may lie in the symbolism that will be explored when dealing with the apparitions at Banneux further on. Briefly, these apparitions are linked to the visions seen by Ezekiel in which he saw a spring flowing out from the east gate of the future Temple, forming a river with trees on either bank. According to the text, these trees would have medicinal leaves, and fruit that would be good to eat (Ezek. 47:1–12). In other words, like the spring at Lourdes they would be a source of healing.

Perhaps the most striking point of comparison, however, is that both God speaking to Moses, and Mary speaking to Bernadette, made known their names, thus revealing their most essential characteristic. God had described himself to Moses as "I AM WHO I AM," that is, as the eternal and infinite self-existent Being who is the cause of all things, when he appeared to him in the burning bush. God renewed this self-declaration when he proclaimed his name before Moses (Ex. 34:6–7). Mary also described her essential self when she said "I am the Immaculate Conception," since this privilege was the immediate cause of her dignity as Mother of God.

This was a point which St Maximilian Kolbe repeatedly emphasized in his theological writings, describing this phrase as "the Immaculata's definition of herself"; and it is worth noting that St Maximilian also made the connection between the passage from Exodus and Lourdes:

> When Bernadette repeated her request the Immaculata revealed her true name by saying, "I am the Immaculate Conception." To no one but her does such a name apply. When God revealed his name to Moses, he declared: "I am he who is" (Ex. 3:14), because God exists from eternity to eternity. His essence is limitless Being, beyond all time and under all aspects.[415]

He also pointed to the importance of Lourdes in relation to the dogma of the Immaculate Conception, and belief in the supernatural in general:

> Since Jesus' Resurrection, from time to time miracles occur to strengthen our faith, such as those which happen at Lourdes. There the Immaculata chose a frail instrument to show her power all the more clearly. At the time there were many objections; people said "it isn't true." But all the while the miraculous water was flowing, and many miracles and conversions took

place. Well then, what did the Most Blessed Virgin do amidst all these marvelous occurrences? In the presence of all these people she declared who she was, thus confirming the dogma of the Immaculate Conception defined in 1854. She said: "I am the Immaculate Conception." If she is the Immaculate Conception, then whatever serves as the groundwork of this truth is also true. Thus this apparition at Lourdes is a confirmation of the whole Catholic faith. This is why these apparitions have such profound importance.[416]

12

Lourdes, Evolution, Marxism, and Vatican I

Criticism of Nineteenth-century French Apparitions

Thomas Kselman argues that Catholic historians who deal with Marian apparitions often adopt an excessively "apologetical approach." He believes that his own scientific–historical attitude is better able to account for the continuing success of shrines such as Lourdes. He sees miracles and prophecies as helping to serve the social functions of religion, but argues that the historian of religion should be concerned with the beliefs surrounding such phenomena rather than reports of miracles.[417] The fundamental problem with his approach, though, is that he fails to deal with the *reality* of possibly miraculous events, and treats them as though they were just the faintly ridiculous beliefs of French peasants rather than examining them in an open-minded way. He uses pejorative terms such as "folkloric practices" to describe these beliefs, in order to imply that no serious person could take the idea of miraculous healings, or other manifestations of the supernatural, seriously.[418] Kselman alleges that visionaries were effectively being controlled by the Church, but this is not the case. Seers such as Bernadette expressly did not seek to produce or tailor their messages in this way: they simply reported what they saw and heard; and if this coincided with church dogma, that is because the apparitions were genuine. Kselman mistakes spiritual direction for some sort of coercive process, but in reality it was the job of the spiritual director to help the seer to determine whether or not a particular apparition was from God, not to tell them what to say or believe.[418]

Kselman outlines a "Social drama of a Miraculous Cure," with the implication that such nineteenth-century cures can be explained through the use of rituals and symbols: "Through the mutual contemplation of sacred symbols during pilgrimages and novenas, the social bond that tied the sick to the world was renewed, and within this state of *communitas* a cure was achieved."[420] So while the medical profession was powerless, this strange social force was able to heal people miraculously. It is surprising that science hasn't been able to discover the precise nature of this marvelous "force" during the last century or so. It is just possible that persons suffering from psychosomatic or nervous illnesses might be "cured" through the emotional effect of religious rituals; but the idea that people with incurable cancers, or the blind, or those paralyzed, or those with other serious diseases, could be cured by this sort of "emotional" healing is stretching things beyond the bounds of common sense.[421]

In fact, even Kselman himself acknowledges that this approach to miraculous healings is inadequate: "Even with the early belief of the clergy, the rapid diffusion and success of the new cults cannot be attributed to anything like the clerical conspiracy pictured in anticlerical propaganda." His explanation for this success, though, is as follows: "the miraculous was a familiar, even necessary part of the world view of many Frenchmen throughout the nineteenth century."[422] The question, though, is *why* they should have had this belief in the miraculous. The simplest explanation surely is that they were aware that people really were miraculously cured at shrines such as Lourdes.

Kselman criticizes those episcopal commissions appointed to deal with the major French apparitions, on the basis that pressure from the public and clergy must have ensured they could only come to one conclusion, that is, in favor of the view that miraculous events had occurred. He also criticizes the fact that such commissions were composed of clergy, but who else would have the necessary knowledge to carry out a thorough *theological and spiritual* inquiry into these events? The fact was that such commissions had to operate in a climate of intellectual hostility towards the miraculous; and so naturally they would have tended to take a defensive position, but there is nothing sinister about that. The idea that the bishops should have been completely neutral observers, who would make up their minds only at the end of the commission's deliberations, does not make sense. Miraculous events were continually coming to light and the bishops could not just pretend they were not happening.

But this does not mean that these episcopal commissions either then, or in more recent years, were *forced* to come out in favor of a particular apparition; and the evidence suggests that most reports of such events have never been accepted by the Church. These commissions, as the century went on, were able to draw on increasing experience of miraculous events; and this explains why there was a greater tendency to believe that supernatural happenings were a possibility. There is a hesitancy in the operations of the early commissions, such as those concerning Catherine Labouré and La Salette, but with more experience there was a greater willingness to take the idea of Marian apparitions seriously. Once again there is not anything sinister about this; it is a perfectly natural development. The Bishops and their commissions were responsible to God, and we can be quite certain that it was this responsibility that was the major factor in their decisions, and not outside pressures.[423]

Darwin, Evolution and Lourdes

Mary's role at Lourdes also seems to be relevant to the whole question of Darwin's theory of evolution. As previously indicated, the various apparitions that have been approved by the Church during the last couple of centuries generally seem to have happened as a sort of prelude, or response, to a revolutionary episode. The events at Lourdes in 1858, however, seem to be an exception to that. But while there were no outstanding political or military events in the years immediately following Lourdes, a significant event did occur the next year, 1859, namely the publication of Charles Darwin's *Origin of Species*.[424]

Regarding Lourdes then, it would seem that just as Mary warned the children at Fatima about the "errors of Russia," so also at Lourdes, apart from her general message of prayer and penance, she was implicitly warning mankind about the dangerous evolutionary ideas that were about to gain prominence; this point becomes apparent from the fact that she described herself as the "Immaculate Conception." In telling Bernadette that this was her title, that she was conceived without sin, she was also reminding mankind that we still suffer from the effects of original sin. And if we suffer from original sin, then we are led back to Adam and Eve and Genesis, and not just in a general way but as an event involving specific individuals at a particular time and place. If Genesis is just mythical, then how do we now suffer from original sin, and even more seriously, why do we need Jesus as our Redeemer? If something has not gone drastically wrong at the beginning of human history, then Jesus' sacrifice and Christianity itself tend to lose their whole meaning.

As previously pointed out, the *Origin of Species* was immediately successful because it was seen as new and exciting, with the potential to do away with the need for God. It also represented the culmination of a long period during which the idea of evolution, and progress generally, had been gaining ground. Buffon, one of the French Encyclopedists, argued as early as 1749 for a gradual process of development, culminating in mankind, as did the German Lessing in the area of religion, seeing Christianity as merely a stepping-stone to a higher form of religion. Herder argued for a gradual development in civilizations, each one dependent on its predecessors, and these views were very influential for the whole Romantic movement. The disruption caused by the French Revolution had shaken the older view that society was essentially static, and so the nineteenth century was generally predisposed to the possibility of change and evolution. Darwin's ideas symbolized and crystallized a whole way of thinking and represented a synthesis of both the rationalistic and romantic world views, and so ultimately can be said to have arisen from the philosophies arising out of the Enlightenment and its ensuing reaction. Liberal religious thinkers assimilated these ideas and began to see God's presence in the processes of evolution within the universe itself, rejecting the traditional distinction between the natural and the supernatural. From a liberal religious standpoint, evolution became the accepted way of describing how God, by means of a long slow process, had brought the world and mankind into existence.[425]

Evolutionary ideas are the logical outcome of that downward process in philosophical thinking, which first reduced the supernatural to the natural, and then the natural to the purely material. These ideas were an outgrowth of anti-biblical, rationalistic Enlightenment thought, and as such form part of the general revolt against Christianity. During the late eighteenth and early nineteenth centuries, the view that man was specially created by God came under attack by degrees, along with all other aspects of Christianity. The discovery of fossils, such as those of Neanderthal man, and cave paintings, seemed to indicate that "prehistoric" men had existed, and this, along with developing geological studies, gradually led many to the view that the biblical account of mankind's origin was unsound. In 1809 Lamarck argued that changes induced in animals by the environment could be transmitted to their progeny, but he faced a firm opponent in Cuvier, who maintained that species were fixed. Charles Lyell advanced the idea of Uniformitarianism in his *Principles of Geology* published in 1830, promoting the idea that the present condition of the earth was due to the operation of natural causes over long periods of time, rather than as a result of such biblical catastrophes as the Fall and the Flood. This was in direct opposition both to the traditional Christian approach and to the Newtonian view of the Universe, which saw it as a completed whole that was only a few thousand years old. It was only necessary for Darwin to include animals, and later men, in this overall approach, and with that the biblical account of the earth's origins appeared to have been overturned.

It was Darwin's *Origin of Species,* then, that resulted in the breakthrough for evolutionary ideas, since its idea of natural selection, based on Malthus's principle that only the fittest survive, seemed to give a scientific basis to evolution. His idea that in the past some species had been transformed over time, while others had become extinct, became the new scientific orthodoxy. Following the publication of Darwin's *Descent of Man* in 1871, these principles were applied to humanity as well, and, in the popular mind, the idea that men were descended from monkeys quickly became very widespread. For atheists, evolutionary ideas were the perfect vehicle for getting rid of the concepts of religion and revelation, in an age when it was felt that science would soon be capable of doing nearly anything, and when man was apparently progressing to a new golden age, but one without God. The nineteenth century thus became an era that saw rationalistic science elevated to the status of a new religion, based on materialism and technology, one diametrically opposed to Christian revelation.[426]

Darwin's work was popularized by Thomas Huxley, who was responsible for introducing the word "agnostic" as a way of describing the position, broadly speaking, of someone who *doubts* the existence of God, as opposed to the atheist, who *denies* it. Through his publications and his energetic promotion of evolution, Huxley did much to make Darwin's ideas scientifically acceptable. Huxley claimed that Darwinism would prove to have much greater ethical value than Christianity with its, as he described them, "superstitious practices,"[427] but the twentieth century has shown that to be a completely false and hollow expectation. If anything, evolution has led to a disastrous decline in morality, of which Communism and Nazism are just two of the most prominent examples—the whole of our modern godless civilization, in fact, is based on an evolutionary view of man, that we are nothing more than advanced animals.

Evolutionary ideas were also applied to social life, and so the older humanitarian ideals of benevolence and brotherhood were replaced by a philosophy that posited an egoistic and often militaristic struggle between individuals and peoples. It is not an exaggeration, then, to say that, just as the eighteenth century was dominated by Newton's thought, so the nineteenth and, indeed, the twentieth centuries have been dominated by the idea of evolution.[428] And just as the Enlightenment was a revolutionary movement, so evolution also involved a complete revolution, an overthrowing of the previously accepted view of how man and the universe had come into being. No shots were fired, no blood was shed, but in reality this was the most deadly revolution of modern times, which prepared the ground for Communism, Nazism, and the currently expanding global atheistic culture. It has also been a very successful revolution, since perhaps the majority of even those who would describe themselves as Christians seem to accept evolution as an explanation of how we got here, despite the fact that it still remains very much an unproved hypothesis.

On this point there is confusion amongst some Catholics, who take the mistaken view that apparent support for evolutionary ideas within the Church is equivalent to acceptance of evolution by the Church as a whole. This is not the case; and in fact the consistent stance of the Magisterium, from Pope Pius XII and his encyclical *Humani Generis* onwards, has been to back up the traditional view of Genesis, that is that the human race is descended from Adam and Eve, whose original sin led to the Fall of mankind. This teaching has been reiterated by both the Second Vatican Council and the new *Catechism of the Catholic Church*, which does not mention evolution either in the text or the index.

For example, Adam is mentioned, as a real individual, in the Vatican II documents, *Lumen Gentium* (1:2), and *Gaudium et Spes* (1:22), while the *Catechism* has this passage: "Among all the Scriptural texts about creation, the first three chapters of *Genesis* occupy a unique place ... Read in the light of Christ, within the unity of Sacred Scripture and in the living Tradition of the Church, these texts remain the principal source for catechesis on the mysteries of the 'beginning': creation, fall, and promise of salvation" (289).[429]

The Darwinian Revolution

Given all this, it does not seem too extreme to see Darwin's book as the beginning of an atheistic intellectual revolution, one to match the more violent revolutions both before and after his time.

His biological approach was applied in many other fields, and Social Darwinism, the application of evolutionary principles to larger groups, became very popular. These ideas were also used to justify the oppression of the weak by the strong, and in this sense became a justification for war and aggression. Darwin's ideas were also exploited to promote theories of racial eugenics, and that certain races were naturally inferior—principles that had deadly consequences in the twentieth century, particularly in the treatment of the Jews by the Nazis. Haeckel was the writer who did most to popularize Darwinian ideas in Germany, where they had a profoundly disturbing influence. German anti-Semitism seems to date from the 1870s, when the idea of natural selection was used to demonize a whole racial group, the Jews, who were stigmatized because they were seen as an alien group not rooted in the German soil.

When the ideas of Darwin and Marx are taken together, along with Sigmund Freud's psychoanalytic movement, which was to emerge around the turn of the century, we can see how the thoroughgoing materialism of the present era developed. Certainly, both Marxism and modern psychology, which have done untold damage in the political and moral fields respectively, base themselves to a great extent on an evolutionary understanding of man.[430] There is also an intimate connection between the thinking of Darwin and Marx. When the *Origin of Species* was published in 1859, Marx saw it as scientific proof for his idea of dialectical materialism: just as the struggle between animals led to higher forms, so, according to Marx, the struggle between classes would lead to a higher form of society.[431]

By any standards, then, the rise of evolutionary thinking was a revolutionary event in nineteenth-century life, which carried the long-drawn-out process of undermining Christianity to the new level of apparently making atheism respectable. Enlightenment thinking truly came of age in the theory of evolution, but this was not the beginning of a new age of reason; the irony is that the theory of evolution is almost completely irrational, not being based on any hard evidence but rather on a blind faith in unworkable evolutionary processes, such as natural selection. In addition, evolution encouraged all sorts of dubious racial and philosophical ideas to circulate with greater freedom, a process that would culminate in the godless ideologies of the twentieth century, and in particular Marxism. Indeed we have probably yet to see the full extent to which evolution will drag mankind away from the truth of divinely-revealed religion.

The Rise of Marxism

Marxism itself was the brainchild of Karl Marx (1818–83), the son of a Jewish lawyer, who developed a philosophy based on deterministic materialism, one that sought to explain both history and mankind. He produced his most famous work on capitalism and Communism, *Das Kapital*, in 1867, but it was only after his death, in 1883, that his thinking was widely adopted. This was because his theories were able to incorporate many contemporary themes, and seemingly provide an answer to nineteenth-century social problems. Marxism, the creed that grew out of his writings, was able to utilize ideas such as scientific progress and evolution, combining them with a dialectical materialistic philosophy to produce a new synthesis. This claimed to give an explanation of all reality, including mankind, and also included a plan of action for changing society. Revolutionary Marxism sought to do this by offering those oppressed by capitalism and industrialization a chance to liberate themselves, but as history has shown, the resulting ideology of Communism inaugurated a far worse form of slavery.[432]

The appeal of Marxism lay in the fact that it managed to give an almost religious dimension to the secularized apocalyptic ideal of an earthly paradise, a materialist heaven on earth in which the wrongs of society would be righted.[433] Marx's hope for a socialist future were not completely illusory; there was a real threat that the chronic injustice of the capitalist system in the West, notorious for its long working hours and poverty, would drive ordinary workers wholesale into the hands of Marxist socialism. Marx's atheism led him to proclaim that "religion was the opium of the people," in other words that religion was just another part of the capitalist system, another way of keeping the workers enslaved by offering them future rewards. The major flaw in capitalism was that it produced a large number of such people, the proletariat, who were politically free but economically dispossessed. By contrast the great strength of Communism was that it constituted a complete system of thought and action, and as such it represented a grave threat to Christianity.[434]

The Church faced problems in coping with such intellectual attacks on its teachings and was thrown on to the defensive; this explains why most Catholic apologetic works from this era, from the Pope downwards, were condemnatory. It took some time for the Church to mount an effective defence, although there were outstanding Catholic thinkers, such as Cardinal Newman, working at this time. This meant that philosophers and writers such as

Comte with his theory of positivism, or Hegel or Marx, did not initially have to face an organized Catholic critique of their ideas.

Hegel (1770–1831) had seen nature and history as part of an evolving process, whose spirit was becoming self-conscious in man. A new attitude to society and history developed, a belief that the German people possessed a "collective soul." This in turn became the basis of the nationalistic ideals that found ultimate expression in Hegel's idea of the "divine" State as "the supreme reality which possesses a plenitude and self-sufficiency of being far surpassing that of the individual."[435] Christopher Dawson describes him as having "one of the most seminal minds of the nineteenth century. He stands behind Karl Marx and ... Communist ideology. He inspired the Russian revolutionary intelligentsia before and after Marx. He [also] had a great influence on Fascism ..." Dawson argues that Hegel was not directly responsible for the rise of Nazism, but maintains that he did a great deal to provide the ideology behind the rise of Prussia.[436]

Pius IX and the Church

It was some time before the influence of Lourdes was fully felt, and the religious situation in France deteriorated quite drastically in the years following 1858, at a time when the government had an ambivalent attitude towards Christianity. The anticlerical press became more clamorous, whilst amongst intellectuals irreligious attitudes were commonplace, a situation exemplified by the publication of Renan's *Life of Jesus* in 1863. This book caused a sensation throughout Europe because of the way it rejected the supernatural in the Gospels, ignored their morality, and generally portrayed Jesus in an unfavorable light. This was an example of the way printed matter began to circulate more widely, and thus propagate ideas which had been confined to small intellectual élites in the previous century; now it began to find a much wider audience and influence public opinion.[437]

Meanwhile, most of the Papal States were annexed by Piedmont in 1860; this caused Catholic opinion in France to protest at the threat to the Pope and the religious situation there to deteriorate further. Pius IX rejected calls that he should abandon all his remaining holdings and was left with a much smaller domain, although he still refused to negotiate. By the summer of 1861, an Italian Parliament proclaimed Victor Emmanuel king of Italy, but he was prevented from taking Rome by the presence of French

troops. The tremendous pressure put on Pius IX had the paradox-
ical effect of a growth in papal prestige, as the Pope increasingly
came to be seen as the true Father of all Catholics, defending the
rights of the Church. So just as his temporal power was being
eclipsed, the Pope's spiritual authority grew stronger, as he
increasingly concentrated on the spiritual battle, aware that the
revolutionaries who had seized the papal territories were influenced equally by French and German philosophical ideas that
exalted the rights of man, but rejected God.[438]

In Russia, in the same year, 1861, an attempt was made to
grapple with serfdom, a practice that had reduced millions to the
level of virtual slavery, through the proclamation of a law of emancipation. Other reforms were also gradually introduced, but in
practice the situation of the peasants remained much the same and
this created a great deal of bitterness, with the country as a whole
remaining unstable. Russia was still an autocratic, and increasingly
bureaucratic, state, but one with a growing revolutionary movement that was quite prepared to resort to assassination and other
terrorist acts. A rebellion in Poland was put down in 1863, and this
led to harsh measures against the Church there.[439]

In December 1864, Pope Pius IX produced a document in two
parts, an encyclical *Quanta Cura* and a *Syllabus,* which condemned
certain errors, at the same time affirming the independence of the
Church from the power of any State. This was a rejection of the
idea that society could exist without religion, or that the sover-
eignty of the people overrode all individual human, or divine,
rights. Similarly, those doctrines and ideas which tended to undermine religion, including extreme rationalism, naturalism,
pantheism, and particularly the recent theories on socialism and
Communism, were criticized. Pius IX prophetically saw these ideas
as being capable, if implemented, of destroying the whole moral
basis of society. He was not, however, rejecting modern civilization
and progress, except where these were used as a way of attacking
religion.[440] But this was not the way the *Syllabus* was received by
European intellectuals, who regarded it as completely reactionary
and unacceptable.

The revolutionary atmosphere that permeated the nineteenth
century, and the threatening way this was perceived by the Church,
however, should also be borne in mind when evaluating the
Syllabus. Pope Pius had to deal with a situation where the Church in
Europe was increasingly coming under siege; in Belgium and
France irreligious attitudes were growing more widespread; and in
Italy itself, a country not recognized by the Holy See, anticlericalism

was rife and many bishoprics were vacant, a problem that led to negotiations involving St John Bosco, the founder of the Salesian congregation. He played an important part in the general revival of Catholicism that took place during the nineteenth century. His main contribution was the foundation and development of the Salesians, a religious congregation dedicated to the education of youth, named after St Francis de Sales, the great Counter-Reformation bishop of Geneva. After Don Bosco became a priest, he worked to start schools for poor boys, and eventually opened his own Salesian homes; similarly, he started technical schools and workshops to give boys experience in a trade, while also selecting and training those with a vocation to form the nucleus of his new order, and to act as teachers. By the time of his death in 1888, there were 250 Salesian houses looking after the needs of over one hundred and thirty thousand children, and his institutions had produced over six thousand priests, of whom twelve hundred had remained in his congregation.[441]

It is in his role as a prophet, though, that he is also of interest for the purposes of this book, and particularly regarding the way some of his prophecies seem to tie in with the words of Mary at Fatima in 1917 to the young seers, Lucia, Jacinta and Francisco. One of Don Bosco's most famous prophetic dreams concerned the future of the papacy and the Church. He saw the Catholic Church as a great ship, with the Pope as its captain in the midst of storms, being increasingly attacked by irreligious forces, as other boats, representing persecutions of all sorts, seemed about to destroy it. But at the last moment the Pope managed to steer his ship towards two great columns, one representing the Eucharist and the other Mary, and a great period of peace then descended on the Church and the world. This prophecy ties in very well with the message of Fatima, that following persecutions and the recognition of Mary's importance, and her association with the Eucharist, the world will be given a period of peace.[442]

Thus the problems facing the papacy and the Church in the nineteenth century can be summed up in terms of a general and growing development of irreligious ideas, and of movements hostile to Catholicism. The major problem was that, unlike the situation at the time of the Reformation, now the whole basis of Christianity was being questioned, as eighteenth-century philosophical ideas began to bear fruit. Pius IX, aware of all the problems developing in society, announced that an ecumenical Council would meet in Rome to decide on the best way for the Church to respond to these threats.[443]

Vatican I and Papal Infallibility

The First Vatican Council began in Rome on 8 December 1869, over three hundred years after the Council of Trent, and just as that gathering had previously undertaken the task of formulating the Church's definitive response to the Protestant Revolution, so Pius IX realized that the Church of his day had to respond authoritatively to the problems of the nineteenth-century world, and also to strengthen the position of the papacy. By refusing to invite representatives of governments, and thus breaking with a tradition that stretched back to Constantine and the Council of Nicaea in the fourth century, Pius IX also sought to make it clear that the papacy would follow a new course in future.

The major achievement of the First Vatican Council was the solemn proclamation of papal infallibility, and although in practice this had been accepted by most Catholics for some time, a number of bishops from France, Germany, America and elsewhere, opposed it. The main debate centered on the exact limits of infallibility, and the text finally adopted in July 1870 spoke of spiritual assistance being given to the Pope in his official capacity, and only when he spoke *ex cathedra*, "from the chair," as the authorized transcription makes clear. In other words, only when the Pope speaks as the supreme teacher of all Christians, and, by means of his apostolic authority, defines a doctrine on faith or morals to be held by the whole Church, is he guaranteed the charism of infallibility. This makes such declarations unalterable in themselves and not dependent on the assent of the Church.

Once this doctrine was proclaimed, the Pope's position was greatly strengthened, and his role as the Chief Shepherd of the Church began to develop in the more modern sense, particularly through the practice of issuing encyclicals. From now on the popes would not be dependent on governments, or subject to their interference when it came to the calling of Councils, and so the papacy gained spiritually even as its temporal power waned.[444] This was an important and timely development, for the increasing power of secular governments called for the Church to have a powerful leader with enhanced authority.

Following the proclamation of the decree of infallibility, Pius IX adjourned the Council due to the departure of the French forces from Rome in August 1870, as tension rose between Prussia and France and war broke out between them. The rapid defeat of France's armies in early September led to the fall of the French Second Empire and the proclamation of a republic soon after. The fact that this defeat completed the unification of Germany under Prussian control and made it the strongest nation, militarily speaking, in the world, indicates the importance of this conflict, and hence of the apparition at Pontmain, which is dealt with in the next chapter. Pius IX was now isolated, and the Italian government could press ahead with the reunification of the country, including Rome. The Pope, after some hesitation, refused the offer to recognize him as ruler of the small area around the Vatican. He thus became a prisoner within the Vatican palace for the remaining seven years of his life, a position that was maintained by his successors until the signing of the Lateran treaty between Pope Pius XI and Mussolini in 1929.[445]

From a modern viewpoint, it might be argued that it would have been better for Pius IX to have surrendered the Papal States earlier. His defeat in this matter, however, had very serious consequences for Catholic life all over Europe in succeeding years, as governments recognized the Church's temporal weakness and acted accordingly. In 1873 Pope Pius pointed to all these troubles and directly linked them to the world-wide activities of Freemasonry, which he saw as actively opposed to the Church. Echoing the words of many of his predecessors, he strongly condemned Masonry and its allied secret societies by means of encyclicals and addresses throughout his pontificate. He blamed them for the grave evils that had arisen in Europe, having previously strongly criticized rulers for not suppressing Freemasonry, which he directly linked to the revolutionary movements that had convulsed the continent. In particular, he rejected the idea that Freemasons were harmless philanthropists, pointing to their secrecy and the frightening oaths they took.[446] The Pope had direct experience of these matters, since some of the leaders of the movement towards Italian unity were Freemasons, and part of an anticlerical irreligious clique.[447]

Pius IX's successor, Pope Leo XIII, (1810–1903), also saw the hand of Freemasonry behind many of the problems facing both Church and state. In his 1878 encyclical, *Quod Apostolici*, he reaffirmed the condemnations of previous popes, arguing that the aim of Freemasonry and its associated sects was the destruction of the Church and the promotion of a new and even more degraded form of paganism. He also produced a further encyclical, *Humanum Genus,* in 1884, and this too censured Freemasonry. He explicitly charged Masons with anarchic and revolutionary activities, with promoting sedition, and with favoring extreme forms of socialism. He particularly condemned their naturalist approach, which saw marriage as just another contract, and which fostered religious indifference and the degradation of youth by secularized teaching and immoral literature. The crux of his censure revolved around the way that Freemasonry, and liberalism generally, sought to remove any sense of moderation or shame from life, to make everything soft and luxurious, so that humanity would end up being governed by its passions, and thus liable to be much more easily manipulated. In short, he accused Freemasonry of actively promoting vice as a way of gaining power indirectly rather than by means of a frontal assault.[448]

Bismarck's Kulturkampf

Meanwhile, in his German Empire dominated by Prussia, Bismarck had begun his *Kulturkampf* against the Church, attacking religious orders and imprisoning clergy. He had cleverly maneuvered France into declaring war on Prussia in 1870, and the conflict very quickly went against the French forces. Their defeat meant that Bismarck's Prussia was able to create a German empire by absorbing other Germanic states, and thus become an even stronger military power, one innately antagonistic to Catholicism. Prussia's victories led to a nationalistic sense of racial superiority, and this, coupled with intellectual pride, led to the mistaken belief that Protestant Germanic culture was threatened by Catholicism. This was the rationale behind the *Kulturkampf*, an attack based on the ideals of the Reformation and modern philosophical thought, an approach that saw Catholicism holding back the progress of civilization. Freemasonry was also involved in the rise of Prussia and the *Kulturkampf*.[449]

This anti-Catholic movement had been growing during the nineteenth century in Germany, particularly in attacks on the Bible. These ranged from critical works which claimed that it had no foundation, or that Jesus was an impostor or trickster, to more subtle approaches such as that of the German theologian Strauss, who had claimed that the Gospel accounts of Jesus were really mythical, that is *stories* based on religious ideas. Another German theologian, Baur, of the Tübingen school, claimed that the Gospels were written at the earliest in the second century, and that there were two competing trends of thought in early Christianity, one based on the teaching of St Peter, the other on that of St Paul. Similar attacks were being made on the authenticity of the Old Testament by writers such as Wellhausen and Graf, with their J, E,

D, P, theory, which split it into different sections supposedly authored at different times, by "Jahwist," "Elohist," "Deuteronomist," and "Priestly" writers, and then edited together into a united whole, at a late date. These were all part of a group of writers, theologians, and philosophers, who made atheism and anti-religious and anti-Christian attitudes respectable in the nineteenth century, and particularly in Germany.[450]

It is also more than likely that the struggle between Bismarck and the papacy led to the growth and acceptance of the idea that St Mark's Gospel was the first to be written, rather than St Matthew's. This has traditionally been believed in the Church, and is expressed in the usual order of the Gospels, *Matthew*, Mark, Luke, John. This idea of Marcan priority had important consequences, since it furthered acceptance of the view that Matthew 16:18–19, Jesus' commission to Peter as the first Pope, was a later addition and not part of the primitive teaching of the Church. Bismarck found this supposed fact very convenient in his drive against the Vatican. This theory was popularized in the 1870s by a young theology professor named Holtzmann, who had inherited it from Strauss, and it allowed him to argue that Mark and a hypothetical document called Q were used in the compilation of Matthew and Luke. No trace of Q has been found to this day.

From Bismarck's attacks against the papacy it seems clear that he was well aware that he had to undermine the position of the Pope, if he was to achieve his end of subjugating the Catholic Church in Germany. Thus it was obviously in his interests, and those of the Prussian State, to ensure that an intellectual counter-argument to Petrine authority was available in the form of the historical priority of Mark's Gospel. It seems that Bismarck and his officials promoted this idea in the German universities, where all professors were appointed by the State, despite the fact that it was no more than a hypothesis without any convincing literary or historical evidence. Within a generation it had become the received teaching within the country, to the extent that to accept the priority of Matthew had come to be regarded as anti-German. From that time, this theory has gone on to exert a determining influence on the whole of modern New Testament theology.[451]

Bismarck's war against the Church threatened to become the policy adopted by other countries as the end of Pius IX's reign approached, with measures hostile to Catholicism being introduced in Italy, Austria and France. Bismarck was opposed by the Catholic *Zentrum* party led by Ludwig Windthorst, as a series of increasingly anti-Catholic laws were passed. But Catholics there stood firm in the face of this persecution and eventually, by 1877, Bismarck realized that his anti-Catholic policy, as a frontal assault on the Church, was a failure and it was abandoned. Nonetheless, in the longer term the work of subverting the Church continued, and was for the most part successful. For Germany as a whole, Bismarck left a tainted legacy in a weak parliament, the *Reichstag,* and a state with a pronounced militaristic and authoritarian character.

By 1879 a Republican regime was back in power in France, and, determined to punish Catholics for supporting the previous right-wing government, it began to introduce anti-religious and anticlerical measures. The century since the beginning of the Revolution had seen an extended struggle between traditional, mainly Catholic, forces and those who supported liberalism; as would elsewhere be the case, the new ideology was at last triumphant, in the form of the Third Republic. At this time France was the only major European power to have a republican government, and at this point too, most governments were either hostile or at best indifferent to Catholicism. There was very little in the way of support, and it seemed that the Church was about to enter a period of eclipse if not conflict. A quarter of a century later, however, by the end of Pope Leo XIII's reign, the situation had greatly improved, and both the Church and the papacy were again able to exert an influence for good on the world.[452]

13

Pontmain, Pompeii, and Knock

Pontmain Apparition – January 1871

By January 1871 France was in a very serious position militarily, with the Prussians controlling two-thirds of the country and Paris besieged. It seemed to be only a matter of time before Mayenne and Brittany, the north-western part of the country, would also be taken. The next attack was expected at Laval, the capital of Mayenne, less than thirty miles from Pontmain, where Mary would appear. At the time, Pontmain was a small village, inhabited by simple and hardworking country folk, who, guided by their parish priest, Abbé Michel Guérin, sought to live as good Christians. The Barbedette family consisted of father César, his wife, Victoire, with their two sons Joseph and Eugène, aged ten and twelve, and another older brother who was away in the army. On 17 January 1871, after going to early morning Mass, the boys spent the day at school as usual. On their return, they were helping their father in the barn when a neighbor, an old lady named Jeannette Détais, called in and began to chat with César. During the conversation, the older boy, Eugène, walked over towards the door to look out; later he said that he had gone to see what the weather was like, on that bitterly cold but clear and frosty winter evening.[453]

As he looked at the star-studded sky Eugène noticed one area practically free of stars above a neighboring house. This puzzled him; but, as he gazed at it, suddenly he saw an apparition of a beautiful woman smiling at him; she was wearing a blue gown covered with golden stars, and a black veil under a golden crown. As Jeannette Détais was about to leave, Eugène asked her if she could see anything, and as she replied in the negative, his father and brother came out to look. Joseph immediately said he too could see the apparition, although their father, like the old lady, saw nothing. He was somewhat afraid the matter would cause people to talk, and so he asked Jeannette to say nothing about it, which she agreed to do, while telling the boys to go inside and continue with their work. But a little later he asked Eugène to see if the Lady was still there, and on being told "Yes," asked him to go and fetch his mother. Victoire arrived but like the other adults she could see nothing, although she was puzzled because her boys were usually very truthful. She suggested that it might be the Blessed Virgin, and that they should all say five Our Fathers and five Hail Marys in her honor.

By this time the neighbors were coming out to see what was going on, and the Barbedettes withdrew into the barn to pray. The family servant, Louise, was called but she too could see nothing; and as it was now about a quarter past six, and time for supper, the boys were ordered inside and told off by their worried mother for imagining things. She must have felt that something really was happening, however, because she gave them permission to go out again soon after, and, on hearing that the Lady was still there, went to fetch Sister Vitaline, the local schoolteacher. Eugène pointed to three bright stars in the shape of a triangle and told her that the Lady's head was in the middle of them. Although Sister Vitaline could see the stars, she saw nothing else, and so she went to fetch three young girls from the school to see their reactions. Immediately they arrived, the two youngest of these, aged nine and eleven, expressed their delight at the apparition, describing it as the boys had done, although the oldest girl saw nothing. The three stars were seen by everyone that evening, but disappeared after the apparition.[454]

It was decided to fetch other children, and another sister called at the presbytery to tell Fr Guérin, who, after some hesitation, decided to come out as well. As he reached the barn with his house-keeper, a child of two and her mother had just arrived. Immediately the infant looked with delight at the apparition, clapped her hands, and called out the name of Jesus, as taught by her mother. The next evening the child was taken back to the same spot at the same time and told to look, but gave no indication of seeing anything.[455]

The adults in the crowd, which had now grown to about sixty people, including the priest, could still see nothing and began to say the rosary, as the children exclaimed that something new was happening. A blue oval frame with four candles, two at the level of the shoulders and two at the knees, was being formed around the Lady, and a short red cross had appeared over her heart. During this time some of the onlookers had become a little incredulous and started to doubt the children, who then reported that the Lady had grown sad. As the rosary progressed, though, her smile returned and the figure and its frame grew larger, until it was twice life size; the stars around her began to multiply and attach themselves to her dress until it was covered with them.[456]

As the Magnificat was being said, the four children cried out, "Something else is happening." A broad streamer on which letters were appearing unrolled beneath the feet of the Lady, so that eventually the phrase, "But pray, my children," could be read. Fr Guérin then ordered that the Litany of Our Lady should be sung, and as this progressed new letters appeared, making the message, "God will soon answer you." As they continued to sing, another message was formed, one that removed any doubt that it was the Blessed Virgin who was appearing to the children: "My Son allows Himself to be moved." The children were beside themselves with joy at the beauty of the Lady and her smile, but her expression then changed to one of extreme sadness, as she now contemplated a large red cross that had suddenly appeared before her, with a figure of Jesus on it in an even darker shade of red. One of the stars then lit the four candles that surrounded the figure, as the crucifix vanished and the group began night prayers. As these were being recited, the children reported that a white veil was rising from the Lady's feet and gradually blotting her out, until finally, at about nine o'clock, the apparition was over.[457]

The following March a canonical inquiry into the apparition was held, and in May the local bishop questioned the children. The inquiry was continued later in the year, with further questioning by theologians and a medical examination. The bishop was satisfied by these investigations, and in February 1872 declared his belief that it was the Blessed Virgin who had appeared to the children. Joseph Barbedette became a priest, a member of the Congregation of the Oblates of Mary Immaculate, while his brother Eugène became a secular priest. One of the girls who had seen Mary assisted him as his housekeeper, while the other, Jeanne-Marie Lebossé, became a nun. A large basilica was built at Pontmain and consecrated in 1900.[458]

In 1919 a second canonical process into Pontmain was initiated during which the surviving witnesses were again interrogated. At this stage, though, nearly fifty years after the event, a problem arose in that Jeanne-Marie Lebossé seemed to retract her evidence and say that she had really seen nothing at Pontmain. Nevertheless, despite this, the judgment given at the conclusion of this second process, in the following year, 1920, confirmed the work of its predecessor, laying emphasis on the evidence given by the two Barbedette boys, who were the initial witnesses of the apparition. Jeanne-Marie said that she had only been reacting to the exclamations of the other children, but it seems that she may have entered a state of mind where she was *afraid* of deceiving people about the apparition, after convincing herself in the course of time that she had seen nothing.

This is apparently not an unusual phenomenon in the lives of the saints, where the fear of diabolical illusion has been ever-present in their minds. Considering that Jeanne-Marie was only nine at the time, and had gone through a troubled childhood with the death of her father, it is perhaps not surprising that, like Maximin at Ars, she should have eventually succumbed to the pressure of events, and of being labeled a "visionary," and come to believe that she had lied. It seems, though, that her original evidence, if anything, was the most satisfactory in comparison with that of the other children, and there were no signs that she had lied and was bearing an intolerable secret in the period immediately after the apparition.[459]

Criticism of Pontmain

In his criticism of Pontmain, Michael P. Carroll, apparently drawing on the booklet *What Happened at Pontmain* by the Abbé M. Richard as a source, implies that the two boys were alone at the barn door for some time. He argues that this would have allowed them to fabricate their story about the Lady. It is clear, though, from the Abbé Richard's text, that Eugène first spoke about what he could see to the old lady Jeannette Détais, who saw nothing:

> Struck by the intensity of the expression in the boy's question, his father and brother, overhearing, quickly came to the door and also glanced in the indicated direction. The father saw nothing. Eugène said to his brother: "Do you see it, Joseph?" "Yes," said the child, "I see a beautiful tall Lady." "How is she dressed?" "I see a tall Lady who wears a blue dress, with golden stars on the dress, and blue slippers with golden buckles."[460]

Obviously the "it" in question here could have been anything, and so we have to assume they both described the same thing separately, without collusion. There is no evidence here, as Carroll states, that they were alone together at the door of the barn. Similarly, Carroll claims that Françoise Richer and Jeanne-Marie

Lebossé were left alone with the boys and so had time to talk to them about the Lady.[461] But once again, as the text makes clear, this was not the case: Sister Vitaline had not given the girls any details of what the boys had reported seeing, she had just told them that they would see "something." The two girls thus went to the place of the apparition with Victoire Barbedette, while Sister Vitaline went to fetch another religious, Sister Mary Edward.

> Arriving at the gable corner of the Rousseau house, Françoise Richer cried out: "But I see something over the house of Augustine Guidecoq, but I don't know what it is." She was looking only from the side while walking along the street. Then they ran to the door of the barn where Eugene was calling them. There, Jeanne-Marie Lebossé and Françoise Richer immediately said: "Oh! The beautiful Lady ... she has a beautiful blue dress ... with golden stars ..." And they repeated exactly what the two boys had said.[462]

Contrary to Carroll's assertion, then, there is nothing here to indicate that the children were left alone, and clearly at least one of them saw something even before she reached the barn. The Abbé Richard's text, published with the *Imprimatur* of Laval diocese, is a very early historical source for details about Pontmain. Just over a month after the apparition he came to Pontmain to question, at length, both the seers and the other inhabitants of the village. He edited their responses and then read these back to those involved, at the site of the apparition, making some changes as necessary; thus his account is very accurate, and it provides no support for the above thesis.[463]

When the children reported the third message, that began, "My Son permits Himself ...," reading out each letter as it appeared, they were interrupted by Sister Vitaline, who thought that it should have read, "My Son *worries* Himself ..." In French the words for "permit," *laisse,* and "worry," *lasse,* are quite similar, and if the children were just making things up, we would naturally have expected them to agree with the Sister and accept her idea. But this did not happen and they went on to insist that it was an "I," spelling out the word together several times.[464] All of this indicates that Carroll's conclusion, that this apparition was just an illusion, and that the children were making it up, either consciously or unconsciously, is not based on a secure argument.

The Prussians never reached Pontmain; instead they unexpectedly turned back, and an armistice was signed soon afterwards. Although the war proved costly to France, at least the slaughter was over and the Barbedettes' eldest son was able to return home. Germany gained the provinces of Alsace and Lorraine, and France was forced to pay a huge indemnity of five billion francs to the victors.

The Ark of the Covenant and the Tabernacle

The Ark of the Covenant was originally housed in a tabernacle or tent, as the Israelites journeyed through the wilderness in the time before the Temple was built, in the Israel of King Solomon, and it would seem that there is a typological connection between this tabernacle, the person and role of the high priest, and the apparition at Pontmain. To understand the significance of this it is necessary to see how one of the early Christian writers compared Mary with the tabernacle. St Ephrem expressed himself thus: "Joseph and also John [the Evangelist] honored Your mother's womb as a symbol. It is the symbol of the Tabernacle, the temporal Tabernacle, in which Emmanuel was dwelling."[465] He also compared Mary with the Ark of the Covenant, utilizing the idea that Jesus as the Word of God, the *logos*, was in Mary just as the Old Testament Word of God, the Decalogue, was in the Ark: "Joseph rose to serve in the presence of his Lord Who was within Mary. The priest serves in the presence of Your Ark because of Your holiness. Moses bore the tablet of stone that His Lord had written. And Joseph escorted the pure tablet in whom was dwelling the Son of the Creator. The tablets were left behind since the world was filled with Your teaching."[466] This idea is also present in the *Akathistos* hymn, in which Mary is described as the "tabernacle of God and the Word," and the "ark gilded by the Holy Ghost."[467] St John Damascene, in describing the burial of Mary, says: "The assembly of the apostles carried you, the Lord God's true Ark, as once the priests carried the symbolic ark, on their shoulders."[468]

After Moses handed on to the Israelites the Law he had received from God on the mountain, he arranged for the building and furnishing of the sanctuary where the Ark of the Covenant would be kept. It had to be moveable, because the people were set to journey through the desert before they reached the promised land. God had already told Moses all that had to be done (Exod. 25–31), and now the work was carried out, after all the necessary materials had been gathered and craftsmen appointed.

Essentially, the tabernacle was a cloth version of the later Temple, with an outer "wall" of hangings as a perimeter or court, and an inner tent or dwelling, that itself had a smaller inner section divided off by a curtain, the Holy of Holies. The dwelling was made up of sheets of linen dyed violet-blue, purple, and red, embroidered with winged creatures or cherubim, over an acacia-wood frame. This was overlaid with sheets of goats' hair, and then a cover of rams' skins dyed red, plus a fine leather covering. The curtain or veil separating off the Holy of Holies from the holy place was also made of linen dyed violet-blue, purple and red, as above, and hung on acacia-wood rods (Exod. 36:8–38).

The Ark, too, was made of acacia wood and overlaid with gold, with a mercy seat on top and two golden cherubim at its ends, with their wings over spreading it. A seven-branched lampstand of pure gold was made and placed inside the holy place, on the left, and an altar was set up in the court. Vestments were made for the priests, with a special set for Aaron, the high priest, from the same dyed linen material. In addition he wore an ephod, a sort of apron tied at the neck and waist, over which was worn the breastplate of judgment, which had four rows of three precious stones on it, corresponding to the twelve tribes of Israel. These items were worn over a blue robe, which had golden bells fixed to its hem and which was decorated with small images of pomegranates. A turban decorated with a flower made of gold was also worn by the high priest on his head (Exod. 39:1–32). Once all this was ready, the sanctuary was erected and everything was consecrated, including Aaron and his sons, the priests. A cloud then covered the tent and the glory of God filled the holy place; it was only when this cloud arose that the Israelites could continue their journey through the desert (Exod. 40).

If we compare the events at Pontmain with this account of the sanctuary, some very interesting points stand out. The Lady seen by the children was wearing a deep blue robe, and slippers with golden ribbons formed into rosettes, while Aaron, as high priest, also wore a violet-blue robe under his ephod and breastplate. This indicates a connection with the unusual color seen in the apparition; the children compared the blue color to indigo pellets which they had seen being used for washing.[469] In the majority of her apparitions Mary has worn white. The golden crown on the Lady's head spread out at the sides and had a horizontal red line across it, and this is reminiscent of the high priest's turban with its colored cord and golden flower. Likewise, the ephod of the high priest was decorated with gold and jewels, suggestive of the stars that the children saw covering the Lady's robe.

It was the duty of the high priest to enter the Holy of Holies once a year to perform the rite of expiation for sin, and this was done by sacrificing a bull for his own sins and those of his family, and a goat for the sins of the people. At the same time he sprinkled some of the blood on the mercy seat over the Ark of the Covenant (Lev. 16). Aaron's entering of the Holy of Holies in this way, behind the veil, seems to explain the symbolism of the blue oval seen by the children, which encompassed the Lady as they saw her in the sky. This oval apparently represents the cloth of the Holy of Holies, which was made from the same material as Aaron's robe, and is a feature that is unique to the apparition at Pontmain. It is also intriguing to note that the children saw a little red cross, "about as large as a finger"[470] over her breast at this point, and to relate this to the fact that the high priest was supposed to sprinkle the blood with his *finger* on the mercy seat. Blood is of course red, and the cross a sign of expiation through bloodshed (Lev. 16:14). A more likely explanation, though, is that this little cross could represent the *urim* and *thummim,* the sacred items for casting lots kept in the high priest's breastplate, and used for divining God's will. These were worn over the heart, as a symbol of judgment (Ex. 28:30), and so in the same way Mary had the symbol of judgment *par excellence,* the cross, over her heart.

Next, the apparition doubled in size as the "stars of the atmosphere" arranged themselves beneath the Lady's feet in rows, two by two, until there were about forty there. These seem to have been stars similar to the three large ones seen around her head.[471] At the same time the stars on her dress began to multiply, causing the children to exclaim, "soon she will be nearly golden."[472] These details recall the golden bells put on the hem of the high priest's robe, and the ephod and breastplate worn by him, which were covered by gold and jewels, and hence must have been very dazzling.

The white banner beneath the Lady, on which the golden letters appeared, also seems to have a counterpart in the linen used for the outer perimeter or court of the sanctuary. Once its message was read this disappeared, and the children saw the Lady contemplating a large red cross surmounted with a red figure of Christ, held in her hands in an attitude of great sadness. This symbol takes on particular significance when the Letter to the Hebrews is recalled. This was written to a Jewish community in an attempt to show them that Christ's sacrificial death superseded the sacrifices of the Old Law; it argued that Christ had initiated a new priesthood, with himself as the new high priest. After describing the worship of the high priest in the sanctuary in the desert, where he went into the inner tent to offer blood for the sins of the people (Heb. 9:1–7), it goes on to state that this was only a provisional rite which awaited fulfillment by Christ. This happened when he ascended into heaven and passed into the heavenly sanctuary, offering his own sacrificial blood, the price of mankind's redemption (Heb. 9:11–14). In the apparition, the red crucifix and the figure of Christ perfectly symbolize his sacrificial death, as the new high priest, during which all his *blood* was poured out for mankind. They also indicate the essentially Christocentric nature of this apparition, that at Pontmain Mary points us to Christ, and particularly to his Cross and sufferings.[473]

While watching this the children saw a star from beneath Mary's feet light the four candles attached to the blue oval; this seems a curious symbolism until the fact that there were three other lights is recalled. These were the three stars positioned a little way from the Lady's head, and this makes a total of seven lights. This number corresponds to the seven-branched lampstand that was put inside the holy place. The lampstand also had four cups shaped as almond blossoms; these may more directly represent the candles, since Aaron's rod or branch, which will be dealt with further on, also has a Marian symbolism; this rod sprouted ripe almonds, so providing another link with the lampstand. The red crucifix then disappeared and two small white crosses appeared on her shoulders. As incredible as it might seem, these also have a counterpart in the dress of the high priest, specifically concerning the ephod, which had shoulder straps to which were affixed two precious stones set in gold with the names of the twelve tribes, six on each stone. All of this seems to indicate that Pontmain has a very clear and striking typological link with this particular biblical account, that of the high priest and the sanctuary of the Ark of the Covenant in the desert.[474]

The passage quoted above from the Letter to the Hebrews (9:1–7), mentions Aaron's branch as one of the items kept in the Ark, and this provides us with a link between Mary and Aaron as high priest. During the journey through the wilderness, there was a rebellion against Moses and Aaron led by Korah, Dathan, Abiram and two hundred and fifty other leaders of the Israelites, for which they were put to death by God. The next day the people began to complain against Moses and Aaron, holding them responsible for the deaths, and this caused God to threaten to destroy the whole community for their perversity. Moses told Aaron to hurry and perform a rite of expiation for the people, and this succeeded in stopping a plague that had broken out among them, although over fourteen thousand had died. To stop further disputes over the status of Aaron and the priesthood, God told Moses to take a branch for each tribe, including one for Aaron's tribe, Levi, and put them in the Tent of Meeting. When Moses returned the next day, he found that Aaron's branch had sprouted, producing buds, flowers and almonds, while the other branches had remained unchanged (Num. 16–17:1–11).

We can now consider some quotations from the early Christian writers on the significance of this blossoming of Aaron's branch. St Ambrose makes this observation about the branch or rod and Mary: "She is the rod which brings forth a flower. For she is pure, and her virginity is directed to God with a free heart and is not deflected by the dissipation of worldly cares."[475] Similarly, St Ephrem sees a connection between Mary and the blossoming rod of Aaron. "The staff of Aaron sprouted, and the dry wood brought forth; his symbol has been explained today—it is the virgin womb that gave birth."[476] St Gregory the Great (c.540–604) also connects Mary's virginity and Aaron's rod or staff: "Consider it carefully, please, and tell me, if you can: ... how did the dry staff of Aaron flower; how did the Virgin, Aaron's descendant, conceive and remain a virgin, even in giving birth?"[477] In addition, Aaron's branch or rod was put in the Ark of the Covenant, further increasing its Marian symbolism.

A "Triptych" of Marian Apparitions

In the account of the apparition at La Salette there are indications of a typological connection between Mary's appearance and the garb of the Jewish high priest. As we have seen, the typology at Pontmain suggests a similar connection, and both apparitions are linked to the two accounts given in Exodus of the sanctuary and its ministers. La Salette thus corresponds with Exodus chapters 25—31, while aspects of Pontmain parallel chapters 35—40. The *description* of vestments of the high priest (Exod. 29), which Moses received on the mountain, provides the biblical typology for Mary's appearance at La Salette in 1846; the actual *construction* of the sanctuary and the institution of the priesthood (Exod. 35—40), provide the typology for Mary's appearance and actions at Pontmain in 1871, twenty-five years later. The fact that the apparition at La Salette took place on a high mountain, while that at Pontmain took place on level ground, further emphasizes the typological link with these sections of Exodus. That leaves chapters 32 to 34 in the middle, and, if the typological ideas followed in this book have any significance, then we should expect those chapters to be related in some way to the events at Lourdes in 1858, and Marian themes generally.

This is exactly what we find. First, in these middle chapters there is the account of Moses successfully acting as intercessor for the people after they had fallen into idolatry over the golden calf, just as Mary acts as an intercessor and mediator for mankind (Exod. 32). Then, we have the account of the Tent of Meeting, which was outside the camp, and to which Moses would go to see God "face to face." As already indicated, this parallels the location of the grotto at Lourdes, which was situated outside the town (Exod. 33:7–11). The next section again shows Moses interceding for the people (Exod. 33:12–17), a process repeated further on (Exod. 34: 8–9). We also have the account of Moses asking God to "show him his glory," to which he replied that it was not possible for man to see his face and live, but that he would put him "in a cleft of the rock," until he had passed by (Exod. 33:19–23).

As has already been pointed out, this reference to a "cleft" in the rock, parallels one of the most distinctive features of Lourdes, that Mary chose to appear in the "cleft" or niche of the grotto at Massabielle. Similarly, the order to Moses that none of the people should approach the mountain (Exod. 34:3) corresponds with the prohibition against the crowds' going near the site of the apparitions made by the authorities at Lourdes. In addition, God pronounced his name before Moses (Exod. 34:5–7), just as Mary pronounced her name, "the Immaculate Conception," before Bernadette. Finally, when Moses came down from the mountain his face was shining, and he continued to wear a veil before the people (Exod. 34:29–35). This accords with the complete change in the aspect of Bernadette's face when she was looking at Mary during the apparitions.

So these three, La Salette, Lourdes, and Pontmain, apparently form a "triptych" of Marian apparitions. A triptych is a three-leaved hinged tablet, often decorated with holy images, of which the middle image is usually the most important. In the same way, Lourdes is the middle apparition between La Salette and Pontmain, and is certainly the most important of the three. Typology suggests that the passages from Exodus dealt with above, chapters 25—31, 32—34, and 35—40, form an ordered sequence which exactly parallels the three apparitions. The central focus at Lourdes was Mary's Immaculate Conception, the focus of nineteenth-century Marian thinking generally. The typology previously examined shows that La Salette and Pontmain are intimately linked with Lourdes, and that Moses and his activities provide a unifying typology and thematic structure for these three apparitions. We can probably also include some of the other Marian apparitions within this general outline. This is certainly the case with the apparitions at the Rue du Bac to Catherine Labouré in 1830, where the theme of the Immaculate Conception was also very prominent.

Catherine Labouré's Last Years and Death

During these earlier apparitions the Blessed Virgin had given Catherine Labouré to understand that the bloody events referred to during the first apparition, that of 18 July 1830, would take place in forty years' time, that is, in 1870. The Third French Republic came into being in 1870, and soon encountered a vicious revolution in Paris, in March 1871, organized by members of the Commune. Although strictly speaking not Communists, they had certainly been influenced by the ideas of Marx and anarchism generally, while a substantial proportion were the intellectual descendants of the Revolution; Freemasonry was also a malign background influence. Whatever their exact beliefs, the ideology of the Communards was distinctly anti-religious. During their short period of power in Paris, they desecrated churches, arrested clergy and were responsible for the deaths of thirty priests, including the archbishop. Although Catherine's community was threatened, as Mary had promised, they were protected from harm; but on Ascension Thursday, 18 May, the church of Our Lady of Victories was broken into and desecrated by a mob. When Catherine heard of it she remarked: "They have touched Our Lady. They'll go no further."[478] In fact the revolution was near its end, and on 21 May, Republican troops closed in on the area controlled by the Commune: once its power was destroyed, Marshal MacMahon became President of the Third Republic.[479] This short-lived socialist insurrection was an attempt to turn the clock back to revolutionary times, as far as the Church was concerned; and the episode, though it was quickly ended, was a salutary reminder that such ideas were a growing and dangerous force.[480]

There was something of a religious revival at this point, and pilgrimages to various shrines, including Lourdes, became popular, while the Miraculous Medal had become very well known:

by this stage it is estimated that more than one thousand million had been distributed world-wide. By 1874, Catherine's health had greatly deteriorated, her arthritis having worsened; and she seems to have had some type of asthmatic condition, as well as heart problems. In 1876, convinced that she would soon die, and having prayed over the matter, she approached the new Superior of her house, Sister Dufès, to break her silence and tell her the whole story of the apparitions. When the Superior remarked that she was highly favored, Catherine replied: "I was nothing but an instrument. It was not for me that the Blessed Virgin appeared. I did not even know how to write ... and if the Blessed Virgin chose me, an ignoramus, it was in order that no one should be able to doubt her." She was asked to write out another account of the apparitions, and predicted that she would die before the end of the year; her death came on 31 December, and, most unusually, she had no death-agony of any kind, passing away peacefully.[481]

It seems that Catherine made many predictions that came true, and one in particular is fascinating because of an apparent link to the prophecy of Mary at Fatima, that the world would eventually be granted a period of peace; although it could also refer to the time after the proclamation of the dogma of the Assumption in 1950. She is reported to have said: "Oh, how wonderful it will be to hear, 'Mary is Queen of the Universe ...' It will be a time of peace, joy and good fortune that will last long; she will be carried as a banner and she will make a tour of the world."[482] Possibly, this may also refer to a future time when Mary's Queenship is proclaimed as a dogma.

Once Catherine was dead, there was no need to keep secret her identity as the seer of the Miraculous Medal, and word quickly spread as crowds converged on the house. Catherine was buried in a vault beneath the chapel, and almost immediately accounts of miracles at her tomb began to circulate, following the healing of a paralyzed boy, who was lowered by ropes into the vault. In 1895 attempts were made to establish a feast day for the Miraculous Medal, and at the same time the first steps were taken towards Catherine's beatification. It was not, though, until the rediscovery of Mgr de Quélen's canonical inquiry of 1836, which had been lost, that real progress was made, and she was eventually beatified in May 1933, just a few months after the apparitions at Banneux and Beauraing in Belgium.

At this point, Catherine's body, which had been in the grave for fifty-seven years, was exhumed and transferred to the Rue du Bac convent, where her coffin was opened in the presence of the Archbishop of Paris. There was general astonishment at finding her body perfectly preserved, her eyes still blue and her limbs supple. Fourteen years later, in July 1947, she was finally declared a saint, not, as Pope Pius XII made clear, because she had seen apparitions of Mary, but because she had done her duties with heroic love and devotion, living a life of supreme humility just as St Bernadette had done. The tremendous impact of the Miraculous Medal, however, was probably of influence, as a proof of her mission and sanctity. Modern church approval for Catherine's apparitions and the Medal came in May 1980, when Pope John Paul II visited the chapel at the Rue du Bac to pray before the statue of the Virgin with the globe, where Catherine's incorrupt body is still preserved in a shrine.[483]

The Miraculous Picture of Pompeii

The events at Pompeii in Italy, which center around a miraculous picture of Mary and the Child Jesus, while not really as prominent as the major Marian apparitions, are of interest, and there are also indications of a link with the typology surrounding the Ark of the Covenant. Pompeii, near Naples in southern Italy, was the ancient city destroyed by the volcanic eruption of Mount Vesuvius in AD 79. During the seventeenth century, the area was affected by malaria and became practically deserted, the haunt of bandits and a lawless and superstitious place, with few practising Catholics. In 1872 Bartolo Longo came to the area to investigate some property, and was shocked to discover how abandoned the valley of Pompeii was. He was also struggling with his own doubts about his Christian faith. While walking through the parish on 9 October, he distinctly heard a voice say to him: "If you seek salvation, promulgate the Rosary. This is Mary's own promise."[484]

Amazed, Bartolo promised to do what he could to promote the rosary; just then the noonday Angelus rang out and he knelt in confirmation of his pledge. He decided to found a rosary confraternity and planned a festive mission for the next year, but for various reasons this was not a success. However, in 1874, and the following year, in November 1875, this festival did succeed in attracting many people, including the local bishop, who proposed that the populace should be ambitious and aim to raise not just a new altar to Mary in their chapel, but a whole new church. He went further and even prophesied that a basilica would also be raised in Pompeii, a prophecy that was later fulfilled.

Bartolo Longo was determined to do something to ensure that

the local people would continue with the recitation of the rosary at the end of the three day mission at the church, and so he decided to buy a picture of Mary to expose for veneration. The first picture he chose, though, did not accord with canon law, since it was not an oil painting on canvas or wood, so on the last day of the mission, he had to travel to Naples and find a new picture. The only suitable painting, however, was far too expensive, and so he was forced to accept a very cheap and inferior work from a friend, which had been bought for a pittance in a junk shop. It was worm-eaten and Mary was depicted with a very coarse-looking face, while the two saints flanking her, St Dominic and St Rose, who was later changed for St Catherine of Siena, were far from satisfactory. Bartolo hesitated about accepting it, but since he had promised the people he would bring back a picture of Mary for them by that evening, he eventually acquiesced.[485]

The painting was too large to be carried by hand, and so Bartolo arranged for it to be wrapped in a sheet and delivered by cart. It eventually reached the chapel in Pompeii, after being transported on top of a load of manure, the only transport available. In January 1876, the picture was partially restored for the canonical foundation of the Confraternity, held on 13 February, and it was further improved in 1879. Meanwhile a reputation for miraculous healings had begun to grow around it. A young girl of twelve, Clorinda Lucarelli, was afflicted by a particularly severe form of epilepsy, which threatened her life. Some of her relatives heard of the proposed building of the new church and vowed to help if she was cured; she was in fact miraculously restored to health. Similarly another young girl, who was dying in agony, was restored to health through the intercession of Our Lady of Pompeii. On the day the cornerstone of the new church was laid, 8 May 1876, a priest who was dying from gangrene, Fr Anthony Varone, was completely cured of his illness, to the extent that he was able to say Mass the next day.

A month later a fourth miracle was recorded when Madame Giovannina Muta was cured of advanced consumption. She was persuaded to put her trust in Mary, and on 8 June, while lying in bed, saw an apparition of her as she appeared in the picture. Mary gazed at Giovannina and threw her a white ribbon with the message: "The Virgin of Pompeii grants your request, Giovannina Muta." Immediately the woman felt herself regaining strength as she was completely cured. These are just some of the many miracles recorded at the shrine, and soon the image was covered with diamonds and gems offered in thanksgiving.[486]

One cure in particular is important, because it concerns a definite apparition of Mary, and also because of the emphasis it gives
to the rosary. A young girl from Naples, Fortuna Agrelli, was suffering from a painful, incurable disease. Doctors had declared her
case hopeless and on 16 February 1884, along with some of her
relatives, she began a novena of rosaries for her cure. On 3 March,
Mary appeared to the girl as Our Lady of Pompeii, sitting on a
throne, with the child Jesus on her lap, and holding a rosary. She
was attended by St Catherine of Siena and St Dominic. Fortuna
marveled at the beauty of Mary and asked her as "Queen of the
Rosary," for her cure. Mary replied that, since she had called her
by a title that was so pleasing to her, she could not refuse her
request; she then told her to make three novenas of the rosary to
obtain all she asked for. The child was indeed cured, and soon
after Mary appeared to her again saying; "Whosoever desires to
obtain favors from me should make three novenas of the prayers of
the Rosary in petition and three novenas in thanksgiving." This is
how the Rosary Novenas devotion to Mary originated. It involves
saying five decades of the rosary each day for 27 days in petition,
and another five decades each day for the succeeding 27 days in
thanksgiving, making a total of 54 days.[487]

The new church was finished and then enlarged as successive
popes honored it, until in 1934 Pope Pius XI ordered that a new
basilica be built; this was completed under Pope Pius XII in 1939,
just in time for World War II, when Italy faced such troubled times.
Pompeii definitely seems to have acted as a herald of Fatima,
particularly in its emphasis on the rosary, and so it seems that it
should rightly take its place amongst the approved apparitions of
Mary, even though the main emphasis is on the miraculous
picture.[488] Pompeii has received more recent support, in that Pope
John Paul II declared Bartolo Longo Blessed on 26 October
1980.[489]

In terms of typology, Pompeii seems to have some affinities with
the account of David bringing the Ark of the Covenant up to
Jerusalem (2 Sam. 6). David and his men transported the Ark on a
new cart from the house of Abinadab, where it had been kept, but,
as has already been outlined, Abinadab's son Uzzah was killed by
God for touching the Ark (2 Sam. 6:7). There is an interesting
parallel here with the way the painting was brought to Pompeii on
a *cart*, just as in the case of the Ark on its original journey to the
house of Obed-edom. The picture itself, with its image of Mary and
the Child Jesus flanked by the two saints, Dominic and Catherine

of Siena, is also suggestive of the Ark of the Covenant with its accompanying cherubim, in that Mary typifies the Ark. The several moves of the picture also seem reminiscent of the way the Ark was moved by David and his heir Solomon: it was moved to the new church in Pompeii, just as David moved the Ark to Jerusalem, and the picture was again moved to the new basilica at Pompeii, as likewise the Ark was finally housed in the Temple built by Solomon.

David is of course closely associated with the Psalter, the one hundred and fifty psalms found in the Bible, some of which he undoubtedly composed himself; these one hundred and fifty psalms are a type of the rosary with its one hundred and fifty Hail Marys. So at Pompeii there is a possible connection between the promulgation of the rosary and the biblical psalms. All of this indicates some sort of typological connection between Pompeii and the Ark of the Covenant at the time of David, but this link is not as strong as in the case of the major apparitions, given that the main emphasis is on the miraculous picture. This seems to equate with the fact that Pompeii is not well known in international terms.[490]

The Apparition at Knock

Ireland had suffered grievously for the Faith in the centuries following the Reformation, and this pattern was to continue in the nineteenth century. The country had been united to England by the Act of Union in 1801, and many attempts, both constitutional and revolutionary, were made to end this union during the nineteenth century, but without success. Catholic emancipation in 1829 brought an improvement in some respects, but the Great Famine of 1845–49 was a major disaster, which changed the face of Ireland permanently. The failure of the potato crop, the staple food of two-thirds of the Irish population of eight million, and the lack of any real assistance from the English Government, meant that over a million and half people died of hunger and disease, and nearly another million emigrated, mostly to America. The century was also marked by conflicts between landlords and tenants, as the Irish tried to establish the most basic human rights for themselves. Disillusionment with English policies led many to see armed rebellion as the only solution to Ireland's problems. That the bitterness felt by many could have been translated into revolutionary violence is not an impossibility given the sufferings of the people. The Fenians, a secret republican group, were formed in America in 1858, and began to use force to gain their ends, blowing up a jail in London in 1867. The Land League was founded by Michael Davitt in 1879, and, by means of rent strikes and boycotts, sought to improve conditions for the poor, who often could not afford rents and were liable to eviction from their homes at any time. Its first great meeting took place in Irishtown, Co. Mayo, in April 1879, only a matter of months before the apparition at Knock, and so it was during this potentially explosive period that Mary chose to visit and console the poor Catholics of Ireland.[491]

At the time Knock was a remote village in Mayo, in the west of Ireland, consisting of a dozen poor houses scattered around the little church, with its people trying to eke out a living in quite harsh conditions, a situation shared by their priest, Archdeacon Cavanagh. He had a reputation for holiness, and it became known later that he had only just completed one hundred Masses for the holy souls in purgatory on the morning of the apparition. He also had a great devotion to Mary.[492] He ministered to his flock from a church dedicated to St John the Baptist, which had been built about half a century previously and given a strangely prophetic inscription: "Matt. 11 Chapt. *My house shall be called the house of prayer to all nations. Ps. 117. This is the gate of the Lord: the just shall enter it.*"[493] A storm had badly damaged the church the previous year, and new statues, including one of Our Lady of Lourdes, had been ordered; these were placed in the simply ornamented building.[494]

Thursday, 21 August 1879, was a working day as usual for the inhabitants of Knock, and Archdeacon Cavanagh spent the day visiting outlying parishioners, arriving home at about seven in the evening, drenched through by the heavy rain that had begun to fall. He sat in front of the fire trying to dry his clothes, and somewhat later his housekeeper, Mary McLoughlin, left the presbytery to visit a friend, walking past the church on her way. As she did so, she was surprised to see strange luminous figures, and an altar, at the gable end of the church, but thought they must have been more statues ordered by the priest. Why he had left them out in the rain was a mystery to her and she thought the whole thing a bit strange, but she continued on to Mrs Margaret Beirne's house. This friend's daughter, also called Margaret, had returned from locking the church at about 7:30, and although she too saw something luminous on the south gable, she likewise hurried on home without stopping. Some time after that another witness, a Mrs Hugh Flatley, a widow, also saw what she thought were more statues as she came round the side of the church; but she too continued without giving the matter further thought. The heavy rain probably discouraged these women from closer investigation.[495]

Mary McLoughlin did not mention what she had seen to Mrs Beirne, since the latter had just returned from a brief holiday and there was plenty of news to catch up with. Apart from young Margaret, those present that evening were Mrs Beirne's twenty-year-old son Dominick, Mary, an older daughter, and another young relative. Mary McLoughlin eventually rose to return to the presbytery and Mary Beirne offered to walk with her part of the way. They set off in the rain, but as they grew nearer the church, Mary Beirne noticed the figures at the gable and cried out: "Look at the beautiful figures!"[496] Mary McLoughlin professed ignorance, but didn't think they had been put there by the priest.[497]

As they got nearer, however, the brilliance of the light around the gable, despite the fact that there was still daylight in the evening sky, made them aware that they were seeing something extraordinary. Both women stood in amazement as they realized that they were not looking at statues at all, but at strange moving figures. A wall enclosed the grassy church grounds, and between it and the gable end they could see three figures, seemingly standing above the tall grass, a few feet away from the church wall. Mary McLoughlin was surprised to notice that neither the wall nor the ground near the figures was wet, despite the steadily falling rain. They immediately recognized the central figure as Mary, and the one on the left as St Joseph, while Mary Beirne thought that the one on the right resembled a statue of St John the Evangelist she had once seen, in addition to the fact that this figure wore a miter. After some time Mary Beirne went off to fetch her family, and they soon came back with her to stand in wonder before the church wall, as it gradually got darker and the rain continued to fall in torrents. Other neighbors were alerted and also joined the group, and it is probable that many of the villagers saw the apparition at various times during that evening, although only fifteen eyewitnesses were officially examined.[498]

They stood entranced as the brilliant golden light, with which the figures were enveloped, shimmered and seemed to rise and subside. Most of them saw an altar behind the figures bearing a large cross in front of a young lamb, and one young boy saw angels with wings fluttering over this tableau. The figures themselves wore beautiful white garments, and Mary also wore a crown and stood with her hands raised almost like a priest when saying Mass, gazing at the heavens, her lips moving in what the witnesses took to be prayer. One old lady, full of joy at what she was seeing, tried to grasp Mary's feet, but, despite the lifelike and natural appearance of the apparition, felt nothing. The witnesses could see St Joseph inclining his head towards Mary in an attitude of reverence, while St John was dressed as a bishop, holding a book in his left hand, with his right hand raised as though preaching or teaching. One boy, Patrick Hill, went close enough to see the writing in the book, but like the other witnesses he heard no sounds or voices.[499]

He gave the most detailed information about the apparition, and those who interviewed him found him an intelligent and helpful witness. This is his description of Mary:

> I distinctly beheld the Blessed Virgin Mary, life size, standing about two feet or so above the ground, clothed in white robes, which were fastened at the neck; her hands were raised to the height of the shoulders, as if in prayer, with the palms facing one another, but slanting inwards towards the face; ... she appeared to be praying; her eyes were turned, as I saw, towards heaven; she wore a brilliant crown on her head, and over her forehead, where the crown fitted the brow, a beautiful rose; the crown appeared brilliant, and of a golden brightness, of a deeper hue, inclined to a mellow yellow, than the striking whiteness of the robes she wore; the upper part of the crown appeared to be a series of sparkles, or glittering crosses.[500]

After about an hour, Mary McLoughlin hurried back to the presbytery to tell Archdeacon Cavanagh what was happening, but for some reason he did not realize the importance of what she was saying, and so remained at home. By about eleven o'clock the witnesses were tired and soaked through, and some of the men went home. One woman, Judith Campbell, was worried about her mother, who was dying, and, after going to check, rushed back to say she was dead. The remaining witnesses followed her, but discovered that she was only unconscious and was actually to live until the next day; but by the time they returned to the church the mysterious light and the figures had disappeared.

Next morning the priest learned what had happened and questioned some of the witnesses; it was also discovered that a local farmer named Patrick Walsh, who lived about half a mile away, had seen a great light on the south gable of the church about nine o'clock the previous evening.[501] This is his description of what he saw:

> It was a very dark night. It was raining heavily. About nine o'clock on that night, I was going on some business through my land, and standing a distance of about half a mile from the chapel, I saw a very bright light on the southern gable-end of the

chapel; it appeared to be a large globe of golden light; I never saw, I thought, so brilliant a light before; it appeared high up in the air above and around the chapel gable, and it was circular in its appearance; it was quite stationary, and it seemed to retain the same brilliancy all through. The following day I made inquiries in order to learn if there were any lights seen in the place that night; it was only then that I heard of the Vision or Apparition that the people had seen.[502]

The Symbolism of the Figures at Knock

Overall, then, unlike the situation with other apparitions such as Lourdes or La Salette, most of the witnesses at Knock were adults, and although they expressed awe and wonder at what they saw, there was nothing in the way of ecstatic experiences, as in the case of Bernadette. It is unlikely that the witnesses could have invented the story of the apparition, since they were fifteen simple and honest people, of all ages, who would soon have been trapped in mistakes and contradictions if they had been lying about their accounts, which they all insisted on until their deaths.[503]

What is even more impressive, though, is that the symbolism of the apparition, when examined in detail, exhibits much greater depth than could possibly be expected from the theologically unsophisticated inhabitants of a small nineteenth-century Irish village. The fact that they saw the figure of Mary on a slightly higher level than either that of St Joseph or St John the Evangelist, correctly expresses her spiritual exaltation over them. Similarly, the altar, lamb, and cross, symbols of Christ and his sacrificial death, were on a still higher level, indicating their supreme position, and yet they were in the background, suggesting that the focus of the apparition was on Mary and her role. The witnesses would have been familiar with statues of the Madonna and Child, or of Our Lady of Lourdes, or the image of Mary found on the Miraculous Medal; but in the Knock apparition, the pose adopted by Mary is more reminiscent of a painting of her in an attitude of prayer found in the catacombs. The position of St Joseph was of someone paying honor to Mary, whose joined hands symbolized prayer and petition. St Joseph had been declared Patron of the Universal Church in 1870 by Pope Pius IX, and so his pose in the Knock apparition could be said to have expressed this ideal.

The figure of the Christ as a lamb occurs particularly in the writings of St John the Evangelist, and he is the only Gospel writer to describe Jesus as the "Lamb of God" (John 1:29–36). John also described a vision he had in the Book of Revelation, where he saw a slain Lamb being given all power and authority. This was a reference to the sacrificial death of Christ, which resulted in his being raised to the highest possible degree of glory (Rev. 5:6–14). John describes the activities of the Lamb on more than twenty other occasions in this book, as well as the altar in the Temple of God in heaven, before which the angels ministered (cf. Rev. 6:9; 8:3, 5 etc.). The cross, of course, is the basic Christian symbol, and so these three elements, cross, lamb, and altar, are very closely associated with the writings of St John the Evangelist.

All the above points are fairly complicated ideas, though, and not the kind that ordinary country people might have invented if the apparition had been false. Moreover, the symbolism of the apparition points to a deeper association than simply that between the figures present and some themes from the New Testament. As is evident, the figure of Mary was central and so she is the main focus of the apparition, standing with her arms raised in an attitude of prayer and intercession, and her eyes turned heavenwards as a *mediator* for mankind with God. Her large crown symbolizes Queenship, and thus indicates her Assumption into heaven; and the attitude of St John, partly pointing towards her, and partly towards the altar, lamb, and cross, indicates that she had, and still has, some sort of *mediating* role in the sacrifice of Christ on the cross. Likewise, Mary's presence in the foreground indicates that we are meant to concentrate on her role, her mediation; although, of course, she in turn depends entirely on Christ, and, from a Catholic point of view, the merits of Christ's sacrifice come to mankind through the Mass. The sacrificial aspect of the Mass, as the unbloody commemoration of the events of the Last Supper and Calvary, is also present in the apparition in the symbolism of the Lamb and the altar. During the Mass, the priest holds up the consecrated host and says: "Behold the Lamb of God, who takes away the sins of the world. Happy are those who are called to his supper." Yet the Mass, important as it is, is not the central point of Knock; it seems reasonable to say that the deeper symbolism of the apparition is concerned with Mary as the Mediatrix of all graces, who has been crowned as queen of Heaven, and who intercedes for the Church.

Fr Michael Walsh, author of *The Apparition at Knock*, points out that the timing of the apparition is also significant: 1879 was the silver jubilee year of the proclamation of the Dogma of the Immaculate Conception, while August 21 was the eve of the octave of the Assumption, so the apparitions took place just before the eighth day after the feast of the Assumption on August 15. Likewise, there is apparently a connection between what happened at Knock and La Salette; on the day of the apparition, 21 August 1879, the statue of Our Lady at the French shrine was solemnly crowned by the Cardinal of Paris, who was also the Papal Legate, before a huge crowd. There is no mention of this among any of the documents concerning Knock, and, in any case, it is unlikely that ordinary country people in Ireland would have had any idea of what was going on in France before the era of the modern mass media.[504] This seems to be an example of the type of subtle links between various authentic apparitions, which often only become apparent much later.

Objections have been made to Knock on the basis that nothing was said to those present, and thus that there is not any certainty that this really was an apparition of Mary. The statements made by the witnesses, though, make it clear they had no doubt that they were seeing her, despite the fact that she was standing in an uncommon pose; similarly, there was no hesitation in identifying St Joseph, and it was only with regard to St John the Evangelist that there were any reservations. But since the symbolism of the apparition is closely associated with elements found in both John's Gospel and the Apocalypse, it is reasonable to accept that the third figure was St John. In addition, Joseph and John were the two figures most closely linked to Mary in the Gospels, Joseph as the husband who looked after her and Jesus, and John as the "beloved" disciple who took care of her after Jesus' death. Hence, if any figures were to appear with Mary, we might expect to find these two. The fact that no verbal message was delivered is not a strong objection to Knock, considering the powerful meaning of the symbols found in the apparition. It would have taken many words from Mary to convey the complicated ideas expressed in the apparition, and the dramatic tableau is a good example of the adage that a "picture is worth a thousand words." In any event, God is completely free to make use of symbolism, rather than words, in order to deliver his message.[505]

Investigating the Apparition

For the rest of his life, Archdeacon Cavanagh regretted that he had not seen the apparition, but consoled himself with the thought that it was undoubtedly God's will that only the ordinary poor people should have had that privilege. The news spread rapidly, despite the fact that the local and national papers accepted a request not to publicize the events at Knock from the local clergy, many of whom were sceptical and disapproving. The archbishop of Tuam, Dr McHale, quickly set up a commission of enquiry, with nine priests questioning the witnesses and recording their answers. Regrettably, the original documents from this commission have not survived, and the accounts we now have, which agree substantially, were first published in booklet form in 1880. This publication, *The Apparitions and Miracles at Knock*, by John MacPhilpin, was accepted by the 1936 commission as faithful to the original accounts. It is apparent from the way the depositions of the witnesses are worded, that they represent summaries of a process of question and answer, and also that some of the vocabulary used would have been supplied by the commissioners. This, however, does not affect their basic validity.[506]

One theory advanced to explain the apparition was that it was due to someone painting the figures on the church wall with some type of phosphorescent or luminous paint. This was an idea favored by a Dr Francis Lennon, a physics lecturer at Maynooth seminary, who was asked by the commission to examine possible ways in which the image could have been made. But this explanation is incompatible with the evidence of Mary McLoughlin, who saw the apparition in daylight, apart from the fact that no trace of any paint was found on the wall. Tests were also carried out with a magic-lantern, a sort of slide projector, which showed that it was impossible that the apparition could have been produced by means of shining an image on the church wall. This did not, however, prevent Dr Lennon from assuming a negative attitude towards the apparition, and as he held an important position, he strongly influenced other clergy.[507]

The evidence given by Mrs Flatley, who saw the figures from the side as full and rounded, also argues against the use of luminous paint or a magic lantern,[508] as does this explicit testimony from Patrick Hill:

> After we prayed awhile I thought it right to go across the wall and into the chapel yard. I brought little [John] Curry with me; I went then up closer; I saw everything distinctly. The figures were full and round, as if they had a body and life; they said nothing, but as we approached, they seemed to go back a little towards the gable.[509]

The commission concluded that the testimony of the witnesses was reliable and trustworthy, but Archbishop McHale, who was aged and unwell, made no definitive statement for or against Knock.[510]

The general situation in Ireland, and an exaggerated prudence on the part of the Irish Church, is the probable explanation, although it seems that the Archbishop personally believed in the reality of the apparition. He died in 1881, in his nineties, and his successor refused to take a definite position regarding Knock.[511] The situation for the church authorities was complicated by the memory of the way Catholics had been so viciously persecuted for their beliefs by successive English governments, without education, unable to own land, barred from the professions, and forbidden even to attend Mass, which was regarded as a "conspiracy." All this had the effect of making people wary of doing anything that would renew persecution; and with some Irish bishops closer than others to the authorities, there were divisions within the Catholic body itself. In such as situation, it is perhaps not surprising that the clergy reacted with indecision and sometimes hostility towards Knock.[512]

Meanwhile large crowds of pilgrims had begun to arrive, drawn by the apparition and the reports of miracles resulting from drinking water in which scraps of the cement from the gable wall had been immersed. One young girl was cured of deafness by having a piece of this cement put in her ear, and within a year it was claimed that up to six hundred miraculous cures had taken place. Although many of them could not be medically verified, medical testimony has been preserved in some cases indicating that extraordinary cures did apparently take place. The general tendency of people, who regarded their cure as miraculous, was not to want to undergo medical tests in case it seemed as though they were doubting what had happened, and thus questioning God's power.[513]

The *Daily Telegraph* sent a reporter who also tried, and failed, to show that the apparition was due to a magic-lantern projection. He and other correspondents were impressed by the quality of some of the witnesses of the apparition, particularly Patrick Hill and Mary Beirne. In 1880, as had happened at Lourdes, there were reports of strange visions and happenings at Knock, and these tended to cause confusion, although they turned out to have no significance. Nevertheless, they gave those opposed to Knock another reason for voicing their antagonism, which became quite marked, especially in the anti-Catholic press, both in Ireland and England. All of this contributed to diminishing the number of pilgrims to Knock towards the end of the century, and it was not until the 1920s that real interest began to grow again,[514] when, in 1929, the then

Archbishop of Tuam took part in ceremonies at Knock for the first time. In a reference to the 1879 commission, he explained that, since the Church had given no definitive ruling on Knock, people were free to accept the apparition if they wished. In 1936, another commission was set up to examine the three surviving witnesses. Mary Beirne, who had now become Mrs Mary O'Connell, was eighty-one years of age when interviewed, but strongly reaffirmed the evidence she had earlier given, ending with the words: "I am quite clear about everything I have said, and I make this statement knowing I am going before my God." Patrick Beirne and John Curry, who were young boys when they encountered the apparition, were again interviewed and both were judged to have trustworthily recollected what they had seen.[515]

This commission examined eight reported cures, including cases of tuberculosis and clubfeet, as well as a lady suffering from Pott's disease, which affects the spine, and which had left her completely incapacitated. She had visited Knock in 1925 and the next day could walk again, eventually resuming an active life. This case had full medical documentation, including the judgment that her condition was inoperable; and some of the other cures were likewise regarded as inexplicable in scientific terms. After three years' work, the findings of the commission were submitted to the Vatican with a request for some form of recognition, although no public statement was issued by the then archbishop, Dr Gilmartin. Over time, this recognition was forthcoming, according to the usual Vatican custom, through the granting of certain privileges to the Shrine, culminating in a special Mass of Our Lady of Knock in 1972. A new basilica was built in the seventies, just in time for the visit of Pope John Paul II in 1979, the centenary year of the apparitions, and an event that indicated effective church approval of Knock.[516]

Mary as the Ark of the Covenant

It might appear difficult to relate the apparition at Knock to a particular biblical theme or incident, particularly since nothing was said and there was no message as such, but it seems, as in the case of Pompeii, that Knock symbolically represents Mary as the Ark of the Covenant; many passages from the Church Fathers and early writers describe her in this way.

St Hippolytus of Rome (d. 235) was the first to link the Ark with Mary: "Now the Lord was without sin, being in his human nature from incorruptible wood, that is from the Virgin, and being sheathed, as it were, with the pure gold of the Word within and of the Spirit without."[517] St Athanasius too compared Mary with the Ark in very fulsome terms:

> Truly, O noble Virgin, you are great above all greatness; who indeed can compare with your greatness; O dwelling-place of the Word of God? With whom shall I compare you among all creatures? You are evidently greater than all of them. O Ark of the covenant surrounded totally and purely on all sides with gold! You are the Ark containing all gold, the receptacle of the true manna, that is human nature wherein the divinity resides.[518]

Chrysippus of Jerusalem (*c.*405–79), also compared Mary with the Ark: "The truly royal Ark, the most precious Ark, was the ever-Virgin *Theotokos*; the Ark which received the treasure of all sanctification."[519] Other writers, including St Andrew of Crete (*c.*660–740), Hesychius, Severus of Antioch, and St John Damascene, similarly applied the typology of the Ark to Mary,[520] as did Proclus, who wrote: "Mary is venerated because she became ... the ark of the Lord."[521]

Solomon became king of Israel after David, inheriting an impressive empire and all the materials necessary for the building of the Temple, as a suitable dwelling-place for God. No expense was spared and a beautiful and elaborate building was erected with an inner *debir* or "Holy of Holies," where the Ark of the Covenant was to be kept. Inside the *debir*, Solomon placed two cherubim, "great winged creatures," with similar decorations, as well as carved rosettes and palm trees on the Temple walls, and everything was covered with gold (1 Kings 6). The Ark was then brought to the Temple, and before all the elders and men of Israel "countless" sheep and oxen were sacrificed, as the Ark, containing only the stone tablets of the Law given to Moses, was placed by the priests in the *debir*, under the wings of the cherubim. Then a cloud, the glory of the Lord, filled the Temple, forcing the priests to leave as Solomon praised God (1 Kings 8:6–7,10–13).

Some interesting comparisons can be made between this account of the arrival of the Ark and the apparition at Knock. Solomon assembled all Israel as the Ark was brought into the *debir*, and in the same way a collection of people, of a wide variety of ages, representing in microcosm Irish Catholicism, was assembled before the *church* wall at Knock. This in itself is very unusual, since at no other recognized Marian apparition do we find both adults and children privileged to see the apparition, nor, apart from Rue du Bac and L'Ile Bouchard, do we find an apparition so closely connected with a church building. This fact indicates that we are meant to understand an underlying theme of *worship* at Knock; and this too is precisely what we find regarding Solomon's Temple, a building that was basically the equivalent of a large church, where God's presence was manifested and he was worshiped. We are told that Solomon sacrificed countless sheep and oxen before the Ark, and at Knock the people saw a young lamb on the sacrificial altar in front of the cross. Inside the Holy of Holies there was an altar overlaid with gold, positioned before the Ark (1 Kings 6:21), and some of the witnesses commented on the brilliant "golden" light they saw surrounding the figures.[522] In addition, Solomon's attitude, as he prayed facing the altar with his arms stretched out towards heaven, (1 Kings 8:22), seems to recall Mary's prayerful attitude at Knock, standing with her hands raised to her shoulders and with her gaze fixed on heaven.

Regarding the cherubim with outstretched wings placed over the Ark, Patrick Hill testified that "around the Lamb I saw angels hovering during the whole time, for the space of an hour and a half or longer; I saw their wings fluttering, but I did not perceive their heads or faces, which were not turned to me."[523]

The priests were responsible for bringing the Ark of the Covenant into the Holy of Holies, and St John, who was standing to one side of Mary, was wearing a miter in the apparition and so represented a bishop, and thus the priesthood. St Joseph might well correspond with the leaders of Israel, since, as "the just man," he certainly summed up in himself the best of the patriarchal tradition of the Old Testament.

Finally, several witnesses commented on how, although it was raining heavily, neither the apparition nor the ground beneath it were wet. One, Dominick Beirne, commented that: "The night was dark and raining, and yet these images, in the dark night, appeared with bright lights as plain as under the noonday sun. At the time, it was pitch dark and raining heavily, and yet there was not one drop of rain near the images."[524] Another witness, seventy-five-year-old Bridget Trench, said that: "It was raining very heavily at the time, but no rain fell where the figures were. I felt the ground carefully with my hands, and it was perfectly dry. The wind was blowing from the south, right against the gable of the chapel, but no rain fell on that portion of the gable or chapel in which the figures were."[525] Perhaps there is an echo here of Gideon's fleece which remained dry when the ground all around it was wet, and thus a subtle connection between Knock and the dogma of the Immaculate Conception.

14

Social Revolution, World War, and Communism

The Nineteenth-Century Assault on the Church

The nineteenth century saw tremendous changes as the political and social effects of the French Revolution, and the subsequent revolutionary episodes in 1830, 1848, and 1871, were carried forward and combined with the results of industrialization. A new technical and scientifically-based society began to develop, one that it was hoped would lead to greater prosperity and happiness for all, but which, in practice, led to a breakdown in traditional social, religious, and moral values, as capitalistic and free market ideals predominated.[526] Great material advances were accompanied by the most extreme exploitation, in which liberal thinkers, supported by the new commercial and industrial interests, pushed for the complete abolition of economic restrictions, as the old order was progressively demolished. The Church tended to support this old order and so there was a continual conflict between Christianity and liberalism, although it should be noted that liberalism itself had assumed different forms in the various European countries.

On the continent, and especially in France, liberalism was often openly anticlerical and opposed to religion, while in England it was strongly influenced by Nonconformism and religious ideals generally; nationalism confused the picture still further, while some liberal elements were moving towards a more openly socialist stance. This general movement, however, involved a belief that social problems could be solved by a realignment of society through a union of science and industry, following the principles of the new rationalized, humanistic religion. These ideas were carried to their logical conclusion by revolutionary Marxism.

The last part of the nineteenth century, then, saw Western culture turn to materialism, as evolutionary theories were applied to the struggles between the various classes and nations, with a belief that only the fittest would survive.[527] This was particularly the case in Germany, a country whose defects became more obvious as time went on. Its appearance of constitutionalism masked the reality of Prussian dominance; the new empire was really an autocracy where the army had far too much power, and this allowed a militaristic ethos to emerge, one that was hostile to the development of true democracy. The principal architect of this state of affairs was Bismarck.[528]

This ethos, though, was also a product of the thinking of men such as Friedrich Nietzsche (1844–1900), who, basing himself on an evolutionary philosophy, abandoned Christian morality in favor of a ruthless attitude to the weak and helpless. He pursued the ideal of the "Superman," one that equated goodness with power and evil with weakness, while exalting war. Nietzsche's radical atheism led him to see Christianity as the most extreme example of the degradation of mankind. He regarded Christian virtues, such as pity for the less fortunate, as meaningless and loathsome, while proclaiming his belief in the "death of God," hoping that all this would lead to the assertion of man in a new climate of pessimistic atheistic humanism. This philosophy was very influential and was used to justify cruelty, hostility, and other forms of inhumanity, including slavery. Ludwig Feuerbach (1804–72) was another important philosopher who saw belief in God as belittling, advocating, in effect, rebellion against God.[529] These pessimistic German philosophies culminated in the negative attitude that gripped the country in the years leading up to the First World War. These theories, and particularly those of Nietzsche, filled the vacuum left by the collapse in religious beliefs in Europe with a new ideology based on his idea of the "will to power," a principle later exploited by totalitarian dictators, such as Hitler (1889–1945).[530]

It is thus not an exaggeration to describe the Church as being practically under a state of siege during this period. Calls for the separation of Church and State, which were really attempts to remove religious influence from society altogether, were repeatedly made and implemented by secular regimes wherever possible. The nineteenth-century attack on the Church, then, was more serious and dangerous than previous onslaughts, and ranged from restricting the Church's rights to outright persecution; but it also had, as a deeper goal, the intention of completely doing away with the idea of religion and God. This had become apparent even at the time of the French Revolution, when the intellectual revolt, begun at the Renaissance and Reformation, reached a further stage in its evolution.[531]

The Social Revolution and the Church

Nonetheless, despite these problems, Pope Leo XIII (1878–1903), wanted to build bridges between the Church and the world, and so he worked to establish contacts with as many governments as possible, while also taking measures to improve Catholic education and to re-establish contact with the ordinary workers, whose living conditions had tended to cut them off from the Church. His encyclical *Rerum Novarum,* published in 1891, advocated social measures to undo the harm caused by the prevailing economic liberalism, which had reduced workers to the level of wage-slaves, and was the main cause of the class divisions being exploited by socialism. He reiterated the age-old concept of the differing areas of concern of the Church and the State, and the basic Catholic principle that the realm of the spirit is superior to the temporal world. He also pointed out that God was the ultimate source of all law and order and that a failure to recognize this was bound to lead to subversion and revolution.[532]

Rerum Novarum was important in that it gave the highest sanction to the principle that the Church should be involved in improving the lot of ordinary workers and dealing with social problems generally; that it should once again become involved in society, even a society much changed in cultural and industrial terms, rather than holding itself aloof, as had been the tendency during the time of Pius IX. That the situation of the proletariat needed improvement, if further revolution was to be avoided, was fairly clear, particularly as worsening economic and working conditions were leading to more strikes as the end of the century approached.[533] By now, though, it was also clear that the Marxist prophecy that capitalism must eventually collapse, because of its inherent contradictions, was not coming true. In this, as in so many other respects, Marx was to prove a false prophet. Whatever its drawbacks, and they were many, capitalism was still a vital force.[534]

Rerum Novarum was a bold analysis of the problem, one that heavily criticized unrestricted capitalism for the way that it had enriched the few at the expense of the majority, who remained in poverty. This had caused increasing social divisions, especially as the workers were not protected, as in the days of the medieval guilds, and in some cases they were living in absolutely dire conditions. Although this analysis was similar to that of socialism, the latter's remedies, which included the promotion of class conflict, the abolition of private property, and a much greater role for the State, were rejected, because they would only make matters worse, as actually happened when Communism gained power in Russia and elsewhere during the twentieth century. Instead, Leo XIII advocated greater co-operation between capital and labor, the recognition of trade unions, and a greater role for the State in protecting the weak, including the provision of a "just wage," one based on the needs of a man's family rather than on purely economic factors. Thus the Pope's proposals were very farseeing and have influenced much social thought, although this has not been readily acknowledged.[535]

In Russia, the Tsar, Alexander II, was assassinated in 1881 and this led his successor, Alexander III, to crack down on liberal movements and Western-inspired ideas generally. Newspapers were banned, censorship was tightened and the Jews in particular became the victims of official repression in the pogroms of the late nineteenth century. During this period, Marxist ideas were circulating widely in the country amongst students and intellectuals, but government action drove many of them underground or into exile. This was rather like driving a disease underground, only for it to reappear in a more virulent form at a later stage, that stage being the Communist Revolution of 1917.[536]

Overall then, this period saw a united Italy, a weakened France, and a much stronger Germany, with the latter beginning to become a serious industrial competitor for Britain. France had developed along republican lines following the overthrow of the monarchy in 1870, but many Catholics felt unable to work with the new regime, maintaining their old loyalties, despite the promptings of Leo XIII. In 1886 education was secularized in France, thus helping to further the split between Catholics and liberals. All of this meant that successive French governments were set on a collision course with the Church, culminating in the closure of many Catholic schools, and the expulsion of the religious orders in 1903. This persecution was opposed to truly democratic ideals and did not last, but was a sign of the power of anticlerical thought in France at the time.[537] Freemasonry was the guiding hand behind this anti-Catholic activity.[538]

Leo XIII's successor, Pius X, (1835–1914), had to deal with the critical situation that led to the complete separation of Church and

State in France in 1905, as the anticlerical regime pushed through measures which ended up stripping the Church of all its property, thus impoverishing the clergy. This situation, however, had its good side, in that it strengthened the link between French Catholics and Rome, as well as ensuring that the priesthood was purified of those elements less concerned with spiritual matters. So, paradoxically, separation, far from destroying the French Church, led to a revival of Catholicism.[539] This revival was also connected with the great growth in devotion to Mary. This had developed particularly after the proclamation of the dogma of the Immaculate Conception by Pius IX in 1854 and the apparitions at Lourdes in 1858, following which many millions made the pilgrimage to the shrine. There was also a growth in the parallel devotion to the Sacred Heart of Jesus, symbolized by the building of the great Basilica of Sacré-Coeur on the hill of Montmartre in Paris; this was finally completed in 1912, in the face of much opposition, as an act of expiation for the evils of anticlericalism.[540] The struggle between the Church and liberalism was in fact particularly intense in France, a struggle between Catholic monarchists and anti-religious republicans, which had been going on for over a century. This "civil war" gravely weakened France, and this was indeed the most lasting legacy of the Revolution.[541]

During the last third of the nineteenth century, the idea of consecrating the world to the Sacred Heart of Jesus had become more popular in the Church, along with a similar consecration to Mary's Immaculate Heart. Various petitions were addressed to the Holy See and in 1899, after close study of the question, Pope Leo XIII decided to consecrate the world to the Sacred Heart. That this was not a mere pious formality is shown by the fact that the Pope thought that this act was the greatest of his pontificate. In the accompanying encyclical, *Annum Sacrum*, Pope Leo, in his position as Vicar of Christ, justified his action on the basis that Jesus, as Son of God and Redeemer of humanity, had both natural and acquired rights over mankind. Therefore the consecration made sense as a further dedication of the human race to Christ, with his Sacred Heart as a tangible sign of his infinite love. This consecration gave an impetus to the idea of consecrating the world to Mary's Immaculate Heart in the early years of the twentieth century, with many petitions to this effect being sent to Rome. Pope St Pius X said that he was in favor of the idea, but was awaiting the right moment, and likewise his successor Benedict XV showed himself supportive in principle.[542] It was to be left, however, to Pope Pius XII to carry out this decisive act in 1942.

"Church and State" before World War I

Since 1815 the "Great Powers" had sought to maintain peace in Europe by agreeing to act together, as far as possible, to maintain the status quo. The system worked reasonably well with uninterrupted peace in Europe until 1830. It was not until the Crimean War in 1854 that there was serious conflict, and this did not affect Western Europe. Bismarck's wars to establish Prussian control over Germany, and German dominance of Europe, in 1864, 1866, and 1870, were localized and limited, and, generally speaking, the century from 1815 to 1914 was remarkably peaceful, at least in comparison with previous eras and the twentieth century. But this situation began to break down towards the end of the nineteenth century, as the European states increasingly sought to maintain peace by a system of alliances. Two competing blocks emerged, with Germany, Austria, and Italy in opposition to the Franco-Russian alliance, which was sealed in 1894. From this point on, peace was maintained through the fear of these close alliances bringing all the armies of Europe into conflict. This acted as a deterrent for twenty years, but such a system of alliances was a retrograde step and almost certain to end in disaster, as happened in 1914 with the outbreak of World War I.[543]

Many governments wanted to create overseas empires, particularly with the idea of securing supplies of raw materials for industry, and this, combined with competition amongst exporting capitalist nations, meant that Europe was now assuming a new orientation with new problems. The jingoism of the Imperial age was really a sort of substitute religion, an attempt to fill the spiritual vacuum left by collapsing religious belief. It was made up of a mixture of emotional nationalism, materialism, and often, a racially superior attitude. All of this filled a psychological need, with most of European intellectual society, and indeed many ordinary people, becoming increasingly alienated from Christianity.[544] Social Darwinists applauded all this as the working out of the principle of the "survival of the fittest"; and, similarly, they saw the colonial triumph of the white races as a natural evolutionary step. There was also a genuine feeling amongst many that the West had a cultural mission to civilize and Christianize the world, but materialism and political factors were the main driving forces behind colonial expansion. Thus the period between the Franco-Prussian war in 1870 and the outbreak of World War I in 1914, saw a complete change in European thinking, particularly once the implications of the theory of evolution had sunk in.[545]

The aftereffects of the French Revolution thus reverberated down through the nineteenth century as, increasingly, secular philosophies gained the popular mind. The Church was attacked both openly, as in the *Kulturkampf*, or more insidiously, by a general assault on Christian morality, but it was particularly in the clash with Marxist ideology that the teaching of the popes would prove most prophetic. But the rise to military power of Prussia was the most pressing political problem for the Church and Europe, a rise that was to come to a terrible climax in 1914.

These problems grew during the reign of Pius X (1903–14), with left-wing groups, including socialists and anarchists, causing trouble in Spain; this led to the accession of a government hostile to the Church in 1909, and a situation that was eventually to lead to the Spanish civil war in the thirties. Conditions in Portugal were even worse, with conflict between those loyal to the monarchy and anticlerical republicans leading to the assassination of King Carlos and his elder son in 1908, and to the establishment of a republic after a military revolt in 1910. The Church immediately came under attack from the forces of Freemasonry, allied with members of some Protestant sects; religious congregations were expelled from the country, church property and the education system were secularized and divorce was introduced. Church and State were separated, despite the fact that the population was almost completely Catholic. These measures led to clashes between Catholics and mobs who attacked churches and convents, with six thousand priests and laymen ending up in prison. Pope Pius X could do little but repeatedly protest, and it was not until 1917, the year of the apparitions at Fatima, that the anticlerical regime was overthrown.[546]

Pius X was accused of being hostile to democracy as such, but this was not the case; rather, he was hostile to that notion of democracy that saw *all* power as coming from the people, and thus leaving out God. Likewise, he was not opposed to intellectual progress within Catholicism; but during his reign he had to face an extremely dangerous threat to the Church in the form of Modernism, a movement which claimed that Catholic dogmas could be changed and that the Bible was not inerrant. Had it been allowed to grow, it would have destroyed Catholicism's supernatural basis and thus it was a very serious threat to the essentials of the Faith.[547]

The rapid spread of Modernist ideas to all sections of Catholic society forced the Pope to act, and in 1907 he produced two documents, an encyclical, *Pascendi*, and a catalogue of errors, both of which condemned Modernism. They showed how its desire to subvert unalterable dogmatic truths was at the heart of its failings, and that this approach ultimately led to a rejection of revelation and a diminishing of faith.[548] Pius X saw Modernism as the synthesis of all heresies and concluded; "The error of Protestantism made the first step on this path; the error of Modernism makes the second; atheism makes the third."[549] These pronouncements had the desired effect and the threat from Modernism was averted. If, though, the frontal assault of Modernism on the Church was repelled in the early part of the twentieth century, it must be said that neo-Modernist ideas seem to have infiltrated the Church to an alarming degree, particularly since Vatican II; once again, its very unity and integrity are coming under threat. This does not, however, negate the positive developments that have come about as a result of the Second Vatican Council; it is a question of separating the wheat from the chaff.[550]

Benedict XV, (1854–1922), followed Pius X as Pope, just as the First World War was beginning in 1914. He made it known that he regarded himself as *impartial* rather than *neutral,* even though this was a much misunderstood policy at the time, with both sides expecting his support. He also said that he did not intend to let the papacy just become a passive spectator before the unfolding carnage. Benedict XV saw his role as helping to stop the fratricidal combat destroying the last vestiges of Christendom in Europe, as Catholics and other Christians fought against each other. He sought a just and equitable peace through negotiation, one that would avoid excessively punishing the losers and thus only storing up troubles for the future. In the event this was a farseeing policy, and if it had been implemented, it might have helped to avoid the Second World War, which partly came about from the way Hitler was able to exploit German resentment at excessive reparations for the previous conflict.[551]

World War I and the Rise of Communism

The First World War began in 1914, ostensibly because of the assassination of the heir to the throne of the Habsburg Austro-Hungarian Empire, Archduke Ferdinand, by a Serb called Princip, who acted with the support of the Serbian authorities. The Emperor Francis Joseph went to war to subdue the Serbians and, inadvertently, dragged the rest of Europe into the conflict. On his death in November 1916, the new heir, Charles Joseph, became emperor.[552] Germany's desire for aggrandizement, and its aggressiveness, must be counted as amongst the major factors in precipitating the First World War, although it was by no means the only guilty party. It seems that the German leaders were obsessed with the idea of being encircled and overwhelmed by a newly industrializing Russia. They wanted to create an enlarged German empire in Europe, and were worried by the weakness of their main ally Austria–Hungary: all of this contributed to an atmosphere where war became more and more likely.[553]

This war, which was not fought for any essential point of national freedom or religious principle, can only be described as a gigantic act of collective madness on the part of the European powers, one fueled by the forces of a perverted exaltation of patriotism and nationalism. Before it was over in 1918, millions of men were to lose their lives in an appalling and pointless slaughter.

Two great military alliances were in existence, the Entente Cordiale, consisting of Britain, France and Russia, in opposition to the Central powers, consisting of Germany, Austria–Hungary and Turkey. Russia's association with Serbia, and its various alliances, ensured that the other European powers were quickly dragged into the conflict. The German assault through Belgium nearly succeeded, but the conflict then settled down into trench warfare on the western front in France, in which the machine gun was supreme. It should have been obvious that the war could not be won without the infliction of massive destruction on European civilization, but the rabid nationalism indulged in by all sides meant that only complete victory was acceptable, and so the war was allowed to run its deadly and futile course. Pope Benedict XV repeatedly raised his voice in forlorn pleas for peace, but was largely ignored, and while President Wilson in America offered to mediate, the war gave a small group of Marxist revolutionaries their opportunity to seize power in Russia.[554]

After two years, men were dying in their hundreds of thousands in savage trench warfare, with no end in sight to hostilities. Although Britain, France, and Germany were under great strain, they still maintained an uncompromising attitude towards their war aims at the end of 1916, despite enormous losses. But for both Austria–Hungary and Russia the situation was critical, since the Austro-Hungarian Empire in particular was becoming very fragile and threatening to split up into its component states, with only its young emperor, Charles Joseph, as a symbol of unity able to hold it together. Russia was an autocratic state, but was led by the rather weak Tsar Nicholas, who was controlled by his wife, who in turn came under the influence of the notorious Gregory Rasputin, an influence that would prove disastrous for the country. By 1916 the Russian government was in a state of crisis, with the country in an increasingly desperate state, as the war dragged on and defeat seemed certain. This produced the sort of atmosphere that the future Bolshevik leader Lenin, (1870–1924), then in exile, recognized as the best chance to introduce Marxist Communism into the country. He realized that only through an almost total breakdown of law and order could he hope to seize power. Meanwhile, Rasputin was killed by four prominent conspirators in the hope that this would save Russia from his baneful influence. But after his death, Nicholas and Alexandra slipped into a state of lethargy, oblivious to repeated warnings that governmental reform was absolutely essential if disaster was to be avoided and Russia saved from catastrophe.[555]

By March 1917 food shortages in the country were being compounded by transportation problems, as Petrograd ground to a halt, with the people on strike and all factories closed. The situation worsened as the Tsar insisted that order be restored, but instead of attempting to work with the Russian Parliament, the *Duma,* to retrieve the situation, he ordered it to be suspended. Rebellious soldiers sided with the people, marching on an arsenal and distributing seventy thousand guns to the public, thus initiating the first stage of the Russian Revolution. A crowd of at least fifty thousand marched on the Duma which was still sitting, and the politician Kerensky managed to take control of the revolutionary movement, promising the formation of a new provisional government. The Communists, though, had their own ideas as to how the revolution would proceed, and they also set up and operated their own "government" from within the Duma. The news of the revolution spread quickly and men such as Stalin, (1879–1953), and Trotsky returned to Russia to take their part in it, while Lenin in Switzerland wondered how he could get back to his own country through war-torn Europe.[556]

Early in 1917 the German leadership had decided on the secret and immoral policy of unrestricted submarine warfare in the hope of finishing the war before America could enter it. Their ally, the Austro-Hungarian emperor Charles, refused to support this policy, but could do nothing to stop its being implemented. German submarines were inflicting increasing losses on British shipping, and while America was still not actively involved in the war, President Woodrow Wilson put forward a proposal for a just peace, which was warmly praised by Pope Benedict XV, but scornfully rejected by the warring nations. Only the Emperor Charles Joseph was genuinely trying to achieve peace through secret contacts with members of his wife's family, who belonged to the royal house of Bourbon–Parma and thus were associated with France. Charles made it clear that he sought peace, because he saw it as his duty before God to try and salvage something of Christian civilization, and he was even prepared to make a separate peace, convinced that his German allies were no longer prepared to listen to reason.[557]

The German leaders and the other European combatants, however, were still more interested in war and nothing was achieved. In April, the German High Command, growing desperate, conceived the idea of removing Russia from the war by fomenting the revolutionary movement there, and to this end they proposed to transport Lenin and his followers to Russia in a sealed railway car, despite the danger of spreading Communist ideas. This move was totally opposed by the Emperor Charles, who refused to allow the train to pass through his territory. But Lenin and his Bolshevik companions duly arrived back on Russian soil via Sweden, ready to take charge of the Revolution and turn it into the most inhuman and soulless movement in the history of mankind.[558]

The fact that Lenin's ambitions for Communism went far beyond simply attaining power in Russia is clear from this address he made on 16 April at Petrograd Station on his return: "Dear comrades, soldiers, sailors and workers! I am happy to greet in your persons the victorious Russian Revolution! I greet you as the vanguard of the world proletarian army. The predatory imperialist war is the beginning of a civil war all over Europe. .... Any day now we shall see the collapse of European imperialism. The Russian revolution you have made has prepared the way and opened a new epoch. Long live the world socialist revolution!"

He quickly condemned the provisional government and worked to ensure that the Bolsheviks gained sole power, relying on sheer force of will to break down any opposition from his fellow Marxists or outsiders, while making common cause with Stalin, the future Soviet dictator.[559] Thus the Communists moved to increase their power in Russia, as a decline in military discipline made the army increasingly ineffective, just as the German High Command had hoped when it had returned Lenin to the country. The provisional Kerensky government was still in control, but the situation was very volatile. The war dragged on in Europe, although there was something of a lull amongst the exhausted combatants.[560]

Meanwhile Benedict XV, realizing that the only hope for

mankind lay in recourse to God, directed that the invocation "Queen of peace, pray for us," be added to the Litany of Loreto early in May 1917, as he turned in anguish towards Mary, asking that she should intercede for the gift of peace for Europe and the world: "To Mary, then, who is the Mother of Mercy and omnipotent by grace, let loving and devout appeal go up from every corner of the earth ... from blood-drenched plains and seas. ... that her most tender and benign solicitude may be moved and the peace we ask for be obtained for our agitated world."

In answer to the Pope's prayer for peace, just over a week later Mary appeared to the three shepherd children at Fatima, at the appropriately named *Cova da Iria* or "Hollow of Peace."[561]

On 26 June Archbishop Pacelli, the papal nuncio and future Pope Pius XII, met with the German Chancellor, Bethmann-Hollweg, who agreed with him on the need for Germany to make concessions, although he was under enormous pressure from the warmongers on his own side. At the end of the month specific proposals were put to the German generals, but General Erich Ludendorff in particular was not interested, and so the most hopeful possibility of obtaining concessions for peace from the German government came to nothing. Soon Ludendorff was to assume effective control of Germany, as Kaiser Wilhelm II's power declined. This was the same man who had advocated the plan to send Lenin to Russia, and who was later to support Hitler's beer hall *putsch* in Munich, his first attempt to seize power in Germany in the twenties. On the Entente side, the British General Haig was pushing ahead with plans for an offensive in Flanders, known by the name of Passchendaele, which would eventually lead to three-quarters of a million men on both sides being killed or wounded, for no appreciable military gain.

Late in July Archbishop Pacelli presented a revised papal offer of mediation to the German government, one quite favorable to Germany and supported by the Kaiser, but again this was rejected by Ludendorff at army headquarters, who, in effect, had the power to veto any initiative. On 12 August, Pope Benedict XV wrote to each of the warring nations, pointing out that Europe was on the point of committing suicide, and calling for a just peace based on moral principles: a reduction of armaments; arbitration of disputes; and a renunciation of claims for war indemnities. As before, though, his plea fell, for the most part, on deaf ears, as a kind of mania for continuing the war gripped the conflicting countries.[562]

Thus a war precipitated by Prussian aggression had brought

Europe to the brink of collapse, as the voice of the Pope, pleading for peace, was ignored. Worse, conditions were being prepared in Russia that would prove ideal for the growth of Communism. Regrettably, the German leadership not only repeatedly refused to countenance any thought of peace, but actually furthered the ambitions of Communism in the pursuit of its own war aims.

The Communist Revolution

Six months after the beginnings of the Revolution, the situation in Russia continued to deteriorate, as the country fell apart and virtual anarchy reigned, a process welcomed by the Communists since it offered them their only real path to power. The army was in crisis—by August over two million soldiers, out of seven million, had simply deserted the Eastern front and attempted to go home. Many ordinary people decided to seize farms, encouraged by Communist agitators who promised an end to private property. An attempted coup in September by the new commander of the Russian army, General Kornilov, ended in failure, and with it any real prospect of halting the spread of Communism in the country.[563]

By October 1917 the situation in Russia was set for the victory of Communism, but Lenin envisaged far more than this and confidently looked forward to the war in Europe wreaking the same havoc in the West as it had in his country. He thought this would allow the Communist Revolution, with him and his party in control, to take hold first in Europe, and then world wide. On 12 October, Lenin, now temporarily in Finland, wrote an article entitled *The Crisis is Ripe*, in which he reiterated his belief that "we are on the threshold of a world proletarian revolution;" he also pointed to all the disorder in Russia and demanded that the Communists seize power immediately, a call soon heeded.

Warren H. Carroll argues that Lenin's optimism was not as far-fetched as it might seem, given that three years of desperate warfare and the loss of millions of lives had brought Europe close to catastrophe: "How many more Passchendaeles could any nation, however disciplined and loyal to its leaders, have endured without breaking?" Already there had been mutinies in the French army, and who could tell what would happen if the war did not end soon? It is questionable if the people of the West would have endured much more suffering before European society would have irretrievably broken down, allowing Communism, with its promises to stop the fighting, to step into the breach, and thus giving Marxism its chance to dominate the whole continent. Carroll comments that the prayers for peace offered at the request of both Benedict XV and the Lady at Fatima, allied to the sufferings of countless millions, undoubtedly played a major part in averting this fate.[564]

On 16 October Lenin slipped back into Russia in disguise, and on 22 October the central committee of the Communist Party met in Petrograd, deciding that the time for an armed uprising had come. Trotsky, meanwhile, went all over the city rousing the crowds to a heightened revolutionary fervor. Significantly, by now the army in Petrograd was prepared to take its orders from the Bolsheviks rather than the provisional Kerensky government. Early on Wednesday, 7 November, Red Guards began to seize strategic points in the city, as Kerensky's pleas for help went unanswered by the Cossack regiments; by morning it was practically all over, as a Bolshevik proclamation of the victory of the proletarian revolution was published all over the city and telegraphed to the furthest corners of Russia. A day later the Winter Palace fell into the hands of the Bolsheviks, and with it Russia, leading to nearly three-quarters of a century of Communist tyranny.[565]

The Bolsheviks moved quickly to nationalize all land in Russia; and, at the end of November, all industry was taken over by the new government. The hopes of the German High Command in sending Lenin to Russia were fully realized when an armistice was agreed with the Communists in early December, thus ending the war between Germany and Russia; this was formally ratified by treaty three months later. Central economic planning was introduced later in the month, as was divorce on demand, while Lenin also created the first Communist secret police service as an instrument of terror; he saw the use of violence as essential to the success of the Revolution and reveled in it. The Communist dictatorship thus established itself and grew in power, basing itself upon the methods of the Jacobins during the French Revolution.[566] Communism was able to succeed in gaining power in Russia because of its centuries-long isolation from the West and the closed nature of its society, conditioned as it was by the Orthodox Church and dominated by the Tsars. The tension created by the clash between Western Culture and this ossified system was resolved by the coming to power of the secular Messianism of Marxism.[567]

During the War, Winston Churchill had compared the return of Lenin to Russia, at the hands of the Germans, with contaminating the water supply of a great city with typhoid or cholera—he had glimpsed what Communism was capable of, if it gained a foothold.[568] British and French forces did have the opportunity to help the White Russian armies in their attempts to destroy Communism at birth, but the political will was lacking, despite Churchill's best endeavors, and it survived the crucial early years when it was most vulnerable to attack.[569]

On 11 November 1918, just over a year after the Russian Revolution, the First World War officially ended, and both the Kaiser and Emperor Charles lost power and were exiled; the Austro-Hungarian Empire was dismantled, leaving only the tiny state of Austria. The Catholic Emperor Charles was the only ruler who had genuinely sought peace during the war, but he died a holy death in poverty on the island of Madeira, a Portuguese territory, in April 1922. Fifty years after his death, in 1972, his tomb was opened as the initial steps in the process of his beatification were taken; his body was found to be almost completely incorrupt, certainly a good sign as regards a possible eventual declaration of his sainthood.[570]

When the Marxist revolutionaries, led by Lenin and Trotsky, overthrew the fragile Russian government in November 1917, no one could have realized that this shattered state would one day assume the status of a world power, threatening Western civilization. But the harshness with which they imposed order, in the years following their victory, was a sign of the way Soviet Russia would act in future, and by 1921 their position was more secure. The assault on religion began immediately, and the Russian Orthodox Church was attacked with great severity by a government that had openly and totally rejected God. New laws echoed the anti-Christian legislation passed during the French Revolution, and in 1919 a network of concentration camps was begun, their numbers reaching 315 by 1923.[571]

Lenin and his followers saw the State as the supreme good, and their goal was the creation of the first modern regime built on totalitarianism. This was rule without individual freedom, morality, or justice, one that aimed at harnessing technology to produce a brutal collective society. This model, in which the State was everything, was taken up by Hitler and Mussolini in producing their own fascist totalitarian regimes in the thirties. But for many people this later development was seen as the only way of halting the spread of Communism, and this fact probably explains the ambivalence of Western governments in their early dealings with Hitler. The world was unprepared for the deceitful propaganda of either Nazism or Communism, and also for the way they would be able to generate a powerful emotional enthusiasm, and counterfeit Christian ideals such as missionary zeal and solidarity with others. These traits, combined with the great power of the totalitarian regimes both to carry out acts of violence and to intimidate their own populations, and eventually those of other countries, meant they would become a far more dangerous threat to Christianity, and civilization, than anything the nineteenth century had seen.

15

The Apparitions at Fatima

The Angel of Portugal and Fatima

For reasons which will become clear, Fatima should be regarded as the most important Marian apparition of the twentieth century, if not the most important event in its own right; as such, it is very significant that it should have occurred just as the Russian Revolution was unfolding. At this time, Fatima was just a small village, about seventy miles north of Lisbon, and the three children to whom Mary appeared came from the small hamlet of Aljustrel, less than a mile away. Lucia, the oldest, was born in March 1907, to Maria Rosa and Antonio dos Santos, while Francisco and Jacinta Marto, born in June 1908 and March 1910 respectively, were the children of her aunt and uncle, Manuel, or "Ti" Marto, and his wife, Olimpia.[572]

Lucia helped to look after her family's flock of sheep and goats from an early age, and it was probably in the summer of 1915, while she was out with some other little girls, that she had her first overt encounter with the supernatural. As they were saying their rosary they saw a cloud "whiter than snow" moving through the air, but transparent and in human form; this was repeated on two subsequent occasions, and these events naturally caused much puzzlement in the community when related by one of the girls. Lucia was questioned by her mother but could only tell her that she had seen what looked like somebody wrapped in a sheet. She was left with an indescribably "ethereal" impression by this event, but would perhaps have forgotten about it if it had not been for her later experiences.[573]

In the spring of 1916, Francisco and Jacinta were allowed to go out with their cousin Lucia as she looked after the sheep; the children would play while keeping an eye on the animals. They were in an area known as the *Loca do Cabeço* one morning when it began to drizzle, causing them to seek shelter. After the rain stopped, they ate their lunches and then said the rosary together. The day became beautifully calm and sunny and they began to play again, only to be surprised by a strong wind shaking the trees. Then they saw "a light whiter than snow, in the form of a young man, transparent, and brighter than crystal pierced by the rays of the sun," coming nearer, until they could see his features and he spoke to them: "Do not be afraid, I am the Angel of Peace. Pray with me." He then knelt and touched the ground with his forehead, the children following his example, before continuing: "My God, I believe, I adore, I hope and I love You! I ask pardon of You for those who do not believe, do not adore, do not hope and do not love You!"

He repeated this prayer three times before rising and saying: "Pray thus. The Hearts of Jesus and Mary are attentive to your supplications." Then he gradually faded away in the sunlight, to leave the children absolutely overwhelmed with a sense of the supernatural, repeating the prayer for hours, until towards evening they returned home. This feeling only diminished gradually over the next few days, and the intimacy of the encounter meant they naturally kept silent about it.[574]

Spring turned into summer with its intense heat, and this meant that the flocks could be pastured only in the morning and evening, leaving the children to rest during the siesta. They were by the well in Lucia's garden one afternoon, when the Angel suddenly appeared before them again: he gently admonished them saying: "What are you doing? Pray! Pray very much! The Hearts of Jesus and Mary have designs of mercy on you. Offer prayers and sacrifices constantly to the Most High." Lucia asked how they could do this and he replied: "Make of everything you can a sacrifice, and offer it to God as an act of reparation for the sins by which He is offended, and in supplication for the conversion of sinners. You will thus draw down peace upon your country. I am its Angel Guardian, the Angel of Portugal. Above all, accept and bear with submission, the suffering which the Lord will send you."[575]

Again the children were completely overcome by their encounter with the supernatural, and when later Francisco, who, as on the first occasion had seen the Angel but not heard his words, questioned the girls, they were still too overwhelmed to talk properly to him, and told him to wait until the next day. Lucia later wrote about the effect of this apparition:

These words were indelibly impressed upon our minds. They were like a light which made us understand who God is, how He loves us and desires to be loved, the value of sacrifice, how pleasing it is to Him and how, on account of it, He grants the grace of conversion to sinners. It was for this reason that we began, from then on, to offer to the Lord all that mortified us, without, however, seeking out other forms of mortification and penance, except that we remained for hours on end with our foreheads touching the ground, repeating the prayer the Angel had taught us.[576]

In the autumn the children again saw the Angel as they were out looking after the sheep. They had said the rosary and the prayer they had been taught, when he appeared before them, holding a chalice in his hands. Above it was suspended a host from which drops of blood were falling into the chalice. The Angel left the chalice suspended in the air and prostrated himself before it, repeating the following prayer three times:

Most Holy Trinity, Father, Son and Holy Spirit, I adore You profoundly, and I offer You the most precious Body, Blood, Soul and Divinity of Jesus Christ, present in all the tabernacles of the world, in reparation for the outrages, sacrileges and indifference with which He Himself is offended. And, through the infinite merits of His most Sacred Heart, and the Immaculate Heart of Mary, I beg of You the conversion of poor sinners.[577]

The Angel then gave the host to Lucia to eat, and let Francisco and Jacinta drink from the chalice whilst saying: "Take and drink the Body and Blood of Jesus Christ, horribly outraged by ungrateful men. Repair their crimes and console your God." Then he prostrated himself again, repeating the prayer he had just recited for the children a further three times with them, before disappearing. The children felt practically annihilated by an intense sense of the presence of God, one which left them physically exhausted, but at peace and happy; these sensations remained with them for a considerable period.[578]

They still did not tell anyone about these visits of the Angel, though, feeling an interior necessity of keeping quiet about these events; without realizing it, they were being prepared for their encounters with Mary during the following summer. The apparition of the Angel was not made public until 1937, with the publication of Sr Lucia's *Second Memoir,* and she has come in for some criticism because of this, with some people questioning whether her recollections are reliable.[579] Considered in context, though, the visits of the Angel, while important, were not crucial to the Fatima apparitions, and they might well have caused confusion had they become known too soon. It appears, too, that she did in time inform the bishop amongst other clerics about the Angel, but was advised to keep silence, as she was to remind Bishop Correia da Silva in her fourth memoir.[580] In any event, it would seem that Lucia's account of the Angel gains support, in a typological sense, when the events surrounding Fatima are compared with the life of the prophet Elijah, and particularly with the account of his meeting with an Angel, as will be demonstrated later (cf. 1 Kings 19:5–8).

The First Apparition – May 1917

By May 1917, Lucia was ten, Francisco nearly nine and Jacinta seven. May 13 was the Sunday before the feast of the Ascension, and after going to early Mass, the three children took their flocks out to pasture on the small area owned by Lucia's parents known as the *Cova da Iria*. Neither they nor the sheep were in any hurry and it was not until about midday that they reached their destination, where, after eating their lunch, they said the rosary together. After this, they took the sheep up a little higher to fresh pasture and began to play at building a house. Suddenly there was a bright flash of something like lightning, and the children looked up, thinking a thunderstorm was coming: but to their surprise the sky was still a cloudless blue and there was no wind. They had just agreed to go home in case it was a storm, when there was another flash; they looked up to their right to see, in Lucia's words, "a lady, clothed in white, brighter than the sun, radiating a light more clear and intense than a crystal cup filled with sparkling water, lit by burning sunlight."[581]

The children stood there amazed, bathed in the light that surrounded the apparition, somewhat surprised and perhaps alarmed, prompting the Lady to smile and say: "Do not be afraid, I will not harm you." Lucia, as the oldest, asked her where she came from. The Lady pointed to the sky and said: "I come from heaven." Somewhat reassured, Lucia asked her what she wanted: "I have come to ask you to come here for six months in succession, on the thirteenth day at this same hour. Then I will tell you who I am and what I want. And I shall return here yet a seventh time."

Lucia then asked if they would go to heaven, and she was told "Yes", she and Jacinta would go to heaven, but Francisco would need to say many rosaries first. As in the case of the apparition of the Angel the previous year, Francisco, for some reason, could only see the Lady and not hear her words. Lucia's thoughts turned to two young women who had died recently, and was told that one was in heaven and the other, her friend Amelia, would be in purgatory "until the end of the world."[582]

The Lady then said: "Are you willing to offer yourselves to God and bear all the sufferings He wills to send you, as an act of reparation for the conversion of sinners?" Lucia as spokesman for all three readily agreed: "Then you are going to have much to suffer, but the grace of God will be your comfort." Lucia recounted that, at the same moment as she said these words, the Lady opened her hands,

> communicating to us a light so intense that, as it streamed from her hands, its rays penetrated our hearts and the innermost depths of our souls, making us see ourselves in God, Who was that light, more clearly than we see ourselves in the best of mirrors. Then, moved by an interior impulse that was also communicated to us, we fell on our knees, repeating in our hearts: "O most Holy Trinity, I adore You! My God, my God, I love You in the most Blessed Sacrament!"[583]

After allowing them to remain like this for some time, the Lady finished with a request: "Say the Rosary every day, to bring peace to the world and the end of the war." With that she began to rise into the air, moving towards the east, until she disappeared. The children remained transfixed, gazing at the sky, and then, having checked on the sheep, and, as at La Salette, found them contentedly grazing, they remained for the rest of the day in a state of wonderment, trying to come to terms with their experiences. Jacinta was overjoyed and kept repeating ecstatically: "Oh, what a beautiful Lady!" Lucia though was sad at the thought of some of the Lady's words, and realized, too, that despite her protestations to the contrary, Jacinta would not be able to keep silent about what she had seen and heard. Francisco, a quiet boy, said little, except to ask what the beautiful Lady had said, as they made their way home that evening.[584]

Lucia said nothing to her family about what had happened, but Jacinta, forgetting her promise, could hardly wait to tell her mother Olimpia, to whom she was very close. She related the events of the afternoon, but her mother did not take what she said seriously. Later, though, her father, Ti Marto, after Francisco had corroborated her story before the whole family, expressed his own view that it was not impossible that Our Lady had appeared to the children, as she had done in places such as Lourdes or La Salette. He seems to have been the first believer in the apparitions at Fatima, partly because he knew that his children just did not have the knowledge necessary to make up such a detailed story, and also because he had never known them to lie. The story went around the houses of Aljustrel very quickly the next day; and so Maria Rosa, Lucia's mother, soon got to know of it, and, unfortunately for Lucia, she did not take very kindly to such news, punishing her severely for what she thought were lies.

The children got together and tried to think of ways they could make sacrifices, as the Lady had asked, resolving to go without lunch and to say the rosary more prayerfully. Lucia was taken by her mother to the local priest in an attempt to force her to confess, but the child would not admit to lying. Fr Manuel Marques Ferreira treated the children's story with reserve, this being the only practical approach he could take, and certainly he did not defend or support them at this stage. He advised Lucia's mother to allow her to go to the Cova da Iria on 13 June, but to bring her to him so that he could question her afterwards. Francisco and Jacinta received more support from their parents, but the attitude of the inhabitants of Aljustrel was sceptical and even derisory; the children had much to suffer, just as the Lady had told them.[585]

The Second Apparition – June 1917

By now the events of the previous month were well known in the vicinity, and about fifty people turned up at the Cova da Iria on 13 June, the feast of St Anthony of Padua, who, being Portuguese, was a very popular local saint. This was a festive day in Fatima, and Lucia's mother hoped that the excitement would take her mind off her appointment with the Lady. The parents of Jacinta and Francisco went off to a fair, leaving them to make up their own minds as to what they should do, while Lucia's mother departed in some trepidation for the *festa* of St Anthony, leaving one of her daughters to keep an eye on Lucia. All three children eventually assembled at the Cova near the holmoak tree where the Lady had appeared, and settled down with the group who had gathered. This "tree" was actually a bush little more than three feet high. Prayers and the rosary were said, when Lucia suddenly cried out to Jacinta that Our Lady was coming. One of the witnesses, a lady called Maria dos Santos Carreira, heard Lucia ask what the apparition wanted, and was amazed to hear a sound like a tiny voice, like the buzzing of a bee, in reply.[586]

Lucia herself later recounted how the children saw a flash of light, followed immediately by the apparition of Mary on the little holmoak tree: Lucia asked what she desired: "I want you to come on the 13th of next month, to pray the Rosary every day, and to learn to read. Later, I will tell you what I want." Lucia then asked for the cure of a sick person: "If he is converted, he will be cured during the year." She also asked Mary to take them to heaven and was reassured in this way:

> I will take Jacinta and Francisco shortly; but you will stay here for some time to come. Jesus wants to use you to make Me known and loved. He wishes to establish the devotion to My Immaculate Heart throughout the world. *I promise salvation to whoever embraces it; these souls will be dear to God, like flowers put by Me to adorn his throne.*[587]

Lucia was sad at the first part of this reply, saying: "Am I to stay here alone?" Mary replied: "No, my daughter. Are you suffering a great deal? Don't lose heart. I will never forsake you. My Immaculate Heart will be your refuge and the way that will lead you to God." Lucia later described what happened then:

> As Our Lady spoke these last words, she opened her hands and for the second time, she communicated to us the rays of that same immense light. We saw ourselves in this light, as it were, immersed in God. Jacinta and Francisco seemed to be in that part of the light which rose towards heaven, and I in that which was poured out on the earth. In front of the palm of Our Lady's right hand was a heart encircled by thorns which pierced it. We understood that this was the Immaculate Heart of Mary, outraged by the sins of humanity, and seeking reparation.[588]

The witness Maria Carreira describes how Lucia then cried out and pointed, as Mary departed: "Look, there she goes! There she goes!" She herself heard a noise like, "a rocket, a long way off," and looked to see a small cloud a few inches over the tree rise and move slowly towards the east until it disappeared. All eyes followed it until Lucia finally said: "There, now we can't see her anymore. She has gone back into Heaven, the doors are shut!" Maria Carreira continued: "We then turned back towards the miraculous tree and what was our admiration and surprise to see that the shoots at the top, which had been standing upright before, were now all bent towards the east, as if someone had stood upon them." The crowd of pilgrims then returned to Fatima, where they reported the amazing things they had seen, thus ensuring that there were between two and three thousand people present for the July apparition.[589]

As soon as the children got home they were subjected to a barrage of questioning, some of it hostile and cynical, although once the details of what had happened at the Cova became known, that there was definitely something to their story, people became rather more thoughtful; but Lucia's mother, Maria Rosa, still refused to believe that her daughter could possibly have seen the Blessed Virgin. It was decided to take all three children to the parish priest again; but he was dissatisfied with their answers and their tendency to keep things to themselves. He ended up by expressing the opinion that it might all be a trick of the devil. Lucia was upset by this thought and even dreamt about the devil, so Jacinta and Francisco had to work hard to reassure her that the beautiful Lady had come from heaven and not hell.[590]

The Third Apparition – July 1917

Lucia, however, still had her doubts, constantly reinforced by her mother, who wanted to avoid the family becoming a laughingstock; and so, on 12 July, she told Francisco and Jacinta that she didn't want to go to the Cova the next day. But on the thirteenth, as noon approached, Lucia felt an interior force practically compelling her towards the Cova and her appointment with Mary. This is reminiscent of what happened to Bernadette, when she too had felt a mysterious force moving her towards the grotto on one occasion. As Lucia made her way towards the Marto house, all her doubts and difficulties vanished. Thus the three children set off for the Cova as Ti Marto followed them, eventually joining the large crowd that had assembled around the holmoak. He described how he got close to the children as the rosary was finishing, and Lucia jumped up telling everyone to close their umbrellas because Our Lady was coming:

> I looked as hard as I could but could see nothing at first. And then I saw what looked like a greyish cloud resting on the oak tree, and the sun's heat lessened and there was a delicious fresh breeze. It hardly seemed like the height of summer. The people were so silent that you could have heard a pin drop. And then I began to hear a sound, a little buzzing rather like a mosquito in

an empty bottle. I couldn't hear any words! I think talking on the telephone must sound like that though I've never done it! What is it?—I said to myself. Is it near or far away? All this was for me a great proof of the miracle.[591]

The children, though, could understand what was happening clearly. Once more they saw the indescribably beautiful Lady over the holmoak, and were filled with a sense of peace and happiness. Lucia was so absorbed with the apparition that Jacinta had to tell her that Our Lady was speaking to her, and again Lucia asked what she wanted. Mary replied: "I want you to come here on the 13th of next month, to continue to pray the Rosary every day in honor of Our Lady of the Rosary, in order to obtain peace for the world and the end of the war, because only she can help you." Lucia then asked her who she was and for a miracle, so that everyone would believe: "Continue to come here every month. In October, I will tell you who I am and what I want, and I will perform a miracle for all to see and believe."[592]

Lucia also made some requests for sick people, to which Mary replied that she would cure some but not others, and that all must say the rosary to obtain such graces, before continuing: "Sacrifice yourselves for sinners, and say many times, especially when you make some sacrifice: O Jesus, it is for love of You, for the conversion of sinners, and in reparation for the sins committed against the Immaculate Heart of Mary." Lucia later revealed that, as she spoke these words, Mary opened her hands and rays of light from them seemed to penetrate the earth, so that they saw;

> ... as it were a sea of fire. Plunged in this fire were demons and souls in human form, like transparent burning embers, all blackened or burnished bronze, floating about in the conflagration, now raised into the air by the flames that issued from within themselves together with great clouds of smoke, now falling back on every side like sparks in huge fires, without weight or equilibrium, amid shrieks and groans of pain and despair, which horrified us and made us tremble with fear. (It must have been this sight which caused me to cry out, as people say they heard me). The demons could be distinguished by their terrifying and repellent likeness to frightful and unknown animals, black and transparent like burning coals.[593]

This vision of hell was the first part of the "secret" of Fatima, which was not revealed until much later. Ti Marto testified that at this moment, "Lucia took a deep breath, went as pale as death," and cried out in terror to Our Lady, calling her by name, while the children themselves looked up to the sad face of the Blessed Virgin, who spoke to them kindly:[594]

> You have seen hell[595] where the souls of poor sinners go. To save them, God wishes to establish in the world devotion to my Immaculate Heart. If what I say to you is done, many souls will be saved and there will be peace. The war is going to end; but if people do not cease offending God, a worse one will break out during the pontificate of Pius XI. When you see a night illumined by an unknown light, know that this is the great sign given you by God that he is about to punish the world for its crimes, by means of war, famine, and persecutions of the Church and of the Holy Father. To prevent this, I shall come to ask for the consecration of Russia to my Immaculate Heart, and the Communion of Reparation on the First Saturdays. If my requests are heeded, Russia will be converted, and there will be peace; if not, she will spread her errors throughout the world, causing wars and persecutions of the Church. The good will be martyred, the Holy Father will have much to suffer, various nations will be annihilated. In the end, my Immaculate Heart will triumph. The Holy Father will consecrate Russia to me and she will be converted, and a period of peace will be granted to the world.[596]

At this point, the second part of the secret of Fatima ends and the third part begins with the words, "In Portugal the dogma of the faith will always be preserved ..." The first two parts of the secret became publicly known only in 1942, when a new edition of a book on Jacinta was planned for the silver jubilee of the apparitions.[597] The third part of the secret has only recently been publicly divulged, and is discussed in a later chapter. Mary specifically told Lucia not to tell anyone about the secret at this stage, apart from Francisco, before continuing: "When you pray the Rosary, say after each mystery: O my Jesus, forgive us, save us from the fire of hell. Lead all souls to heaven, especially those who are most in need." There was a moment of silence before Lucia asked if there was anything else, and after assuring her that there was nothing more, Mary disappeared off into the distance.[598]

At this point Ti Marto and the other witnesses heard what sounded like a clap of thunder, and saw the little arch, which had been put up near the holmoak tree and hung with two lanterns, tremble as if in an earthquake. The little cloud also disappeared from the tree and the people began to crowd round the children, furiously putting questions to them, asking Lucia what had made her so sad. She replied that it was a secret, and this only caused more commotion, so that it was only with some difficulty that the children were taken back to the village.[599]

They tried, without much success, to get back to their work as shepherds, so as to avoid those who sought them out to question them further, and also to have the solitude to pray and think over what the Lady had said to them. Jacinta, in particular, was very worried at the thought of all the sinners going to hell, and between them they sought ways to make sacrifices, including not drinking during the hottest part of the day. A good example of the simplicity, and even naïveté, of the children is found in the fact that they thought that "Russia" was an unfortunate person, for whom they would have to pray and make sacrifices.[600]

The Fourth Apparition – August 1917

As 13 August approached, the story of the apparitions had reached the anti-religious secular press, and while this ensured that the whole country knew about Fatima, it also meant that many biased and negative reports were circulating. The authorities, too, were worried at this rise of religious "fanaticism," and the administrator at Vila Nova de Ourem, Arturo Santos, a Freemason and the most prominent local figure, decided, as the authorities had done at Lourdes, that it was necessary to stamp out this medieval nonsense. He had an interview with Lucia, during which he threatened her with death if she did not tell him the secret, but without success, as she said nothing. He then turned up on the morning of 13 August with an offer of a lift in a carriage to the Cova da Iria for the children, but tricking their parents, he took them to his house for questioning.

Meanwhile, at the site of the apparitions, a large crowd had gathered, having come on foot, horseback, bicycle, and even in some cases, by car. People were praying and singing hymns around the holmoak, when around noon news was brought that the children had been abducted. Immediately a great commotion began, interrupted by a noise like a loud clap of thunder and a flash of "lightning." As the crowd watched, a small white cloud settled over the tree before rising into the air and disappearing. Maria Carreira then described how everything about them began to reflect all the colors of the rainbow, and the leaves on the trees began to look like flowers. The crowd, estimated at between five and six thousand on this occasion, realized that Mary had come and they became angry with the Mayor and his henchman for imprisoning the children; some wanted to vent their anger on them.[601]

The children, meanwhile, had spent the morning at the Mayor's house at Ourem being interrogated about the secret; but despite his threats and promises of money, they refused to divulge it. In the afternoon they were moved to the local prison and threatened with being put into a cauldron of boiling oil, but were determined that they would die rather than reveal the secret. They were taken off one by one and fully expected martyrdom, knowing the fearsome reputation of the Mayor, but eventually they were reunited in another room. Santos had one last attempt to break their resolve and threatened to throw them all together into the oil, but failing in this, he gave up and the children were taken back to Fatima.[602]

A few days later Lucia, Francisco, and his brother João, were with the sheep at a place near Aljustrel called *Valinhos*, when, at about four o'clock in the afternoon, she noticed the characteristic changes in atmospheric conditions that indicated an apparition of Mary; the air became fresher, the sun dimmer, and there was a flash of light. These changes were also noticed by Lucia's sister Teresa and her husband, in Fatima itself. Lucia told João to go and get Jacinta, and as she arrived there was another flash of light and she could see Mary on a different, slightly bigger, tree. Lucia again asked what she wanted and was told: "Go again to the Cova da Iria on the 13th and continue to say the Rosary every day." Mary also said she would perform a miracle, so that all would believe, and that, if they had not been abducted, it would have been even better known.

Lucia then asked how the growing shrine should be administered, and requested cures for the sick, being told that some would be cured during the year. Mary, looking very sad, then said: "Pray, pray very much, and make sacrifices for sinners; for many souls go to hell, because there are none to sacrifice themselves and pray for them." With that she rose into the air and moved towards the east before disappearing, leaving the children to take home the branch she had been standing on as a souvenir. Members of both sets of families testified that the branch was perfumed by the most beautiful fragrance, and this was one factor in persuading Lucia's parents to take what she was saying more seriously.[603]

By now, the children had thoroughly absorbed Mary's plea for prayer and penance, and did everything they could to answer it. They prayed the prayer of the Angel for hours while lying prostrate on the ground: "My God, I believe, I adore, I hope and I love You.

I ask forgiveness for those who do not believe, nor adore, nor hope, nor love you." They went as long as they could without drinking in the burning heat of the Portuguese summer, and also went without food as a sacrifice for sinners, to save them from hell, the vision of which had so profoundly affected them. They even knotted some pieces of old rope around their waists as a form of mortification, not removing them day or night.[604]

The Fifth Apparition – September 1917

At Fatima, despite the apparently supernatural nature of the phenomena, which had been experienced by many spectators at preceding apparitions, the children still had to face a lot of hostility and mockery, as well as intense questioning in attempts to discover the secret. But while local people were sceptical, those from farther afield were more enthusiastic, and so on 13 September, very large crowds began to converge on Fatima from all directions. As noon approached, the people began to settle down and the rosary was recited, with the men uncovering their heads. A number of seminarians and priests mingled with the crowd, although the latter held themselves aloof in case the whole business turned into a fiasco. One of the priests who was present that day, but who was very favorably impressed by what he saw, was Mgr John Quaresma, later a member of the bishop's canonical inquiry into the events at Fatima. He and a fellow priest went to the Cova da Iria in a horse-drawn carriage, positioning themselves so they could see whatever happened; he described events as follows, in a letter written soon after:

> At midday there was complete silence. One only heard the murmur of prayers. Suddenly there were sounds of jubilation and voices praising the Blessed Virgin. Arms were raised pointing to something in the sky. "Look, don't you see?" ... "Yes, yes I do!" ...With great astonishment I saw, clearly and distinctly, a luminous globe, which moved from the east to west, gliding slowly and majestically through space. My friend also looked and had the good fortune to enjoy the same unexpected and delightful vision. Suddenly the globe, with its extraordinary light disappeared. Near us was a little girl dressed like Lucia and more or less the same age. She continued to cry out happily: "I still see it! I still see it! Now it's coming down ...!"

Other witnesses testified that they experienced phenomena

similar to those at earlier apparitions, such as the sudden freshening of the atmosphere, or saw the sun becoming paler until the stars could be seen, or saw points of light resembling "flower petals" which fell, disappearing as they came near the earth.[605]

The children had been besieged by crowds of people since early morning, all making requests and asking for cures; this continued all along the way from their houses to the Cova da Iria, and so they experienced great difficulty in making any progress. Finally, though, they arrived, and after the customary flash of light, they saw Mary on the holmoak tree. In reply to Lucia's usual question as to what she wanted, Mary said: "Continue to pray the Rosary in order to obtain the end of the war. In October Our Lord will come, as well as Our Lady of Dolours and Our Lady of Carmel. Saint Joseph will appear with the Child Jesus to bless the world. God is pleased with your sacrifices. He does not want you to sleep with the rope on, but only to wear it during the daytime." It is interesting and somewhat sobering to note that this is apparently one of the few times Mary actually smiled at Fatima, that is when speaking of God being pleased with the children's sacrifices; contrast this with the apparitions at Lourdes where she frequently smiled at Bernadette. This is surely an indication of how important such sacrifices are, and also of the seriousness of the situation the world finds itself in, with so many people in grave danger of going to hell.[606]

Lucia then began to put forward the petitions for cures, to be told: "Yes, I will cure some, but not others. In October I will perform a miracle so that all may believe." With that she began to rise and disappear towards the east.[607] Mgr Quaresma described the reaction of the child in front of him at this point:

> After a few minutes, about the duration of the Apparitions, the child began to exclaim again, pointing to the sky: "Now it's going up again!"—and she followed the globe with her eyes until it disappeared in the direction of the sun. "What do you think of that globe?" I asked my companion, who seemed enthusiastic at what he had seen. "That it was Our Lady," he replied without hesitation. It was my undoubted conviction also. ... I must emphasise that all those around us appeared to have seen the same thing, for one heard manifestations of joy and praises of Our Lady. But some saw nothing. Near us was a simple devout creature crying bitterly because she had seen nothing. We felt remarkably happy. My companion went from group to group in the Cova and afterwards on the road, gathering information.

Those he questioned were of all sorts and kinds and of different social standing, but one and all affirmed the reality of the phenomena which we ourselves had witnessed.[608]

After this the children were again inundated with questioners; this became a severe strain on them and their families, since most of the questions were either foolish or asked just to satisfy curiosity. At this stage, too, they were examined by a priest who was a professor at the local seminary, Dr Manuel Formigão, who had been present at the apparition. On 27 September, he interrogated Francisco and Jacinta separately, in quite some detail, finding that their replies substantially agreed. He then spoke with Lucia, touching on the matter of the secret, but seeing her discomfort, he did not pursue that line of questioning. He was not able to catch her out in mistakes or contradictions and became convinced that the children were sincere in what they were saying. He held open the possibility, though, that they might be the victims of hallucination or of satanic influence. The small discrepancies he found in their accounts did not touch any major points, and could be explained by their mental tiredness due to the constant questioning.

Dr Formigão returned later to Fatima to speak with the children, also asking Lucia's mother whether she had ever read the story of La Salette to her. She answered that she had, but that Lucia had never mentioned it afterwards or given any indication that it had made any great impression on her. He then put further questions to Lucia in front of four witnesses, before going to the Marto house and speaking with Jacinta and Francisco. Again he was favorably impressed by their sincerity and their determination not to reveal anything of the secret, apart from the fact that it was for the good of all three, and that people would be sad if they knew it.[609] Dr Formigão later drew up a psychological profile, in which he maintained that the children were sincere, acting in good faith, and apparently not telling lies or deceiving themselves. When the new bishop of Leiria, Bishop Correia da Silva, was installed in 1920, he wrote to him expressing his support for the reality of the apparitions.[610]

13 October 1917 – the Miracle of the Sun

The proclamation of a public miracle caused the most intense speculation throughout Portugal: for opponents of the Church this seemed like the perfect opportunity to deal a death blow to religion, which would surely be the case once nothing happened at the Cova da Iria on 13 October. The journalist Avelino de Almeida published a satirical article on the whole business in the anti-religious newspaper *O Seculo,* and this succeeded in drawing even more attention to the apparitions. People from other parts of the country descended in their tens of thousands on the Cova, using all possible means of transport, in spite of the terrible storm that lashed the mountain country around Fatima on the eve of the thirteenth. Many pilgrims went barefooted reciting the rosary as they went, all crowding into the area around the Cova, as by midmorning the weather again turned bad and heavy rain began to fall.[611] Once more the children were surrounded by crowds of people, and had great difficulty in making their way to the Cova. Despite the rain still falling in torrents, and lying inches deep, people knelt in the mud before the children, presenting petitions. Eventually, though, they reached the holmoak around noon, as the crowd began to grow calmer and more expectant under the darkened cloudy sky.

Lucia, moved by an interior impulse, told everyone to put down their umbrellas and say the rosary. The children then saw the flash of light and Mary appeared before them, as, for the last time, Lucia asked what she wanted: "I want to tell you that a chapel is to be built here in my honor. I am the Lady of the Rosary. Continue always to pray the Rosary every day. The war is going to end, and the soldiers will soon return to their homes." Again Lucia made some requests, being informed that people must amend their lives and ask forgiveness for their sins, if they wanted healings or conversions. She reported too that Mary grew very sad and said: "*Do not offend the Lord our God any more, because He is already so much offended.*" Then, rising into the air and opening her hands towards the sun, growing more brilliant as she did, she disappeared from sight, being replaced by various apparitions of Mary, Jesus, and St Joseph, seen only by the children.[612]

While Lucia was seeing all this, she cried out "Look at the sun," and the vast crowd saw something very different, a true miracle. All eyes turned skyward to see the black clouds parting and the sun, looking like a dull gray disc, become visible. The crowd found they could look directly at it quite easily, as the secular Lisbon paper *O Dia* reported:

> ... the silver sun, ... was seen to whirl and turn in the circle of broken clouds. A cry went up from every mouth and the people fell on their knees on the muddy ground. ... The light turned a

beautiful blue as if it had come through the stained glass windows of a cathedral and spread itself over the people who knelt with outstretched hands. The blue faded slowly and then the light seemed to pass through yellow glass. ... People wept and prayed with uncovered heads in the presence of the miracle they had awaited. The seconds seemed like hours, so vivid were they.[613]

In *O Seculo* Avelino de Almeida adopted a very different tone from his earlier satirical article on Fatima, going into even more detail;

...one could see the immense multitude turn towards the sun, which appeared free from clouds and at its zenith. It looked like a plaque of dull silver and it was possible to look at it without the least discomfort. It might have been an eclipse which was taking place. But at that moment a great shout went up and one could hear the spectators nearest at hand shouting: "A miracle! A miracle!" Before the astonished eyes of the crowd, whose aspect was Biblical as they stood bareheaded, eagerly searching the sky, the sun trembled, made sudden incredible movements outside all cosmic laws—the sun "danced" according to the typical expression of the people. ... People then began to ask each other what they had seen. The great majority admitted to having seen the trembling and dancing of the sun; others affirmed that they saw the face of the Blessed Virgin; others, again, swore that the sun whirled on itself like a giant catherine wheel and that it lowered itself to the earth as if to burn it with its rays. Some said they saw it change colors successively. ...[614]

Another important witness was a young lawyer, Dr José Almeida Garrett, who wrote to the priest who had interviewed the children, Dr Formigão, describing what he had seen: "It must have been nearly two o'clock by the legal time and about midday by the sun. The sun, a few moments before, had broken through the thick layers of clouds which hid it and shone clearly and intensely. I ... saw it as a disc with a clean-cut rim, luminous and shining, but which did not hurt the eyes." He then went on to describe how it did not resemble the moon, and could not have been confused with the sun as seen through fog, and that he was amazed to find he could look at it directly without any pain to his eyes:

The sun's disc did not remain immobile. This was not the sparkling of a heavenly body for it spun round on itself in a mad whirl. Then, suddenly, one heard a clamour, a cry of anguish breaking from all the people. The sun, whirling wildly, seemed to loosen itself from the firmament and advance threateningly upon the earth as if to crush us with its huge and fiery weight. The sensation during those moments was terrible. During the solar phenomenon, ... there were changes of color in the atmosphere. ... I saw everything an amethyst color. Objects around me, the sky and the atmosphere, were of the same color. ... I turned away and shut my eyes, keeping my hands before them to intercept the light. With my back still turned, I opened my eyes and saw that the landscape was the same purple color as before. ... All the phenomena which I have described were observed by me in a calm and serene state of mind and without any emotional disturbance.[615]

Other witnesses too, such as Maria Carreira, testified to the terrifying nature of the solar miracle:

It turned everything different colors, yellow, blue, white, and it shook and trembled; it seemed like a wheel of fire which was going to fall on the people. They cried out: "We shall all be killed, we shall all be killed!" Others called on Our Lady to save them and recited acts of contrition. One woman began to confess her sins aloud, saying that she had done this and that. ... At last the sun stopped moving and we all breathed a sigh of relief. We were still alive and the miracle which the children had foretold had taken place.[616]

These are powerful testimonies, but perhaps one of the most interesting witnesses was an Englishwoman, Mabel Norton, who was a Protestant. She had been living in Portugal for seven years and was spending some time at the home of a Marchioness, speaking English with her children. She did not see the miracle in as much detail, perhaps because she was not a Catholic, and indeed was somewhat disappointed when she realized what other people had seen, but nevertheless, her account is very important, especially as she had not really been expecting anything to happen. Mabel went with the family to Fatima early on the morning of 13 October, arriving at the Cova at about midday, just in time for the miracle. She describes how Lucia's cry "Look at the sun!" was taken up by the people until it rolled from the center to the edges of the crowd as a "great wave of sound," and is careful to note that this was the first indication of the *kind* of miracle that could be expected, that is, that it was something to do with the sun. Then the rain suddenly stopped and she found she could look at the sun, which appeared as a "luminous disc, on which it was possible to gaze without blinking." She is emphatic about the speed with which the rain stopped, and is clear in her description of events: "I saw the rain cease, suddenly, not as rain usually ends. Then the clouds were pushed back from the sun in every direction, as if by invisible hands, and the sun appeared, in color like the blade of a knife, luminous but not dazzling. Then, as I looked, the sun described a swift circle, paused; described another, paused; described yet a third. And then the clouds began to sweep over it again."[617]

Other people witnessed the solar miracle from a distance, thus ruling out the possibility of any sort of collective hallucination, as in the case of the poet Alfonso Lopes Vieira who lived over thirty miles away from Fatima: "On that day, 13th October, 1917, without remembering the predictions of the children, I was enchanted by a remarkable spectacle in the sky of a kind I had never seen before." Inácio Lourenço, who was to become a priest, was a school child of nine when he saw the miracle at a village about twelve miles from Fatima. He described how the children and their teachers were attracted outside by a commotion in front of the school to see the miracle of the sun:

> I looked fixedly at the sun, which seemed pale and did not hurt the eyes. Looking like a ball of snow revolving on itself, it suddenly seemed to come down in a zig-zag, menacing the earth. Terrified, I ran and hid myself among the people, who were weeping and expecting the end of the world at any moment. ... During those long moments of the solar prodigy objects around us turned all the colors of the rainbow. We saw ourselves blue, yellow, red, etc. All these strange phenomena increased the fear of the people. After about ten minutes the sun, now dull and pallid, returned to its place. When the people realized that the danger was now over there was an explosion of joy and everyone joined in thanksgiving and praise of Our Lady. ...[618]

Another witness, who was aware of the dangers of possible hallucination, the Baron of Alvaiázere, was certainly not expecting a miracle, and took precautions to ensure that he was not affected by "suggestion." But in his deposition to the canonical committee which investigated Fatima, he made the following statement: "An indescribable impression overtook me. I only know that I cried out: 'I believe! I believe! I believe!' And tears ran from my eyes. I was amazed, in ecstasy before the demonstration of divine power ... converted in that moment."[619] A final intriguing point was that many people reported that the heat of the sun, as it descended to the earth, also had the effect of drying their clothes and the ground, so that they went from being completely soaked to being dry in about ten minutes.[620]

That same evening Dr Formigão managed to question the children further. Lucia described the various apparitions she had seen of Jesus, Mary and Joseph, and went through the conversation she had with Mary; but under the strain of everything they had been through that day, made the mistake of thinking that she had remembered Mary as saying that the war would end *that* day, rather than end *soon*. Jacinta agreed with her and for this reason Dr Formigão went back to Fatima on 19 October to speak to them again and clarify this point. When he arrived, though, he found the children being interrogated by a group of priests, and discovered they were completely exhausted. Although their replies were unsatisfactory and somewhat contradictory because of their tiredness, it would seem that, when everything is taken into account, including the extraordinary nature of their experiences, it is not surprising that they could not stand up to the sustained emotional strain of continual questioning, making some mistakes in their answers.[621]

After the Apparitions

An influenza epidemic swept Europe in the autumn of 1918, just as the War was finishing, and both Jacinta and Francisco fell ill. Francisco recovered somewhat and there were hopes that he might become well, but he realized that he was destined to die young, as Our Lady had foretold, and his condition worsened again. He offered up all his sufferings as a way of consoling God for the sinfulness and ingratitude of mankind, becoming so weak that eventually he could not even pray. He received his first Communion, and on the next day, 4 April 1919, he died.[622] Jacinta, too, was confined to her bed during the long winter months, and although she recovered, was struck down with bronchial pneumonia, while also developing a painful abscess in her chest. She was moved to the hospital in Ourem in July 1919, where she underwent the painful treatment prescribed for her, but without much effect, returning home in August with an open wound in her side. It was decided that another attempt should be made to treat her; and so, in January 1920, she was taken to Lisbon, where she was diagnosed as having purulent pleurisy and diseased ribs. While waiting to go into hospital, she stayed at an orphanage, where she impressed those who looked after her by her patience in suffering and with a wisdom well beyond her years.[623]

Eventually, in February she was admitted to hospital, where she underwent another painful operation to remove two ribs; this left her with a large wound in her side that had to be dressed daily, causing her agony. On the evening of 20 February, the local priest was called and heard her Confession, but he insisted on waiting till the next day to bring her Communion, despite her protests that she felt worse; as Mary foretold, she died that night, alone, and far from her family. Her body was returned to Fatima and buried with that of Francisco, until both were later moved to the basilica built at the Cova da Iria.[624] During her time in hospital, Mary apparently appeared to Jacinta and told of the grave punishments that God would send the world unless a sufficient number of people made reparation for the sins of mankind. Jacinta told this to Dr Formigão, the priest who had interviewed the children after the apparitions, and this was apparently the inspiration behind his decision to found a congregation of religious sisters at Fatima to live a life of prayer and sacrifice.[625]

Lucia was naturally heartbroken at the loss of her two cousins, and the new bishop of the restored diocese of Leiria decided that it was best if she was removed from Fatima, both to spare her the continual questionings she had to endure, and also to see what effect her absence would have on the numbers coming as pilgrims. Her mother agreed to her being sent away to school, and she left in May 1921, in great secrecy, for Porto, where a school run by the sisters of St Dorothy was situated, and where she was under strict orders not to speak about what she had experienced.

The Church, meanwhile, had maintained silence about the apparitions during the years from 1917, and it was not until May 1922 that Bishop Correia issued a pastoral letter on the subject. In it he described how great numbers were now coming to Fatima, following the phenomena witnessed by thousands of people at the Cova, and how he had questioned Lucia, now aged fourteen, and found her a truthful and reliable witness, despite her lack of education. He also pointed out that the civil authorities had done everything they could do stop pilgrims from going to Fatima, but without effect, and that the Church had acted with prudence and so could not be falsely accused of encouraging people to believe in the apparitions. He then indicated that he would set up a commission of enquiry into the events at Fatima.

Prior to this, a small chapel had been built at the Cova, although official hostility towards the growing pilgrimage to Fatima was still intense and threatened to become violent. In March 1922, the chapel was destroyed with bombs planted by local Freemasons, but even this did not prevent pilgrims from making their way to the shrine. In simple faith, people began to take earth away from the site and make infusions which led to miraculous healings, and this only served to make Fatima more popular still. In October 1926, the bishop visited the Cova for the first time and saw for himself that the great crowds now coming to Fatima needed an adequate water supply, and so asked for a well to be dug. This, as at Lourdes, immediately became the focus of attention and many miraculous cures were reported there.

In 1926, too, the Papal Nuncio visited the site; and in 1927, ten years after the apparitions, the bishop presided at an official ceremony at the Cova for the first time, as other Portuguese bishops began to organize pilgrimages. Eventually the commission set up by Bishop Correia finished its work and in 1930 he issued another pastoral letter on the apparitions, which, after recounting the events at Fatima, contained the following brief but important statement:

In virtue of considerations made known, and others which for reasons of brevity we omit; humbly invoking the Divine Spirit and placing ourselves under the protection of the most Holy Virgin, and after hearing the opinions of our Rev. Advisors in this diocese, we hereby: 1. Declare worthy of belief, the visions of the shepherd children in the Cova da Iria, parish of Fatima, in this diocese, from the 13th May to 13th October, 1917. 2. Permit officially the cult of Our Lady of Fatima.[626]

The image of Our Lady of Guadalupe on the tilma.

Juan Diego witnessing the apparition of Our Lady.

Left: Contemporary painting of the apparition of Our Lady to Catherine Labouré on 27 November 1830.

Below: Miraculous Medal – the obverse shows Our Lady as Mediatrix with rays coming from her hands. The reverse shows the Cross and 'M' surrounded by twelve stars.

Statue of Aaron the High Priest, in Milan, Italy.

Statue of Our Lady of la Salette showing clear points of resemblance to the dress of the Jewish High Priest, Aaron.

Early postcard of Our Lady of Pontmain. Note the resemblance to the attire of the Jewish High Priest.

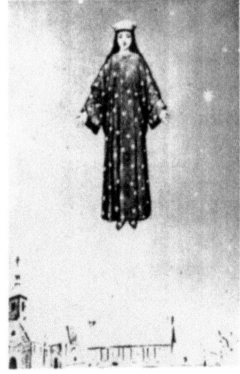

The first stage of the apparition at Pontmain.

The Basilica at Lourdes.

Statue of Our Lady
in the grotto at
Lourdes.

Left: Bartolo Longo, the seer and promoter of Pompeii.

Right: Oil painting of Our Lady of Pompeii, showing her with the Child Jesus and flanked by St Dominic to the left and St Catherine of Siena to the right.

Right: Bartolo Longo, with the band formed by him, and made up of the sons of prisoners.

Left: Knock Parish
Church with
apparition
gable.

Left: Processional statue of Our
Lady of Knock, inside the
Basilica.

Below: Apparition tableau at gable
end of Knock Parish
Church. Statues of Our
Lady, St Joseph and St John,
with altar, lamb, Cross and
angels in the background.

Left: Lucia, Francisco and Jacinta Marto at the time of the apparitions in 1917.

Below: The crowd at the Cova da Iria look at the sky during the miracle of the sun on 13 October 1917.

Left: Front page of *O Seculo* of 15 October 1917, two days after the miracle of the sun. It carried a report of the events at Fatima. The headline on the right reads, "How the sun danced in the middle of the day in Fatima."

Right: View of the Sacred Heart
statue in front of the
Fatima Basilica.

Below: The children at the site of
the apparitions at a later
date – by then a primitive
shrine had begun to
develop.

Right: A large crowd
throngs the
Recinto in front of
the Basilica. The
Capelhina is to the
left of the picture.

Left: The children of Beauraing at the spot where they saw the first apparition of Our Lady, on 29 November 1932 – back row, left to right – Andrée Degeimbre, Fernande Voisin and Gilberte Voisin. Front row – Gilberte Degeimbre and Albert Voisin.

Right: The statue of Our Lady of Beauraing at the site of the apparitions.

Below: View of the convent gate, with the hawthorn tree of the apparitions to its right. The railway bridge is in the background.

Left: Mariette Beco at the time of the apparitions at Banneux in 1933.

Below: The Beco house in Banneux, with a couple praying in the garden where Our Lady appeared to Mariette Beco.

Left: Painting of Our Lady of Banneux. Note the sash, reminiscent of the sash worn by Our Lady at Lourdes.

Below: The route taken by Our Lady from the Beco house to the miraculous spring. Mariette Beco followed her on a number of occasions.

The Cornacchiola family, with Bruno to the left, at the time of the apparition. Bruno's parents and grandmother are to the right of the picture.

The grotto at Tre Fontane at the time of the apparitions in 1947.

Left: Pope John Paul II at the
site of the miraculous
spring, during a
pilgrimage to Banneux
in 1985.

Right: Statue of Our Lady
of Revelation at Tre
Fontane grotto.

Left: The four children of L'Ile Bouchard – left to right – Jacqueline Aubry, Nicole Robin, Laura Croizon, and Jeanette Aubry.

Below left: The site of the apparitions in 1947. Our Lady appeared to the left of the altar, near the flowerpot on the stand to the left.

Statue of Our Lady at the site of the apparitions in the parish church. The long hair, reaching the knees, which was apparent in the first apparition, is clearly visible.

Left: The parish church of St Gilles, L'Ile Bouchard, site of the apparitions of Our Lady in December 1947.

16

Fatima: Typology and Criticism

Fatima and the Typology of the Story of Elijah

It is now a question of comparing the events at Fatima with the biblical story of Elijah to see how they parallel each other. Elijah appears suddenly in the Bible, having been sent by God to announce to Ahab, the wicked king of Israel, that because of the sinfulness of the people, there would be no rain in the land until he gave the word (1 Kings 17:1). At the time of the Fatima apparitions, Portugal was suffering a spiritual drought, as the anti-religious government did everything it could to stamp out Christianity in the country. The only thing that could save it was a rain of grace, something which would give the people the courage to proclaim their faith in God. In the light of this, it is significant that one thing which even the adult onlookers were able to see during the apparitions was the little gray or white cloud that settled on the holmoak tree. Maria Carreira and her friends saw this little cloud at the end of the 13 June apparition, as did Ti Marto during the July apparition. It was seen by many more during the August apparition when the children were abducted, as Maria Carreira recounted: "After the thunderclap came the flash of lightning, and then we began to see a little cloud, very delicate, very white, which stopped for a few moments over the tree and then rose in the air and disappeared."[627]

So this little cloud was seen on a number of occasions by onlookers during the apparitions, taking the place of Mary on 13 August. This makes sense, when we consider how Mary is linked to clouds in the Bible by the early Christian writers, as, for instance, in this prophecy about Egypt in Isaiah; "Behold, the Lord is riding on a swift *cloud* and comes to Egypt; and the idols of Egypt will tremble at his presence" (Isa. 19:1). For many of the early writers, including St Jerome and St Proclus,[628] this was a reference to Mary as the *light cloud.* The Hebrew word used here, *qal,* can mean either "swift" or "light," (in the sense of weight, not brightness). St Jerome says: "surely we ought to see in the light cloud holy Mary, who was not weighed down by any manly seed."[629] St Ambrose develops this idea, linking it to the events of the Exodus, when the Israelites traveled through the desert:

> That pillar of cloud, did, in its outward appearance, go before the children of Israel, but as mystery it signified the Lord Jesus, who was to come in a light cloud [*levis,* swift or light, taken by Ambrose in the latter sense], as Isaiah said; that is in the Virgin Mary, who was a cloud on account of the inheritance of Eve, but light because of her virginal integrity.[630]

Ambrose also compares Mary to a cloud in another passage: "Oh, the riches of Mary's virginity. ... As a cloud she waters the earth with the rain of Christ's grace. ... Receive, then, receive, O consecrated virgins, the spiritual rain that falls from this cloud, ... Run after this good cloud, for within her she has brought forth a fountain to water the face of the earth."[631]

All of this becomes more interesting when we look at the reference to the "little cloud" in the story of Elijah, which comes just after the account of the miracle of the fire from heaven that consumed the sacrifice, (1 Kings 18:16–40), and describes how the drought in Israel would be ended by torrential rain. After giving Ahab this news, Elijah climbed to the top of Mount Carmel and bowed to the ground, telling his servant to go and look out to sea; this request was repeated seven times, until, on the last occasion, the man reported that he could see a cloud as small a man's hand rising from the sea. Elijah then told his servant to run and tell Ahab that a storm was imminent (1 Kings 18:41–46). Just as the little cloud seen by Elijah's servant represented the end of the drought and the beginning of the rains, so also, following the early Christian writers, it can be seen as symbolic of the Blessed Virgin, the one who was given the task of ending mankind's spiritual drought by bearing Christ. Perhaps, too, the torrential rainstorm which followed this incident finds a parallel in the storm which lashed Fatima before the miracle of the sun.

Elijah on Mount Carmel

But the relationship between the story of Elijah and the events at Fatima becomes even clearer when the solar miracle of 13 October is compared with Elijah's great sacrifice on Mount Carmel. Belief in the Jewish religion in the Northern Kingdom of Israel had fallen to a low ebb because of the influence of pagan religions: Elijah was thus sent by God to bring the people back to the truth. He met King Ahab and told him to gather all the people of Israel around him on Mount Carmel, as well as the four hundred and fifty prophets of Baal attached to his wife Jezebel. Ahab agreed to this, and the people were gathered together and addressed by Elijah, who told them to chose between God and Baal. He offered a test as to which was the true God: both he and the prophets of Baal would prepare two bulls and lay them on wood, but not set fire to them. Then, in turn, they would call on their god and the one who answered with fire was the true God. The people agreed and the prophets of Baal set to work. They prepared their bull, but despite calling on Baal from morning till noon nothing happened. At this point Elijah mocked them, saying, amongst other things, that perhaps Baal was asleep. The prophets of Baal redoubled their efforts and for the rest of the afternoon raved around their bull, cutting themselves with their swords and lances until their blood flowed, but still nothing happened (1 Kings 18:17–29).

In a similar way, the Portuguese people were "called" to Fatima by the promise of a great public miracle, and at least seventy thousand responded, by no means all of them believers. There were many followers of "Baal" there too, in his current incarnation as a godless, revolutionary government—those who also wanted to get rid of the very idea of the true God. But just as in the case of the prophets of Baal, who called on their god to show himself and received no answer, so also the corrupt government could not answer the true needs of the Portuguese people; instead, by persecution, they sought to deny them their religious heritage.

Now it was Elijah's turn. He called the people to him and repaired the altar of God with twelve stones, before making a trench around it. He then put wood on the altar and cut his bull in pieces and laid it on the wood. Then he called three times for four jars of water to be poured on the burnt offering, so that it was completely soaked and the trench was filled with water. At the time of the evening offering, he called on God and in response the "fire of the Lord" fell from heaven, consuming the bull and the wood and even licking up the water in the trench. This caused the people to fall on their faces and cry out, "The Lord, he is God; the Lord, he is God" (1 Kings 18:30–39).

Through the children, Mary invited the people to her at Fatima, just as Elijah had done on Mount Carmel, and proceeded to show them that her apparitions were truly of God through the tremendous miracle of the sun. Elijah had prepared the sacrificial victim, placed it on wood, soaking it in water, so that no fraud in setting fire to it was possible; similarly, Mary, too, was careful to appear on the "wood" of the little holmoak tree, after it and the whole countryside had been soaked through by the terrible storm that struck the area overnight. Elijah called on God to make himself known to the people by means of the miracle of fire from heaven consuming the sacrificial animal, while God proved his existence for those present at Fatima, and us too, by the miracle of the sun at the Cova da Iria, a really unprecedented miracle in Christian history. Just as the water was licked up from the trench by the heavenly fire, so also the people and the ground at the site of the apparition were dried in a matter of minutes by the heat of the whirling, plunging, sun. Like those on Mount Carmel, the witnesses at Fatima were forced to proclaim the greatness of God by the awesome nature of what they saw.[632]

But the parallels between Fatima and the story of Elijah do not end there. Just as the authorities in Portugal remained obstinately opposed to the apparitions, despite the overwhelming evidence of the supernatural in the solar miracle, so too Jezebel, the wife of Ahab, despite being aware of the miraculous fire called down by Elijah from heaven, decided to kill him rather than accept that the Lord was greater than her god Baal (1 Kings 19:1–2). Elijah became afraid at this and fled for his life into the desert, where he became discouraged and fell asleep, only to be woken by an angel, who told him to get up and eat the scone at his head and drink the jar of water with it. He lay down again and the Angel had to insist he ate once more, so as to have the strength to walk for forty days and nights to Mount Horeb (1 Kings 19:5–8). It is interesting to compare this episode to the encounter between the children and the Angel of Portugal: instead of giving them a scone and water, he gave them the Body and Blood of Christ in the summer of 1916, as the food to strengthen them for all the troubles they would face following their encounters with Mary during the following year. Although the appearance of the angel to Elijah happened *after* the events on Mount Carmel, it fits in typologically, since the children's experiences with the Angel only became publicly known *after* the apparitions in 1917.

When Elijah arrived at Mount Horeb, he went into a cave, where the word of the Lord came to him and told him to stand outside. Then a mighty wind came by, followed by an earthquake, and then fire, though God was not in any of those, but rather in the gentle, murmuring sound, or voice, that followed (1 Kings 19:9–12). So too, the children saw Mary as a vision of gentleness and love, preceded by something like thunder and lightning.

Another Marian symbol is found in the account of the call of Elisha by Elijah, when he threw his cloak over him as a sign of his authority (1 Kings 19:19–21). Elisha was Elijah's disciple and eventually took his place as a prophet and holy man, after Elijah was taken up to heaven in a whirlwind (2 Kings 2). This, incidentally, illustrates how Elijah can also be seen as type of Mary, who was also assumed into heaven. There has been a long tradition in the Church that Mary "covers" her devotees with her mantle to protect them; here we have Elijah, who represents Mary, covering Elisha with his mantle or cloak, as a sign that he had become his follower. Lucia had to leave her parents, as Elisha had done, and eventually became a Carmelite sister, thus indicating a point of comparison. Elijah's cloak can also be seen as symbolizing the brown scapular. There is, in fact, a long-standing connection between Mary and the Carmelite order, which claims continuity with Elijah and the hermits who followed him on Mount Carmel in Israel.[633]

It should also be noted that, while the vast crowd at Fatima was experiencing the miracle of the sun on 13 October, the children were seeing a series of apparitions of Jesus, Mary and Joseph. They saw St Joseph and the Child Jesus appearing to bless the world, and this was followed by an apparition of Jesus and Mary, with her being shown as "Our Lady of Sorrows." Finally they saw Mary as Our Lady of Mount Carmel. This last point became clear because of the way Mary was carrying the brown scapular in this last apparition, which Lucia in her innocence described as the "two cards."[634] In none of the other recognized apparitions do we find Mary appearing under a form representing a different "tradition" within the Church, and so this is quite significant. It indicates that there is a definite connection between Fatima and Carmel, and thus between Mary and Elijah, underscoring the typological points made above.

The Sun at Fatima: a Meteorological Miracle?

Fr Stanley Jaki seems to adopt a critical attitude to the received idea that there really was a miracle proper at Fatima involving the sun, and prefers to speak of a "meteorological miracle," although he does acknowledge that something clearly "miraculous" did take place, especially given that it was predicted months in advance. He is quite critical, with some justification, of the fact that not enough was done to collect contemporary eyewitness accounts of the miracle; but this was not the major concern of those involved at the time, and, in any case, there are enough testimonies to attest to the reality of the miracle, even though, ideally, it would have been better to have had more. Apart from the fact that the Church in Portugal still faced hostility, gathering reports of healing miracles at Fatima was seen as more important than collecting accounts of the miracle of the sun. The emphasis was more on spreading the spiritual message of Fatima through ongoing accounts of healings.[635]

Fr Jaki's thesis seems to be that ice-particles in the clouds in the region of the sun may well have acted to refract the rays of the sun and break them up into the colors of the rainbow. He points to the evidence of witnesses such as Inácio Lourenço, who saw the sun descend very low as indicating that the miracle was definitely "meteorological" in nature, that is, presumably, as a result of "weather." It is evident, though, that a truly miraculous image of the sun could have descended near the crowd at Fatima, without the need to invoke a naturalistic explanation involving meteorology.[636]

One problem with Fr Jaki's approach is that he seems to be at pains to call into question some well-known biblical miracles, such as the Old Testament miracle of the sun involving Joshua (Josh. 10:12–15). In this, Joshua commanded both sun and moon to stand still, so that the Israelites could pursue and defeat their enemies. The text tells us quite clearly that, at his command both sun and moon stopped in the sky, and that the sun actually delayed its setting for nearly a day. Fr Jaki, though, dismisses this idea and replaces it with his own hypothesis that, "the 'stopping' of the sun for a day may indeed be a metaphorical phrase to convey a purely psychological sense of the lengthening of one afternoon."[637] This causes him to overstate his case and claim that because, in his view, many of the biblical miracles should be reinterpreted in the light of modern "science," therefore this should also happen with the miracle of the sun at Fatima. For example, he also feels that the biblical plagues described in Exodus should be interpreted as a "chain of natural events." As he says:

> In view of the lessons provided by biblical exegesis, there should be nothing sacrilegious in trying to see in the miracle of the sun an unforeseeable occurrence of meteorological factors whose intensity was greatly enhanced by a direct divine intervention. In fact, any careful study (or exegesis) of the eyewitness accounts imposes such an approach to the miracle of the Sun.[638]

The fact is, though, that the eyewitness accounts do not impose such a view, and indeed the strong impression is given that we are dealing with something which is clearly miraculous. It is true that many of the witnesses speak of "clouds" being in the sky at the time of the miracle, but it is a big jump from this to conjecturing that the whole thing can be explained in terms of weather. Fr Jaki hypothesizes that the miracle was an "optical image in whose formation the screening effects of clouds or of vapor or of a layer of ice crystals could play a part."[639] He goes on to argue that the colors produced during the miracle are those of the spectrum, and thus not necessarily miraculous, and that the formation of an image of the sun on the clouds may have been due to "lens-like condensations of the air." Apparently, such a "lens" may start rotating in a tornado-like fashion, and he thinks that a "sudden temperature inversion" may explain the movement of the sun towards the earth three times. We are then told that this "lens" of air could move along a curved path, thus giving the illusion of a rotating sun, while similarly, movements by the ice-crystals are held to have possibly caused the shafts of light which were projected on to the ground. Even so, he is hard pressed to explain the drying of the ground and clothes experienced by many witnesses, and is forced to conclude that all these considerations "constitute a hypothesis and nothing more."[640]

It is hard to see how a "natural" phenomenon such as Fr Jaki's "air-lens" could have acted in the manner indicated in many of the eyewitness accounts of the solar miracle. Tornados and other air turbulences are, by their very nature, chaotic, constantly moving in an unpredictable way, in contrast to the ordered way in which the Fatima miracle unfolded. It is just possible that such phenomena could have produced a momentary distortion of the sun, but this would be prone to sudden change. By contrast, the consensus of the eyewitness accounts speak of the crowd being able to look directly at the sun, which then began to rotate and throw out colored streamers of light like a Catherine wheel, a process repeated three times. The majority of those present saw it change color successively, yellow, blue, red, purple, not in a random chaotic way, but in a slow gradual way. Then it seemed to grow in size and plunge towards earth, throwing out great heat, before returning to its proper place and aspect, the whole process lasting about ten minutes.

It is very difficult to see how all this could have been produced in any "natural" way; and, indeed, the miracle of the sun seems to have been expressly designed to exclude such a possibility. In fact, the strong impression given by the eyewitness accounts is of a phenomenon which was seen in broadly the same way by most of the crowd, but with numerous exceptions, with some seeing nothing at all. This point in itself seems to exclude a naturalistic explanation for the miracle of the sun, because if it had just been a case of weather, then we would have expected all to have seen more or less exactly the same thing, even while making allowances for the natural discrepancies which arise between any collection of testimonies about a particular event.

Overall, then, it seems that Fr Jaki has carried his tendency towards reinterpreting biblical miracles rather too far in respect of the miracle of the sun at Fatima, and has ended up devaluing it and reducing it to the level of an essentially "meteorological" incident. This is in clear contrast to the view of the Bishop of Leiria in his 1930 pastoral letter ratifying the apparitions, who wrote as follows:

> The phenomenon of the Sun on October 13, 1917, described in newspapers of the time, was simply marvellous and caused the greatest impression on those who had the happiness to witness it. ... This phenomenon, which went unnoticed by astronomers, and hence was something unnatural, was witnessed by people of all sorts and social classes—believers and unbelievers, journalists of the principal Portuguese daily newspapers, and even by individuals who were miles away; which destroys all explanations of collective illusion.[641]

One of the central aspects of Fatima is that it is a rejection of the theological reductionism so prevalent today. In contrast to the approach which seems to think that sacred history can be reinterpreted to fit in with modern ideas, the message of Fatima involves a strengthening of belief in elements such as miracles, angels, the reality of heaven and hell, the role of Mary and, indeed, all the basic Catholic principles. It is a repudiation of "neo-Modernist" theories, which seek to empty the miraculous of its divine content, and thus an implicit rejection of such ideas.

In reality the miracle of the sun seems to be just that, a miracle, and the most likely explanation is that it was some form of "apparition," albeit on a gigantic scale. That it was seen only within a certain distance from Fatima, and that the sun was observed as normal elsewhere, seems to indicate that it was a "local" phenomenon. But it was not "imaginary," in that many people felt the heat of the sun as it approached the earth, and the reports of the landscape changing color also indicate that something was really happening. If we recall the Guadalupe account where Mary rearranged the flowers for Juan Diego with her own hands, or Rue du Bac, where Catherine Labouré put her hands on Mary's lap, or Knock, where one of the witnesses felt the grass under the apparition to be dry, despite the rain, and another saw it as ball of light from a distance, then clearly we are dealing with apparitions which impinged on reality, and felt real to those involved. As will be seen with the accounts of the apparitions at Beauraing and Banneux in 1930s Belgium, similar aspects were present. At Beauraing many witnesses saw a "ball of fire" in the place of the apparitions on one occasion, while at Banneux, the mother of the seer also saw a mysterious shape. What seems to have happened at Fatima is an extension of these principles to cover a much larger area, so that the final apparition, the miracle of the sun, was seen by the tens of thousands who thronged the Cova. Thus, at Fatima we seem to be dealing with a genuine miracle and not a meteorological phenomenon.

Other Modern Critics of Fatima

Hilda Graef's criticism of Fatima likewise centers around the miracle of the sun, but is far more serious in that she seeks to deny its validity altogether. After her description of the events at Fatima, which is full of disparaging references, and the obvious point that the sun could not really have moved from its position in space, which is not in dispute, she goes on to say:

> How else are the phenomena—which it must be stressed, were not observed by all present—to be explained? There is, first of all, the fact known to us all that if we stare at the sun we see all sorts of colors. Further, there are many phenomena that occur in the atmosphere after a heavy rain—these, of course, would have been seen by everyone, but this was not the case. Thirdly— and this explanation seems to cover many of the phenomena given in the various accounts—mass suggestion produced by Lucia's cry "Look at the sun!" and the fervent expectation of a miracle by the crowds may account for the "dance of the sun." These difficulties, combined with the error about the end of the war have caused a certain amount of doubt about the authenticity of the apparitions.[642]

This passage, perhaps better than any other, displays the superficiality of such criticisms of Fatima. The point about people staring into the sun and seeing colors is disappointingly weak, while Graef refutes her second point herself. Her third point, that mass suggestion following Lucia's cry was responsible for the crowd seeing the sun dance, is likewise very implausible. It has to be remembered that the miracle of the sun was seen by at least seventy thousand people—would the overwhelming majority of such a huge crowd have all given such similar reports if they were not reporting the truth? They went expecting a miracle, but had no idea what was going to happen, that it would actually involve the sun. That is to say nothing of those who were miles from the Cova, and so could not possibly have been subject to any sort of mass suggestion. The last point about the error concerning the date of the end of the war has been dealt with above: there was no error, just a misunderstanding. This was the greatest miracle of the twentieth century, and to treat it in this fashion is, sadly, to abdicate any idea of treating the events at Fatima fairly or with the seriousness they deserve.

Sandra Zimdars-Swartz adopts a phenomenological approach towards Fatima, one that seeks to focus on the "human processes and interactions" of the seers and the communication of their messages, rather than the "devotional" approach which is more concerned with the actual messages themselves.[643] While there is obviously sense in this, surely there is a danger with such an approach of losing sight of the central meaning of the apparition, as a concrete reality with a real message. Religious phenomenology, in investigating Fatima, seems more concerned with peripheral or hypothetical points, such as how the seers interacted with each other, or the fact that the secrecy of the confessional *may* have influenced Lucia's later attitude towards the Fatima secrets. Likewise, Zimdars-Swartz believes that problems in Lucia's family, and the sufferings she had to undergo personally, are some sort of "explanation" for what happened at Fatima: "It would seem that before 1917 Lucia had developed a way of seeking and finding religious meaning in the midst of adversity, that is, by sharing unusual experiences in near-secrecy with a few friends—and this set the pattern for what was to become the apparition of Fatima."

Granted that Lucia's particular family circumstances were trying, there is no way that they alone can *explain* the many clearly miraculous events which happened at Fatima. Similarly, like many secular commentators on Fatima, Zimdars-Swartz points to the fact that Lucia did not write her memoirs until the period between 1935 and 1941, when in the convent. At the same time, she describes, but totally fails, to give an any sort of non-religious explanation for the miracle of the sun, which was surely the guarantor of Lucia's integrity, both at the time and in later years.[644] It is not as if Lucia's testimony stood alone without any sort of supporting evidence, which is what is usually implied by critics of Fatima.

After alluding to the message of La Salette and its concern with particular sins, such as blasphemy and Sabbath-breaking, which Zimdars-Swartz describes as "transgressions against a ritually defined sacred order," she goes to argue that: "In the Fatima messages too, the epitome of sin and evil is a kind of violation of such a sacred order. In the warning about Russia in the second part of the secret, the great calamity threatening the world is seen as the spread of atheism, i.e., the collapse of the ritual of confession of faith in God. There is also offered here, however, a prescribed ritual which would restore something of the sacred order."[645]

The "prescribed ritual" here, of course, is the consecration of Russia to Mary's Immaculate Heart. This quote really illustrates the gulf in thinking between those who advocate this particular secular phenomenological viewpoint towards Fatima and those who adopt a genuine religious approach. It is a serious misunderstanding of religion, and indeed reality, to see the spread of atheism as only, "the collapse of the ritual of confession of faith in God." We are not dealing with ritualistic or unimportant beliefs, but with the development of atheistic Communism during the twentieth century, a system responsible for the persecution of people simply for believing in God, and one resulting in millions of deaths and the virtual enslavement of a large portion of the earth's population. These were not the activities of some isolated tribe whose religious beliefs were of no real importance for the rest of the world, but of militant atheistic Communists who sought world domination. The consecration of Russia to Mary's Immaculate Heart, far from being just another "prescribed ritual," comes from a genuine divine intervention, and involves a promise of future peace for the world. The reality of its effects certainly seems to be indicated by the collapse in Communism that has taken place since the collegial consecration was performed by Pope John Paul II in 1984.

This sort of analysis, then, indicates the main deficiencies of this particular phenomenological approach, that is it is essentially descriptive and divorced from reality, and thus fails to take religious belief seriously. Likewise, there is a tendency in the book to mix up true and false apparitions, as though they all have equal validity, despite the fact that Zimdars-Swartz correctly discriminates between actual cases of true and false apparitions.[646]

Ultimately, all this means that this particular type of religious phenomenology can tell us little of any value about Fatima or its message.

Protestant Evangelical Criticism of Fatima

Kenneth R. Samples includes Fatima in a brief survey, from a particular Protestant Evangelical viewpoint, of the main Marian apparitions, but his comments are wholly descriptive and rather superficial. As in the case of some of the secular writers, there is also a tendency to lump together approved and non-approved apparitions.[647] What is interesting, though, is that in essence his ideas are not that different from some of the well-known secular researchers, in the sense that, like them, he too comes to the subject with his own set of preconceived ideas. Rather than being open to the possibility that the Marian apparitions really do come from God, that is, being prepared to look at the evidence dispassionately, he argues that they must be false, because they only back up the Catholic position on Mary. He believes that they clash with the Protestant biblical view of Mary and so must be rejected.[648]

He then goes on to argue that this does not mean he is rejecting apparitions *a priori*, but in reality that is exactly what he is doing. The whole problem with this particular Protestant approach to Christianity, with its exclusive emphasis on the Bible, is that it is one-dimensional. History and tradition are largely ignored in favor of a narrow, literalist interpretation of the text, often without reference to its context. There is much inconsistency, though, in this approach: the text is taken literally until it clashes with the "tradition" handed down by Luther and Calvin, when its real meaning is interpreted away. It is only necessary to point to Jesus' words at the Last Supper, "This is my Body" and "This is my Blood," and the rejection of their literal meaning by Protestantism, in favor of a "spiritual" (but erroneous) interpretation, to realize this.

The Bible was compiled and authenticated by the Catholic Church. It did not fall from heaven in its completed form; but rather the Church, under the guidance of the Holy Spirit, gradually discerned which writings were revealed by God and which were spurious. Therefore the Bible does not "stand alone," but must be interpreted by an external authority, the Church. The history of Protestantism, with its continual splits and divisions, only serves to illustrate the fact that, of itself, the Bible cannot stand as a suitable authority. This is not to say that there is anything wrong with biblical teaching, just that its authentic interpretation is the prerogative of the Magisterium of the Church.

Samples thus rejects both Catholic Mariology and the Marian apparitions, on the *a priori* grounds that they do not conform with his own understanding of Scripture.[649] In other words, Samples starts with the Bible and then goes out to look at the real world of apparitions and miracles, and since these do not conform with his particular interpretation of the Bible, they are rejected. It is certainly true that we can gain information about matters concerning faith and morals from the Bible, but to extend universally this principle to other matters is to turn reality on its head. If somebody is miraculously cured at Lourdes, we cannot say that particular type of miracle isn't mentioned in the Bible, hence we can ignore the overwhelming evidence in its favor—medical reports, x-rays, and so forth—and say that nothing miraculous has happened. To adopt such an attitude does not make sense. On that basis, the Pharisees and scribes who rejected Jesus would have been justified in doing so; he was not performing the right sort of miracles for them, they held he was a sinner, and so he obviously was not from God. His teaching and actions did not fit in with their preconceived ideas, and so they plotted to kill him. Thus, the position of Samples, in rejecting apparitions, is uncomfortably close to that of the Pharisees in their repudiation of Christ. This is perhaps not surprising, since, in many respects, Calvinistic Protestantism, given its unbalanced emphasis on the Bible, represents a return to that sort of mentality.

This point comes out clearly in the next section of Samples' book. He begins by acknowledging that he is unable to account for all aspects of the events surrounding Marian apparitions, but feels much can be explained in natural terms. The difficulty of doing this in the case of those apparitions approved by the Church will be clear to the reader by now. He then considers the possibility of a supernatural explanation in the following terms: "because of the unbiblical nature of Marian apparitions, if the cause is supernatural in origin then we can only be dealing with the demonic, not with God. I realize that this line of reasoning will be offensive to many Catholics; nonetheless, I believe it is a necessary theological inference."[650]

There is some truth in his argument about the possibility of false miracles, but ultimately it is clear that Satan cannot produce *genuine* miracles and signs. At best, he can perform counterfeit miracles: this must be the case, because otherwise we would have no way of telling him apart from God. It is certainly possible that some unapproved apparitions *may* ultimately have a satanic origin, but this cannot be true of apparitions approved by the Church.

The main point which comes out from his analysis, though, is how it parallels the criticisms of Jesus made by the Pharisees. He was accused of being in league with Beelzebul, the ruler of the demons, and that this was the source of his power in casting out demons. Jesus, though, pointed out to them that, if this were the case, the "kingdom of Satan" was divided and must fall; but in fact, his ability to cast out demons indicated that his power must come from God (Matt. 12:22–29). The Pharisees could see this but refused to accept Jesus. Now, the miracles worked by Jesus were the proof of his mission, as he himself stated during his disputes with the Jews: "If I am not doing the works of my Father, then do not believe me; but if I do them, even though you do not believe me, believe the works, that you may know and understand that the Father is in me and I am in the Father" (John 10:37–38).

The criticisms of Marian apparitions put forward by Samples follow exactly the same pattern; he is duplicating the error of the Pharisees by adopting a biblical frame of reference, which automatically excludes Marian apparitions and miracles: The Pharisees said Jesus' miracles were due to Satan, and Samples says the Marian apparitions and miracles are also due to the devil. Unfortunately, although he specifically mentions Lourdes and Fatima when discussing alleged miracles, it is clear that, in the main, he is thinking of the sort of miracles which are claimed for unapproved apparition sites, such as crosses spinning or rosaries changing color, "miracles" which, admittedly, are rather trivial and unworthy of God. But this is not the case with Lourdes, where the miraculous healings have been subject to detailed scrutiny. Similarly, seventy thousand people at Fatima could not all have been deceived when they said they saw the sun revolving and then plunging towards earth. What seems to have happened is that Samples has investigated unapproved apparitions and found them wanting—not without good reason—and then applied this negative appraisal to the approved apparitions. Clearly, this is not a legitimate procedure: each apparition has to be judged on its own merits and not subject to a blanket condemnation. This again demonstrates the necessity of carefully distinguishing between approved and unapproved apparitions.

Samples then goes on to make the following point which implies a satanic origin for Marian apparitions; "since Scripture instructs us to test the spirits, ... the fact that the lady at both Lourdes and Fatima refused initially to identify herself, raises great suspicion as to her real identity."[651] With this sort of reasoning, perhaps we should call Jesus' credentials into question, on the grounds that he too refused to confirm his identity as the Messiah in the early part of his ministry. Samples also alleges that "millions of people, including many of the pilgrims at Lourdes, actually worship the Virgin—perhaps ignorantly, and certainly against official church teaching. This is idolatry. Where there is idolatry, satanic activity is certain ..."[652] He then goes on to link Lourdes with necromancy; but there is really no evidence for either idolatry or necromancy at Lourdes, as anyone who was really familiar with that shrine would realize. In sum, his anti-Catholic attitude prevents him from really looking at Marian apparitions with an open mind; and, just like the Pharisees with Christ, that means it is impossible for Samples to understand or appreciate them.

It is instructive to compare his ideas, and those of the secular critics dealt with above, with the Catholic position, because once again it shows how the intellectual legacy of the Reformation and the secularism which, at least indirectly, resulted from it, is with us to this day. The Catholic view is that miracles and apparitions occurred in biblical times, and have continued to occur periodically to this day. At the time of the Reformation, however, Protestantism largely abandoned the idea that miracles and apparitions could still occur, and certainly neither Luther nor Calvin, unlike Jesus, displayed any miraculous proofs of their alleged mission to reform the Church. The secularists have taken this weakened position to its logical conclusion, and said that not only do miracles and apparitions not happen now, but they have *never* occurred; the Bible is just a fabrication. These approaches, of course, ignore the reality of miraculous events. So really, Samples' version of Protestantism, and secularism, are in the same camp, broadly speaking, of opposition to Marian apparitions, the first on the grounds that they are *a priori* "unbiblical," and the second on the grounds they are *a priori* "impossible." Both approaches demonstrate the fallacy of approaching modern miraculous phenomena with a closed mind, which is not being prepared to look honestly at the evidence; and thus they must be rejected.

17

The World between the Wars

The Postwar World and the Church

The First World War and its aftermath had brought about tremendous changes in the world. Millions had died in the most appalling circumstances, as Europe was taken to the limit of its resources, and beyond. The whole of Eastern Europe was in turmoil and Communism was beginning its grisly rise. Western Europe too was shattered, with relief in Britain and France that it was all over, but a relief tempered by the realization that Germany would one day rise from its ruined state and perhaps again menace Europe. Only America emerged from the war in a strengthened condition; and it was its conception of democracy that seemed to provide the key to the future. Old autocratic regimes were swept away and replaced by new democracies; but, regrettably, many of these were to fall by the wayside in the upsurge of authoritarianism and fascism in the years leading up to the Second World War.[653]

The peace that followed World War I not only helped to prepare for another war, while ushering in the era of Communism, but was also directly hostile to Catholicism. Italy had entered the war on the allied side only on condition that the Vatican was excluded from the peace negotiations of 1919, and these talks were tainted by hostility to the Church, as the old Catholic Austro-Hungarian Empire was swept away, leaving Protestant Germany intact. Despite this, the Pope did everything he could to foster a spirit of reconciliation; and his approach was later given concrete form in the League of Nations, although regrettably this organization was to be terminally weakened by the absence of the United States. Elsewhere, the Church was suffering persecution, as in Mexico, where the new rulers attacked ordinary Catholics with a ferocity reminiscent of the Aztecs, a very sad situation for the country that had witnessed the beauty of Guadalupe.[654] Portugal enjoyed a brief period of normal Catholic life at this time, but the assassination of the president and a series of coups meant that the country remained unstable until 1926, when an authoritarian government came to power after years of unrest and economic problems, with Salazar becoming Prime Minister in 1932.

Behind the scenes, Vatican diplomats, including Archbishop Pacelli, exerted what influence they could to prevent Germany from being ruined by excessive war-reparations payments, while the defeated country entered a period of turmoil, as it faced the threat of Communism. The Spartacist revolutionary movement, however, was crushed by the army in 1919 and the liberal democratic Weimar Republic established; this event, incidentally, showed that Communist risings in the West were more than just a possibility. Unfortunately, a myth that the German military had been betrayed by civilian cowardice, and that this was responsible for Germany's defeat, was widely propagated. Given the overwhelming military influence in the country during the war, that was quite ridiculous, but it meant that later civilian governments were tainted with the dishonor attached to the Versailles treaty, by which Germany had forfeited much territory, particularly in the East. A sense of grievance was born that Hitler was later able to exploit successfully. Germany was not able to assimilate the rapid change from its previous autocratic form of government to parliamentary democracy, and thus Weimar was doomed to failure. The prevailing mood in 1920s Germany was dominated by nationalism and anti-Semitism, rather than toleration and a desire for democracy.[655]

In Russia, Lenin's Communist state was under attack in its early years, but managed to survive with all the terrible dangers this would present for the future. In 1920, Communist armies focused on Poland, well aware that, if they could defeat that country, the rest of Europe, exhausted after the war, lay within their grasp. Defeat for the Poles seemed inevitable, but in what has been described as a "miraculous" victory, General Pilsudski's forces overcame the Red Army at the River Vistula near Warsaw in August 1920, forcing its retreat. Poland was thus saved from invasion for nearly twenty years, and once again, as in the days of John III Sobieski in the seventeenth century, the Poles played a major part in preventing the invasion and destruction of the rest of Europe.[656]

Meanwhile, in Russia itself mistaken policies led to the first of the great Soviet famines, and may have caused as many as three million deaths in the winter of 1921–22. Lenin died in January 1924, poisoned, probably on Stalin's orders, but by then the all-encompassing dictatorship of Soviet Communism was firmly established.[657] The victory of Communism in Russia was a terrible blow to that country, and also had the unfortunate side-effect of galvanizing the belief of Communists in other countries that a world-wide revolution was possible. This led to the formation of the Third International or Comintern, which issued directives binding on Communist parties everywhere, encouraging the progress of Communism by any means.[658]

Pius XI, (1857–1939), had become Pope in January 1922, following the death of Benedict XV, and is probably best known for his part in the negotiation of the Lateran treaties with Mussolini's regime, in which the status of the Vatican as a city-state was finally agreed, allowing the papacy to assume its modern role. He was to have the unenviable task of ruling the Church as the world entered another period of upheaval, following the economic crisis of 1929 and the growth of the totalitarian governments of the thirties. He saw these growing international problems as a profound threat to the little of what remained of the ideals of Christendom, and, indeed, to civilization itself, which was not an exaggerated view as events were to confirm. He clearly saw the danger of fascism and Communism, and condemned both in encyclicals in the thirties, while also doing everything in his power to re-Christianize society and promote peace, despite the difficulties involved.

In 1931 Pope Pius spoke out in his encyclical *Quadragesimo Anno*, on the fortieth anniversary of Leo XIII's encyclical *Rerum Novarum*. He forcefully criticized the way that workers were still being treated like objects, and argued strongly for a just wage, whilst also condemning economic liberalism and socialism. He pointed out the injustice of the way the principles of capitalism were being abused, leading to a situation where a small number of the very rich selfishly controlled the destiny of the rest of society, leading to gross exploitation and a loss of human dignity.[659]

Later Apparitions to Sr Lucia

By 1925, Lucia, who was now aged eighteen, had become a postulant with the Sisters of St Dorothy at Pontevedra in Spain, and on Thursday, 10 December, the Blessed Virgin, accompanied by the Child Jesus on a little cloud, appeared to her in her cell. Lucia recounted that Mary rested her hand on her shoulder, while showing her a heart encircled by thorns in her other hand. The Child Jesus spoke first: "Have pity on the Heart of your Most Holy

Mother. It is covered with the thorns with which ungrateful men pierce it at every moment, and there is no one to remove them with an act of reparation." Then Mary said:

> My daughter, look at My Heart surrounded with thorns with which ungrateful men pierce it at every moment by their blasphemies and ingratitude. You, at least, try to console me, and say that I promise to assist at the hour of death, with all the graces necessary for salvation, all those who, on the first Saturday of five consecutive months go to confession and receive Holy Communion, recite five decades of the Rosary and keep me company for a quarter of an hour while meditating on the mysteries of the Rosary, with the intention of making reparation to me.[660]

The Child Jesus again appeared to Lucia in February 1926 to encourage her to propagate this devotion,[661] and additionally, on the night of 29–30 May 1930, as she was praying before the Blessed Sacrament, she received an interior locution from him explaining why it was necessary to make a communion of reparation on *five* Saturdays.[662] She explained later that she had been given to understand that this related to the five main types of blasphemies and offenses committed against the Immaculate Heart of Mary: that is against the Immaculate Conception; against Mary's Virginity; against her Divine Maternity and her spiritual motherhood of mankind; for the offenses of those who encourage in the hearts of children indifference, contempt and even hatred of her, and finally, as reparation for those who outrage her in her holy images.[663]

On 13 June 1929, Lucia saw another important apparition involving Mary as she was making a Holy Hour in the convent chapel at Tuy in Spain, as was her custom on Thursday nights from eleven to twelve. She was alone, praying the prayers of the Angel in the dim light of the sanctuary lamp when

> Suddenly the whole chapel was illumined by a supernatural light, and above the altar appeared a Cross of light, reaching to the ceiling. In a brighter light on the upper part of the Cross, could be seen the face of a man and his body as far as the waist; upon his breast was a dove of light; nailed to the Cross was the body of another man. A little below the waist, I could see a chalice and a large Host suspended in the air, onto which drops of blood were falling from the Face of Jesus Crucified and from the wound in His side. These drops ran down onto the Host and

fell into the chalice. Beneath the right arm of the Cross was Our Lady and in her hand was her Immaculate Heart. (It was Our Lady of Fatima, with her Immaculate Heart in her left hand, without sword or roses, but with a crown of thorns and flames). Under the left arm of the Cross, large letters, as if of crystal clear water which ran down upon the altar, formed these words: "Grace and Mercy."

At this point Lucia explained that she understood the apparition was a representation of the Holy Trinity, as she heard Mary speak to her:

> The moment has come in which God asks the Holy Father, in union with all the Bishops of the world, to make the consecration of Russia to my Immaculate Heart, promising to save it by this means. There are so many souls whom the Justice of God condemns for sins committed against me, that I have come to ask reparation: sacrifice yourself for this intention and pray.

Lucia told all this to her confessor who ordered her to write it down, and she also said that, later on, Jesus had spoken as follows to her: "They did not wish to heed My request. Like the king of France, they will repent and do it, but it will be late. Russia will have already spread her errors throughout the world, provoking wars and persecutions of the Church; the Holy Father will have much to suffer."[664] It was just before this time, in early 1929, that persecution of Christians in Russia was revived and intensified. All public religious activities were banned, and Sunday as a day of rest was abolished. By 1932 a five-year "anti-religious" plan was being promoted with the aim of totally erasing any sign of religion in the Soviet Union.[665] The reference to the French king is to the delayed consecration of France to the Sacred Heart, made by Louis XIV in the seventeenth century.[666]

Sr Lucia wrote to her confessor at the time, Fr Gonzalves, reiterating the message about the First Saturday devotion of reparation and giving details of what was necessary to ensure the salvation of Russia:

> If I am not mistaken, Our Dear Lord God promises to end the persecution of Russia, if the Holy Father condescends to make, and likewise ordains the Bishops of the Catholic World to make, a solemn and public act of reparation and consecration of Russia to the Most Holy Hearts of Jesus and Mary. In response to the ending of this persecution, His Holiness is to promise to approve of and recommend the practice of the already mentioned devotion of reparation.[667]

There were many difficulties in the way of such a consecration, however, not least the fact that Sr Lucia was a little hesitant in expressing herself on this matter, mainly because she did not see Jesus in person; rather she felt his divine presence as an interior communication. Apart from that, as has previously been pointed out, Jesus had already indicated to Sr Lucia other problems. Nevertheless, she continued to write to Fr Gonzalves and also contacted the bishop a number of times, to urge that the consecration be taken seriously.[668]

The Twenties and Thirties

During the twenties and thirties there were many important social and religious changes, as the Christian basis of Western industrialized culture further weakened. Ordinary workers were progressively de-Christianized, partly as a result of further technological progress. This process reduced people to the status of cogs in a gigantic machine, a situation not helped by the effects of growing urbanization and a consequent breakdown in the old social patterns. By the thirties, religious indifference had become widespread in industrialized Europe amongst all sections of society, with laws permitting divorce and a growing moral decline.[669] Pius XI issued his encyclical *Casti Connubii* in 1930, as a reminder to Catholics that all artificial methods of contraception were wrong, but there were many signs that a contraceptive and hedonistic mentality was growing in Europe. Weimar Germany in particular was notorious for its tolerance of all manner of sexual deviance. Freud's destructive theories were having as great an influence as had Darwin's previously, helping to cause further intellectual upheaval in Europe and also increasingly affecting the moral attitudes of ordinary people.[670]

Conditions in Germany grew steadily worse after the war, with the country slipping further into trouble, as the national debt nearly quadrupled between 1920 and 1923. An inflationary spiral developed, with citizens losing confidence in money and trying to exchange it for goods, which they hoped would keep their value. Eventually a new gold mark, each one worth a billion old paper marks, was introduced in November 1923, to replace the inflated currency. This had the effect of canceling the government's debts to the banks, but still left it owing colossal sums in reparations to the Allies, which, however, were eventually rescinded. The effect of all this on the German public was to lessen confidence in the

Weimar government, with the blame being put on the Treaty of Versailles and Jewish financiers for the mess the country found itself in. This was precisely the sort of atmosphere in which Hitler's ideas were most likely to succeed.[671] France, meanwhile, was worried at the prospect of a German military revival, unlike the British, who felt such a risk was exaggerated at this time. French society was divided, with secular interests, including Freemasons and socialists, involved in a cultural struggle with Catholic elements, a struggle which weakened and demoralized the country in the years leading up to the Second World War.[672]

When Western economies were thrown into turmoil by the collapse in trade and mass unemployment following the Wall Street crash of 1929, many people saw capitalism as terminally weakened, especially given the apparent progress made by Russian Communism. But this progress was an illusion, and in reality Stalin was cementing his terrifying dictatorship more firmly into place. He began to build a personality cult around himself, renaming places all over Russia, such as Stalingrad for Tsaritsyn, while pressing on with his plan for rapid industrialization and the destruction of the independent peasants through their forced collectivization. The ordinary people, given the choice, would have returned to a market economy, and so, if the Communist revolution was to continue, their independence had to be destroyed. Poor harvests in 1927 and 1928 led to more and more pressure being put on the peasants and their food being seized. The supposedly rich peasants, the *kulaks*, were singled out for extermination, but huge numbers of ordinary peasants were forced on to collective farms, and soon anyone who objected to this policy was classed as a kulak.[673]

Large-scale violence was used from 1929 until the mid thirties, which resulted in probably ten million people losing their lives, and many millions more ending up in the camps. This death total was Stalin's own estimate given to President Roosevelt at Yalta in 1945. This situation led to a great man-made famine during 1932–33, as the peasants destroyed their food rather than surrender it. Those who remained were herded on to the collective farms and reduced to the level of virtual slaves, forbidden to travel to the towns in search of work, a situation that remained in force until the 1970s. This terrible repression brutalized the Communist Party still further and provided a blueprint for Hitler. Likewise, the large scale use of slave-labor in Russia, with at least ten million people in concentration camps from 1933 onwards, also provided a model for the Nazis. The high death rate in such camps meant that a constant supply of new prisoners was necessary, and thus the awful tyranny of the Soviet State was compounded by the fact that no one felt safe from arrest. During the thirties Stalin purged the party itself, so that eventually he attained a position of absolute dominance, holding a terrifying power of life or death. By the late thirties, communism had claimed something like twenty million victims. A climate of fear was created, one which was maintained until the demise of the Soviet Union in recent times. None of this was accidental; it was inherent in the inhuman system created by Lenin and perfected by Stalin.[674]

While all this was going on, Western intellectuals, such as George Bernard Shaw, were praising the Soviet system as a great advance for the world. In 1932, at the height of the famine, the visiting evolutionary biologist Julian Huxley, grandson of the Thomas Huxley who had done so much to promote Darwin's ideas, thought that the general level of health in Russia was superior to that found in England. Sidney and Beatrice Webb, the English socialists, toured Russia during this period and spread the view that there was no famine: at the same time Stalin was deliberately engineering a famine in the Ukraine, which led to the deaths of at least five million people. All this was part of a general movement amongst many Western intellectuals, seemingly a combination of self-delusion and deliberate deception, which promoted the lamentably mistaken view that Communism would lead to a new promised land. This attitude was helped by the tendency to concentrate on Nazi brutality during the thirties, rather than Marxist terror. Their pro-Communist writings were translated and published by Stalin, and in this process of "supping with the devil," Western thinkers were corrupted, and with them Western society itself. This was evident in the way that liberal thought forms, that is, those most influenced by socialist and Communist ideology, came to be so fashionable in the West in the postwar era.[675]

Britain's status as a world power depended on her empire, but imperialism was a declining force during the thirties, and the prevailing left-leaning mentality in the country was more concerned with disarmament. This was the period when intellectuals, such as Anthony Blunt and Guy Burgess, were working to undermine the British security services at the behest of Soviet interests. In general, there was an unwillingness to accept that another war could occur, an attitude which moved from pacifist inertia to actual appeasement during the thirties. It always has to be borne in mind, though, that the fear of Communism was greater than that of Nazism at this stage, and this tended to make Western governments see Hitler as the lesser of two evils.[676]

Thus the twenties and thirties saw increasing immorality in a growing climate of pacifism and appeasement. The Soviet Union continued its blood-soaked rise, aided by Western intellectuals, who seemingly cared little for the truth, while the inequity of the Versailles Treaty became increasingly evident, as Germany struggled to pay its war debts, leading to a further destabilization which Hitler would later turn to advantage.

18

The Apparitions at Beauraing and Banneux – 1932–33

Beauraing: November 1932 – January 1933

During the twenties and early thirties, the Church in Belgium had done much work to reintroduce Catholic ideals into the lives of ordinary workers, particularly through an apostolate of the laity. It was recognized that the working-class environment was hostile to Christianity, and so a completely new approach was developed during the twenties, one which sought to reinvigorate society through the laity, to win back ordinary people to the Church, a plan that had the full approval of the Pope. This form of "Catholic Action" spread to other countries during this period, although it was no easy task to reach people who faced constant economic hardship and to whom the easy answers of socialism and Communism were a constant temptation.[677]

Beauraing is a small town in the southern, French-speaking, part of Belgium, and it was here that the Blessed Virgin appeared to a group of children between late November 1932 and January 1933. The five children involved in the apparitions came from the Voisin and Degeimbre families, neither of which was particularly Catholic. Hector and Marie Louise Voisin sent only one of their daughters, Gilberte, who was thirteen and a very religious girl, to the Catholic school run by the local sisters, the Academy, as a semi-boarder. Their other two children, Fernande, a fifteen-year-old girl, and Albert, aged eleven, went to state schools. Gilberte stayed on in school until 6:30 to study, and on 29 November 1932, her brother and sister were making their way to the Academy to walk home with her. On the way, they called at the Degeimbre house and were joined by two of the daughters, fourteen-year-old Andrée and another Gilberte, aged nine.[678]

The four children, the three girls and Albert, made their way to the convent door to meet Gilberte Voisin, entering the grounds and passing a small Lourdes grotto in front of the railway embankment that skirted the convent garden. While waiting for the front door bell to be answered, Albert, with an expression of surprise on his face, looked towards the embankment over the grotto and cried out: "Look! The Blessed Virgin, dressed in white, is walking above the bridge!" The girls looked and could see the luminous figure of a lady dressed in white walking in midair, her feet hidden by a little cloud. Meanwhile the door was answered by one of the Sisters, who called to Gilberte, while noticing the agitated state of the children. They told her they could see the Virgin walking over the grotto, but Sister Valeria could see nothing and thought the children were confused about the statue of Mary in the Lourdes grotto. As soon as Gilberte Voisin reached the door she too saw the figure. Frightened, they all ran home, turning back once to see the glowing figure still above the bridge, but their parents refused to believe their story.[679] A point of interest, however, is that Gilberte Degeimbre's mother heard her talking in her sleep that night saying: "Look, Albert, how beautiful she is!"[680]

Next evening, 30 November, their parents, convinced that it was all a case of overactive imaginations, allowed the children to escort Gilberte home again, and as they were walking together towards the convent gate, they once more saw the Lady walking over the railway embankment. They ran to the house of the widowed Mrs Degeimbre crying out: "We've seen her! It *is* the Blessed Virgin, and she is so much more beautiful than any of her statues!" On the following evening, 1 December, suspecting a trick, she went with the children and some friends and neighbors to the convent, and even before they reached it, the children saw the Lady in the garden. She disappeared almost immediately, and as the children went to fetch Gilberte, the adults looked around to see if they could catch someone playing a practical joke, but without success. Gilberte, meanwhile, had just come through the door of the convent when she too saw the Lady, who had her hands joined and eyes raised to heaven; she smiled at the children and then disappeared. As the children moved towards the gate, they saw her again as she moved from some shrubs near the gate towards the grotto, before disappearing. The youngest child, Gilberte Degeimbre, was so overcome by what she had seen that she was taken home and looked after by Gilberte Voisin, while the other three children returned to the convent with their parents.[681]

Even before they reached the gate, though, they again saw the Lady and fell to their knees, as if struck down, according to witnesses; in high-pitched voices they then began to say the Hail Mary, as they gazed at a hawthorn tree inside the garden near the fence. Madame Degeimbre moved towards the tree but halted instantly as Andrée cried out: "Stop! you are going to tread on her." She later said that this was the moment when she began to believe the children. They later told how they saw a beautiful Lady on one of its branches, wearing a white gown and holding her hands together as in prayer, with rays of light surrounding her head.

After she disappeared, the local priest, Fr Lambert, was consulted by the mothers of the children, and he advised silence, although this proved difficult, as the story began to spread around the town. Next evening, 2 December, Mother Théophile, the convent superior, put two dogs in the yard and locked the convent gates, having severely scolded some of the girls for what she described as "telling lies," during the day. But the children still saw the Lady, as they fell to their knees in unison outside the garden in the street. It is significant that they had approached the convent not as a group, but separated from each other and mingled in with the adults, and thus it is difficult to see how they could have faked an apparition, especially in the dark. Albert asked her if she was the Immaculate Virgin, to which she smiled and nodded her head, and, when asked what she wanted, she said simply: "Always be good," words which prompted the reply "Yes, we'll always be good."

Mary then disappeared, and the children began to make their way home, but one of the neighbors, a M. Marischal, decided to stay and examine the area with the aid of a torch. Albert turned back to wait for him and again saw Mary. This prompted M. Marischal to return to the other adults and suggest that he fetch his own young son, since it appeared that only children were able to see the apparition. Thus the children returned to the scene with young Leopold Marischal, but although the children dropped swiftly to their knees, Leopold only knelt slowly and after the others. He saw nothing. Mary's words to the children on this occasion were: "Is it really true that you will always be good?"

On 3 December, Mother Théophile asked Gilberte Voisin to describe the Lady she had seen, and was told that "She had a white dress with blue reflections. Her feet were hidden by a white cloud. She held her hands joined while looking at heaven or at us. She smiled. On her head she had a white veil that fell on her shoulders and descended to the middle of her legs. She had rays all around her head, many rays, all straight, very fine, all the same size."[682]

That evening Mother Théophile locked the gate, again having

forbidden the children to come to the garden, as a crowd of about one hundred and fifty gathered outside the convent. Next day Madame Voisin called to see Mother Théophile and told her how her husband had taken Fernande aside and impressed on her the seriousness of their position, if it turned out that the children were lying, that their own reputations would be ruined and that the families would become a laughingstock in the town. Fernande replied that it was impossible for her to change her account, even if threatened with death, and Madame Voisin finished by saying: "I wish you could have seen the calm assurance with which she spoke. My husband and I could say nothing more to her."

Somewhat reassured, Mother Théophile agreed to let the children pray outside the convent garden, but still locked the gate, and so a pattern developed for subsequent apparitions, in which the children would see Mary by the hawthorn tree, from *outside* the garden.[683] The children would simultaneously drop to their knees on the cobble-stoned street with a force that made bystanders wince, and yet they suffered no injury, indeed they said they felt as though they were kneeling on cushions, and moreover, people were astonished at the quality of the children's voices when they prayed, a quality that seemed to go beyond the merely natural.[684]

On the evening of 4 December the children once more saw the Lady, and she again, when questioned, indicated that she was the Immaculate Virgin. She said nothing, however, when some cures were requested, but told the children to return on 8 December, the feast of the Immaculate Conception. When asked by Fernande if she wanted a chapel built, she replied, "Yes," before disappearing. On Tuesday, 6 December, the children, at Fr Lambert's suggestion, said the rosary during the apparitions for the first time, and were rewarded by seeing a rosary on the right arm of the Lady, a practice continued during the remaining apparitions.[685] The next evening, the children again saw the Lady, who, they reported, had said nothing, and following this they were examined by four doctors. They testified to their good mental and physical health and the apparent honesty of their answers.

On Thursday, 8 December, a crowd of about fifteen thousand assembled expecting a great miracle, but they only saw the children in ecstasy, impervious to lighted matches held underneath their hands, pin pricks, or lights shone in their eyes. This was the only occasion when the children entered an ecstatic state. One of the doctors present, Fernand Mastriaux, testified that no trace of any burning was found on the children's hands, although they should have sustained first-degree burns. At one stage, he asked

Gilberte Degeimbre why she was crying, to receive the reply; "She is so beautiful." He asked the same question a few moments later but received no reply. When the apparition was over the Virgin had not spoken to the children, and many in the crowd were disappointed that there had been no great cure or sign. Meanwhile Fr Lambert, Mother Théophile, and the church authorities generally, were taking a very prudent and circumspect attitude towards events at Beauraing, and refusing to get involved: the local bishop ordered his priests not to go to the site of the apparitions.[686]

From this point on the apparitions did not occur every night, although the children assembled and said the rosary as usual; if Mary did appear, they would fall to their knees in unison. They were closely watched to ensure they could not talk to each other, and when the apparition was over, were questioned separately as to what they had seen. A lawyer named Adrien Laurent took notes of these examinations and they constitute a faithful record of events. Many found the fact that their accounts agreed on all major points impressive, although some sections of the Belgian press were sceptical.[687] On 17 December, in response to a question in the name of the clergy, the children reported that the Lady reiterated her request for a chapel, while on both 22 and 23 December Albert did not see the Lady, although the girls did. When questioned, he assumed that this was because he had used someone else's rosary beads. There were no apparitions on 25 and 26 December, but on 28 December the children said that Mary had told them that: "My last apparition will take place soon."[688]

The next day Fernande saw the Blessed Virgin with a heart of gold surrounded by rays, and this was seen by two of the other children on 30 December, as Mary repeated the phrase: "Pray, pray very much," which was only heard by Fernande. On the last day of 1932, 31 December, all the children saw Mary's golden heart. This has been seen as indicating a connection between Beauraing and Fatima, with its emphasis on devotion to the Immaculate Heart of Mary, although at the time few people in Belgium had heard of the events in Portugal, and they did not become widely known until 1936 or 1937.[689]

On 1 January 1933, Mary spoke to Gilberte Voisin asking her to "Pray always," with the emphasis on *always*; the next day she told them that on 3 January, at what was to prove to be the final apparition, she would speak to each of them separately. A very large crowd, estimated at between thirty and thirty-five thousand people, assembled that evening as the children began their rosary. After two decades, four of them called out and fell to their knees, leaving

Fernande, the oldest, in tears because she could see nothing. The children later reported that Mary looked even more magnificent than usual and smiled radiantly, as she spoke first to the youngest child Gilberte, telling her a secret she was not to reveal, before saying: "Goodbye." She then spoke to Gilberte Voisin, imparting to her what has been seen as the main promise of Beauraing, "I will convert sinners," as well as also giving her a secret and saying: "Goodbye." Albert was likewise given a secret and bidden farewell, while to Andrée she said: "I am the Mother of God, the Queen of Heaven. Pray always," before taking leave of her in the same way as the others, showing her golden heart before disappearing.

Fernande remained kneeling while the other children went inside for questioning, when suddenly she, and many in the crowd, heard a loud noise like thunder and saw a "ball of fire" on the hawthorn tree. Mary appeared and spoke to Fernande, asking her if she loved her Son and herself; when Fernande replied that she did, the response was: "Then sacrifice yourself for me." At this the Blessed Virgin glowed with extraordinary brilliance, and extended her arms, so that the girl could see her golden heart, before saying, "Goodbye," and disappearing, to leave Fernande weeping.[690]

Criticisms of Beauraing

Criticism of the events at Beauraing was not slow to appear, but in addition to the anti-Catholic press, there were attacks from unexpected quarters. The French Carmelite Fathers, in the April 1933 edition of their magazine, the *Études Carmélitaines*, published four unfavorable articles on Beauraing. Two of these articles were by priests and two by doctors; they were later published in book form. While the criticisms of the priests were not particularly weighty, since neither of them had been present at any of the apparitions, those of the two doctors from Louvain were initially regarded as more substantial. The first, Dr van Gehuchten, apparently took exception to Albert yawning and being distracted during the only apparition he was present at, leading him to conclude that the boy had seen nothing. The second, Dr De Greeff, was likewise only present for one apparition, that of 17 December, and claimed that the children had made the whole thing up, after being frightened by the light of a car over the railway bridge. When it was pointed out, however, that this was physically impossible, he refused to modify his negative opinion. Similarly, he was practically the only witness to claim that the children had *not* fallen to their knees simultaneously, arguing for an interval of nearly half a second between them.

Fr Herbert Thurston in his *Beauraing and other Apparitions*, subtitled *An Account of some Borderland Cases in the Psychology of Mysticism*, published in 1934, expressed agreement with Dr De Greeff in his contention that the ball of fire in the hawthorn tree, seen by Fernande during the last apparition, actually "had its origin in the magnesium flashlight of a photographer who was trying just then to take a picture of the scene." He goes on to say in a footnote, "The flashlight and the vision must have occurred within a few minutes of each other, and Fernande, in her emotional state, may easily have confused them."[691] On the face of it, this seems like a plausible suggestion, but once the facts are examined its inadequacy is apparent. This is how Sharkey and Debergh describe this event: "Suddenly, it seemed to Father Maes, a huge bolt of lightning illuminated the garden. Other witnesses, closer to the hawthorn, said a ball of fire about five feet in diameter burst in the shrub and sent sparks flying high. There was also a loud noise, like a clap of thunder."[692] Clearly the "psychologically convenient" idea of the flashlight, giving a momentary flash, is not sufficient to explain how witnesses could have seen a large ball of fire which sent sparks flying. Regrettably, this sort of reductionism, as we have seen in the case of Fatima, is prevalent in attempts to explain away, or at least minimize, the undoubtedly miraculous elements that have been a part of many of the Marian apparitions.

Michael P. Carroll theorizes that, as a general principle with apparitions, the accounts of the seers tend to diverge over time, with this being taken as evidence that as each series of apparitions develops, and more spectators are present, it is more difficult for the seers to collude in their accounts. As evidence for this, he points out that the children saw and heard different things, particularly during the latter apparitions. The simplest reason for this, though, is not that the children were making things up, but that they were simply reporting what they saw and heard. There is no reason why they should all have seen and heard exactly the same thing at each apparition. It is quite plausible that Mary should have said something different to each child at the last apparition—there is nothing particularly remarkable about that. At Fatima Francisco only saw Mary and did not hear her speak. There is thus no real evidence here to suggest that the children were lying.[693]

In general, Carroll sees Marian apparitions as due to "natural causes," most probably hallucinations, on the basis that observers present, unlike the seer or seers in question, did not see Mary. In other words, he approaches the problem with his mind made up that supernatural manifestations are simply not possible, and so the only explanation is that we are dealing with some sort of hallucination.[694] But the situation is more complicated than that: if, after taking every reasonable step to eliminate fraud or error, it becomes apparent that the only *rational* and logical explanation for a reported Marian apparition is that the person really did see what he claimed to see, then it is unscientific to rule this out, as Carroll does. Like other investigators, he also makes the mistake of equating approved apparitions with unapproved ones, assuming they are all false. When individual cases are dealt with, for the most part his analyses are superficial and biased against the supernatural. He claims that he does not believe that the children involved were lying, but that, once one started "hallucinating," the others either consciously or unconsciously colluded in this process, also claiming to have seen something.[695] As has been shown, though, this position is untenable and all the evidence suggests that the children involved did *not* collude in making up any stories.

In support of Carroll's position, though, it is to be admitted that the vast majority of reported Marian apparitions over the centuries are probably false, since only a relatively small number, since the time of the Reformation, have developed an appreciable cult and been approved by the Church. It is certainly debatable how many of these others should be categorized as hallucinations or illusions, and how many are due to plain fraud, madness or even diabolical influence. The fact that most reported "Marian" apparitions, though, are probably false, does not mean that they *all* are, an important point that has not been taken seriously by modern critics. The Church does not say that Marian apparitions are necessarily common, but where all the evidence suggests that some have happened, it does say that it is unreasonable to dismiss them out of hand.

The Eastern Gate and Beauraing

It would appear that Ezekiel's description of the Eastern gate of the Temple complements the above account in a very convincing way. The identification of Mary with the Eastern gate in the vision of Ezekiel, a gate which must always be kept shut, (Ezek. 44:1–2), was very popular with the Fathers and the early Christian writers, including St Amphilochius of Antioch, St Cyril of Alexandria, Severus of Antioch (c.465–538), and Chrysippus.[696] St Ambrose makes the following comparison:

Who then is this gate unless it is Mary? It is closed because she is a virgin. The gate therefore is Mary because Christ entered this world through her, when he is poured forth in a virginal parturition, and does not destroy the sexual enclosure of the virginity. The receptacle of her purity remains untouched, and the signs of integrity continue inviolate; when he comes forth from the virgin, the world cannot contain his great heights. "This gate," he says, "will be closed and not opened." Mary is this good gate which was closed and was not opened. Christ passed through it, but did not open it.[697]

St Jerome makes a similar identification as follows, "She is the East Gate, spoken of by the prophet Ezekiel, always shut and always shining, and either concealing or revealing the Holy of Holies; and through her 'the Sun of Righteousness,' our 'High Priest after the order of Melchizedek,' goes in and out. ... A mother before she was wedded, she remained a virgin after bearing her son."[698]

A number of the Fathers of the Church, then, clearly identified Mary with the Eastern gate of the Temple, so it is necessary to look at the biblical account itself in some detail to see how it relates to the events at Beauraing. Ezekiel was a sixth-century BC prophet who was taken to Babylon as one of the exiles, and as he recounts, while there had a tremendous vision of God near the River Chebar, during which he was commissioned as a prophet (Ezek. 1–3). The first two parts of his book are taken up with prophecies against Judah, Jerusalem, and the Gentiles, while the last part deals with Israel's restoration, its new covenant, Temple, and forms of worship. The section from chapter 40 onwards has been designated as the "Torah" of Ezekiel because it describes a vision the prophet had of the new Temple, as he was taken all around it and told to note carefully its dimensions. Each of the gates, including the Eastern gate, was to have palm trees as a form of decoration on its piers (Ezek. 40:31, 34, 37). Ezekiel then described how, in vision, he saw God returning to his temple by the Eastern gate (Ezek. 43:1–5), followed by this passage, which the early Christian writers applied to Mary: "Then he brought me back to the outer gate of the sanctuary, which faces east; and it was shut. And he said to me, 'This gate shall remain shut; it shall not be opened, and no one shall enter by it; for the Lord, the God of Israel, has entered by it; therefore it shall remain shut. Only the prince may sit in it to eat bread before the Lord; he shall enter by way of the vestibule of the gate, and shall go out by the same way' " (Ezek. 44:1–3).

Now it is a question of seeing how this and other passages from

Ezekiel relate to the events at Beauraing. An interesting feature of these apparitions, in contrast to earlier major ones, is that they took place in a built-up area, in a convent garden, whereas La Salette, Lourdes and Fatima all took place in the countryside. When the children first saw Mary she was walking in the air over the railway embankment, with a cloud at her feet: the children could see her knees move and so were sure she was walking. As has been pointed out, the cloud has a symbolism of its own, but this walking movement is unique to Beauraing. In the context of Ezekiel's experience, however, it makes sense; he was shown all around the Temple, *traveling* through it, following the Angel who was measuring it.

Likewise, regarding the closed Eastern *gate*, the first time the children saw Mary was while waiting at the *door* of the convent, and it was only when Gilberte Voisin passed through the same *door* that she saw the apparition. The second time they saw her they were walking through the convent garden between the *gate* and the front *door*, and again on the third night Gilberte saw her as she closed the convent *door* behind her, with all the children later seeing her just before they reached the front *gate*. Perhaps stranger still is the fact that Mother Théophile's decision to close the convent gates meant that the children saw Mary for the rest of the time under the hawthorn tree and through the fence, as they knelt in the street on the other side of the *closed gate* of the convent. Just compare this with the above text from Ezekiel, which speaks of the Eastern gate remaining shut and no one going through it (Ezek. 44:1–2). Clearly the unusual topography of these apparitions— particularly the children seeing Mary through the closed convent gate—was not due just to chance.

The first recorded request of Mary, on 17 December, was for a chapel, and, of course, the whole last section of the book of Ezekiel, from chapter 40 onwards is concerned with the future Temple, which at heart is a chapel, if we take "temple" in its basic meaning of a building where God is present and which is specially dedicated to him. Similarly, Mary asked that people come on pilgrimage to Beauraing, and one of the highlights of Temple worship was the processions or pilgrimages associated with it (cf. Ps. 42:4). Other elements of the apparitions also suggest worship, for example the way that the children fell on their knees before the apparitions, just as Ezekiel prostrated himself before the glory of God (Ezek. 43:3). Likewise the children prayed the Hail Mary in high-pitched voices, reminiscent of a liturgical chant. This type of chanting went on in the Temple, and, of course, the rosary itself is a representation of the Psalms, which would have been recited as part of the Temple cult. Mary's repeated requests for prayer also fit in with the liturgical emphasis in Ezekiel, and obviously the Temple itself was a house of prayer, as a number of the psalms make clear.[699]

The Church and Beauraing

Not surprisingly, the apparitions caused immense excitement and debate throughout Belgium, as reports were circulated in newspapers and magazines, with the anticlerical press generally taking a negative line. Most of their reporting, though, was shoddy or secondhand, and was countered quite easily. The same can be said about the articles that appeared in the French Carmelite magazine mentioned previously, and which cast doubt on the apparitions. Over time, however, opposition tended to subside, as ordinary Belgians were impressed by the apparent sincerity of the children, and also by the conversions and cures that had undoubtedly taken place. The growth of the shrine was due to lay initiatives, since it was the laity rather than the clergy who organized the initial pilgrimages, and, indeed, over two million people visited Beauraing in the first year.[700]

One of the most celebrated physical cures was that of Maria Van Laer, who had been an invalid for nearly half her life. Besides being tubercular, she had a twisted spinal column, a diseased leg, and tumors which had become open sores. No medical treatment was possible and as a last resort she insisted, in June 1933, and despite the objections of her family, on being taken to Beauraing. She was carried on a stretcher to the hawthorn tree for a number of visits, and suddenly felt well enough to move and eat. On the way home in the ambulance, she steadily recovered her strength, although it had been feared that the trip would kill her. By the time she arrived home, she was completely cured, with no tumors or deformity. This cure attracted much attention in Belgium and Maria became a nursing nun in 1936.[701]

Confusion, though, was caused by a number of false visions that occurred during and after Beauraing; these sowed doubt in some people's minds, as was the case with previous recognized apparitions. Some of those present on 8 December, who had been standing on the railway embankment, claimed to have seen a vision of, "a whitish light having a human form." When questioned the next day, they were in a frightened and emotionally upset state, and some said they had seen something like Our Lady of Lourdes, but others gave different accounts. It is difficult to decide the exact cause of these "visions," but perhaps some form of multiple hallucination was responsible, or, more seriously, perhaps they are evidence of demonic intervention. In the highly-charged atmosphere of that evening, when many expected a miracle or sign, these are certainly possibilities, and show that the greatest prudence is needed in investigating such phenomena.

The difference between these events and the experiences of those who saw the miracle of the sun at Fatima are subtle but decisive. At Fatima, a miracle had been promised and people had gone there with the expectation of seeing something, but without knowing exactly what would happen. But at Beauraing on 8 December the feeling had grown amongst the crowd, because it was the feast of the Immaculate Conception, that a miracle would be performed. The Lady, though, had said nothing about a miracle, and so we can probably explain what was seen as resulting from an intense expectation, which affected certain members of the crowd, to the extent that they believed they saw something which was not there, that is, they were subject to some form of emotional hallucination, (if not a demonic episode).[702] It is the difference between being told a miracle *will* happen and in *expecting* a miracle to happen, situations involving two completely different mental, spiritual, and emotional states.

Opposition to Beauraing had practically ceased by the time the bishop appointed a commission of inquiry in 1935, with the work continuing under his successor. In February 1943 Bishop Charue authorized public devotions to Mary at Beauraing, but it was not until July 1949,[703] following the turmoil of the Second World War, that the shrine was officially recognized and two important documents issued. The first dealt with two of the many cures that had taken place at Beauraing, declaring them to be miraculous, one being that of Maria Van Laer, as referred to above. This cure had been thoroughly examined and was backed up with extensive documentation and x-rays, as well as evidence taken under oath. The second document was a letter to the clergy in which the bishop said, "we are able in all serenity and prudence to affirm that the Queen of Heaven appeared to the children of Beauraing during the winter of 1932–1933, especially to show us in her maternal Heart the anxious appeal for prayer and the promise of her powerful mediation for the conversion of sinners."[704]

Even before that decision, though, the shrine had grown and developed, with a chapel being built and the convent and school being converted into a home for sick pilgrims. The children all married and had families of their own, trying to keep in the background as much as possible; they saw themselves only as the instruments for making Mary's message known.[705]

Banneux: January – March 1933

When it became known in mid-January 1933 that a girl from Banneux, another Belgian village, fifty miles north-east of Beauraing, was also claiming to have seen the Blessed Virgin, doubts were raised by those who knew something of Lourdes and the false visionaries who flourished there after Bernadette. This was certainly the view of the local priest, Fr Louis Jamin, when confronted with the news that young Mariette Beco, an eleven-year-old girl, had seen the Blessed Virgin on Sunday 15 January; but subsequent events were to show that this new set of apparitions would also be accepted by the Church.

That evening, at about seven o'clock, Mariette was in the kitchen with her mother, looking after the youngest child of the family while waiting for her younger brother Julien to arrive home. She looked out of the window into the dark night once more, to see if he was coming, and was surprised to see a young lady out in the yard, seemingly made of light and smiling at her. Mariette noticed the oval light that surrounded her body; she was bent slightly forward and inclined to the left, and was wearing a long white gown with a blue sash, as well as a transparent white veil on her head. Mariette could see a golden rose on her right foot, and a rosary with a golden chain and cross hanging on her right arm, which was joined to the left in prayer.

Mariette was unsure what to make of this; she moved the oil lamp in case it was causing a reflection on the window, but the beautiful smiling Lady remained and so she turned to her mother and said: "Mama, there's a woman in the garden!" The immediate reply was, "Nonsense!" but Mariette persisted saying, "A lovely lady, beautifully dressed: a completely white dress, a blue sash." Jokingly her mother replied, "Oh yes! Perhaps it is the Blessed Virgin;" but, becoming a little worried, she looked out through the window and was disturbed to see a white light shaped like a person, with what looked like a sheet over its head; she closed the curtain and declared that it must be a witch. Mariette, though, took another look and still saw the Lady smiling at her, and, taking courage, she began to pray with the rosary beads she had only recently found on the road. She recited several decades and saw the apparition's lips move in prayer, before the Lady beckoned her with her finger to come outside. As she moved towards the door, though, her mother, alarmed by now, locked it, and by the time Mariette had returned to the window, the Lady had gone.[706]

Both her brother and father, also called Julien, dismissed the whole business as nonsense on their return, but Mr Beco became more thoughtful when his wife told of what she had seen, and he asked them to show him the spot where they said the Lady had been. The Beco family were not particularly religious, having fallen victim, like many others at the time, to indifference in spiritual matters. Julien Beco thought that the light had probably been a reflection from the oil lamp, but, like his daughter, he was not able to reproduce anything that looked like a white lady. The next day, Mariette told a school friend what had happened and was persuaded she should tell the priest. He, naturally, reacted with some scepticism, and Mariette ran off, defiantly proclaiming that she *knew* what she had seen and was certain of it.

Nothing happened that evening, Monday, 16 January but Fr Jamin was surprised to see Mariette at Mass on the Tuesday morning for the first time in months. She also came to his catechism class and, impressed, he asked her to give her account of what had happened, which he noted down immediately afterwards. He tried to catch her out by claiming she had seen the statue of Our Lady of Lourdes, but Mariette insisted that the Lady she had seen was inclined forward and much more beautiful.[707]

On Wednesday 18 January, Mariette left the house at seven o'clock in the evening and knelt to say the rosary near the front gate as her father watched, worried because it was cold and dark. Suddenly, she raised her arms, because, as she was later to recount, she could see the Blessed Virgin descending towards her between two tall pine trees, a tiny figure growing larger and more luminous as she approached, stopping near her on a small grayish cloud about a foot from the ground. She joined in Mariette's prayers, but did not touch the rosary that hung from her arm. Julien Beco had meanwhile been trying without success to rouse his daughter from her trance-like state; he slammed the door and even shouted at her but with no effect, and, quite worried by now, set off on his bicycle to fetch the priest. Fr Jamin was out, however, and instead he brought his cousin, quickly hurrying back to see Mariette still praying, and then rising and going out through the gate and on to the road. She later said that the Lady had again beckoned her with her finger and she had followed her out; to her father's anguished question as to where she was going, Mariette simply replied: "She calls me!"[708]

They followed her out, seeing her fall to her knees with a thud on two occasions, before she turned to the right and finally knelt for a third time on the ditch, placing her hands in some water there. She said later that the Lady had told her to do this, and they heard her repeat aloud: "This stream is reserved for me," and "Good evening." As the apparition disappeared over the pines, growing ever smaller, Mariette came to herself and noticed her father and his cousin. She was then questioned about what she had seen during the thirty-five minutes she had been in ecstasy. In a later testimony, Mariette described what happened on this and similar occasions: "The Virgin stayed so long and always smiled at me. She said nothing to me all this time. ... Then she called me to the spring, signalling with her finger. She glides backwards, never turning around. She stops twice. At the spring she said to me, 'Push your hands into the water.' ... The Virgin leaves the same way she came, withdrawing and growing smaller, like a lamp going out ..."

Fr Jamin and another priest, Fr del Marmol, were informed, and arrived at the Beco house at nearly ten o'clock, and although Mariette was asleep by then, the visit bore fruit in that Julien Beco told the priest that he wanted to come to Confession and receive Holy Communion the next day. Fr Jamin was still more surprised because, on the way, he had mentioned to the other priest that he wanted a sign about Mariette's behavior, such as the conversion of her father! Despite this, the priest thought it prudent not to be present during further apparitions, relying instead on reports from people he could trust.[709]

Next evening, Thursday, 19 January, Mariette again left the house at about seven, with an old overcoat over her shoulders as protection against the cold, and knelt down in the snow to pray. After a couple of decades of the rosary, she again saw the Lady, stretched out her arms and said: "Oh, she is here!" before asking her who she was, to hear the reply: "I am the Virgin of the poor." As the small crowd who had gathered watched, she took the same path to the spring by the ditch, again falling to her knees on a total of three occasions. Mariette had mistakenly thought the spring was set aside for *her* personally, but Mary had actually said, "This spring is reserved for all the nations—to relieve the sick." Even though the young girl was not exactly sure what a "nation" was, nor of the precise meaning of "relieve," *soulager*, she understood that it was good news and was thankful. Finally she repeated the last words of the Lady for this apparition, which only lasted about seven minutes: "I shall pray for you. *Au revoir*."[710]

Next evening, Friday, 20 January, her parents, seeing her tiredness and nervous exhaustion at the events of previous days, and the contradiction she was facing from those who did not believe, wanted to keep Mariette indoors; but she insisted on going out as usual to where a small crowd had gathered. Her father watched as she again knelt on the path, and once more greeted with outstretched arms the wonderful apparition that she alone could see. The witnesses heard Mariette say, "What do you wish, my beautiful Lady?" and then: "Oh, a small chapel," before she collapsed and remained unconscious for a few minutes. She revived quickly, though, with the aid of a doctor who was present, replying to the questions being put to her. Mariette told them that the Blessed Virgin had placed her hands on her head and blessed her with the sign of the cross, and that she had fainted at that point.

Next day, after a good night's sleep, she went to see Fr Jamin to report on what had happened, as she did after each apparition; but it seems that he was not convinced, and his unbelief upset Mariette greatly. That evening, she again prayed outside in the snow, feeling that the blessing she had received was a sign of the end of the apparitions since she saw nothing. She continued though on subsequent evenings to pray, on her own sometimes, but often with her father too, and it was only after three weeks of disappointment that the Lady again appeared to her on 11 February, the feast of Our Lady of Lourdes.[711]

Six people were present on this cold, moonlit Saturday evening, and after she had said her rosary, unusually she decided to continue praying standing up: she had reached the fifth decade of her second rosary when she once more dropped to her knees, before rising and making for the road. She did not seem to hear a priest, who asked her where she was going; and, after reaching the spring, with similar genuflections as before, she plunged her hand into the water and blessed herself, while appearing to listen intently to someone. A nurse who was present took her pulse at this point and found it quite normal. After a few minutes, Mariette thanked her unseen visitor and tearfully made her way back to the house. She had not understood the French words used by the Lady, *Je viens soulager la souffrance*, "I come to relieve suffering," and had to get her father to translate them into the local dialect. Afterwards they went to see Fr Jamin; and Mariette gave him a full account of what had happened.

There were no more apparitions until 15 February, when several ladies and Mariette's mother were with her in the garden. The rosary was recited and then Mariette again saw the beautiful Lady, reporting that the priest had asked her for a sign and then listening intently for several minutes before bursting into tears. She could only say that the Lady had said: "Believe in me, I will believe in you. Pray much. *Au revoir.*" Later it was revealed that she was given a secret that she was not to reveal, and this probably explains Mariette's sadness that night.[712]

On Monday, 20 February, she was praying as usual, when suddenly she held out her hands as her voice changed and speeded up; she then rose to make her way to the spring just over a hundred yards away. Once again she fell to her knees twice on the way, and continued praying as she reached the ditch, before kneeling again, only to burst into tears when the Lady finished speaking to her. Mariette reported that Mary had said, "My dear child, pray much," and then looking very sad had simply said: "*Au revoir.*"

The final apparition, the eighth, took place on 2 March 1933, and as Mariette knelt in the rain, one of the bystanders held an umbrella over her. After praying for a while, the skies cleared and then Mariette's voice and appearance changed, as she held out her arms towards her beautiful Lady. In reply to Mary's words, "I am the Mother of the Savior, Mother of God, Pray much," Mariette could only say, "Yes, yes." Mary then blessed Mariette as she had done during the fourth apparition and indicated that this was indeed the last apparition by saying "*Adieu,*" instead of, as before, "Au revoir."[713]

The Temple Stream and Banneux

Less than two weeks separated the apparitions at Banneux from those at Beauraing, and so, if the pattern of apparitions corresponding to biblical events is consistent, then we should expect to find something further on in the book of Ezekiel which relates to Banneux. This is actually the case, and it is only necessary to go forward a few chapters, to the account of the spring flowing from the Eastern gate of the Temple, to find a situation that fits exactly.

After reporting various regulations for the use of the Temple and in the liturgy, Ezekiel describes a further vision, in which he was accompanied by the same angel; he saw water flowing out from below the threshold of the Temple, and the "man" measuring off the stream with a measuring line. After a thousand cubits, he stopped and led Ezekiel through the water: it was ankle-deep; after another thousand cubits, it was knee-deep; after another thousand cubits, it was waist-deep; but after a further thousand cubits, it had become a river too deep to cross (Ezek. 47:1–5).

As in the case of Beauraing, there is a clear connection between Mariette's actions and this text from Ezekiel. In the initial apparition, Mariette had seen the Lady through the window and attempted to go through the *door* to reach her, only to be stopped by her mother. After that she always knelt down in the garden near the *gate* and had to pass through this *gate* in following the Lady to the spring. Just as Ezekiel followed an angel, as he measured off the stream that flowed out from the Eastern gate, so also Mariette followed Mary. What is more remarkable, though, is the fact that Mariette was seen on several occasions to fall to her knees *three* times between the gate and the spring, and this corresponds precisely with the *three* measurements made by the Angel to the stream as it grew into a mighty river. Similarly, Mary told Mariette to "push your hands into the water," just as the Angel made Ezekiel wade across the stream. The connection lies in the fact that both involve the idea of bodily entering water. Strangely enough, even the position of the spring, directly *east* along the road from the Beco house, parallels the way the water flowed out to the *east* from the Temple.[714]

Regarding the second part of Ezekiel's text, the correspondence is equally marked. In this he describes how he was led back along the bank and saw a great number of trees on each side of the river. His guide told him how the stream would make salt water fresh, and how the trees growing on the river banks would not wither. Through the water from the sanctuary, they would bear fruit every month, while their leaves would have healing properties (Ezek. 47:6–12). The request for a chapel corresponds with the fact that we are dealing with a stream coming from the *Temple*, the house of God. Mary indicated to Mariette that the spring pointed out to her was for all the nations, to relieve the sick, and one of the properties of the trees that were to grow on the banks of the river seen by Ezekiel was that they should have medicinal or *healing* leaves. This river was to make the waters of the Dead Sea wholesome, which suggests that, in itself, it would have healing properties, as was certainly the case with the miraculous waters of Banneux. The fact that Mary appeared to Mariette from between two pine *trees*, over a forest, also suggests a connection to the trees seen by Ezekiel.

Another interesting point is the way the figure of Mary gradually grew larger as she approached Mariette, which seems to parallel the way the stream grew larger as it flowed from the Temple. Mary becomes, in symbolic terms, the river of grace flowing from God's Temple, a very apt picture of the reality of her being the Mediatrix of all graces. In fact, Hesychius of Jerusalem, a fifth-century writer, described Mary as a fountain sealed, "because the *river of life* that goes forth from you has filled the earth; ..."[715] This probably is principally a reference to Christ, but can also be applied to Mary. A further point of interest is the blue sash worn by her, which, apart from being in itself quite a good symbol of water, and even a stream or river, is also reminiscent of the similar sash seen by Bernadette at Lourdes; both Lourdes and Banneux are the two Marian shrines particularly linked with miraculous cures coming through springs.

Mary specifically described herself at Banneux as the "Virgin of the poor," and although Ezekiel has an emphasis on the necessity of helping the poor (cf. Ezek. 16:48–50; 18:10–13; 22:29), it is fair to say that the same could be said of several other prophets too. It is more probable that she used this title because she really did want to identify herself with the poor. Certainly the Beco family, like Bernadette's family, were extremely poor, even to the extent that the curtain on their kitchen window was an old sheet. Similarly, although the term "virgin" does appear in this part of Ezekiel (44:22), it is probable that the significance of the term, as used at Banneux, comes from the fact that it illustrates another facet of Mary's person, that, as well as being a Mother, she was also a Virgin. But it is also possible that there may be an oblique reference here, too, to the use made by some of the Church Fathers, as indicated above in discussing Beauraing, of the texts involving the Eastern gate in demonstrating Mary's virginity.

Banneux was investigated from 1935 until 1937 by an episcopal commission, after which the evidence collected was submitted to Rome. Meanwhile growing numbers of pilgrims came to the shrine; and in March 1942 Bishop Kerkhofs of Liège announced that Rome had cleared the materials relating to the apparitions, leaving all further matters of investigation and approval in his hands. In May of that year, he approved the cult of the Virgin of the Poor, and in 1947 the apparitions themselves received preliminary approval, with this becoming definite in 1949. Like the children at Beauraing, Mariette married and had a family, being content to remain in the background.[716]

Beauraing, Banneux, and Nazism

In keeping with one of the main themes of this book, that the Marian apparitions are intimately connected with important secular events, it is possible to see links between Beauraing, Banneux, and the rise of Nazism. It is surely significant that the two Belgian apparitions, in a country bordering Germany, should have occurred at the very moment that Hitler was gaining power. In July 1932, the Nazis had become the largest party in the Reichstag, with 230 seats; but this was not enough to give them an absolute majority, when placed against the Communists with 89, the Socialists with 133, and the Center party with 97 seats. This more than doubling of the Nazi representation, from the situation in September 1931, has to be seen in the light of more than 5 million unemployed. In the November 1932 elections, though, the total of Nazi seats dropped to 196, while the Communists now held 100. It looked as though Hitler was beginning to lose support.[717]

This was the moment when Mary intervened to appear to the children at Beauraing. They first saw her on 29 November 1932, and she first spoke to them on 2 December, saying, "Always be good." On 30 December her message was, "Pray, pray very much," while on 1 January 1933 she simply said, "Pray always," with the emphasis on *always*. The last apparition was on 3 January, and Mary spoke to each of the children telling Gilberte Voisin that she would "convert sinners." To Andrée she said: "I am the Mother of God, the Queen of Heaven. Pray always." The last child, Fernande, was asked by Mary to "sacrifice yourself for me."

In the context of Hitler's imminent accession to power, these messages take on a profound meaning. To "always be good," in Nazi-occupied Belgium would not prove easy, while the requests to "pray, pray very much," "pray always," and "sacrifice yourself for me," indicated the urgent necessity of prayers for the German people and their politicians, that they should not make the terrible mistake of allowing Hitler to come to power. But the prayers of those at Beauraing and elsewhere in Belgium were unavailing and Hitler legally became Chancellor on 30 January 1933, appointed by Hindenburg in the mistaken belief that he would form a national government to rescue the country from its problems.

The theme of the paramount necessity for prayer was also present in the apparitions at Banneux, which went on until early March. On 15 February, Mariette reported that Mary had said: "Believe in me, I will believe in you. Pray much." On 20 February, Mary simply said, with a look of great sadness, "my dear child, pray much," while at the final apparition, on 2 March 1933, she told Mariette:" I am the Mother of the Savior, Mother of God, Pray much." Mary's words, too, that the spring was, "reserved for *all the nations*—to relieve the sick," were also an implicit rejection of the crude Nazi racial theories.[718] Instead of relieving the sick and handicapped, Hitler was planning to get rid of them.

Mary thus repeatedly appealed for fervent prayer during the weeks after Hitler had become Chancellor, when the German people were under such great pressure in deciding who to vote for in the new elections. In the event, they largely succumbed to that pressure, as was clear by 5 March, when the electoral results came in; they gave the Nazis 288 seats with just under fifty per cent of the vote. With help from the Nationalists, Hitler had a parliamentary majority, and was able to introduce an Enabling Act giving greater powers to the cabinet.

Thus, summing up, we can say that Beauraing and Banneux seem to represent Mary's response to the incipient threat of Nazism, but the German people were not prescient in regard to Hitler, and he was able to become Chancellor by democratic means. Hitler's evil racial system, based on evolutionary and eugenic thinking, and propelled by a fear of Communism, of which Nazism was the mirror image, was thus able to assume power in the heart of Europe and begin the march towards war.

Hitler's acquisition of power also came against a background of four years of economic depression, and mass unemployment, and thus many people felt dissatisfied with government under the Weimar Republic; the temptation to choose a strong leader was difficult to resist, given that the alternative was either socialism or communism. Hitler needed a two-thirds majority in the Reichstag to gain full emergency executive powers under the constitution, and he was able to achieve this only with the support of the Catholic Center party, the *Zentrum*. Pius XI had been particularly concerned that German Catholics and the Center party, split as it was between left and right, with one side concerned with social action and the other enticed by nationalism, had not seemed to recognize the inherently evil side of Nazism. The action of its leader, Chancellor Brüning, in dissolving parliament in 1930, had allowed the Nazis to become the second largest party and facilitated their rise to power. There had been many warnings from Catholic leaders about the dangers of National Socialism all through the twenties and early thirties, with believers being told they could not be members of the party, but it seems that Catholics generally were somewhat naïve in not recognizing where Hitler would lead the country.[719]

But the situation seemed so desperate that many must have felt there was no alternative to this course in March 1933. With hindsight, we can see this was a tragic mistake since it allowed Hitler's dictatorship to begin, but the general view was that between them, President von Hindenburg and the vice-chancellor, von Papen, would be able to moderate Hitler's approach and that power would make him more responsible: they underestimated Hitler's ruthlessness and cunning. This was a view also held be many people in Britain and America, equally afraid of the threat from Communism; at this stage few could have imagined that the Nazis would prove barbaric enough to carry out Hitler's program in *Mein Kampf*. Thus the German people traded their freedom for an illusory political stability, preferring the prospect of jobs to a morally upright government.

Within a matter of months, German democracy was dead, removed virtually without opposition, as people were frightened into acquiescence. Hitler was then able to set up his police state and begin his moves towards re-militarization. The Germans did not realize that Hitler intended to take them down the road to World War and disaster, that when he spoke of Germany being a "world power," he really meant an attempt at world domination. His plan was to attain mastery in Europe before attacking and destroying Russia, so as to provide "living space" for a vast German Empire covering the whole Eurasian continent. Once this was achieved, he planned to make Germany an oceangoing superpower and then take on and defeat America, thus assuming control of the whole world. Given that America had cut itself off, in protectionist mood, since 1930, and Russia's apparent inherent weakness under Communism, this was perhaps not such an impossible plan as might be imagined.[720]

19

The Second World War

The Rise of Totalitarianism

As the thirties progressed, it was thus becoming clear that the democratic world was facing a frightening threat from the new totalitarian states, Russia, Germany, Italy and Japan. These were all quite prepared to overturn the rule of law and impose their will by force, in pursuit of their respective aims of regional or, indeed, world domination.[721] Pius XI found himself coming into conflict with these regimes in Europe, as he sought to apply religious principles in a difficult political climate. Although Mussolini's Italian Fascism was not completely hostile to the Church, both Russian Communism, with its atheistic ideology, and German Nazism, with its neo-paganism, were determined enemies of Christianity. Pius XI refused to take sides and criticized both forms of totalitarianism, especially when extreme nationalism was involved, and where the State was regarded as an idol which had complete control over men's lives.[722]

The Lutheran Church, as an essentially state Church, did not really provide any serious opposition to Nazism, further illustrating the basic weaknesses in Luther's theology in its exaltation of the State. Christopher Dawson points out how Lutheranism and Calvinism, despite their similarities, ended up "producing or helping to produce" completely different attitudes and societies. He contrasts the passivity of Lutheranism with regard to the State with the revolutionary effect of Calvinist thinking, particularly in the English-speaking world. To some extent these differences can be explained by geography; that is, Lutheranism was largely confined to Scandinavia and Germany, while Calvinism was more closely involved with the bourgeois cultures of the West.[723] But there are deeper reasons too; Lutheranism's passivity has to be balanced against the violent strain which is particularly apparent in

Luther's own writings. These have an "instinctive tendency to aggression and violence," and helped to foster a "cult of power," with this power being held by the State. As Dawson says:

> This Lutheran tradition, with its strange dualism of pessimism and faith, other-worldliness and world affirmation, passive quietism and crude acceptance of the reign of force, has been the most powerful force in the formation of the German mind and the German social attitude. It played a considerable part in the development of German idealism. It [also] lies behind Hegel's exaltation of the Prussian state as the supreme expression of Absolute Spirit ...

He further argues that Luther's cult of force and his "natural law of irrationalism" were transformed into a "cult of militarism," one based on "power politics," which increasingly sidelined traditional morality from the time of Bismarck onwards.[724]

So there is apparently a link between Luther's revolt and the final degradation of Germany in allowing itself to be captivated by Hitler and Nazism. In 1517 Luther began his revolt against the Church, and exactly four hundred years later, in 1917, the Communist Russian Revolution was fomented with German encouragement, during a World War essentially caused by German aggressiveness. As Dawson points out: "Strong as Germany was, she never felt herself to be strong enough, and the progressive increase of her military and naval power drove the rest of Europe down the fatal road of competitive re-armament, which culminated in the First World War."[725] The refusal of the German Generals, such as Ludendorff, to modify their war aims meant that the First World War dragged out to a bitter end, and thus prepared the way for the rise of Hitler, and another even more terrible war.

Surely there is a connection between the revolt begun by Luther and consummated by Hitler, between the Germany enfeebled by Luther's revolt and the hideous condition inflicted on that same country by Nazism, as it sought to make up for lost time and become a powerful nation with a vast empire? Tragically, the Germans chose a leader who was to create a regime which would be the epitome of evil. The actions of men, whether for good or for evil, live on after them and can have the most glorious or the most ghastly consequences; and, in all this, Luther cannot escape censure. The Protestant Reformation was to prove to have a very long shadow indeed.

Hitler also embodied Nietzsche's idea of the "will to power," an ideal that contemptuously rejected right and wrong, in its attempt to replace liberty by slavery in a new totalitarian world order.[726] He was able to capitalize on the fact that inherent weaknesses in German society, dating from Bismarck's rule in the late nineteenth century, made it possible for one man to gain complete power in the country.[727] Nazism took Nietzsche's atheist philosophy of racial superiority and allied it to ideas developed by the writer Houston Stewart Chamberlain, the author of *The Aryan Concept of the World*. This view saw the moral and intellectual qualities of the individual as a product of his racial origins, of *blood*, while rejecting racial equality, arguing that the "lowest" human races were closer to the animals than the highest Aryan races. We can see the clear influence of evolutionary ideas here.

It was necessary then for an Aryan master race, the Germans, to take control of the entire world and shape it in its own image. Just as Communism sacrificed the individual to the State, so Nazism made an idol of race and a virtue of hate, particularly hatred of the Jews, who were demonized as a subhuman race. It is clear that the destruction of the Jews was part of Hitler's plan right from the beginning, and sprang from his bizarre belief that the Germans had been poisoned by alien blood. All of this illustrated the illogical nature of Nazism, while also making it clear that it was a neo-pagan rejection of Christianity, in its appeal to all the worst instincts of ordinary Germans.[728]

Hitler's fascism was thus built around a biological racial determinism. These principles were ultimately derived from Social Darwinism, and, in the case of Hitler, also from Hegel's idea of the supremacy of the State. Communist ideology called for the extermination of entire classes, while the Nazis advocated breeding programs to eliminate unwanted races.[729] However, such ideas were not popular only in Hitler's Germany.

The Application of Darwinism

Francis Galton (1822–1911), a cousin of Charles Darwin, had promoted eugenics as the principle of supposedly improving the condition of humanity by controlling reproduction. He applied natural selection to the human race as a whole, blaming misguided charity for allowing the poor to bear too many children, and thus lower the quality of mankind. In 1904, Galton had endowed a Chair of Eugenics at London University, and was also responsible for introducing statistical methods in the area of intelligence. Studies into eugenics were also undertaken in Germany and

America, with the first International Eugenics Congress being held in 1912. In practical terms, eugenics went hand in hand with the promotion of birth control, with this being seen as the best way of preventing the "unfit" from breeding. The American Eugenics Society was founded in 1922, and some of its founder members were closely involved in the white supremacist movement. In short, in the early part of the twentieth century the eugenics movement had an aura of respectability, even though it advocated euthanasia and the sterilization of the handicapped, amongst other barbaric ideas.[730]

Thus Germany under Hitler was by no means the only country to introduce eugenic practices: by the mid thirties, sterilization laws were passed not only in Germany but also in Switzerland, Norway, Sweden, Denmark, and in twenty-seven states of the United States. This sort of legislation seems to have been most favored by the northern Protestant countries, another example of the negative effects of secularization on this part of Western society. Hitler, with the help of German eugenicists, was determined to produce his "Master Race;" but with his defeat, such ideas went into eclipse, going underground to surface in the pro-abortion, pro-euthanasia, "culture of death," we are presently witnessing, a culture which promotes birth control and abortion, while circulating largely groundless scare stories about population growth.[731]

But Darwinism, racism and anti-Semitism were not the only roots of Nazism, and we can also definitely see the influence of Communism on Nazi ideology. In many respects, although fascism was deeply hostile to Communism, they both had roots in Marxist thinking. They were really two sides of the same totalitarian coin, with Stalin's Communism making possible the success of Hitler's Nazism. In the Europe of the thirties, they forced people to make terrible choices, and in the process, democracy was contemptuously cast aside and trampled underfoot. Hitler saw the Nazi party, the National *Socialist* German Workers' Party, as a socialist party, in the sense that he was not motivated by bourgeois or capitalistic ideals; he certainly modeled the Nazis on Lenin's centralized Communist Party, as the following quotation makes clear:

I have learned a great deal from Marxism, as I do not hesitate to admit. ... I have learned from their methods. ... The whole of National Socialism is based upon it. Look at the workers' sports clubs, the industrial cells, the mass demonstrations, the propaganda leaflets written specially for the comprehension of the masses; all these new methods of political struggle are essentially

Marxist in origin. All I had to do is take over these methods and adapt them to our purpose.[732]

Again, in all this we can see the working out of Mary's prophecy at Fatima, that, unless converted, Russia would spread its errors throughout the world. Not only Communism, but its offshoot Nazism, were set to cause the world terrible suffering.

The Road to War

From 1934 onwards, Hitler consolidated his position, and by March 1936 he felt strong enough to remilitarize the Rhineland, having begun to rearm in contravention of the Treaty of Versailles the previous year. At this stage, he could still have been stopped if the French had confronted him, but the will to do this was lacking, with Britain and France engaged in a quarrel over Mussolini's invasion of Abyssinia. Once this opportunity had passed, it would prove impossible to stop Hitler without all-out war. Pius XI had meanwhile reluctantly started to negotiate with Hitler's regime, well aware of the dangers of such a move, but also conscious that to do nothing would have left German Catholics completely at the mercy of Nazi propaganda. Negotiations were not completed until 1937, and, although the resulting concordat earned the Nazi regime international prestige, it was an unfortunate necessity. It strengthened the position of the Church during the struggle with Nazism, allowing it to protest at violations, as well as tying Hitler's hands, at least to some extent.[733]

Meanwhile, the rise of the Republican left-wing government in Spain in 1936 had graphically demonstrated the evils of Communism, as mobs attacked and burned churches, particularly in Catalonia. This led to the Church, in self-defence, taking the side of the Nationalists, led by Franco, when the civil war began in July 1936. By 1938, in Republican areas, a great number of church buildings had been destroyed in a destructive orgy, which also saw the deaths of thousands of priests, religious, and lay people at the hands of the Communists. There were Nationalist reprisals, but it was their enemies who began the bloodshed. Franco was not controlled by either Hitler or Mussolini, but was forced to accept their aid in the face of Soviet help for the Republicans, many of whom were Communists. No one else would help him. Eventually, Franco's superior military and organizational ability won the day for the Nationalist cause, and ensured that Spain was both saved from Communism and able to keep out of the Second World War.[734]

In March 1937, Hitler's duplicity and his persecution of the Jews, along with the theories of Aryan racial supremacy inherent in Nazism, led Pope Pius XI to condemn it in his encyclical *Mit Brennender Sorge*. This was a complete denunciation of the regime, the text of which was smuggled into Germany, secretly printed, and read from church pulpits. Although he was infuriated by this, Hitler did not attack the Church more openly until after the outbreak of the war, when he carried out a series of imprisonments and executions. Up till then, he still needed the support of Catholics, and many were fooled by the sophisticated Nazi propaganda machine. The worst horrors in Europe were reserved for the Catholic people of Poland, who along with the Jews, had to bear the full brunt of Nazi barbarism.[735]

The Pope also, in his encyclical *Divini Redemptoris*, likewise published in March 1937, tackled Communism, which he described as a menace undermining the foundations of Christian civilization, whose perversity was due to its being based solely on materialism and a false Marxist interpretation of history. He argued that its wickedness was evident in the way that it imposed itself by violence and totalitarianism, and also because of its inherently anti-religious nature. The encyclical then went on to put forward the Christian vision of man as a being with rights which the State could not override, while rejecting ideas such as the class struggle, and arguing that the only basis for a just economic order and society was that of Christian charity. Pius XI also pointed out that neither socialism nor Communism would have arisen if the warnings of previous popes had been heeded.[736]

Sr Lucia's Mission Continues

In September 1935, the remains of the youngest seer of Fatima, Jacinta, who had died in 1920, were removed to Fatima, and, on opening the coffin, her face was found to be intact. Photographs were taken, and Bishop Correia da Silva arranged to send some of these to Sr Lucia, who, in expressing gratitude, mentioned Jacinta in terms of sanctity. This caused the bishop to ask Sr Lucia to write what she knew of Jacinta, and this is how she came to compose her *First Memoir*, which recounted the basic facts about Fatima, and was ready by Christmas 1935.[737] Following the outbreak of the Spanish Civil War, apparently a fulfillment of the prophecy about Russia spreading its errors, Fr Gonzalves wrote to Sr Lucia asking what should be done. She replied in May 1936, and again pointed out the necessity of the Holy Father's making the consecration of Russia, describing how she had asked Jesus in prayer why he would not convert Russia without it. She received the following answer as an interior locution: "Because I want My whole Church to acknowledge that consecration as a triumph of the Immaculate Heart of Mary, so that it may extend its cult later on, and put the devotion to this Immaculate Heart beside the devotion to My Sacred Heart."

To this Sr Lucia replied: "But my God, the Holy Father probably won't believe me, unless You Yourself move him with a special inspiration." She then heard the following answer: "The Holy Father. Pray very much for the Holy Father. He will do it, but it will be very late. Nevertheless the Immaculate Heart of Mary will save Russia. It has been entrusted to her."[738]

Sr Lucia went on to express her fear in the letter that it might all have been an illusion, but this should be balanced against her certainty that she really was speaking with Jesus: "When I speak intimately with God, I feel His presence to be so real that there is no doubt in my mind, but when I have to communicate it, all I have is fear of illusion." It is apparent that her main concern was not to deceive herself or anyone else on this important matter. She repeated her fears on this score in another letter to Fr Gonzalves in June, but, in mystical theology, such doubts about communications between the individual and God are not uncommon, and are indeed a sign of truthfulness. If Sr Lucia had expressed absolute certainty in these matters, it would not have been a good sign.[739] After consulting a colleague, Fr Gonzalves wrote to Bishop Correia da Silva urging him to contact Rome on the matter of the consecration of Russia, and this the bishop did early in 1937.[740]

In 1931 the Portuguese bishops had collectively consecrated Portugal to Mary's Immaculate Heart, and in 1936, at the site of the apparitions, with the prospect of the country's being afflicted with Communism as a result of the conflict raging in neighboring Spain, they made a vow to organize a national pilgrimage to Fatima, if Portugal was delivered from this fate. Their country was indeed preserved from Communism, and as a result they were able to return in May 1938 to fulfil their vow and renew the previous consecration, being joined by half a million ordinary Portuguese. Following a spiritual retreat, under Fr Pinto, the spiritual director of Alexandrina da Costa, a Portuguese mystic, the Portuguese bishops also petitioned the Pope, asking that he consecrate the whole world to the Immaculate Heart of Mary, so that it could be saved from disaster, just as Portugal had been delivered from the threat of Communism.[741]

By now, however, Pius XI was in his eighties, less than a year from death, and overwhelmed with the difficulties facing the Church on all fronts. If we ask why he did not perform the requested consecration, it should be remembered that the apparitions at Fatima had only happened twenty years previously, and were virtually unknown in the Church as a whole; in many respects, neither the Church nor the world would have been ready for such a pronouncement. The papacy is very slow to act in accordance with private revelations, even when as well-attested as Fatima: it took the Church two hundred years to assimilate the devotion to the Sacred Heart of Jesus as propagated by St Margaret Mary in the seventeenth century. The sad fact is that humanity was not ready for such a consecration, since, despite Mary's warnings, and the great miracle of the sun at Fatima, people were not turning to God. As Mary had said on 13 July 1917: "God wishes to establish in the world devotion to my Immaculate Heart. If what I say to you is done, many souls will be saved and there will be peace. The war is going to end; *but if people do not cease offending God*, a worse one will break out during the pontificate of Pius XI." People had not ceased to offend God and so the threat of a second World War was looming ever larger.[742]

Sr Lucia continued to live quietly during this period, and in response to another request from the bishop of Leiria, wrote about her own life and the apparitions. He realized that, although the apparitions had been approved by the Church, there still remained much that needed to be told. She thus completed her second memoir in November 1937, and this caused something of a shock, since it was the first indication that the children had been visited by the Angel of Portugal in 1916.[743]

On 25 January 1938, a strange light filled the skies of northern, as well as, most unusually, southern Europe. It was described as a particularly brilliant display of the aurora borealis, but Sr Lucia realized that it was the "unknown light" foretold by Mary during the July apparition: "When you see a night illumined by an unknown light, know that this is the great sign given you by God that He is about to punish the world for its crimes, by means of war, famine, persecutions of the Church and the Holy Father. To prevent this, I shall come to ask for the consecration of Russia to my Immaculate Heart, and the Communion of reparations on the First Saturdays."[744]

The *Daily Telegraph* reported on this event the next day, describing how, "the sky was illumined by a crimson glow which deepened to violet" over a large part of Europe, including Portugal. The *New York Times* similarly described how the "aurora" was seen even in Gibraltar and Bermuda.[745]

Sr Lucia apparently informed the bishop of the importance of this sign and again referred to it in her third memoir.[746] There has been further criticism regarding the unknown light on the grounds that the war did not officially start until 1939, after the death of Pius XI. But Hitler's actions in Austria and particularly Czechoslovakia in 1938 were hardly peaceful, and it should be realized that any chastisements foretold by Mary were conditional. Some progress had been made in propagating the devotion of the Five First Saturdays, and according to Sr Lucia, because of this, Mary had intervened to postpone the "scourge of war" to a later date.[747]

Sr Faustina and the Divine Mercy Devotion

On 5 October 1938, Sr Faustina Kowalska, a religious sister who had lived out a mission of hidden suffering for a number of years, died at her convent in Poland. She passed on the Divine Mercy devotion, which like the revelations to St Margaret Mary Alacoque about the Sacred Heart, came directly to her from Jesus. This new devotion received a tremendous boost with the canonization of Sr Faustina, who became St Faustina, in April 2000. For reasons that will become clear, the message of Fatima and this devotion belong together, since they complement each other. Just as Our Lady of Fatima promised peace for the world, if true devotion to her Immaculate Heart became widespread, so Jesus told St Faustina that mankind would not have peace until it turned with trust to his mercy. This is just another example of the way that these twin devotions to the Hearts of Jesus and Mary are inseparable.

On 22 February 1931, Jesus appeared to Sr Faustina in her convent cell, clad in a long white garment, with two large rays of light, one red and the other pale, issuing from his breast. He said to her: "Paint an image according to the pattern you see, with the signature: Jesus, I Trust in You. I desire that this image be venerated, first in your chapel, and [then] throughout the entire world. I promise that the soul that will venerate this image will not perish." Jesus later told her that the two rays denoted blood and water, symbols of his precious blood and of baptism.

Sr Faustina reported this to her confessor, who said it referred to her soul. But when she came out of confession, she heard the following words: "My image is already in your soul. I desire that there be a Feast of Mercy. I want this image, which you will paint with a brush, to be solemnly blessed on the first Sunday after Easter; that Sunday is to be the Feast of Mercy." When Sr Faustina reported this to her Mother Superior she said that they would need a sign about this; but Jesus told Sr Faustina that the sign would be the graces granted through the image.[748]

On Friday, 13 September 1935, Jesus revealed the Chaplet of Divine Mercy to Sr Faustina, as a means of obtaining God's mercy for the world. She described what happened:

> In the evening, when I was in my cell, I saw an Angel, the executor of divine wrath. He was clothed in a dazzling robe, his face gloriously bright, a cloud beneath his feet. From the cloud bolts of thunder and flashes of lightning were springing into his hands; ... When I saw this sign of divine wrath which was about to strike the earth, ... I began to implore the Angel to hold off for a few moments, the world would do penance. But my plea was a mere nothing in the face of the divine anger. Just then I saw the Most Holy Trinity. The greatness of Its majesty pierced me deeply, and I did not dare to repeat my entreaties. At that very moment I felt in my soul the power of Jesus' grace, ... [and] When I became conscious of this grace, I was instantly snatched up before the Throne of God. ... I found myself pleading with God for the world with words I heard interiorly.
>
> As I was praying in this manner, I saw the Angel's helplessness; he could not carry out the just punishment which was rightly due for sins. Never before had I prayed with such inner power as I did then ...

When Sr Faustina entered the chapel the next morning, she heard an interior voice telling her to recite the prayer she had been taught the previous day every time she came into the chapel. Jesus said to her:

> This prayer will serve to appease My wrath. You will recite it for nine days, on the beads of the rosary, in the following manner. First of all, you will say one *Our Father* and *Hail Mary* and the *I Believe in God*. Then on the *Our Father* beads you will say the following words: "Eternal Father, I offer you the Body, Blood, Soul and Divinity of Your dearly beloved Son, Our Lord Jesus Christ, in atonement for our sins and those of the whole world."

On the *Hail Mary* beads, you will say the following words: "For the sake of His sorrowful Passion, have mercy on us and on the whole world." In conclusion, three times you will recite these words: "Holy God, Holy Mighty One, Holy Immortal One, have mercy on us and on the whole world."

Jesus asked that this chaplet be said by Sr Faustina's community, and then spread throughout the world.[749] The parallel between the above vision and part of the contents of the third secret of Fatima, as recorded by Sr Lucia, and revealed in June 2000, is quite striking:

at the left of Our Lady and a little above, we saw an Angel with a flaming sword in his left hand; flashing, it gave out flames that looked as though they would set the world on fire; but they died out in contact with the splendor that Our Lady radiated towards him from her right hand: pointing to the earth with his right hand, the Angel cried out in a loud voice: 'Penance, Penance, Penance!'

Note also the date of Sr Faustina's vision—13 September—the anniversary of the fifth apparition at Fatima on 13 September 1917.

In late September 1936, Jesus amplified the message about the Feast of Mercy:

My daughter, tell the whole world about My inconceivable mercy. I desire that the Feast of Mercy be a refuge and shelter for all souls, and especially for poor sinners. On that day the very depths of My tender mercy are open. I pour out a whole ocean of graces upon those souls who approach the fount of My mercy. The soul that will go to Confession and receive Holy Communion shall obtain complete forgiveness of sins and punishment. ... The Feast of Mercy emerged from My very depths of tenderness. It is My desire that it be solemnly celebrated on the first Sunday after Easter. Mankind will not have peace until it turns to the Fount of My mercy.

Later on, she heard Jesus say: "I want to grant a plenary indulgence to the souls that will go to Confession and receive Holy Communion on the Feast of My Mercy." The official celebration of the Feast of the Divine Mercy by the Church, on the Second Sunday of Easter, was publicly announced by Pope John Paul II during the homily for Sr Faustina's canonization on 30 April 2000, and an official decree to this effect was issued on 5 May 2000.[750]

The substance of this message was repeated at least fourteen times to Sr Faustina, indicating its importance,[751] and again there seems to be a definite connection to Fatima, one which emphasizes the bond between the Hearts of Jesus and Mary. It will be recalled that during the apparition on 13 July 1917 the Blessed Virgin had said: "In the end, my Immaculate Heart will triumph. The Holy Father will consecrate Russia to me and she will be converted, and a period of peace will be granted to the world."

Thus, we can see a clear link between the Divine Mercy revelations given to Sr Faustina and the message of Fatima. Jesus said, "Mankind will not have peace until it turns to the Fount of My mercy," that is his Sacred Heart, while Mary emphasized that there would only be peace when devotion to her Immaculate Heart was world-wide.

It seems that Sr Faustina had a clear premonition of the coming of World War II, and was aware that it would mean particular suffering for Poland, a thought which led her to redouble her prayers for her homeland. In May 1938, as she prayed, she heard these words: "I bear a special love for Poland, and if she will be obedient to My will, I shall exalt her in might and holiness. From her will come forth the spark that will prepare the world for My final coming."[752]

This prediction would seem to have been fulfilled in the pontificate of John Paul II, the Pope from Poland, but also in the Divine Mercy devotion itself, and in the example and sanctity of saints such as Maximilian Kolbe, the martyr of Auschwitz, one of the many Poles who gave their lives for the Faith during the Second World War.

The Start of World War II

In March 1938, Hitler completed his takeover of Austria, the *Anschluss* or union between the two Germanic countries. At the famous Munich conference in September of that year, Chamberlain, the British Prime Minister, came away proclaiming that he had secured peace. But this was at the price of the virtual handing-over of Czechoslovakia to Hitler through the redrawing of its borders, to facilitate the absorption of German elements in the country. This ensured that the balance of power in Europe now decisively favored Hitler, though, at this point, he had probably reached the limit of the German people's desire to rectify the perceived wrongs of the Versailles treaty, and there was apparently no real desire for war in the country. Hitler thus went forward knowing that he could only succeed through terror and force, and not with any genuine popular enthusiasm for war. Meanwhile, the British people were waking up to the reality of what Hitler's expansionist aims would really mean, and so the idea of appeasement receded as the likelihood of war grew greater. In April 1939 Britain undertook to guarantee Poland's independence, a move reluctantly accepted by France.[753]

When Pius XII, (1876–1958), became Pope in March 1939, following the death of Pius XI in February, his main emphasis was on the need to preserve peace. Like Benedict XV during the First World War, he refused to take sides, hoping to act as an arbiter between the opposing European powers and to negotiate some sort of settlement. In May 1939, through his nuncios, he attempted to arrange a conference between France, England, Germany, Italy, and Poland, to solve the various disputes threatening peace. But already at this stage Hitler was negotiating with Stalin, having previously negotiated a pact with Mussolini, and when Pius XII saw that his efforts were in vain, he concentrated on trying to keep Italy out of the future conflict. He still advocated a general five-point peace plan, which included measures such as guarantees to all nations of their integrity; a general reduction in armaments; peace maintained by international institutions; treaties revised without violence; and a general appeal to all Christians to act on the basis of the Gospel principles of justice and charity. But the Pope's call went unanswered, and events were set in train that would allow the war to take its grim course. In August 1939, Hitler and Stalin concluded their nonaggression pact, which included a deal to dismember Poland, and the delineation of respective German and Russian spheres of influence in Western and Eastern Europe.[754]

This pact was a great boost to both Hitler and Stalin, with both tyrants praising each other's statesmanship: on a practical level, too, it gave Hitler free access to Russia's raw materials, a vital necessity for the German war machine. But, behind all this, Hitler's real aim was still the destruction of Russia, and he was determined on a course that would bring either complete victory or total ruin for his country. When he invaded Poland in September 1939, Britain and France came into conflict with Germany, and the Second World War proper began.[755] Hitler's armies made short work of France in its desperate state, in a lightning campaign of only six weeks, which ended in June 1940. The British Expeditionary Force only just managed to escape at Dunkirk, and the Vichy regime, which was then created in France, became an appendage of Germany.

Hitler would have preferred not to fight Britain, but he misjudged the depth of hostility towards him under Winston Churchill, (1874–1965), the new Prime Minister. Churchill, however, was realistic enough to know that Britain, even with its empire, could not defeat Germany, so he placed his hopes on America coming into the war and a breakdown of the Nazi–Soviet pact. In the summer of 1940, Britain's fighter aircraft defeated the attempt by the German Air Force to destroy RAF airfields in southern England, and so put off any attempt at a German invasion, giving the country a much-needed breathing-space. In her desperate situation, virtually alone against the might of Hitler, who now controlled most of Europe, Britain's only possible offensive weapon was the bombing of German cities.[756] If Britain had been defeated at this stage, it would have been difficult, if not impossible, to defeat Germany, since America would have had no foothold with which to attack Nazism in Europe. As it was, victory in the Battle of Britain gave the alliance with the United States time to grow and mature, and held out the hope of ultimate triumph.[757]

Sr Lucia and the Consecration of 1942

Although Sr Lucia still did everything she could to press for the consecration of Russia, in a letter written to Fr Gonzalves in July 1940, she spoke of it in the following manner: "As for the consecration of Russia (to the Immaculate Heart of Mary), it was not done in the month of May as you expected. It will be done, but not at the moment. God wants it this way for now to punish the world for its crimes. We deserve it. Afterwards He will listen to our humble prayers."[758]

In December 1940, Sr Lucia, under obedience, also wrote to the new Pope, Pius XII, telling him that part of the secret that concerned the consecration of Russia and the Communions of reparation. She had originally composed a letter to the Pope on 24 October, explicitly asking for the consecration of Russia, but her superiors thought it more likely that Pius XII would agree to a general consecration of the world, with Russia being mentioned secondarily. Hence the revised letter that was written and sent in December. In this she asked the Pope to extend the First Saturdays devotion to the whole world, and revealed that Jesus had made it known to her that he would shorten the "days of tribulation" that mankind was then undergoing. But this was on condition that Pius XII, "consecrate the world to the Immaculate Heart of Mary, with a special mention for Russia, and order that all the Bishops of the world do the same ..."[759]

The time was not ripe then for the particular consecration of Russia, but God was prepared to accept a general consecration of the world, with mention of Russia, as a means of shortening the war. This approach fitted in with the request to Rome from Alexandrina da Costa that the world be consecrated to Mary's Immaculate Heart, made by her through her spiritual director, Fr Pinho, in 1936. As already detailed, this request was repeated by the Portuguese bishops in 1938. Alexandrina had a reputation as a mystic, having been paralyzed and bedridden since 1924. She offered up her great sufferings, including participating in Christ's passion every Friday, and during the last thirteen years of her life, ate or drank nothing, surviving only on Holy Communion. To those who came to see her she reiterated the message of Fatima, the necessity of prayer and penance, and she herself lived the principle of reparation for the sins of mankind.[760]

In this letter to the Pope, Sr Lucia also made the following statement, which included a reference to the consecration of Portugal to Mary's Immaculate Heart made in 1931, and renewed in 1938, as the situation in Europe worsened: "Most Holy Father, if in the union of my soul with God I have not been deceived, our Lord promises a special protection to our country in this war, due to the consecration of the nation by the Portuguese Prelates, to the Immaculate Heart of Mary; as proof of the graces that would have been granted to other nations, had they also consecrated themselves to Her."[761]

The fact that Portugal was able to keep out of the Second World War, in contrast to its involvement in World War I, was undoubtedly a sign for the Pope and the bishops of the world of the power of this consecration, and probably contributed to Pius XII's decision to go ahead with the consecration of the world in 1942. In 1940 it looked as though Hitler's forces would soon overrun the whole of Europe, including Portugal, and so this was no empty promise on Sr Lucia's part. The danger of Spain entering the war, and the pressure Portugal was under from the Allies to be allowed to use its territories, meant that, all through 1941, the threat of the country being forced into the war was certainly real.[762]

The first two parts of the secret were not revealed until the publication of the *Third Memoir* in 1941, and Sr Lucia came in for more criticism following its publication, for some people felt she had kept silence for too long. In reality, however, it would have been difficult, if not impossible, to have revealed the first two parts of the Fatima secret during the pontificate of Pius XI, given that he was specifically mentioned in them. This is to say nothing of the revelations about the future role of Russia and the Second World War. Having just experienced the carnage of World War I, would people have been able to accept a prophecy of a new and more terrible war, and the future spread of Communism?

Sr Lucia had received a further request from her bishop to tell anything more she could about Jacinta for a new edition of a book about her, one which contained excerpts from Sr Lucia's first two memoirs. She understood that the time had come to reveal publicly the first two parts of the secret, the vision of hell and Mary's request for the consecration of Russia, as well as the necessity of establishing devotion to her Immaculate Heart, if there was to be true peace in the world.[763] Bishop Correia da Silva then decided that it was best for Sr Lucia to reveal everything else she could remember about events at Fatima, and hence she began her fourth memoir in October 1941, finishing it on 8 December.[764] A year later, the new edition of the revised book on the apparitions, *Jacinta,* by Canon Galamba, was published; this quoted from the third and fourth memoirs, revealing to the general public all the essential parts of the Fatima message, including the first two parts of the secret. Only the third part of the secret still remained hidden.

On 31 October 1942, Pope Pius XII spoke to the Portuguese people in a radio message. In this he alluded to the way that his predecessor, Pius XI, had acknowledged the miraculous intervention of Mary in Portugal, and how this had led to the transformation of the country. He invited them to trust in Mary's maternal protection and pray for an end to the war, before continuing with the formula of consecration, which included Russia, but did not mention it specifically by name: "To you, to Your Immaculate Heart ... we confide, we consecrate, we deliver, not only Holy Church, ... but the whole world, ... To peoples separated by error and discord, namely those who profess to You singular devotion where there was no house that did not display Your holy icon, today hidden perhaps until better days, give them peace, and lead them again to the only flock of Christ under the true and only Shepherd."

Thus, in this act Pope Pius XII consecrated the whole world to Mary's Immaculate Heart, whilst also going on to recall the consecration of the world to the Sacred Heart of Jesus, made by Pope Leo XIII in 1899. This was not the complete consecration asked for by Mary, but it was sufficient for God to intervene and shorten the war.[765] This is apparent from a letter written by Sr Lucia to Fr Gonzalves in May 1943, where she stated that the true penance that God demanded was for everyone to fulfill their religious and civil duties, going on to say: "He promises that the War will soon end, on account of the action that His Holiness deigned to perform. But since it was incomplete the conversion of Russia has been put off to later."[766]

It certainly seems that Churchill thought that the turning-point in the war came a few days after the date of the consecration,[767] a reference to the Second Battle of El Alamein, in North Africa, between 23 October and 4 November, 1942, which saw the defeat of Rommel's forces. Of course, it will be maintained by critics that it is impossible to prove that the 1942 consecration really did shorten the war, but the circumstantial evidence suggests that the war could certainly have gone on for much longer. In this respect, the collapse of Russian Communism following the 1984 consecration by Pope John Paul II is much more clear-cut. To give just one example, if the D-day landings in June 1944 had not been attended by such calm weather, it is conceivable that the Allied invasion of German-occupied Europe could have been repulsed by Nazi forces. It would not have taken much of a storm, just a bit of bad weather, to seriously disrupt the invasion. Such things are in the hands of God, whatever modern weathermen may say. It is only necessary to remember the fate of the Spanish Armada to realize the knife-edge between success and failure in these matters. If the June 1944 invasion had failed, it would have meant at least another year of war, with further immense suffering for the whole of Europe.

The Course of the War

The state of the War changed dramatically when in June 1941 Hitler decided on his suicidal policy of invading Russia, in violation of his pact with Stalin. He believed that, once he had defeated the Communists, he would have access to virtually unlimited resources and become practically unbeatable. Hitler was determined to pursue his genocidal policy of exterminating or enslaving millions of Slavs, as inferior peoples, and conquering and colonizing the vast Russian heartland. He erred in underestimating the strength of the Russian army, and the ability of the country to absorb almost unimaginable losses. This invasion was a decision fraught with tremendous consequences for the world, since it led to the defeat of Germany and allowed Communism to swallow up half of Europe.

The realization by ordinary Russians that Hitler intended to obliterate them as a people saved Stalin's regime, and allowed him to portray the struggle with Germany in terms of a Great Patriotic War. Religious practice was again allowed and this greatly boosted the national spirit. Stalin's regime survived through his own absolute ruthlessness and by means of material help from the West. The Russians were able to mount a counter-offensive against the German armies in December 1941, and it was at this point that the tide of the war began to turn against Hitler, especially after his decision to support the Japanese attack on America at Pearl Harbor. He began a U-boat offensive against the United States, but this only served to bring America into the war against Germany, thus sealing its fate.[768] Once the German U-boat code had been broken, Hitler's potentially most dangerous weapon was neutralized, and Britain's sea link to America was effectively secured by 1943. But there was fear amongst the allies of the possibility that Germany might develop atomic weapons, and so some responsibility for the subsequent development and use of the bomb can be laid at the door of Hitler. He was determined to fight to the finish even if he destroyed Germany in the process, and determined, too, that the elimination of Europe's Jews should go ahead at all costs; this had begun on a large scale from 1941 onwards, in an atmosphere of great secrecy.[769]

When the end came, with the Allied invasion of Europe from the West, and that of the Russians from the East, the continent was reduced to ruins, and worse, it was the Soviets who were to emerge with the greatest spoils. The Allies had been forced to deal with them as a matter of sheer survival. Poland, for whose cause the war had ostensibly been fought, was to end up under Soviet rule, but at least, thanks to Churchill, the Mediterranean was saved from Soviet domination. Following the crucial meetings at Tehran in November 1943 and Yalta in January 1945, however, it was to emerge that Franklin Roosevelt, (1882–1945), the American President, had been duped by Stalin. He mistakenly believed that Russia had no further territorial ambitions in Europe, and only the fact that Stalin overplayed his hand regarding Poland prevented the return of the entire US army to America shortly after the war. But by then it was too late to do much to alter a situation on the ground that saw Communist forces occupying half of Europe, and even the fate of Western Europe was by no means guaranteed.

But with the election of a new President, Truman, the planned

American withdrawal was canceled, and the Cold War became a reality, following Churchill's famous speech in March 1945. Even Churchill, however, had been blind to the evils of Stalin's regime, given the desperate struggle with Nazi Germany, and he too lost sight of the danger of an expanding Soviet Union during the dark days of conflict. The Allies ended up handing much of Eastern Europe to Stalin, descending to shameful moral depths in the process, particularly in the repatriation of unwilling Soviet citizens to prison, torture, and in many cases, death.[770] The war in the East finished with the dropping of two atom bombs by the Americans on Japan.

Postwar Politics

Thus began the uneasy standoff between America and Russia, which was to last over forty years. Following the Russian blockade of Berlin in 1948, the Western defensive alliance, NATO, was set up in February 1949. American isolationism was ended, as it assumed the role of the world's policeman, whilst the US also brought about the physical reconstruction of Europe through the Marshall Plan. After Russia built and exploded a nuclear device of its own, from plans obtained by Communist traitors in the West, a new arms race sprang up between the two superpowers in the late forties and early fifties, as the United States sought to contain any further Russian expansion. From the time of the Korean war onwards, a full-scale arms race developed as Communist expansionism began to turn the world into two divided and heavily-armed camps. Nor was there any improvement for the people of the Soviet Union, where the Gulag continued to expand; in the years leading up to the death of Stalin, in 1953, at least another ten million prisoners met their deaths in the hellish slave labor camp system.[771]

By 1949, China under Mao Tse-Tung had also fallen to Communism, and so a powerful block, totally opposed to Western ideals and Christianity, seemed to be growing ever stronger. The Chinese Communists emulated, and even surpassed, their comrades in Russia, in putting to death anything up to forty million people. Mao repeated Stalin's mistakes in formulating his Great Leap Forward in the late fifties, an attempt at social engineering on a gigantic scale. It affected at least seven hundred million people and in 1959 led to a massive man-made famine that lasted till 1962, in which millions died. Ominously, by the early sixties, China, using Russian technology, had developed a nuclear capability of its own, and under Chairman Mao had a leader who seemed to believe that a nuclear war could be won, even if it meant the deaths of three hundred million of his own people.[772]

Following the Second World War, there was also a danger in Europe that Communist parties might gain power in Italy, and more particularly in France, and this was obviously a special concern for Pope Pius XII, who knew that the aim of Russian Communism was complete dominance in Europe. Without American aid, this might well have happened, but eventually Christian Democratic governments were able to emerge in Italy and West Germany, and so European freedom was preserved; France, with its Fifth Republic, likewise eventually saw a renewal under De Gaulle (1890–1970). At the end of the war, though, this optimistic scenario had not been expected and the general mood in Europe had been grim. The continent was in ruins and there seemed little hope for the future, but the very nature of the absolute devastation wrought by Nazism meant that it was possible to make a new beginning.

Into this vacuum stepped a series of truly Christian leaders who worked to rebuild postwar Europe. In Italy and Germany, Alcide de Gasperi and Konrad Adenauer respectively took charge in 1945. They were both Catholics who had resisted fascism, believing in the rule of law, the centrality of the family, and in keeping the powers of the State as limited as possible. De Gasperi was the only major untainted Italian political figure at the end of the war, and he was able to form a stable Christian Democratic government; under his leadership, Italy was fully reintegrated into European life by the fifties. Likewise, Adenauer in Germany fashioned a Christian Democratic movement that was remarkably successful in rebuilding the country. His major achievement was in integrating Germany as closely as possible into the Western cultural sphere, and particularly his collaboration with France, a move that laid the foundations of the European Community.[773]

At one stage, in late 1947, it seemed as though there might be civil war in France, but as we will see, the apparitions of Mary at L'Ile Bouchard were instrumental in preventing that happening. France had faced a difficult period after the war, when the Communists capitalized on their tardy participation in the resistance movement, and the general sense of disillusionment following the Vichy regime. French intellectual life was blighted by the emergence of existentialism, "a theology without God," which saw man alone in a godless universe, one he was obliged to shape by his own political activism. Existentialism was based on the ideas of Kierkegaard, a radical nineteenth-century theologian, but was popularized by two German philosophers during the 1920s, Karl Jaspers and Martin Heidegger.[774] Existentialism was promoted by writers such as Jean-Paul Sartre, who defended the use of totalitarian violence. His longtime companion, Simone de Beauvoir, was one of the founding spirits of modern feminism, particularly through her book *The Second Sex*.

De Gaulle found that he could not work with the Communist Party and resigned in 1946, allowing the Communists and Socialists to foist a disastrous constitution on the country. It was left to Jean Monnet to rebuild France's industrial base, despite a lack of support from unstable governments under the Fourth Republic, and to promote the idea of the European community. But the sort of partnership between France and Germany which this involved required a stronger government in France, and this was eventually provided when De Gaulle returned as President in 1958 and introduced a new constitution.

It is striking then to see the way that most of Western Europe regained democratic norms, and a degree of prosperity, in the postwar period. Given that two terrible, all-out conflicts had been fought out on the continent in the first half of the century, such an outcome was by no means guaranteed, and the presence of America, and American support in the form of Marshall Aid, was crucial in ensuring this stability.[775] The progress of Communism, then, was blocked in postwar Europe, but it still remained a very powerful force as the Cold War began in earnest. The way that risings in Hungary in 1956, and Czechoslovakia in 1968, were brutally put down, showed the uncompromisingly evil nature of Soviet rule. It had firmly established itself across a great swathe of Eastern Europe and Asia, as a militantly anti-Christian power, and retained control over hundreds of millions of people, until the beginnings of its collapse in the eighties, which has left a poisonous legacy still tainting the formerly Communist countries.[776]

20

Tre Fontane, L'Ile Bouchard, and the Assumption Dogma

Tre Fontane: 12 April 1947

As indicated above, both France and Italy faced difficult transitions to normality in the aftermath of the War. Both experienced a reaction against the their previous regimes which had supported Hitler, Mussolini's fascists in the case of Italy, and in the case of France, Pétain's Vichy government. In 1947, both countries saw fascinating, but little known, Marian apparitions, which seem to have all the hallmarks of authenticity.

Tre Fontane takes its name from a Trappist monastery on the outskirts of Rome, which is the site of the martyrdom of St Paul. According to tradition, after he was beheaded his head bounced three times, with a fountain springing up at each of these points. There is also a connection with St Bernard, who is said, in 1138, at a nearby church, to have had a vision of a ladder with angels ascending and descending—this, of course, is a Marian type, as was discussed in the section on the Patriarch Jacob and the apparitions at the Rue du Bac.

The principal seer of Tre Fontane, Bruno Cornacchiola, was born on 9 May 1913, and thus he was 33 at the time of the apparition on 12 April 1947. He came from a poor background, and had received only rudimentary religious instruction. After military service, at the age of 23, he married Iolanda Lo Gatto, and to earn money decided to fight on the Nationalist side in the Spanish Civil War, although he was actually more inclined towards Communism. Once in Spain he came under the influence of a German Protestant, who managed to convince him that the papacy was the cause of all the world's ills. Bruno at once conceived a hatred for the Church and vowed that he would kill the Pope; nor was this an idle threat—he bought a dagger in Spain especially for this purpose, carving on it the words: "Death to the Pope."

His wife was not enthusiastic about his new Protestant beliefs and he began physically to abuse her. He also destroyed all the Catholic mementos and pictures around the house. Bruno then decided to join the Protestant Adventist church in Rome, and tried to persuade his wife: she agreed on one condition, that first he should make the Nine First Fridays devotion, and that, if at the end of this, he was still determined to become a Protestant, she would join him. Iolanda trusted that God would somehow convert her husband, but at the end of the nine months he was still set on joining the Adventists, and so she reluctantly followed suit.[777]

From 1939 to 1947 he worked as a tram conductor in Rome, and by the latter date they had three children, two boys, Carlo, aged seven, and Gianfranco, aged four, and a girl, Isola, aged ten. Unfortunately, his physical abuse of his wife continued, causing much distress to both her and the children, while by now he was a convinced Communist, who still had plans to kill the Pope. On the Saturday after Easter, 12 April 1947, he set off for the afternoon with his children—on the following day, Sunday, he was due to give an anti-Catholic, and indeed anti-Marian, talk, and he wanted a chance to plan out what he would say. Note that this Sunday is the date of the feast of Divine Mercy, and thus the apparition to Bruno happened on its eve. They took the bus to Tre Fontane, where the shop at the Trappist monastery was famed for its chocolate. Once there, while waiting for the shop to open at about four o'clock, after the siesta, he sat down in the shade to plan his talk, while the children played with a ball on some waste ground nearby.

At about 3:20 he was disturbed by the children shouting for their lost ball, but as he helped with the search, the youngest, Gianfranco, promptly went missing himself. Bruno discovered him in a small cave or grotto, smiling, with hands joined as he knelt and repeated the words, "Beautiful Lady! Beautiful Lady!" Bruno could not make anything out, and so called first to Isola, and then to Carlo, who both came and saw the "Beautiful Lady." All three children were entranced, and oblivious of his shouts. He became frightened after he was unable to lift them, and called out angrily into the empty cave. Finally, in desperation, he cried out, "God help us!"

At this, Bruno saw two transparent hands which touched his face and wiped his eyes, causing him pain. Then, he saw a tiny light in the cave which grew more luminous, as he felt an interior sensation of great joy. Finally he saw a beautiful woman, with a motherly but sad expression, wearing a green mantle over a white dress, and with a rose-colored sash around her waist. In her hands she held an ash-

gray book close to her breast, while at her feet he could see a crucifix which had been smashed, on top of a black cloth.[778] She called
herself the "Virgin of Revelation," and spoke to Bruno slowly and
rhythmically for about an hour and twenty minutes; he could
remember every word afterwards, it was like a recording he could
replay time and time again. But the children only saw her lips move
and heard nothing.

Our Lady revealed herself thus: "I am she who is related to the
Divine Trinity. I am the Virgin of Revelation. You have persecuted
me, now is the time to stop! Come and be part of the Holy Fold
which is the Celestial Court on earth. God's promise is unchange-
able and will remain so. The nine First Fridays in honor of the
Sacred Heart, which your faithful wife persuaded you to observe
before you walked down the road of lies, has saved you."

She counseled him: "Live the divine doctrine. Practice
Christianity. Live the Faith," while also saying, "The Hail Marys that
you pray with faith and love are like golden arrows that go straight
to the heart of Jesus," and, "Pray much and recite the Rosary for
the conversion of sinners, of unbelievers and of all Christians." She
indicated future conversions and cures with these words: "I
promise this special favour: With this sinful soil (the soil of the
grotto) I shall perform great miracles for the conversion of unbelievers and of sinners." The grotto actually had a bad reputation as
a place of immorality. She also spoke of future problems: "Science
will deny God and will refuse His calls." In particular, she spoke of
her Assumption into heaven, outlining her life during her eighty
minute talk: "My body could not and did not decay. I was assumed
into Heaven by my Son and the angels."

She gave him, too, a secret message for the Pope: "You must go
to the Holy Father, the Pope, the Supreme Pastor of Christianity,
and personally tell him my message. Bring it to his attention. I shall
tell you how to recognize the one who will accompany you to see
the Pope."

Finally, it was over, and after smiling at Bruno and the children,
Mary turned around, walked through the wall of the grotto and
disappeared. Bruno was in a daze, although the children were
excited as they all made their way to the Trappist Church to pray
in thanksgiving. Before going home they all went back to the cave,
where they encountered a beautiful fragrance, all the more surprising because its floor was covered with filth. Bruno cleared a space
and used his door key to scratch this message: "On 12th April 1947
the Virgin of Revelation appeared in this grotto to the Protestant
Bruno Cornacchiola and his children and he was converted."

Bruno told the children to say nothing, but this was a forlorn request and as soon as they got to their apartment block they told everyone they met. Arriving home they were greeted by Iolanda who could smell a beautiful perfume emanating from them, and after the children were in bed, Bruno told his wife all that had happened. He begged forgiveness on his knees for the way he had treated her.

Following Mary's directions, Bruno eventually found a priest to advise him, so that he and Iolanda could rejoin the Church, as the story spread and the numbers of pilgrims grew, with articles on the apparition beginning to appear in the press. He and the children were even questioned separately, at length, by the police, but they were unable to find any significant differences in their accounts. Mary apparently appeared to Bruno on several other occasions at the grotto, but did not speak.[779] The local church authorities also carried out an investigation, and the cult of the Virgin of Revelation was approved with unusual speed by the Vicariate of Rome. As the number of pilgrims grew the area around the grotto had to be altered to make it safer and more accessible. A special statue, representing Mary during the apparition, was blessed by Pope Pius XII on 5 October 1947, and then taken in procession, amidst huge crowds, from St Peter's Square to Tre Fontane.

Just over two years later, on 9 December 1949, Bruno was part of a group invited to pray the rosary with Pius XII in his private chapel, as part of the beginning of the 1950 Holy Year celebrations. After the rosary, the Pope asked if anyone wanted to speak to him. Bruno immediately came forward and knelt at his feet and, with tears in his eyes, showed the dagger with which he had intended to kill him, and his Protestant Bible. He begged forgiveness, which Pius XII unhesitatingly gave.

In fact, according to one account,[780] it seems that Pius XII had an awareness of what was going to happen for at least ten years, since, in 1937, while still a cardinal, he had a meeting with a holy woman who had apparently seen Mary in a vision at Tre Fontane. She related how the Virgin had told her that she would return to the grotto and convert a man who wanted to assassinate the Pope, and moreover, that he, Cardinal Pacelli, would himself be Pope. His reply was cautious, and in effect he said he would wait and see, but in 1939 Eugenio Pacelli duly became Pope Pius XII. Given all this, it is understandable that the cult of the apparitions at Tre Fontane was approved so rapidly.[781]

The background to all this was the postwar struggle between the

Catholic Church and the Communists in Italy, with this being played out in political terms between the Christian Democrat party, led by de Gasperi, and the Communist party, led by Togliatti. The Communist strategy, unusually, was to attempt to work along largely democratic lines, and then gradually to undermine the cultural position of Catholicism. In 1945, a coalition government was formed, and following elections, the Christian Democrats had 32.5 per cent of the vote, the Socialists 20.7 per cent and the Communists 18.9 per cent. Thus the parties of the left were numerically stronger at this point. But, in May 1947, following the earlier formation of a splinter group from the Marxist Socialists, the Christian Democrats expelled the Communists and socialists from the coalition government.

This was just a month after the apparition at Tre Fontane. It is difficult to say exactly how influential this event was, but clearly the reports of a Marian apparition so close to Rome, and of healings, along with an enthusiastic public reception, cannot but have been helpful for the Church, and thus for the Christian Democrats and democracy generally during this crucial period. There was quite a degree of disruption involving strikes, but Parliamentary elections were held the following year, in April 1948, with the Church actively supporting the Christian Democrats against the Communist challenge. The result was an absolute majority for the Christian Democrats with 48.5 per cent of the vote, and this was an extremely important victory since it ensured future stability in Italy.[782]

L'Ile Bouchard: 8–14 December 1947

The postwar situation in France, regarding the threat from Communism, was much more serious. Here, in the months leading up to the apparitions at L'Ile Bouchard, in December 1947, there was a serious threat of civil war. By the end of the Second World War the Communist Party had become amongst the biggest and best-organized in France, representing over five million voters, and was completely Stalinist in tone, taking its line from Moscow. Over time this "state within a state" made the governance of France extremely difficult, and meant that there was a real threat of a Communist takeover.[783]

L'Ile Bouchard (Bouchard Island) is a small town in northwestern France, on the River Vienne, a tributary of the Loire, situated a little over twenty miles south of Tours, and about ten miles east of Chinon. Here, in the parish church of St Gilles, from 8 to 14 December 1947, about eight months after Tre Fontane, unfolded a little-known series of apparitions of Mary, which, despite a slow process of approval, show every indication of being authentic. L'Ile Bouchard has many historical associations, but perhaps the most important involves Joan of Arc, who called here on her way to meet Charles VII at Chinon Castle in March 1429. She stopped at the church of the apparitions, and a side door is named after her. Joan of Arc was canonized in 1920 and declared a secondary patron saint of France.[784] She had played a large part in saving France in the early part of the fifteenth century, and now, over six centuries later, the country again faced terrible problems, and possible civil war. The Communists were causing havoc by means of assassinations, train derailments and widespread strikes. The political and economic situation was very serious and seemed to be getting out of control as the year drew to a close.[785] But, unknown to nearly all, the remedy was at hand.

Several hundred miles away to the south-east, near the small village of Châteauneuf de Galaure, which is about thirty-five miles south of Lyons, lived a remarkable woman in her forties called Marthe Robin. She had been paralyzed and bedridden since 1930, reliving the Passion of Christ each Friday, and this went on till her death in 1981. Every week she received Holy Communion, generally on a Wednesday, and incredibly this was her only sustenance for the next fifty years—she neither ate nor drank anything else.[786] She collaborated in an apostolate with Fr Georges Finet, which involved setting up lay Christian Communities called *Foyers de Charité*, "hearths or homes of love," whose main work is the giving of week-long silent retreats. These have now spread around the world, and Marthe's cause is proceeding in Rome.

Fr Finet, though, was in a somber mood when he paid a visit to her on the morning of 8 December 1947. He confessed that he thought it was the end for France, and that civil war was inevitable. Marthe's reply, though, was firm and consoling: "No Father, the Virgin Mary is going to save France through the prayers of little children."[787]

The first apparition in the church at L'Ile Bouchard took place on the afternoon of that same day, the feast of the Immaculate Conception, a cold and gray winter's day. Given the tense political situation in France, the sisters who ran the local school had, that morning, particularly asked the children to pray for the good of the country. At about one o'clock in the afternoon, Jacqueline Aubry, aged 12, her sister Jeanette, aged 7, and their cousin,

Nicole Robin, aged 10, were on their way back to school after lunch in the Aubry house, when, at Jacqueline's suggestion, they stopped at the church of St Gilles to pray. They went to the altar of the Virgin and began to say a decade of the rosary; but they were not quite halfway through when Jacqueline suddenly saw a beautiful Lady before her, all in white, with hands joined in prayer and a rosary over her right arm. To the left was an angel holding a lily, eyes fixed in contemplation of the Lady. Then Nicole and Jeanette also looked up, and exclaimed in wonder at the marvelous scene before them.

As the Lady smiled at them, Jacqueline whispered that they must tell other people what was happening, so they ran out together and saw a school friend, Laura Croizon, aged 8, and her 13-year-old sister, Sergine. Returning to the church, the five girls made their way towards the altar, as Laura cried out that she could see a beautiful lady and an angel. Sergine, though, saw nothing, and the others had to describe the scene for her. The altar of the Virgin had a stained glass window featuring Our Lady of Lourdes to its left, and a statue of Our Lady of Victories directly above it. The apparition was situated several feet off the ground in the corner between the altar and the window. The girls described a beautiful Lady, surrounded by a golden light, wearing a brilliant white dress edged with gold, and a blue sash, and carrying a white rosary. Her veil was a white of a different hue and fell down to near her feet, while the girls could see her striking long blond hair falling down the front of her body, in two parts, to her knees. Her smile was wonderful, and they thought her to be aged about 16 or 17. The girls were struck not just by her beauty and grandeur, but also by her kindness and naturalness; as the week went on, a relationship developed between the Lady and them, which was like that between a supremely loving mother and her children.

The angel, surrounded by an intense white light, was kneeling on his right knee in profound contemplation, and wore a rosy-white robe, also edged with gold. Like the Lady he had blue eyes and blond hair. In his right hand he held out a lily stalk, while his left hand was placed upon his heart. He had white wings, also trimmed with gold, whose feathers shone and moved slightly in a "breeze" the children could not feel. The two figures were in a rocky grotto. The Lady stood on a rectangular stone block, decorated with a garland of five pink roses, while on the rocks just below were the following words in letters of gold, about three inches high: "O Marie conçue sans péché, priez pour nous qui avons recours à vous." (O Mary conceived without sin, pray for us who have recourse to you). As the reader will recall, this is the invocation made famous at the Rue du Bac.

Once the girls had explained all this to Sergine, the Lady disappeared, and they all made way their way out of the church. Jacqueline and Jeanette rushed home to tell their mother, but she did not believe them. Once back at school the news spread very quickly, as Jacqueline excitedly recounted to one of the sisters, Sr Marie de L'Enfant Jésus, that she had seen a beautiful Lady in the Church, but wondered who she might be—was she the Blessed Virgin? The Sister believed instantly, but feared a negative general reaction. The parish priest, Fr Clovis Ségelle, and the head teacher, Sr Saint-Léon de la Croix, came into the school yard just then, and were not impressed by these reports. Fr Ségelle said that Jacqueline must have been seeing double through her thick glasses—and indeed, because of her poor vision and chronic conjunctivitis, Jacqueline did have to wear glasses and continually wipe her eyes. Every morning her mother had to open them with warm water, as they would be glued shut overnight by a thick crust of dried pus.

Jacqueline explained that the other girls had also seen the Lady, and so Fr Ségelle and Sr Saint-Léon decided to question them separately. Each gave the same account, and as school began again, Jacqueline spoke once more with the head teacher, who dismissed her curtly, while managing to give her the impression that she should have stayed in the church if the Lady was really so beautiful. Jacqueline took up this idea, and lost no time in fetching the other girls and leading them back to the altar of the Virgin, where they were delighted to be beckoned by the smiling Lady. As they knelt before her, though, her expression became extremely sad as she slowly uttered her first words: "Tell the little children to pray for France, for her need is great." Jacqueline, still not sure who the lady was, then whispered to Jeanette and Laura to ask the Lady if she was their "Maman du Ciel," (Heavenly Mother[788]). They did so, and the reply was "But of course I am your Maman du Ciel!" Jacqueline then asked about the angel. The Lady looked at him, and he turned towards the girls and said: "I am the angel Gabriel."

Mary then turned back to the girls and asked for their hands to kiss, bending low to reach the hands of Jacqueline and Nicole. But the other two girls were much smaller and could not reach high enough. Jacqueline took them up, one after the other, and lifted them up at arm's length, as though they were practically weightless. All four testified to the solidity and warmth of Mary's hand and the touch of her lips. Before disappearing in a cloud of silvery dust, she asked them to return that evening at five o'clock and the next day at one o'clock. After the girls left the church, they noticed a shining white oval on their fingers, but before they got back to school these traces, which they did manage to show to a local woman, had faded.

Jacqueline and Nicole spoke of what had happened, and after class they were separated and asked to write out accounts of their experiences, which were matching. Once the girls got home they found their parents not inclined to believe them, and only Jacqueline was able to return to the church, for the rosary and Benediction of the Blessed Sacrament in honor of the feast of the Immaculate Conception. Mary appeared and beckoned to her, but as she debated whether to go forward or not, looking back toward Sr Saint-Léon for permission, assuming that she too could see the apparition, the bell rang for Benediction, and when she looked back the apparition was gone. But once the Blessed Sacrament had been returned to the tabernacle, Mary reappeared. Later on this made Fr Ségelle look at the whole affair more closely, since he realized that it was not credible that Jacqueline could have made up this subtle theological point related to the Real Presence of Christ. Although devout, thanks to a pious neighbor, Jacqueline was not from a religious household, and had received little religious instruction.

The next day, Tuesday, 9 December, at one o'clock, all four girls assembled in the church, and so the general pattern for the week's events was set. They knelt by the Virgin's altar and began to pray Hail Marys, when suddenly a shining golden sphere, about three feet across, came out of the wall and unfolded itself as a rectangular curtain of silvery light, on which the rocky grotto stood out in relief. Mary's long golden hair, which had so impressed the girls on the first day, was now hidden underneath her veil. The angel was kneeling on the other side, while the words on the rocks had changed. Now they read: "Je suis l'Immaculeé Conception" (I am the Immaculate Conception). Again they were being presented with important words from a previous Marian apparition, this time Lourdes. They could also see parts of a word written in letters of gold across Mary's breast: "Ma . . . cat," but didn't understand what they meant; her hands hid the middle part of what would be revealed later as, "Magnificat," the traditional name given to Mary's song of praise uttered during the Visitation to Elizabeth, (Luke 1:46–55), which took place shortly after the Annunciation.

The girls were then joined by a certain Madame Trinson, who owned a shoe shop in the town. Mary, with a grave expression, showed the girls the golden cross of her rosary, and asked them to kiss it. Jacqueline and Nicole both stood up to do this, and Madame Trinson was amazed to see Jacqueline repeat her feat of the previous day, lifting up the two younger girls as though they were dolls, as light as a feather, in order that they too could kiss the golden cross. The metal was cold to their lips and they were penetrated with a sense of Mary's grief. The Virgin then made a beautiful, but extremely slow, sign of the cross. It took two minutes to complete, and the girls copied her movements, with Madame Trinson looking on in astonishment. Once this was over Mary said that she would tell them a secret that they could reveal in three days, and with great emphasis said: "Pray for France, which in these days is in great danger." Then she asked that the priest come at two o'clock, with the children and a crowd, so that they could all pray. She also asked for a grotto, and that her statue and that of the angel should be placed in it, promising to bless them once this was done. With that the apparition disappeared.

Fr Ségelle, however, refused to come at two, and so Jacqueline, Jeanette and Laura, with about twenty other children, and thirty adults, assembled in the church. After they had said ten Hail Marys, the Virgin and the angel appeared as before, out of the golden ball. She asked for hymns and prayers, before telling them to return each day at one o'clock, until everything was over. At 5:30 Fr Ségelle informed the archbishop of the day's events. That same day, to general surprise, the Communists decided to call off their general strike.[789]

On the third day, Wednesday, 10 December, one hundred and fifty people waited in the church for the next appearance of Mary. Suddenly the Virgin was present, and again she requested a sung version of the Hail Mary, before asking the girls to kiss her hand. The crowd, like Madame Trinson, were amazed to see the frail Jacqueline repeat her feat of lifting the two smallest girls. Then Jacqueline's mother called out to her daughter requesting a miracle so that all would believe, to which Mary replied: "I have not come here to perform miracles, but to tell you to pray for France. However, tomorrow you will see clearly and you won't need to wear glasses any more." Then Mary told the girls that she was going to tell them a secret, which they must promise not to reveal. They agreed to this, and, after the secret the Virgin asked them to return again the next day at the same time, before disappearing into the golden ball. This apparition had lasted about a quarter of an hour. As in the case of other authentic apparitions, the girls could not be persuaded, by any means, to divulge the secret.

Naturally enough, the people wanted to know what the answer to the request for a miracle had been, and the girls related that Mary had said that from tomorrow Jacqueline would see clearly and not need glasses. At five o'clock, Fr Ségelle interviewed Jacqueline, and poured scorn on the idea that her eyes, which were really in a dreadful condition, could possibly improve overnight. He thought this ridiculous idea would finally reveal that the whole thing was an absurdity. Nevertheless, a miracle had been promised, and few of the adults closely associated with these events had a sound night's sleep. Jacqueline went home in tears, and was met by her father and mother who were also in tears.

Jacqueline's parents were in something of a quandary; they were non-practicing Catholics, and her father had been embarrassed by remarks concerning his daughter, and become angry. But the transparent sincerity of his eldest daughter had struck him deeply, and now they would have to wait and see what the morning brought. When Jacqueline woke up, she was able to open her eyes without any difficulty and had normal vision. She called to her parents in delight, who were overjoyed at seeing their daughter's eyes cured so miraculously. Her father rushed to get Fr Ségelle, who exclaimed on seeing Jacqueline: "So it's true that She has descended among us!" The priest immediately contacted the archbishop and was told to be present at the next apparition.

This was the fourth day, Thursday, 11 December, and by one o'clock the report of this miracle had ensured a full church. Mary appeared and requested that they sing the Hail Mary, before asking: "Do you pray for sinners?" They replied that they did, and then she led them through ten Hail Marys, but only said the first part of each prayer, the angel Gabriel's message, and not the second part. Jacqueline asked her to heal people who had petitioned the girls for cures, to which the Virgin replied that she promised that there would be "happiness in families." Before disappearing she again asked about the grotto. After this, the girls were questioned separately in the sacristy.

On the fifth day, Friday, 12 December, three hundred people were in the church for the one o'clock rendezvous. When Mary appeared, the girls could see something new: now she was wearing a "crown" made up of twelve shining rays, each about a foot long, two narrow blue ones in the center and then five wider ones to each side, colored red, yellow, green, pink and a brownish red. Now the Virgin held her hands lower so the word "Magnificat" could be read. The girls thought the crown resembled a rainbow.

She then asked them to sing the Hail Mary, before leading them, as on the previous day, in ten spoken Hail Marys. After this she said: "Do you pray for sinners?" to which they replied "Yes, Madame," and then she continued: "Good, above all pray a lot for sinners." Jacqueline asked for a miracle, but Mary repeated her previous statement that she had not come to perform miracles, but to ask for prayers for France. After another decade of the rosary she disappeared, and again the girls were questioned separately as to what they had seen and heard.

For the sixth day of the apparitions, Saturday, 13 December, five hundred people were in the church at one o'clock, as the Virgin appeared again, but this time without the crown. Mary again asked for prayers, invocations and hymns, as Jacqueline repeated her request for a miracle, to hear the reply, "Later." Then after more prayers and invocations, the Virgin told them that she would appear the next day for the last time. Again the children were interrogated afterwards.

The last day of the apparitions, Sunday 14 December, saw L'Ile Bouchard crowded with pilgrims and the church of St Gilles jammed solid with two thousand people, while more gathered outside. While waiting for the girls, the congregation prayed the rosary—many had not prayed in years—as the young seers took their places for the last time. Once more, Mary and the angel were before them, for an apparition which lasted over half an hour. Again prayers and hymns were requested, after which Jacqueline read some messages that had been given to her, including one from Sr Marie which said: "Madame, what should we do to console our Lord for the suffering sinners cause him?" The response was: "Pray and make sacrifices."

After more prayers and invocations, Mary requested that the congregation sing the Magnificat, and Fr Ségelle led everyone in this, and later still she re-emphasized the need to pray for sinners. Realizing that the apparition would soon be over, Jacqueline asked the Virgin to give some proof of her presence, to which Mary responded with a smile: "Before I go I will send a bright ray of sunlight." With that, she began to bless the crowd, and as she did so, a mysterious ray of sunshine streamed in through a pane in the south-west window of the choir, illuminating the precise spot of the apparition. It grew in strength and began to cover a larger area, forcing those near the altar of the Virgin to shield their eyes. Those affected also remarked on the heat of this ray. The girls had their backs to the light, but those placed so they could see their faces, and the flowers they held, saw them gently lit by marvelous sparkles and colored lights, as if by reflection from the jewel-like interior of the grotto.

This ray of sunlight was inexplicable in natural terms, since normal sunlight does not spread out like a fan from a single point—for this to happen the sun would need to have been situated virtually outside the window. Moreover, this ray, given its point of entry, should have been blocked by some of the pillars of the choir. In addition, subsequent tests would show that it was physically impossible for a normal ray of sunlight to have illuminated that particular part of the church on the winter's day in question, and so we are in the presence of a miracle.

After it was over, Fr Ségelle gave the congregation, many of whom were in tears, Benediction of the Blessed Sacrament, and once more the girls were closely examined. They faced much further questioning over the next few months from the curious, and many other trials, but remained faithful to their testimony. Several ecclesiastical investigations into the apparitions were held, with that of the Vicar-General of the diocese, Mgr Fiot, being the most important. Although there has been no official recognition of the events at L'Ile Bouchard, there has been a *de facto* recognition by successive archbishops of Tours, in that they have allowed a grotto, and statues of Mary and the angel, to be placed in the church of St Gilles, and also sanctioned the growing pilgrimages to L'Ile Bouchard. In addition, the French theologian Fr Vernet, published a lengthy study favorable to the apparitions in 1992,[790] and on 8 December 2001 in a public decree, the Archbishop of Tours, André Vingt-Trois, authorized "pilgrimages, and the public cult celebrated in the church of St Gilles of L'Ile Bouchard, to invoke Our Lady of Prayer."

Regarding the critical political and economic situation in France, the fifth day of the apparitions seems to have coincided with the point at which the crisis in France was over, and it is difficult to avoid the conclusion that the prayers said at L'Ile Bouchard church, and elsewhere in the country, were instrumental in preventing the outbreak of a possible civil war that would have had catastrophic results for both France and Europe. If Communism could have gained a foothold in France, then the whole future course of European history would undoubtedly have been changed—for the worse. Thus, from a historical point of view, the apparitions at L'Ile Bouchard occurred at a highly significant moment, and so accord with one of the general themes of this book, that Marian apparitions and important historical—even revolutionary—events are closely linked.

The Typology of Tre Fontane and L'Ile Bouchard

Tre Fontane and L'Ile Bouchard are here considered together in typological terms, because like Beauraing and Banneux in 1932–33, they occurred within quite a short space of time—about eight months—and within the same year, 1947. This is somewhat unusual as authentic Marian apparitions, between 1830 and 1933, have generally taken place on average about every ten or twelve years. And, as we have seen, just as there is a close typological link between the two Belgian apparitions, with both finding a biblical counterpart in the book of Ezekiel, in sections only a few chapters apart, so here too, there seems to be a close link between Tre Fontane and L'Ile Bouchard in terms of typology.

This link, however, is not so much a question of space, but of *time,* or perhaps it should be said, of timelessness! That is, there seem to be elements from the biblical book of Daniel, in the case of L'Ile Bouchard, and of sections from the second book of Maccabees, in the case of Tre Fontane, which overlap and reinforce each other, in a quite fascinating way. There also seem to be points of contact between both apparitions and the book of Revelation. Even a casual reading of the books of Daniel and Revelation reveals many points of correspondence, and when one digs a little deeper, the resemblances are even more marked. Specifically, both are strongly apocalyptic, that is specifically concerned with the events leading up to the end of the world.

It might seem that, in this respect, the second book of Maccabees is out of place, since it is an historical account, and, according to Catholic tradition, can be dated to the second century BC, whereas the traditional date for the prophet Daniel's activities is the sixth century BC. But in reality, although Daniel lived and prophesied during that period, the book of Daniel did not reach its final form until approximately the same time as 2 Maccabees, that is sometime during the second century BC. The canonical book of Daniel is quite complicated, comprising three languages, Hebrew, Aramaic and Greek, and it seems that a later inspired writer is responsible for its present form. The result of all this is that 2 Maccabees and Daniel are more or less contemporary, as regards the date of their final formation. The book of Revelation, though, comes from the time after Christ, and can be dated approximately to the end of the first century AD.[791]

Elements from Tre Fontane seem to correspond with the passage from 2 Maccabees which deals with the prophet Jeremiah's concealing the Ark of the Covenant on Mount Nebo—the mount climbed by Moses in order to view the promised land—in a cave or grotto of some sort, and then sealing up the entrance. Some of his companions went back to try and find the place but were unable to, and Jeremiah reproached them, telling them that the place would remain unknown, and the Ark hidden, until towards the end of the world (2 Macc. 2:4–8).[792] As has been indicated several times in this book, the Ark of the Covenant was one of the most popular biblical types of Mary for the Church Fathers, and its last appearance here in the Old Testament, in one of the last books to be written in that section of the Bible, seems to correspond well with events at Tre Fontane. Here, it was specifically in a small cave or grotto, that Bruno Cornacchiola, along with his children, was privileged to see Mary. In addition, one of the main themes of her words to Bruno was her assumption into heaven, and in the Virgin's case too, her final resting place before this event remains in dispute.

But Mary expressly described herself at Tre Fontane as the "Virgin of Revelation," and so, logically, we really need to look forward to the book of Revelation in order properly to understand her message and appreciate its significance. If we move to the end of chapter 11 in this, the last book of the Bible, we read of the following prophetic vision: "Then God's temple in heaven was opened, and the ark of his covenant was seen within his temple..." (Rev. 11:19). Thus between 2 Maccabees and Revelation, the Ark is seen as being finally transferred to heaven, and this, in typological terms, is a perfect description of the Assumption of Mary, the new Ark of the Covenant, into heaven. In April 1947, Mary gave Bruno a secret message to give to the Pope, and a little over three years later, in November 1950, Pius XII solemnly proclaimed the dogma of the Assumption. It seems a reasonable conjecture that this secret message may have been connected in some way with the promulgation of this dogma, perhaps as an encouragement to the Pope to press ahead with the matter.

Mary's self-designation as "the Virgin of Revelation," also points to the passage immediately following, which begins with a description of the "woman clothed with the sun, with the moon under her feet, and on her head a crown of twelve stars." This then goes on to portray the way that this "woman" would give birth to a child, who would be taken up to God's throne despite the attempts of the devil to devour him. The woman, meanwhile, is taken to a place of safety in the wilderness, facing pursuit from Satan, (Rev. 12). This passage has been traditionally understood as referring to both the Virgin Mary and the Church,[793] and refers to the final persecution which the Church will face at the time of Antichrist. The general tenor of some of Mary's remarks at Tre Fontane also seems to fit in with this interpretation. For instance, in saying; "You have persecuted me, now is the time to stop! Come and be part of the Holy Fold which is the Celestial Court on earth," we have the above themes of the woman being persecuted, and the relationship between the Church on earth and heaven. Similarly, during the apparition, Mary pointed to the broken crucifix and black cloth at her feet, and these too seem to be symbols of persecution, with the cloth probably representing normal priestly dress.

Thus, in describing herself as "the Virgin of Revelation," Mary was making a very clear statement about the "signs of the times" in which we are living. Just compare this chapter with the content of the third part of the secret of Fatima, revealed in June 2000, with its description of the sufferings of the Church during the twentieth century. This is not to suggest that the end of the world is imminent, but just that these persecutions are a proximate sign of these "end-time" events; and we also have to bear in mind that, as Mary promised at Fatima, mankind will be given a "period of peace" when, amongst other things, devotion to her Immaculate Heart is practiced throughout the world.

Apart from the connections between Tre Fontane and Revelation, there also seems to be a link with events in the book of Daniel. For example, in order for Bruno to be able to see the "beautiful lady" his children were looking at in the grotto at Tre Fontane, it was necessary for two transparent hands to wipe his eyes; then he could see Mary. If we read the account of Belshazzar's feast in Daniel, we see there an account of a disembodied hand which wrote on the palace wall, giving the king notice that his kingdom was about to fall (Dan. 5). Or again, most unusually, Mary at Tre Fontane was wearing a light green mantle, which enveloped her from head to toe. There is really only one proper reference in the Bible to someone "wearing" light green, and that reference is to Daniel's vision of a heavenly visitor, who is almost certainly the angel Gabriel, although he is not named.[794] He is described as: "a man clothed in linen, whose loins were girded in gold of Uphaz. His body was like *beryl*, his face like the appearance of lightning, his eyes like flaming torches, his arms and legs like the gleam of burnished bronze, and the sound of his words like the noise of a multitude," (Dan. 10:5–6). Beryl is described as, "a clear, pale, sea-green precious stone."[795] Thus there may be a correlation between the appearance of the angel's body and the "beryl-like" color of Mary's mantle at Tre Fontane. In addition, like Mary, who wore a sash around her waist, this angel was also girded with a belt. Since this appearance of the angel heralds his description of future events, leading up to the "time of the end," (Dan. 11:40–12), which parallels a number of passages in Revelation, this identification may not be as far-fetched as would first appear.

This section of Daniel also has mention of "the Book," (Dan. 12:1, 4), a reference to the *Book of Life*, the record of the actions of every person according to which they will be judged by God. This, also, may find a parallel with the "gray" book that Bruno saw Mary holding close to her breast, gray perhaps because gray is the color of ashes, and thus of mourning and repentance, as in the ashes used on Ash Wednesday. That Mary was holding this book in both hands, close to her heart, may be symbolic of her deep concern for the eternal salvation of all mankind. As Mediatrix of all graces, she can, in some sense, be said to have a mediating role in what is written in this book. This apparition feature of her holding a book is absolutely unique to Tre Fontane. "Books" are also mentioned earlier on in Daniel, in his description of the Last Judgment:

> As I looked, thrones were placed and one that was ancient of days took his seat; his raiment was white as snow, and the hair of his head like pure wool; his throne was fiery flames, its wheels were burning fire. A stream of fire issued and came forth from before him; a thousand thousands served him, and ten thousand times ten thousand stood before him; the court sat in judgment, *and the books were opened* (Dan. 7:9–10).

The Book of Revelation has a complementary passage:

> Then I saw a great white throne and him who sat upon it; from his presence earth and sky fled away, and no place was found for them. And I saw the dead, great and small, standing before the throne, *and books were opened*. Also another book was opened, which is *the book of life*. And the dead were judged by what was written in the books, by what they had done (Rev. 20:11–12).

So the book seen in Mary's hands by Bruno, may well have been a representation of the Book of Life, an important theme in both Revelation and Daniel.

L'Ile Bouchard and Daniel's Dream

Regarding L'Ile Bouchard, it seems that there is a clear Marian typology in that part of Daniel which deals with the strange dream of Nebuchadnezzar, in which he saw a mysterious statue. None of his assorted magicians and sorcerers was able to tell the king the contents of his dream, and all were threatened with death. Daniel, however, offered to interpret the dream, and was taken to meet Nebuchadnezzar, telling him that his dream pointed to future events. Daniel described a huge statue of extreme brilliance, with a head of gold, chest and arms of silver, belly and thighs of bronze, and legs partly made of iron and partly of clay. He then continued:

> As you looked, a stone was cut out by no human hand, and it smote the image on its feet of iron and clay, and broke them in pieces; then the iron, the clay, the bronze, the silver, and the gold, all together were broken in pieces, and became like the chaff of the summer threshing floors; and the wind carried them away, so that not a trace of them could be found. But the stone that struck the image became a great mountain and filled the whole earth (Dan. 2:34–35).

Daniel then explained to Nebuchadnezzar that the dream was a prophetic description of four kingdoms, beginning with the king's and ending with a future kingdom of iron which would rule the whole world as the "time of the end" drew near. But this kingdom would itself be destroyed by God, who would set up his own eternal kingdom. Nebuchadnezzar was astounded that Daniel had been able to reveal and interpret his dream and, like Pharaoh with Joseph, gave him many honors (Dan. 2).

The Marian typology of this dream is very revealing. St Jerome dealt with this figure of the mountain, and the stone cut from it, in one of his letters thus, applying it to Christ and Mary: "He is foretold to be 'a stone cut out of the mountain without hands,' a figure by which the prophet signifies that He is to be born a virgin of a virgin."[796] Here, St Jerome is describing Mary as a mountain, and Christ as the stone, which in turn becomes another mountain which fills the earth. In fact, Jesus compared himself to a stone who would crush those opposed to him (Luke 20:18), which certainly strengthens this connection. Ephrem of Syria, too, explored this idea, in describing Mary as, "Mountain of God, holy mountain, wherein it was the good pleasure of God to dwell ..."[797] Severus of Antioch also employed a similar typology.[798]

St Cyril of Alexandria (370/380–444), in commenting on a passage from Isaiah, (Isa. 2: 2–3), has this to say about Mary:

> Under the name of this mountain may also be signified the most Blessed ever-Virgin Mary Mother of God: since a mountain was she, who by the dignity of her election transcended all height of

elected nature. Is not Mary a lofty mountain, who, to reach to the conception of the Eternal Word, raised the summit of her merits above all the choirs of angels, even to the throne of the Deity? Isaiah, prophesying of the all-surpassing dignity of this mountain, says: *In the last days the mountain of the house of the Lord shall be prepared on the top of the mountains.*[799]

Thus, this idea of comparing Mary with biblical mountains, including the mountain of Daniel's dream, is quite well supported by some of the early writers, and this mountain would actually appear to be the last major Marian type of the Old Testament, assuming that the final canonical version of Daniel is later than 2 Maccabees.

Clearly, this mountain and the statue seen by Daniel are closely connected, and there seem to be definite links between these elements and events at L'Ile Bouchard. The statue was made up of four distinct "layers," a head of gold, chest and arms of silver, belly and thighs of bronze, and legs, from the knees downward, partly made of iron and partly of clay. Mary's initial apparition at the church of St Gilles has some very interesting parallels with the appearance of this statue. Her whole appearance was in the midst of a brilliant and shining "golden" light, and she had long blond or "golden" hair which fell in two parts to her knees. This golden hair is an apparition feature unique to L'Ile Bouchard, but when, in addition, its length is taken into account it agrees extraordinarily well with the division between the bright upper parts of the statue and its duller lower limbs. In fact, this feature of long hair down to the knees would seem to be slightly bizarre *without* this sort of typological explanation.

Moreover, we have the general manner in which the whole apparition deployed on later days, that is, Mary and the angel appearing out of a *golden* sphere, which unfolded to reveal a curtain of *silvery* light, on which the sparkling rocky grotto surrounding the figures was displayed. Incidentally, the fact that Mary and the Angel appeared in a *grotto*, provides a further interesting link to the grotto at Tre Fontane. Perhaps more telling, though, is the fact that the Virgin appeared standing on a rectangular stone block, just like the pedestal of a *statue*, and this, too is an apparition feature which is only found at L'Ile Bouchard. In addition, apart from Rue du Bac, this is the only time when Mary has specifically requested that a *statue* of her be made.

The angel, too, can be closely linked with Daniel. He revealed that he was Gabriel, the same angel who was sent by God to announce the Incarnation to Mary. Gabriel is expressly named in the book of Daniel, and surprisingly enough, it is only in this book, out of the whole Old Testament, that he makes any named appearance. He was sent on a number of occasions to explain the meaning of the various visions which Daniel experienced (Dan. 8:15–17; 9:20–23). In no other series of authentic Marian apparitions does an angel have a position of such prominence, where is he seen directly with Mary throughout their whole course. At the Rue du Bac, the angel who accompanied Catherine Labouré only seems to have had the task of taking her to Mary, while at Knock, only one of the witnesses reported seeing angels over the altar, as an essentially background feature.

Finally, the fact that the apparitions at L'Ile Bouchard took place inside a church, in the presence of the Blessed Sacrament, and thus of God, seems to provide a further link with both Daniel and the book of Revelation, given their emphasis on the last judgment and heaven.

L'Ile Bouchard: the Final Apparition?

But it seems that the significance of L'Ile Bouchard goes well beyond the typological points made above, and that it may well be the last authentic Marian apparition of the series which began with Guadalupe in 1531. This is because L'Ile Bouchard seems to act as a typological summary of preceding apparitions, with aspects of some of these being recapitulated, particularly those which took place in France—but Guadalupe and Fatima also seem to be prominent. The first point is that the apparitions began on 8 December, the feast of the Immaculate Conception, and in the same way, the apparitions of Our Lady of Guadalupe began on that feast day in December 1531. Obviously this is not just a coincidence.

Then we have the golden letters which were spelled out beneath Mary's feet on the first day, "O Mary, conceived without sin, pray for us who have recourse to you." These are the words of the invocation which appeared on the image of the Miraculous Medal, which Catherine Labouré saw at the Rue du Bac, in November 1830. This reference to a previous apparition is a very important point, which Mary clearly wants us to note.

Later on that same first day, when the girls had returned to the church, and again saw Mary, her message concerned the great need of prayer for France, while she described herself as their

Maman du Ciel, their Heavenly Mother. This seems to resonate quite well with the message given to the children at La Salette in September 1846, with its emphasis on the need for prayer, and Mary as the heavenly Mother, who is unable to hold back her Son's arm any longer. Mary's whole attitude to Mélanie and Maximin was extremely "maternal" during this apparition; she called them "my children" on at least three occasions.

The next day, 9 December, the inscription on the rocks had changed to read: "I am the Immaculate Conception," the title Mary had given herself at Lourdes, and which had earlier been applied to her dogmatically in 1854. This is thus a clear reference to the apparitions of 1858, and again it must be stressed that this is extremely unusual, and therefore significant. We do not find authentic Marian apparitions giving this sort of explicit reference to other apparitions, except at L'Ile Bouchard.

The girls could also see the letters "Ma ...cat" on her breast, and the hidden word "Magnificat" only became fully visible on the fifth day. This idea of something hidden being revealed finds a close counterpart in the apparition at Pontmain in January 1871. Here, it will be recalled, the children who saw Mary in the night sky also saw a streamer beneath her feet, on which letters gradually formed the words, "But pray, my children," "God will soon answer you," and "My Son allows himself to be moved." Moreover, a little later, Mary at L'Ile Bouchard held out the golden crucifix of her rosary, with a figure of Christ in relief on it, and asked the girls to kiss it, and they reported that she looked at the cross with a mixture of love and grief. This is matched by the incident at Pontmain where Mary, with a look of extreme sadness, contemplated a large red cross which appeared before her.

On the fifth day at L'Ile Bouchard, it seems that we can possibly find a specific correlation with the events at Fatima in the "many-colored" crown which the girls saw on Mary's head. This had twelve shining rays colored blue, red, yellow, green, pink and brownish-red, and was described as being like a beautiful "rainbow" by the girls. Perhaps here we have a link to the colors given off by the sun during the famous miracle of 13 October, when witnesses saw the whirling sun give off successive shafts of different colored light, which made the landscape change color. There may also be an echo here of Mary's appearance at both La Salette and Pontmain, when she was wearing headgear which has been previously identified with the turban worn by the Jewish high priest. The woman with a crown of *twelve* stars is, of course, the motif found in the first part of chapter 12 of Revelation, and provides a link with that book, and also with Tre Fontane.

On the final day of the apparitions, the whole congregation experienced the miraculous ray of sunlight which illuminated the place of the apparitions, and this seems to be an even clearer link with the miracle of the sun at Fatima. As has been indicated, there is no natural explanation for this event, and so we have a parallel to the way that the sun at Fatima appeared to come down towards the earth. Incidentally, in more recent times, there have also been reports of "miracles of the sun" at Tre Fontane. On 12 April 1980, the thirty-third anniversary of the original apparition, with about three thousand people, including Bruno Cornacchiola, present, many reported seeing the sun apparently turning backwards in the sky and coming towards the earth. Something similar happened on 12 April 1982. Thus these too were apparently repetitions, on a smaller scale, of the Fatima miracle.[800]

The above points strongly suggest that L'Ile Bouchard represents a recapitulation of elements from some previous Marian apparitions, and thus it may be more important than is generally realized. When this idea is linked to the general one that there seems to be a typological progression, from the biblical books of Genesis to Revelation, which matches the sequence of apparitions from Guadalupe to L'Ile Bouchard, then there is further support for this strong stream of comparative evidence which backs up the historical arguments advanced in this book.

The Church, Tre Fontane, and L'Ile Bouchard

As previously mentioned, the Church has adopted a favorable attitude to both Tre Fontane and L'Ile Bouchard, with both falling into that category of apparitions which have seen their "cultic" status recognized, something which often leads to formal approbation. Nevertheless, this has not yet been granted, although the signs are good, and so it is necessary to look at the probable reasons for this.

In the case of Tre Fontane, apart from the positive points already mentioned, the Franciscan Conventual Friars Minor were given custody of the grotto in July 1956, and asked to construct a chapel at the site, in addition to administering the shrine. Since then, a prayer to the Virgin of Revelation has been given an imprimatur by the Vicariate of Rome, and the cult was so well recognized that, during Vatican II, numerous prelates went to Tre Fontane to pray. In 1987, on the fortieth anniversary of the apparition, Cardinal

Poletti, the Cardinal Vicar of Rome, and thus the Pope's official episcopal representative for the diocese, came to the shrine to celebrate Mass. However, a definitive judgment, either positive or negative in regard of Tre Fontane, has not been made.[801]

This is probably due, at least in part, to the character of Bruno Cornacchiola; it seems that he went on to claim a total of twenty-eight further apparitions by 1986, with messages which became increasingly apocalyptic in tone, including predictions of various evils which have not materialized. It also seems that he has not been completely truthful in his biography. This is like the tragic history of Mélanie at La Salette; her initial experience was trustworthy, but she allowed events to go to her head in later years.[802]

With L'Ile Bouchard, we again have these positive signs of approval of the cult, and a lack of a definitive judgment one way or the other. The Bishop authorized the construction of a grotto, following Mary's request, and also permitted pilgrimages to the church. The cult of *Notre-Dame de la Prière*, "Our Lady of Prayer," has been recognized, a recognition reaffirmed in November 1988 by Mgr Honoré, the Archbishop of Tours, in a letter published in the L'Ile Bouchard parish bulletin.[803] Regrettably, however, it seems that, following the retirement of Fr Ségelle, until the spring of 1998, a succession of priests unfavorable to the apparitions were in charge of the parish, and this retarded matters. In addition, it seems that there has been a policy of silence and restraint, which may be linked to various troubles the children had afterwards, including persecutions, which only stopped following the intervention of the police.[804] In any event, with the advent of the new archbishop of Tours, it seems that the process of recognition has been accelerated.

It should be remembered, too, that it took Knock a hundred years to gain full approval by the Church and so this slowness is not necessarily a bad thing.

The Dogma of the Assumption

Over a long period, theologians had developed arguments based on the idea that Mary, being sinless, did not suffer from the effects of sin, which include bodily corruption, and that her assumption into heaven could be *deduced* from her Immaculate Conception and sinlessness. Mary was described as the "most blessed of all women" by Elizabeth at the time of the Visitation, and this blessedness was seen as including her freedom from original sin and the consequent curse of being subject to bodily corruption and death. Similarly, this blessedness also included her anticipated resurrection and ultimate glorification, body and soul, in heaven. It was argued that Mary had shared in the most perfect manner in Christ's victory over sin and death, and so should join in his Resurrection and glorification as soon as possible, and not have to wait for the general resurrection. From a practical point of view, this argument finds support in the fact that there are no relics of Mary, and also that we might expect her to be more favored than those saints who have died, but whose bodies have remained incorrupt, including St Catherine Labouré, the Curé d'Ars, and St Bernadette.[805]

If Mary's body had just remained incorrupt on earth, this would only put her on the same level as the above, when in fact she was immeasurably greater than any other saint, or, indeed, all the saints put together. Hence, we might expect God to go one step further, and both preserve her body and also anticipate her resurrection and glorification. This argument really stands at the opposite end of the spectrum to those concerning the Immaculate Conception, that is, the way that Mary's sanctification at conception *preceded* that of Jeremiah and John the Baptist, who were both sanctified in the womb (Jer. 1:5; Luke 1:44).[806]

Since the time of the definition of the dogma of the Immaculate Conception by Pius IX in 1854, many petitions had been gathered, from all parts of the Church, arguing for a dogmatic definition about Mary's Assumption. These were examined during the reign of Pope Pius XII, and in 1949 he asked the bishops of the world whether they thought it was opportune to proclaim the bodily Assumption of Mary into heaven as a dogma of the faith, that is, as something divinely revealed. Ninety-eight per cent of the 1,194 bishops who were asked responded favorably, and Pius XII rightly took this as an affirmation that the Assumption was indeed a truth revealed by God, expressed in the action of the Holy Spirit guiding the episcopate and keeping them from error.

It was already widely accepted as a belief of the Church, having been held for many centuries, but the dogmatic definition clarified and strengthened this position. In making this proclamation, the Pope quoted from the writings of three seventh- and eighth-century Eastern Church Fathers, St John Damascene, St Germanus of Constantinople, and St Modestus of Jerusalem; but he did not mention apocryphal accounts of the Assumption, even though they do bear witness to popular belief on this matter.[807] Essentially, the Pope based this dogmatic definition on the intimate union between Jesus and Mary, on her Divine Maternity and on her co-redemptive role at the Crucifixion; all of this put her in a unique position, to the extent that her anticipated resurrection and glorification are the only logical outcome for someone who had lived such a life of total union with God.[808] And so, on 1 November 1950 he solemnly proclaimed the dogma in the following words: "We proclaim, declare and define it to be a dogma revealed by God that the Immaculate Mother of God, Mary ever Virgin, when the course of her earthly life was finished, was taken up body and soul into the glory of heaven."[809]

There is also a link between the proclamation of this dogma and Fatima, as Cardinal Tedeschini, the Pontifical Legate, revealed at the shrine on 13 October 1951. During his homily, he recalled the miracle of the sun, before going on to describe how Pope Pius XII had himself seen a repetition of this miracle in Rome, on four occasions during the previous year:

> In the Vatican Gardens, the Holy Father looked towards the sun, and then there was renewed before his eyes the prodigy which, years before, this same valley witnessed, on this same day. The solar disc, surrounded by its halo—who can gaze on it? He could, during those four days; beneath the hand of Mary, he could observe the sun coming down, moving, convulsing, palpitating with life, transmitting, in a spectacle of celestial movements, silent but eloquent messages to the Vicar of Christ.[810]

The Weeping Madonna of Syracuse

The last Marian prodigy to be dealt with in this book involves a small plaster figure of Our Lady showing her Immaculate Heart, which in the city of Syracuse, for four days from 29 August to 1 September 1953, wept tears on numerous occasions, and attracted thousands of pilgrims. Although not an apparition as such, this seems to have been a very important development, which was quickly recognized by the Church as authentic. It might even be possible to describe it as a "postscript" to the series of apparitions between Guadalupe and L'Ile Bouchard.

Syracuse is in Sicily, the large island at the foot of Italy, and in one of its poorest parts lived a young couple, Angelo and Antonina Jannuso, who were given the plaster plaque of Our Lady as a wedding present; this they fixed to the bedroom wall. It showed Mary's heart as in the message of Fatima, that is surrounded by thorns and flames. It is worth noting that the Communist party still had quite strong support in Sicily, and that Angelo Jannuso was a follower of Togliatti; neither was Antonina a particularly good Catholic.

On the morning of Saturday 29 August, the octave day of the feast of the Immaculate Heart of Mary at the time, 22 August, Antonina was in bed, suffering due to the effects of a difficult pregnancy, and also from some mysterious sickness something like epilepsy, when, to her amazement, she noticed that the eyes of the figure were shedding tears. Her sister-in-law, Grazia, also saw this happening, as did an increasingly large number of neighbors who gathered. The weeping was not continual, but happened about six or seven times that morning, and also again in the evening, when the husband had returned home. By now it was apparent that Antonina's illness, which had puzzled her doctors, was cured, and all this led to the conversion of the couple, and many others. Over the next two days the weepings continued at intervals, and were witnessed by thousands of people, even when the plaque was moved from the bedroom to a little altar outside the house.[811]

On Tuesday 1 September, a commission appointed by the archdiocese arrived to investigate. They compiled a report under oath, following a careful examination of the figure to ensure that nothing untoward was evident. While they were present there were more tears, and so they were able to collect some specimens for analysis. They could find no natural explanation, or means by which tears might have been fraudulently produced. The plaque was small enough to be held in the hands and the plaster was only between half an inch and an inch thick. Once their work was over the tears ceased. The local archbishop arrived the next day to make inquiries and to speak to witnesses, as reports of miraculous healings began to spread, a development which would result in the formation of a medical commission. Archbishop Baranzini returned on 8 September with other ecclesiastics to say the rosary, and to explain to the crowd the meaning of these tears. He said that they were tears of sorrow and distress, a sign to a society and culture which had gone astray. On 9 September, the laboratory analysis was published, and this confirmed that the liquid was exactly like human tears. The facts of the case were sent to Rome on 10 September, to Cardinal Pizzardo, secretary of the Holy Office.[812]

Archbishop Baranzini returned on 19 September, to preach again to the growing crowds, telling them that these were the tears of a mother, weeping because of the persecutions her children were suffering in the East, and because of the loss of faith in the West. During September and October over a million pilgrims visited the plaster figure of Mary, which had been moved to a more prominent location. Archbishop Baranzini went to Rome on 24 September, and met Pope Pius XII on 27 September. In December, the bishops of Sicily met to pass official judgment, and their leader, Cardinal Ruffini, explained their positive decision in the following statement:

> The bishops of Sicily, gathered together for their regular conference at Palermo, have heard the full report by His Excellency, Archbishop Ettore Baranzini of Syracuse, on the weeping of an image of the Immaculate Heart of Mary. Having weighed carefully all the related evidence contained in the original documents, the bishops have unanimously judged that the reality of the weeping cannot be held in doubt. We express the desire that such a manifestation of the Heavenly Mother may inspire all to salutary penance and to a livelier devotion towards the Immaculate Heart of Mary and that there may be the prompt construction of a sanctuary to perpetuate the memory of the miracle.[813]

There is obviously a clear link, given the image of Mary's Immaculate Heart on the plaque, between the supernatural tears of Syracuse and the message of Fatima, one which Church authorities were anxious to point out; and indeed Pope Pius XII was moved to ask if people understood "the mysterious language of these tears." It is as if this was the final appeal of Mary, who had said all she had to say at Fatima and in her other recognized apparitions, and now, because her pleas were being largely ignored, was reduced to silent tears.

21

The Collegial Consecration and the Fall of Communism

Further Consecrations to Mary

In 1952, as a further sign of the importance he attached to Fatima, Pope Pius XII had specifically consecrated Russia to Mary's Immaculate Heart, on 7 July, the feast of Saints Cyril and Methodius. This, however, was not done in union with all the bishops of the world, and so it did not qualify as the full collegial consecration asked for by Mary. Pope Paul VI recalled the 1942 consecration of Pius XII and also referred with approval to Fatima, during the Second Vatican Council, but he chose not to make the collegial consecration demanded by Mary, even though he was in the presence of the world's bishops. This was probably due to the somewhat turbulent nature of Vatican II, as well as an unwillingness to be seen as critical of Russia, at a time when Christians in the Soviet Union were still suffering greatly under communism. During the sixties the Vatican was conducting a policy of *Ostpolitik,* of trying to work with Communist regimes, whenever possible, in contrast to the former more condemnatory approach of previous popes. Paul VI, however, did declare Mary "Mother of the Church" at the close of the third session of the Council, on 21 November 1964. In 1967 he went to Fatima, on 13 May, the Golden anniversary of the first apparition, and presented Sr Lucia to the assembled crowds, thus giving further papal approval to Fatima. At this stage, no reigning Pope had even been to Lourdes, let alone the shrine of any other modern Marian apparition, so this was quite a significant move.[814]

The Third Part of the Secret: Criticism of Sr Lucia

Regarding the third part of the secret, it was thought that Sr Lucia's fourth memoir had added somewhat to knowledge of its overall context. The sections on the secret in both the third and fourth memoirs were identical, apart from a further sentence that she added to the latter: "In Portugal the dogma of the faith will always be preserved ..." This led to speculation that the third part of the secret concerned a loss of faith elsewhere within the Church, but as we now know, its main theme is rather the persecutions that the Church and the Holy Father had to face in the twentieth century. In that same memoir, she also explicitly stated that she was not allowed to reveal the third part of the secret at that time.[815] There was a good deal of speculation and, indeed, expectation, that the third part of the secret would be made public in 1960, but the Holy See apparently decided that this would not be in the best interests of the Church or the world, and it remained undisclosed until June 2000.[816]

Regrettably, a degree of scepticism grew up concerning Fatima in some theological circles, particularly after the war, an attitude expressed, for example, in Fr Karl Rahner's book *Visions and Prophecies*. Even he, however, maintains that "anyone who absolutely rejects the possibility of special revelations offends against faith; and anyone who denies that they may occur even since the apostolic age offends against a doctrine which is theologically certain." He also goes on to point to the importance of the prophetic element in private revelations, which cannot be replaced by theological speculation or the actions of the hierarchy. In other words, such revelations, when authenticated, have a definite role in the life of the Church, despite the fact that public revelation was concluded at the time of the apostles.[817]

In fact, Fatima enjoyed growing approval by the papal magisterium as the twentieth century progressed, particularly in the more recent papal statements and visits to the shrine, and the onset of the twenty-first century seems to show no signs of a diminution in this support.

Below is the view of Fr Garrigou-Lagrange, one of the foremost Catholic theologians of the twentieth century, regarding the sort of "inner locutions" experienced by Sr Lucia. His use of the word "imaginary" does not mean that such communications are illusory, but that, through them, God acts on the imagination, rather than on the intellect, of the individual concerned:

Imaginary supernatural words are heard by the imagination, when the person is either awake or asleep. They sometimes seem to come from heaven; at other times from the depths of one's heart. They are perfectly distinct, although not heard with bodily ears. *They are not easily forgotten; those especially which contain a prophecy remain graven on the memory.* To recover the exact statement of the words heard, it is sometimes necessary that the person who has heard them should recollect himself and make mental prayer; in this way he can avert [prevent] the slightest variation.[818]

He distinguishes between the above and *formal intellectual words,* which are "free from illusion" because they act directly on the intellect: "the understanding cannot contribute anything to them, and the devil cannot act immediately on the intellect."[819] It is difficult to say which of these forms of heavenly communication were received by Sr Lucia, but these statements do throw some light on her experiences, and indicate that it is quite feasible that she could have accurately remembered what was said to her.

In any event, that the idea of Sr Lucia's receiving later revelations was present almost from the beginning of the events at Fatima is clear from the following considerations. The second interrogation of Lucia by her parish priest, Fr Ferreira, on 14 June 1917, the day after the second apparition, contains the following words of Mary to Lucia: "I want you to come back here on the thirteenth and that you learn to read so that I can tell you what I want." Clearly this cannot just refer to the apparitions up to October, since a child such as Lucia, who had never been to school, could not have been expected to learn to read in only four months. Even in October 1917, she had not yet begun to learn to read because of opposition from her mother. Therefore this is a clear early reference that Lucia was to receive later revelations, of sufficient complexity that it would be necessary for her to learn to read (and write) in order to convey them adequately.[820] Similarly, in her writings Sr Lucia clearly states that she continued to receive communications from God long after the 1917 apparitions, and this is hardly surprising, given the ongoing nature of her mission, that of promoting devotion to Mary's Immaculate Heart in the world, and of working and praying for the collegial consecration.[821]

All of this indicates that the revelations later made to Sr Lucia cannot be dismissed virtually out of hand, as has been the case, unhappily, with some writers. It is true, however, as Fr Messias Coelho, SJ, a leading Fatima authority, has pointed out, that "the apparitions and their messages are charisms, that is, acts of the Holy Spirit," and that hence, "their interpretation—to be correct— also has to be an act of the Holy Spirit. He is the Soul of the

Church. So, the only correct interpretation is that of the Church and not that of the seers. Usually the charism of the seers consists only in telling the Church what they saw and heard." Within the Church, it is the Pope, guided by the Holy Spirit, who has supreme authority to judge a particular message which comes from an apparition.[822]

Pope John Paul II and the Consecration of 1984

Pope John Paul II's formal association with Fatima stems from the attempt made on his life in Rome on 13 May 1981, the anniversary of the first apparition at Fatima, when he was shot in St Peter's Square. There is strong evidence to suggest that Mehmet Ali Agca carried out the assassination attempt under orders from the Bulgarian secret service, which was itself working with the KGB. It seems that the Communists were worried at the increasing influence of the Pope, particularly in Poland, and had decided to eliminate him; but the whole area has become so murky that the truth may never be fully known.[823] Providentially, the bullet wounds were not fatal, and while in hospital recovering, the Pope apparently reviewed all the documents on Fatima. He certainly felt that Mary's intercession had saved his life, and his reading apparently convinced him that the consecration of Russia to Mary's Immaculate Heart was an absolute necessity if the world was to be saved from war and atheism.

Consequently on 13 May 1982, exactly a year after the assassination attempt, John Paul II went to Fatima, both to thank Mary for saving his life, and also to carry out a public act of consecration of the whole world, including Russia, to her Immaculate Heart. After this was accomplished, however, it became apparent that many of the world's bishops had not been informed in time. Thus this consecration had not fulfilled the conditions of collegiality asked for by Mary at Fatima, that is that the Pope, in union with the bishops of the world, should consecrate Russia to her Immaculate Heart. Sr Lucia, still living in the Carmelite convent at Coimbra, apparently made this known later to the Apostolic Nuncio in Portugal.[824]

Interestingly, in this 1982 consecration, John Paul II specifically described Fatima as a place "chosen" by Mary, thus indicating official confirmation of its status and intimating that we are to understand it as the major "prophecy" of the twentieth century.[825] During his homily the Pope made the following remarks:

If the Church has accepted the message of Fatima, it is above all because that message contains a truth and a call whose basic content is the truth and call of the Gospel itself. "Repent, and believe in the Gospel" (Mark 1:15). These are the first words of the Messiah addressed to humanity. The message of Fatima is, in its basic nucleus, a call to conversion and repentance, as in the Gospel. This call was uttered at the beginning of the twentieth century, and it was thus addressed particularly to this present century. The Lady of the message seems to have read with special insight the "signs of the times," the signs of our time.[826]

John Paul II also spoke of Fatima during this homily in these significant terms: "The appeal of the Lady of the message of Fatima is so deeply rooted in the Gospel and the whole of Tradition that the Church feels that the message imposes a commitment on her."[827]

The Pope decided to renew the consecration in March 1984, with letters being sent to all the world's bishops in good time, including the Orthodox, asking them to join him in this action. On 25 March 1984, the feast of the Annunciation, John Paul II duly renewed the act of consecration in St Peter's Basilica in Rome, before the statue of Mary from the site of the apparitions at Fatima, which was specially brought over for the occasion. Although the text used did not mention Russia, the Pope did specifically recall the acts of consecration made by Pope Pius XII in 1942 and 1952, the latter being essentially concerned with Russia. It also appears that John Paul II paused during the ceremony, and, according to the bishop of Leiria-Fatima, Alberto Cosme do Amaral, quietly included Russia in the consecration. This action is understandable, given the delicate political situation, and, it has been argued, with the understanding that God was leaving the Pope, as head of the Church on earth, to decide the precise form the act should take.

Certainly, Russia was in the Pope's mind in the following reference: "in a special way we entrust and consecrate to you those individuals and nations which particularly need to be thus entrusted and consecrated." Although not all the world's bishops joined in the act of consecration, it appears that a "moral totality" did, thus satisfying the request of Mary. Following this consecration, Sr Lucia was again visited by the Apostolic Nuncio; this time, she told him that it was her prayerful conviction that the consecration of Russia had indeed been accomplished, and that God had accepted it.[828] After nearly seventy years, it appeared that the act of collegial consecration had finally been carried out.

The Validity of the Consecration

Others, though, have taken the view that this was not the case, and this opinion cannot be dismissed out of hand. If we look at the various requests and statements made by Mary to Sr Lucia in literal terms, then it can certainly be argued that the 1984 act of consecration did not completely fulfill these requests.

But it should be noted that in the discussion which follows on Sr Lucia's role regarding the consecration, this has to be understood in the light of the fact that no Pope is obliged to carry out any request conveyed through a private revelation, nor is it Sr Lucia's role to judge the validity of any papal or collegial act.

In July 1917, after showing the children hell, and describing what would happen if people did not repent, Mary continued:

> To prevent this, I shall come to ask for the consecration of Russia to my Immaculate Heart, and the Communion of Reparation on the First Saturdays. If my requests are heeded, Russia will be converted, and there will be peace; if not, she will spread her errors throughout the world, causing wars and persecutions of the Church. The good will be martyred, the Holy Father will have much to suffer, various nations will be annihilated. In the end, my Immaculate Heart will triumph. The Holy Father will consecrate Russia to me and she will be converted, and a period of peace will be granted to the world.

Fr Messias Coelho, argues that, although the text used in the 1984 consecration mentioned the world rather than Russia, as Mary requested, since Russia is part of the world, then it is included in the consecration by implication. As he states: "Nobody can prove that the words Our Lady used, asked for a consecration of Russia alone; Russia is part of the world. If the world is consecrated, Russia becomes consecrated."[829] This is obviously a true statement, but there also seems to be a danger of distorting Mary's words, as documented above, beyond their natural meaning.

It is clear that, at present, Russia has not been converted, in the sense of being truly converted to Catholicism or even Christianity in general. Nor is there much evidence of peace in the world. There also seems to be a definite link here between the consecration of Russia and the First Saturday Communions of Reparation, to the extent that it could be argued that they are jointly necessary. This connection is also found in the following passage, which arose out of the 1929 apparition of the Trinity at the convent at Tuy, after which Sr Lucia corresponded with Fr Gonzalves:

> If I am not mistaken, Our Dear Lord God promises to end the persecution of Russia, if the Holy Father condescends to make, and likewise ordains the Bishops of the Catholic World to make, a solemn and public act of reparation and consecration of Russia to the Most Holy Hearts of Jesus and Mary. In response to the ending of this persecution, His Holiness is to promise to approve of and recommend the practice of the already mentioned devotion of reparation.

If taken literally, both parts of this request have not been complied with, in that Russia was not specifically named in the 1984 act of consecration, and similarly, the Pope has not approved and recommended the First Saturdays devotion of reparation in any official public sense. If these two points are organically linked, as seems to be the case, then perhaps the consecration will not become fully effective until the First Saturdays devotion is officially promulgated by the papacy; this may help to explain why the "conversion" of Russia and true peace for the world are so slow in coming. The theological consensus seems to be that the Pope has done as much as he can at present, and that therefore official promotion of the First Saturdays devotion is something for the future. If the above position is correct, it is possible to see the 1984 papal consecration as somewhat similar to that of Pius XII in 1942, which shortened the Second World War. In other words it has led to the fall of Communism and the end of immediate persecution in Russia and its former satellites, and the restoration of the freedom of the Church to evangelize, but it does not completely fulfill the requests made by Mary, although this does not mean that it is necessary to repeat it.

In the mid nineteen-thirties, Sr Lucia asked Jesus why it was necessary that Russia be consecrated to Mary's Immaculate Heart, receiving this reply: "Because I want My whole Church to acknowledge that consecration as a triumph of the Immaculate Heart of Mary, so that it may extend its cult later on, and put devotion to this Immaculate Heart beside the devotion to my Sacred Heart." Again it is clear that, at present, the "whole Church" is far from acknowledging Mary's role and seeing the 1984 act of consecration as a triumph of her Immaculate Heart, and this too is probably a factor in limiting the effectiveness of the consecration.

At a meeting in Fatima in 1989, the Bishop of Fatima was asked if Mary's request regarding the consecration of Russia had been fulfilled. He replied to the effect that this matter was the "business of the Holy Father," who, as head of the Church, was ultimately responsible for it. Fr Frederick L. Miller, who was also present, comments thus on the bishop's reply: "I would certainly say that the Pope has done all that he can possibly do to fulfill Our Lady's request." As he points out, the essential concern of Catholics should be to live the message of Fatima rather than worry over whether the consecration has been done or not, a matter which is in the hands of the Pope alone.[830] These points were reiterated by the Bishop of Fatima in 1990, in the support he gave to visiting prelates, such as Cardinal Meisner, who expressed their belief that the consecration had indeed been done.[831]

We also have the testimony of Sr Lucia, in 1989, in a handwritten letter to the *Fatima Family Messenger*, a Fatima magazine edited by Fr Robert Fox, which apparently does confirm that the consecration made in 1984 was valid. In this letter she points out that previous consecrations were not fully efficacious, because they had not been made in union with the bishops of the world.[832] Sr Lucia produced another signed note, dated 3 July 1990, in response to a specific question from Fr Fox, of which the following excerpt is a translation from the Portuguese:

> I come to answer your question, "If the consecration made by Pope John Paul II on March 25, 1984 in union with all the bishops of the world, accomplished the conditions for the conversion of Russia, according to the request of Our Lady in Tuy on June 13 of 1929"? Yes it was accomplished, and since then I have said that it was made. And I say that no other person responds for me, it is I who receive and open all letters and respond to them.[833]

She reiterated this position in November 2001, when, in a meeting with Archbishop Tarcisio Bertone, the secretary of the Congregation for the Doctrine of the Faith, the details of which were published by the Vatican, she confirmed that it was her conviction that the consecration of 1984 had been as Our Lady wanted, and that it had been accepted by heaven. This statement was made to counter claims made by certain groups that the consecration had not been carried out.[834]

Thus we have to weigh these categorical assertions against the negative points detailed above. Fr Fox further argues that the Pope was very careful to ensure that the wording of the act of consecration guaranteed collegiality. He points out that John Paul II explicitly recalled the two consecrations of Pope Pius XII, in 1942, when he consecrated the world to Mary's Immaculate Heart, and in 1952, when he consecrated Russia to her, offering these previous consecrations with his own act of consecration. As Fr Fox states: "To say that the Pope was not consecrating Russia in union with the bishops of the world does violence to logic. It makes a taskmaster of God who nit-picks for fine details or wording rather than the intention of hearts."[835]

On balance, then, the most important authorities, including the Pope, the local bishop, prominent theologians, and finally Sr Lucia herself, hold the view that the 1984 act of consecration of Russia was properly carried out. Perhaps it is not surprising that there is such controversy over this point, given the difficulties the various popes have encountered in attempting to make the collegial consecration. Pius XII could have requested the bishops of the world to join him in both his 1942 and 1952 consecrations, but chose not to. Similarly, Paul VI could have made the collegial consecration during the Second Vatican Council, when he was in the presence of the world's bishops, but he too chose not to or felt unable to take this step. He may have felt that opposition to the message of Fatima, amongst certain members of the hierarchy, particularly the bishops of Germany and France, and prominent theologians, rendered the carrying out of the full consecration impossible during his pontificate.[836] This seems to be the import of Jesus' words to Sr Lucia after the 1929 apparition of the Trinity: "They did not wish to heed My request. Like the king of France, they will repent and do it, but it will be late. Russia will have already spread her errors throughout the world, provoking wars and persecutions of the Church; the Holy Father will have much to suffer."

Paul VI would also have weighed the effect of the full collegial consecration of Russia, and its apparent condemnation of the atheistic Communist regime, on the lives of ordinary Christians, who would undoubtedly have faced further persecution. It is also probable that not enough people were living the Fatima message to make these earlier consecrations viable. And regardless of the view one takes of the 1984 consecration, it is clear that there are still not enough people who are taking Fatima seriously. Until this happens the full power and beauty of Fatima will not become apparent in the world.

There have also been some criticisms of the whole idea of consecration to Mary, with some arguing that it is improper to speak in such terms, since it obscures the essential idea of consecration to God. This position, though, seems to go against the traditional approach, as exemplified by St Louis de Montfort, one that has been essentially accepted and acted upon by both Pius XII and John Paul II during their pontificates. If it was unacceptable to consecrate the world to Mary's Immaculate Heart, then obviously the above popes would not have done so. To criticize the principle of Marian consecration is also to lose sight of the central reality of the various Marian apparitions, that they concern Mary rather than Jesus. If Jesus had only wanted a consecration to his own Sacred Heart, then clearly he, rather than Mary, would have appeared repeatedly over the last few centuries. The fact that it is Mary who has appeared in so many places, and that the Church at its highest level has accepted this, indicates the importance of Mary's role and that consecration to her is not illogical, providing it is clearly understood that "belonging to Mary is a privileged means of belonging to Christ."[837]

In reality, because of the strong analogy between Jesus and Mary, the consecration to Mary's Immaculate Heart is closely linked to the consecration to Jesus' Sacred Heart, although it is subordinate to and dependent on it.[838] In other words, although the act of consecration is ultimately addressed to God, it is an act that is made through Mary. This point is illustrated by the strongly Christocentric nature of both the 1982 and 1984 acts of consecration, made by Pope John Paul II. Because Mary is so closely linked to Christ, and because she is mankind's spiritual mother, he felt fully justified in carrying out the act of consecration to her Immaculate Heart.[839] The Pope referred to Jesus' words of self-consecration during the Last Supper, as found in St John's Gospel: "And for their sakes I sanctify myself, so that they also may be sanctified in truth." Here the word *sanctify* has the meaning of "consecrate oneself to God," and Jesus' self-consecration to the Father is taken as the model for the way that we, too, should be consecrated to God. This is to be accomplished by a consecration to Mary, since she is wholly consecrated to her Son. By joining with her, we join with Jesus, based on the way that she united herself with Jesus' sufferings on the cross in the most intimate manner possible.[840]

The Continuing Threat from Communism

The history of Communism since the Second World War illustrates just how big a change there was in the late eighties and early nineties, thus helping us to appreciate the effect of the act of consecration in 1984. One of the legacies of the erroneous French

intellectualism of the fifties was a generation of Communist ideo-
logues in south-east Asia, who sought to put into practice a
thoroughgoing Stalinist program of massive social engineering.
They had studied in France and were influenced by Sartre's exis-
tentialist theories, which advocated violence in the pursuance of
revolutionary ends. A group of them seized power in Cambodia in
1975, and, with terrifying brutality, began their program of destroying the whole structure of the country, which they regarded as
tainted by Western ideas. They wanted to create a radical
Communist society, and attempted in one jump what Mao in China
had spent decades trying to achieve. City dwellers were pushed into
the countryside and a fearful reign of terror commenced, which
led to an estimated two million people losing their lives by 1977.
Similar schemes were carried out in Laos and Vietnam, although
on a smaller scale. These successes for Communism in south-east
Asia were made possible by America's defeat by Vietnam under Ho
Chi Minh, an event which gave the atheistic ideology a new lease of
life, and which was thus a disaster for the world.[841]

During the seventies, Communism continued to make progress
world-wide, since it appeared that America had entered on a period
of relative decline. This was a time of widespread anti-Americanism,
particularly in the UN, and it coincided with a resurgence in
Marxist theories amongst intellectuals in the West, and particularly
in France, where determinist philosophies in history, anthropology,
psychology and literature, became popular and influential. The
idea was emphasized that human societies were governed by universal laws that left little room for free will, and so, here too, Marxist
thinking was exercising a pernicious effect. In 1971, Russia overtook America in the numbers of certain categories of nuclear
missiles, and its global military power, and particularly its navy,
expanded steadily throughout the seventies. This enabled
Communism to tighten its grip on those parts of Africa, particularly
Ethiopia and Angola, that had fallen under its influence, thus
adding millions to the total of refugees found throughout the
world. Meanwhile the Soviet Union was also encouraging the
growth of international terrorism though the training of terrorists
at a military academy in Russia; these then went on to cause chaos in
the developing world. Communist training and ideology, even
when not direct, benefited many of the best-known terrorist groups,
including the Baader-Meinhof gang, the IRA, and ETA. All of this
helped to destabilize both the West and the developing world.[842]

Portugal, the home of Fatima, also came under direct threat of
Communism in 1974. A coup had brought a Communist-backed

government to power, and its authority was further strengthened by an abortive countercoup in March 1975. The seizure of the Catholic radio station in late May presaged a serious clash with the Church. It seems that this move may have been prompted by an exceptionally large pilgrimage to Fatima on 13 May 1975, the fifty-eighth anniversary of the first apparition in May 1917. By early July, the true nature of the regime became more apparent, as it pressed on with plans to make Portugal a "revolutionary workers' state." The situation was very serious, because many army officers supported the revolution. Open resistance on the part of Catholics in the face of Communist rule began on 13 July 1975, the anniversary of the third apparition of Mary in which she had warned of the errors of Russia and of persecutions of the Church. Large groups of Catholics gathered in the north of the country, destroying Communist party headquarters in many towns in a totally spontaneous counterrevolution, but one with little bloodshed. There was a great deal of popular support for these actions and, in general, the army in the north did not intervene. On 10 August, the Archbishop of Braga addressed an anti-Communist rally, urging people to oppose this alien system of government which was being imposed on the country by a minority of revolutionaries. On 18 August an attempt by a thousand Communists to hold a rally in the town of Alcobaça, not far from Fatima, was resisted by force, and this was a turning point, a sign that Portugal would not fall to Communism. Within a year, Communist influence had greatly decreased in the country, and Portugal was saved from the threat of revolution.[843]

It had seemed as though Russian Communism would soften somewhat, following Stalin's death in 1953 and his denunciation by Khrushchev in 1956, but, in practice, nothing much changed either for the ordinary Soviet citizen, or regarding Communist expansionist policies. Persecution of Christians continued. With Brezhnev's reign in the seventies and early eighties, absolute rule through a small Communist élite was maintained, as Russia continued to spend vast amounts on arms. It was a "lawless" society run by a ruling class concerned only with perpetuating its privileges, and harsh punishments for dissent continued to be handed out during the seventies and eighties, often in the form of incarceration in psychiatric hospitals. As a system, this form of punishment had been in place since the thirties, and involved torture, beatings, and the illegal and dangerous use of drugs, especially against Christians and other "enemies of the State."

Even as late as 1977, Brezhnev ruled out any possibility of liberalization in Russia, and, in fact, the system was tightened up to make dissent even more difficult. His successor, Yuri Andropov, as a former head of the KGB, was not a man to countenance radical change. It is true that there were signs that belief in Marxism was decaying amongst Communist intellectuals, and, during the sixties and seventies, religious belief stubbornly retained its attraction for many people. Similarly, on a practical level, Russian consumers were still having to endure shortages and shoddy goods, while the failure of Soviet agricultural policies was marked and showed that the system was breaking down.[844] But of themselves, these factors would have been unlikely to bring about the demise of Communism.[845]

During this period, the Soviet Union was bolstered by the ill-judged process of *détente*, promoted by the American diplomat, Henry Kissinger. This was supposed to relax tensions between the superpowers through military, economic and political agreements, but despite this, Soviet military spending continued almost unabated. This process of détente was crowned by the Helsinki agreements of 1975 between Western governments and the Warsaw pact countries. In return for supposedly improving their appalling human rights record and allowing freer debate, the Communists insisted that the West accept their control of both the Soviet Union and Eastern Europe as a permanent state of affairs, regardless of the wishes of the inhabitants. This was the so-called "Brezhnev Doctrine."

Predictably, the "Helsinki Watch" human rights groups that had arisen in Communist countries were eliminated by the early eighties, and there was precious little free debate. The West had learned very little in over half a century of dealing with Communist governments, and in particular did not seem to have grasped that lies and deceit were second nature to them. Meanwhile, the Communists benefited from improved trade with the West, and used it to further their military capability. It seemed that this willingness to put profit before everything would be the West's undoing, and the fulfillment of Lenin's prediction: "When we are ready to hang the capitalists, they will be the first to sell us the rope." One bright moment in this catalogue of woe was the publication of Alexander Solzhenitsyn's three-volume *Gulag Archipelago*, his indictment of the appalling Communist slave-labor camp system. The full depths of the Stalinist horror were exposed, and many Western intellectuals were at last forced to recognize the true nature of Communism.[846]

In the late seventies, though, the Communist Party was still in control of the Soviet Union, and there did not seem to be any signs that the system was about to fail. Given the political will and the sort of ruthlessness shown by previous Soviet leaders, the regime could have been maintained for years, possibly decades, and so its collapse, virtually overnight, is difficult to explain in conventional terms. With hindsight, we can say that the accession of Polish Cardinal Karol Wojtyla as Pope John II, in 1978, must now be seen as the harbinger of the passing of Communism in Eastern Europe, however unlikely this might have appeared at the time. Poland had survived attempts by both the Nazis and Communists to destroy the Church during the Second World War and in succeeding years; the strong Catholic ethos of the people proved a national rallying-point, giving Poles the courage to withstand, with the Pope showing his support for the Solidarity trade union led by Lech Walesa. Poland was thus brave enough to challenge the might of Communism during the early eighties, thereby showing the way for the other countries of Eastern Europe in their own struggles to free themselves from its stranglehold. The Catholic faith of the Poles was undoubtedly the major factor in giving them the strength to resist,[847] and the intervention of Mary to obtain their deliverance can be traced back to the consecration of Poland to the Immaculate Heart of Mary, made on 8 September 1946. This was done at the Marian shrine at Jasna Gora in the presence of 700,000 Poles and using the same form of words as Pius XII used in his consecration of the world to Mary's Immaculate Heart in 1942. Poland was thus the first country to follow the example of Portugal in making this consecration.[848]

The Collapse of Communism

It is ironic that 1984, the year so often associated with the imposition of tyranny in the popular imagination, as a result of George Orwell's famous book, should become an important milestone in the demise of Russian Communism. Indeed it is hard not to see a connection between the consecration made in 1984 and the rise to power of Mikhail Gorbachev in March 1985, when he became General Secretary of the Communist Party. Realizing the dangerous situation of the Soviet Union, he began a program of reform based on restructuring and openness. This led to greater democratization in Russia, a more tolerant attitude to religious believers, and fruitful arms reductions talks with America; but also, ultimately, to the collapse of Communism in Russia. Gorbachev turned away from the Communist imperative of world domination, not having the stomach for the inevitable mass bloodshed that the maintenance of totalitarian rule demanded. He thought the system could be reformed, not being willing to accept that this was impossible, and this eventually led to his own downfall and replacement by Boris Yeltsin. He did not realize (or want to accept) that, once Soviet Communism abandoned its territorial ambitions, it was on the road to oblivion.

This, though, was for the future; and, from 1988, Gorbachev was able to introduce major political changes, including a democratic Russian parliament. At the same time, he began to ease restrictions on religion, on the pragmatic basis that the country needed the energies of believers if it was to rebuild itself. This was probably also an acknowledgment of the way that Communism had been unable to crush Christianity, despite exercising total control over it for more than eighty years. Meanwhile, popular unrest in Eastern Europe, in protest at Communist rule, led to the end of the Warsaw pact, in 1989, as Gorbachev made it clear that Russia was not going to intervene to repress emerging democratic movements in countries such as Poland. In December 1989, President Gorbachev met the Pope at the Vatican, surely an unbelievable scenario only a few years previously.[849]

Fatima had received further papal support when, earlier in the same year, on 13 May, Pope John Paul II declared Jacinta and Francisco "Venerable," the first stage in the canonization process.[850] In May 1991, a decade after the assassination attempt, the Pope returned to Fatima to give thanks to Mary for the marvelous fruits of the 1984 consecration and for saving his life. But he warned that, although Marxism was losing its influence, there was a danger of its being replaced by another form of atheism equally hostile to Christian morality, a reference to Western materialism.[851] Later in the same year, in August 1991, an attempted coup against President Gorbachev failed, the Communist Party was banned, and the Soviet Union as a belligerent world power began to collapse. Given Russia's military might, this dissolution was far more peaceful than had been feared.[852]

These massive changes in Russia and Eastern Europe support the view that the consecration of 1984 was carried out largely in accordance with Mary's wishes. Mary promised the conversion of Russia if her wishes were complied with, but she did not say that this would happen overnight. Seventy years of Communist misrule could not be put right in a few years. The conversion of the Roman Empire took decades if not centuries to accomplish, although the decisive blow was struck by Constantine early in the fourth century at the battle of the Milvian bridge. A curious contrast can be made between this event and the miracle of the sun at Fatima. Before that famous battle, in October 312, Constantine is said to have seen a vision in the sky of a cross in front of the sun, with the words "In this sign you shall conquer." He duly made the cross the standard of his army and went on to his famous victory, which changed the whole course of history.[853] So a pagan emperor saw a cross in front of the sun and this led to the Roman Empire becoming Christian, while, by contrast, the Christian people of Portugal, at Fatima, saw the miracle of the sun and the country was saved from irreligious disaster, and a return to paganism. But Fatima's significance was meant not only for Portugal, and it is right to see both events as turning-points. Constantine's vision and victory pointed to the triumph of Christianity over Roman paganism, and Fatima points to a future great victory for the Church when, as Mary promised, her Immaculate Heart will triumph and a period of peace will be given to the world.

There is still much to be done, but it is difficult to argue that there have not been huge changes in Russia in recent years. Russian society is by no means tranquil, there is a great deal of corruption and the threat of a return to some form of authoritarian government, but at least the vicious persecutions of the past are over, and there is an opportunity for a new beginning. Whether that opportunity is grasped in the near future is another matter.

The Beatifications and the Third Part of the Secret

In 1999 there was great excitement when it was announced that Pope John Paul would beatify Francisco and Jacinta in Fatima on 13 May 2000. On the evening of 12 May, a crowd of 650,000 greeted the Holy Father as he arrived at the Cova da Iria on his third pilgrimage to the shrine as Pope. He placed a ring he had been given by Cardinal Wyszynski at the foot of the statue of Our Lady in the Capelhina, an act which was seen as having some significance by informed commentators, although few could have imagined that the next day would bring news of the long-awaited third part of the secret.

The next morning, the Pope returned to the Cova da Iria for the Beatification Mass, stopping off at the Basilica to meet privately with 93-year-old Sr Lucia. This Mass was concelebrated with a large number of bishops in front of the Basilica before the vast crowd. Sr Lucia received Holy Communion from the Pope, as did Maria

Emilia dos Santos, the Portuguese woman whose miraculous cure from osteo-tuberculosis, in 1987, was attributed to the intercession of Francisco and Jacinta. This was the miracle required for the beatifications of the youngest non-martyr Blesseds in the history of the Church. During the Mass, the Holy Father read out the text of beatification, which allows the celebration of a local feast for the two children on 20 February each year. Assuming they are eventually canonized, this will become a feast of the universal Church and they will have the title of Saint.

Towards the end of the Mass, Cardinal Sodano, the Vatican Secretary of State, unexpectedly announced, at the Pope's behest, the imminent publication of the third part of the secret of Fatima along with an official commentary. He revealed, too, that part of the text dealt with the Holy Father,[854] and described it as a "prophetic vision similar to those found in Sacred Scripture," which had to be interpreted in symbolic terms. He further described the contents as being concerned with the persecutions suffered by the Church and successive Popes during the twentieth century, and particularly that "the bishop clothed in white," seen shot down by the children, was Pope John Paul II. Thus he regarded the assassination attempt on him on 13 May 1981, as something prophetically foreseen in this vision, and indicated that the contents of the third part of the secret could now be revealed, as they seemed to refer to past events.[855]

A little over a month later, the full text of the third part of the secret, originally set down by Sr Lucia in January 1944, was released by the Vatican, along with a commentary by Cardinal Joseph Ratzinger. Its contents were as follows:

I write in obedience to you, my God, who command me to do so through his Excellency the Bishop of Leiria and through your Most Holy Mother and mine.

After the two parts which I have already explained, at the left of Our Lady and a little above, we saw an Angel with a flaming sword in his left hand; flashing, it gave out flames that looked as though they would set the world on fire; but they died out in contact with the splendor that Our Lady radiated towards him from her right hand: pointing to the earth with his right hand, the Angel cried out in a loud voice: "Penance, Penance, Penance!"

And we saw in an immense light that is God: "something similar to how people appear in a mirror when they pass in front of it" a Bishop dressed in White "we had the impression that it was the Holy Father." Other Bishops, Priests, men and women Religious going up a steep mountain, at the top of which there was a big Cross of rough-hewn trunks as of a cork-tree with the bark; before reaching there the Holy Father passed through a big city half in ruins and half trembling with halting step, afflicted with pain and sorrow, he prayed for the souls of the corpses he met on his way; having reached the top of the mountain, on his knees at the foot of the big Cross he was killed by a group of soldiers who fired bullets and arrows at him, and in the same way there died one after another the other Bishops, Priests, men and women Religious, and various lay people of different ranks and positions.

Beneath the two arms of the Cross there were two Angels each with a crystal aspersorium in his hand, in which they gathered up the blood of the Martyrs and with it sprinkled the souls that were making their way to God.[856]

Two months previously, the Pope had sent a special envoy, Archbishop Tarcisio Bertone, along with the Bishop of Leiria-Fatima, Bishop Serafim de Sousa Ferreira e Silva, to visit Sr Lucia at her Carmelite convent in Coimbra, and discuss how the third part of the secret should be interpreted. Sr Lucia confirmed that the text presented to her was indeed the secret and that it was her writing, and that the vision had to be interpreted symbolically. She also confirmed that it represented the persecutions that the Church and the papacy had faced in the twentieth century. When asked if the main figure was the Pope, Sr Lucia immediately replied that it was, and apparently she also agreed with the interpretation which saw the assassination attempt on John Paul II as part of the vision. She also said that the idea, that the envelope should not be opened until after 1960, was not from Our Lady but was her own "intuition."[857]

The importance of Fatima in the life of the Church was further confirmed by the decision of the Holy Father, on 8 October 2000, to entrust the Third Millennium to Our Lady. The statue of Our Lady of Fatima at the Capelhina was again specially brought to Rome for the occasion, a move of particular symbolic importance in the Jubilee Year. As in the case of the 1984 collegial consecration, all the bishops of the world were encouraged to join in this new act of entrustment. In addition, the latest version of the Roman Missal, which was presented to the Press in March 2002, has a new feast day for the Virgin of Fatima, on May 13. Thus these developments, the beatifications, the revelation of the third part of the secret, the new celebration on 13 May and the dedication of the Third Millennium to Our Lady, indicate that Fatima has assumed a position of center-stage in the life of the Church in the first years of the new century, a position which can only grow in strength.

Summing up the importance of Fatima, we can say that it has underlined some important points in the teaching of the Church which were in danger of being forgotten, particularly that all Christians have a duty to join their own sufferings with those of Christ and so call down God's grace on the world. In 1916, the Angel asked the children to "make everything you can a sacrifice, and offer it to God as an act of reparation for the sins by which He is offended, and in supplication for the conversion of sinners." In July 1917, Mary repeated this theme: "Sacrifice yourselves for sinners, and say many times, especially when you make some sacrifice: O Jesus, it is for love of You, for the conversion of sinners, and in reparation for the sins committed against the Immaculate Heart of Mary."

Our Lady also emphasized the importance of the daily rosary, mentioning this in all six of her apparitions at Fatima: "Say the Rosary every day, to bring peace to the world ..." (May); "...pray the Rosary every day," (June); "...continue to pray the Rosary every day in honor of Our Lady of the Rosary, in order to obtain peace for the world," (July); "...continue to say the Rosary every day ... Pray, pray very much, and make sacrifices for sinners; for many souls go to hell, because there are none to sacrifice themselves and pray for them," (August); "Continue to pray the Rosary ... God is pleased with your sacrifices," (September), and finally, "I am the Lady of the Rosary. Continue always to pray the Rosary every day. ... Do not offend the Lord our God any more, because He is already so much offended" (October).

These points comprise the central teaching of Fatima, in contrast to such elements as the third part of the secret or the collegial consecration, as important as these factors are. This is because a life of sacrifice and prayer is within the capability of all, whereas those other matters are outside the control of individual Catholics. Likewise, Fatima points to the importance of Eucharistic reparation, particularly through the Five First Saturdays devotion, the details of which were revealed by Mary to Sr Lucia in December 1925:

> ... look at My Heart surrounded with thorns with which ungrate-ful men pierce it at every moment by their blasphemies and

ingratitude. You, at least, try to console me, and say that *I promise to assist at the hour of death, with all the graces necessary for salvation,* all those who, on the first Saturday of five consecutive months go to confession and receive Holy Communion, recite five decades of the Rosary and keep me company for a quarter of an hour while meditating on the mysteries of the Rosary, with the intention of making reparation to me.

Indeed, all the major traditional points of Church teaching are emphasized at Fatima, including the Trinity, heaven, hell, purgatory, the soul, angels, demons, the papacy, and the intercessory role of Mary.[858]

Despite all this, Fatima has continued to be a "sign of contradiction," with some theologians denying its validity and the fact that Sr Lucia has had a continuing "prophetic" mission of establishing devotion to Mary's Immaculate Heart in the world. It is clear, though, that the message of Fatima was not confined to one period of time, as in the case of other apparitions, but rather has continued to develop over the course of the twentieth century, and, indeed, it is not complete yet. The implications of the message of Fatima still have to be taken up by the Church as a whole. Only when that is done will there be a true renewal within the Church, and will the world have an opportunity for real peace.[859]

Church and World: the Future?

As indicated in the introduction, it is hoped to deal, in a further volume, with the current critical state of the Church and the world, as well as the place of modern alleged Marian apparitions in the light of history and Fatima.

In the past, the threat to the Church has been largely external, but now there is a new situation which is to a large extent unprecedented. The Church in the West is experiencing a grave falling away for which there does not seem to be any quick remedy—a full recovery from the culture-shock arising from the moral and intellectual assault on Catholicism in the twentieth century is not readily apparent, although there are signs that the confusion following the Second Vatican Council is passing. Despite this, and despite the great work of John Paul II, it does not seem that the Western Church, in large part, is passing on the Faith to the next generations, and this has essentially been the situation since Vatican II. The religious orders are in steady decline, liturgical banality is widespread, and there is a worrying lack of discipline and doctrinal orthodoxy in many sectors of the Church. Pope Paul VI spoke of the "smoke of Satan" entering the Church, and this does not seem to have been an exaggeration.

On a broader level, despite some useful preparatory work, there has not been much real progress in recent years in ecumenical terms—with regard to the Orthodox and Protestant churches—which means that the Christian world as whole remains a "house divided," and is thus not nearly as effective as it should be. The same can be said for the Marian movement as a whole; instead of Catholics uniting to proclaim the message of Fatima, there has been a process of division, as support for alleged apparitions, the majority of which do not have any form of Church approval, grows apace. In addition, persecution at the hands of Islam in numerous parts of the world is a growing concern, while Communist regimes are still in place in China, North Korea, Vietnam, and Cuba, and still harassing, if not openly persecuting, Christians.[860] While the Communist structures of government in the former Soviet Union and Eastern Europe have disappeared, it cannot be said that these areas are experiencing a great spiritual rebirth. In some cases, although the structures are gone, the old Communist mind set is still present, and thus Christians still face severe problems in these areas.

The moral threat from the new technological world-society is immense. As predicted, the acceptance of abortion as "normal," has led to a corrupting of medical science, and now we face the prospect and reality of embryo experimentation, cloning and other forms of exploitation, which recall the medical programs of the Nazis—but with immeasurably greater potential for evil, because these are not being done now merely by individual "rogue" states, but threaten to become worldwide activities.

It may well be that the Church in the West is heading for confrontation with this increasingly neo-pagan society: certainly Catholics in many other parts of the world are facing hardships of all sorts, including outright persecution. Historically, such persecution, as in the cases of Ireland in the past, and more recently Poland, is capable of leading to a renewal and deepening of the Faith in the societies thus affected, and that may well be what will happen in the West.

In her third memoir, Sr Lucia recounts visions which Jacinta alone had of a future Pope. She was with the other children one day, during the siesta, when she called out to Lucia, asking if she had also seen the Holy Father, before continuing:

I don't know how it was, but I saw the Holy Father in a very big house, kneeling by a table, with his head buried in his hands, and he was weeping. Outside the house, there were many people. Some of them were throwing stones, others were cursing him and using bad language. Poor Holy Father, we must pray very much for him."

Another time, while the children were praying the prayers of the Angel, prostrate on the ground, Jacinta again told Lucia what she had just seen in a vision: "Can't you see all those highways and roads and fields full of people who are crying with hunger and have nothing to eat? And the Holy Father in a church praying before the Immaculate Heart of Mary? And so many people praying with him?"[861]

The second of these visions can be interpreted as applying to the upheaval caused by the Second World War—although it may well have a future application too—but the first seems to apply definitely to a future time of persecution affecting the Pope directly. And if the Pope is to be persecuted, it is more than probable that the Western Church generally will also suffer.

There are, though, some positive signs. Pope John Paul II's pontificate, coming in the wake of Vatican II, has laid the basis for a future renovation of the Church. In his support for the Council, his encyclicals, and through the *Catechism of the Catholic Church*, the Pope has given the Church the necessary tools with which to ensure future renewal and growth. Similarly papal support for the new movements and communities means that they will be in a good position to assist in the work of revitalization.[862] But at the moment, these are signs of hope for the future, rather than present realities having an appreciable impact. There is a need for an effective re-evangelization of the Western Church in particular, and a much more effective, and a more spiritual and evangelical, local leadership. There is also a need for a much greater emphasis on the Bible and for more reverent forms of worship, points which would also contribute to ecumenical progress with conservative Protestants and the Orthodox respectively.[863] The message of Fatima suggests, however, that this new evangelization will only succeed if it has a strong Marian element, one which is able to spread devotion to Mary's Immaculate Heart throughout the Church and the world.

The Pope has constantly emphasized the need for hope and trust, and a rejection of irrational fears. Amongst his first words at his inauguration was the following statement:

Be not afraid to welcome Christ and accept his power. Help the Pope and all those who wish to serve Christ and with Christ's power to serve the human person and the whole of mankind. Be not afraid. Open wide the doors for Christ. To his saving power open the boundaries of states, of economic and political systems, the vast fields of culture, civilization, and development. Be not afraid. Christ knows "what is in man." He alone knows it.[864]

John Paul II returned to this theme of the need for mankind not to succumb to a paralyzing fear of the future, in a speech to the United Nations General Assembly in 1995:

> ...*we must learn not to be afraid,* we must discover a spirit of hope and a spirit of trust. ... *We must not be afraid of the future. We must not be afraid of man.* It is no accident that we are here. Each and every human person has been created in the "image and likeness" of the One who is the origin of all that is. We have within us the capacities for wisdom and virtue. With these gifts, and with the help of God's grace, we can build in the next century and the next millennium a civilization worthy of the human person, a true culture of freedom. *We can and we must do so!* And in doing so, we shall see that the tears of this century have prepared the ground for a new springtime of the human spirit.[865]

Conclusion

In closing we can say that, as established above, the most important point to make about the major Marian apparitions is that the Church has given them its support, and thus deemed them both beneficial in coming to a better understanding of public revelation, and also a healthy stimulus to living a better Christian life.

In addition, the general mental stability and soundness of the various seers makes it intrinsically unlikely that they were the victims of illusion or hallucination. Many of the Marian apparitions have involved children, often quite poor and humble children, and this in itself militates against the idea that they were fraudulent. They have occurred over a period of nearly five hundred years now, spread over a wide geographical area, and thus the idea that the seers, or the Church, could have fabricated these incidents becomes impossible to believe. In most cases, there was some tangible proof of what was happening, evident even to bystanders, and so we are not dealing with cases of hallucination either.

It has also been demonstrated that there are definite links between the Marian apparitions and important revolutionary events, such as the Reformation, and the French and Russian Revolutions. The Protestant Reformation, far from leading to a renewal of Christianity, had precisely the opposite effect, in that it allowed the rise of secularism, and of modern godless materialism in particular. Catholicism was a stronghold against secularism, but its destruction in northern Europe opened the floodgates to the present degenerate modern world. The process of questioning authority, which Luther's Revolution quickened, has continued unabated to this day, as its attempt to put the Bible above the Church backfired, leading to a progressive devaluation of the Scriptures.

This critical and rational spirit led on in turn to the Enlightenment, as the Church was progressively pushed to the margins of society in the years leading up to the French Revolution. This itself involved a full-blooded attempt to do away with Christianity and impose a "rational" religion on the people, but after the defeat of Napoleon, Europe turned its back on revolutionary ideas. The evil seeds, however, had been sown and they proceeded to germinate in the various outbursts which affected Europe in the nineteenth century—ideologies and philosophies hostile to Christianity, and particularly evolution and Marxism, began to grow in strength and influence. At the same time, Prussia aggressively developed its Germanic empire, becoming the leading military power in Europe, eventually precipitating the First World War. This war allowed Marxist Communism its chance to seize power in Russia, and ultimately, as the twentieth century progressed, to enslave half the world. The rise of Communism, in turn, allowed Hitler his chance to come to power in Germany and plunge the world into a second, even worse, conflagration.

As has been indicated, these revolutionary events are paralleled by the major Marian apparitions, and so, since these developments seems to go beyond mere coincidence, it can be legitimately argued that the apparitions form a divine response to those developments. It is important to note, however, that this response has not been because of the mainly political nature of these revolutions, but because the ideologies they have promoted threaten the salvation of souls. The period since the Reformation has seen a definite moral and spiritual decline in the world, which must be obvious to any unbiased observer, and this process has only been accelerated by more recent revolutions. There has been great progress in material and secular terms during this period, but regrettably this has involved a turning away from Christianity and the rise of neo-paganism.

The modern world is thus a product of the various revolutions which have occurred over the last five hundred years or so, and we are seeing the cumulative effects of these in the present debased and immoral modern global civilization, a "culture of death," where abortion, pornography and drug abuse are rampant, where basic human rights are still often trampled upon and where millions still live in extreme poverty in the face of the massive affluence of the West.

The individualism promoted by Luther's Reformation has been allied with the spirit of rationalism of the Enlightenment, and given added impetus by the evolutionary theories of Darwin. In addition, the latter half of the twentieth century saw the fruition of Freud's ideas on sex, which have played such a large part in undermining traditional morality. Since the 1960s these trends towards neo-paganism have accelerated, with the hostility towards Pope Paul VI's encyclical on birth control, *Humanae Vitae*, symbolic of the modern world's rejection of the Church's teaching. As the Pope correctly predicted, however, the use of artificial contraception has led to a widespread breakdown in family life, while abortion has greatly corrupted society in general. Humanly speaking, there does not seem to be any way of arresting this trend towards greater and greater evil, and so mankind must have recourse to God and Mary.

As demonstrated above, the power of Fatima has been seen in the remarkable changes which have taken place in the former Soviet Union since the collegial consecration of 1984. It is easy to forget that, as late as the 1970s, Communism was still making progress world-wide. Until the late 1980s, most of Eastern Europe was still under Communist sway. The overt threat of Communism, though, has been replaced by a godless modern ideology, based on evolutionary thinking and materialism, which is proving just as subversive, and, if anything, more deadly.

The Marian apparitions remove the Bible and Christianity from the realm of the mythical, and make us realize that events similar to the miraculous incidents recounted in the Scriptures have happened again in the fairly recent past. Just as the Old Testament prophecies have found fulfillment in world history, and will continue to do so until the end of time, so the Marian apparitions represent the fulfillment of the "prophetic" Marian types found in the Bible. Mary was not given the title "Queen of Prophets" without reason. The typological evidence presented in this book indicates that they seem to have been foreshadowed by Old Testament events, which were often taken by the Church Fathers as types of Mary.

Without this typological connection, it is hard to see why Mary has appeared in such dramatically different ways in her recognized apparitions. It surely cannot have just been for effect, and so there must be a deeper reason. Her apparently "eccentric" mode of dress, and her activities on some of these occasions, seems to be best explained by the typological similarities discussed above, however unusual this idea may seem at first glance.

Mary revealed herself at Guadalupe as the new Eve, and at Rue du Bac as the Mediatrix of all Graces and the ladder of Jacob which unites mankind to God. At La Salette she came as a new Moses, warning humanity of the need for repentance. At Lourdes she proclaimed herself to be the Immaculate Conception, while at Pontmain and Knock she came as the new Ark of the Covenant. At Fatima, like a new Elijah, she again warned mankind of the dangers it faced, particularly the "errors of Russia," and at Beauraing and Banneux she appeared as the new "Eastern Gate," the Virgin Mother of God, to beg for fervent prayer. At Tre Fontane she came as the "Virgin of Revelation," thus indicating the importance of our recognizing the "signs of the times" in which we live. These types and titles are not just pious themes, but represent the truth of Mary's intercessory role, which in reality is almost infinitely greater. She is the spiritual mother of mankind, the mother of the mystical body of Christ, and thus she is the mother of every human being in the order of grace.

The role of the Marian apparitions in helping to revitalize Catholicism has not been acknowledged properly in modern times; rather, there has been a tendency to disparage and belittle them, to the consequent impoverishment of the Church. The apparitions seem to have acted as catalysts, particularly in the renewals of the Catholic Church which took place during the sixteenth, nineteenth, and early twentieth centuries. Without an adequate response from ordinary Catholics, their message and fruitfulness would have fallen on stony ground, but this response was largely forthcoming in the past, and thus the Marian apparitions, although they have been largely ignored by the world, have had an important influence on the Church. In reality, though, the response by Catholics, as a body, more recently, and particularly to Fatima, has not been wholehearted enough; more is required if the deliverance from present evils, that has been promised by God through his mother, is to be fulfilled.

It might seem that all this is putting too much emphasis on the role of Mary and exaggerating her importance. But the message of Fatima, which has been accepted at the highest levels of the Church, and advanced significantly by Pope John Paul II in particular, should leave us in no doubt that Marian devotion is of crucial importance. During the second apparition, in June 1917, Mary told the children that God "wishes to establish the devotion to My Immaculate Heart throughout the world. I promise salvation to whoever embraces it; these souls will be dear to God, like flowers put by Me to adorn his throne." Similarly, the next month, after showing the children the vision of hell, she reiterated and amplified this message: "You have seen hell where the souls of poor sinners go. To save them, God wishes to establish in the world devotion to my Immaculate Heart. If what I say to you is done, many souls will be saved and there will be peace." So the devotion to Mary proposed at Fatima is both a guarantee of individual salvation and a necessity for the world if there is to be true peace. Only when the Church as a whole acknowledges Mary's unique position, and responds to her repeated appeals, will that happen.

When she comes down from heaven to appear to particular individuals, she is both warning and consoling the world: warning it that mankind must change its ways, and consoling it with a reassurance that the Christian promise of eternal life is not a fable, but the only solid reality we can look forward to. The Marian apparitions, and particularly Fatima, are a decisive call to listen again to Christ and the Church, and it is the great promise held out by them, that the world will see true peace, and a new civilization of love, that should encourage us for the future.

Further Reading

Batten, Don, ed., *The Updated & Expanded Answers Book* (Answers in Genesis Ltd, Acacia Ridge, 2001).

Behe, M., W. Dembski, S. Meyer, eds., *Science and Evidence for Design in the Universe* (Ignatius Press, San Francisco, 2000).

Behe, Michael, *Darwin's Black Box: the Biochemical Challenge to Evolution* (The Free Press / Simon & Schuster, 1996).

Bowden, Malcolm, *The Rise of the Evolution Fraud* (Sovereign Publications, Bromley, 1982).

———, *Science vs Evolution* (Sovereign Publications, Bromley, 1991).

Cooper, Bill, *After the Flood: The Early post-Flood History of Europe traced back to Noah* (New Wine Press, Chichester, 1995).

Cuozzo, Jack, *Buried Alive: The Startling Truth about Neanderthal Man* (Master Books, Green Forest, 1999).

Davis, Percival and Dean Kenyon, *Of Pandas and People: the Central Question of Biological Origins*, Second Edition (Haughton Publishing Company, Dallas, 1999).

Denton, Michael, *Evolution: a Theory in Crisis* (Adler & Adler), 1986).

Harrison, R. K., *Introduction to the Old Testament* (Eerdmans, Grand Rapids, 1977).

Humphreys, D. Russell, *Starlight and Time: Solving the Puzzle of Distant Starlight in a Young Universe* (Master Books, Green Forest, 2000).

Johnson, Phillip E., *Darwin on Trial* (InterVarsity Press, Downers Grove, 1991).

Keane, Gerard J., *Creation Rediscovered: Evolution and the Importance of the Origins Debate* (TAN Books and Publishers, Rockford, 1999).

Kitchen, K. A., *Ancient Orient and Old Testament* (The Tyndale Press, London, 1966).

Milton, Richard, *The Facts of Life: Shattering the Myth of Darwinism* (Corgi Books, 1993).

Morris, Henry, *The Long War against God: The History and Impact of the Creation/Evolution Conflict* (Master Books, Green Forest, 2000).

Oard, Michael J., *An Ice Age Caused by the Genesis Flood* (Institute for Creation Research, Santee, 1990).

Sarfati, Jonathan D., *Refuting Evolution* (Answers in Genesis, Acacia Ridge, 1999).

Shute, Evan, *Flaws in the Theory of Evolution* (Craig Press, New Jersey, 1980).

Steidl, Paul, *The Earth, the Stars, and the Bible* (Presbyterian and Reformed Publishing Company, Phillipsburg, 1979).

Steinmueller, John E., *A Companion to Scripture Studies,* 3 vols. (Joseph F. Wagner, New York, 1946).

Whitcomb, John, and Henry Morris, *The Genesis Flood: The Biblical Record and its Scientific Implications* (Baker Book House, Grand Rapids, 1981).

Wiseman, P.J., *Clues to Creation in Genesis,* ed. D.J. Wiseman (Marshall, Morgan & Scott, London, 1977).

Woodmorappe, *John, Noah's Ark: A Feasibility Study* (Institute for Creation Research, Santee, 1996).

Notes

1. *Catechism of the Catholic Church,* 105, 107.
2. "Homily of Pope John Paul II at Fatima, May 13, 1982," cited in Appendix III, Timothy Tindal-Robertson, *Fatima, Russia and Pope John Paul II,* Revised Edition (Gracewing, Leominster, 1998), pp. 245–46.
3. See Dietrich von Hildebrand, *Trojan Horse in the City of God,* (Sands & Co. Ltd., London, 1969), pp. 89–92.
4. See, for example, *Theotokos: A Theological Encyclopedia of the Blessed Virgin Mary,* 2d ed., s.v. "Apparitions," and Rev. Eamon R. Carroll, O Carm, "Must Catholics believe in Fatima? The place of Private Revelation in the Church," in *Exploring Fatima,* (AMI Press, New Jersey, 1989), p. 3. See also John Delaney, ed., *A Woman clothed with the Sun,* (Doubleday, New York, 1961), where all but Pontmain are dealt with.
5. Warren H. Carroll, *Our Lady of Guadalupe and the Conquest of Darkness,* (Christendom Press, Front Royal, 1983), pp. 19–24.
6. Francis Johnston, *The Wonder of Guadalupe,* (Augustine Publishing Company, Devon, 1981), p. 14.
7. Carroll, *Our Lady of Guadalupe,* pp. 25–27.
8. L. McAlister, *Spain and Portugal in the New World, 1492–1700,* (University of Minnesota Press, Minneapolis, 1984), pp. 78, 79–81.
9. Ibid., p. 87.
10. M. Meyer and W. Sherman, *The Course of Mexican History,* (Oxford University Press, New York, 1983), pp. 87–89; Carroll, *Our Lady of Guadalupe,* pp. 19–20. More recently, the idea that the Aztecs were expecting the return of Quetzalcoatl has been questioned. Michael E. Smith argues that this idea was contrived by the surviving Aztec nobility *after* the conquest, as a way of explaining Montezuma's strange actions. The modern preference seems to be to call him "Motecuhzoma," rather than Montezuma. See Michael E. Smith, *The Aztecs,* (Blackwell Publishers Ltd., Oxford, 1996), pp. 37, 283–84.
11. Meyer and Sherman, *The Course of Mexican History,* pp. 95–113; Br Francis Mary, "Guadalupe in Spain," in *A Handbook on Guadalupe,* (Academy of the Immaculate, New Bedford, 1997), p. 26.
12. Meyer and Sherman, *The Course of Mexican History,* pp. 115–17, 185; Carroll, *Our Lady of Guadalupe,* pp. 47–53.
13. Meyer and Sherman, *The Course of Mexican History,* pp. 117–28; Carroll, *Our Lady of Guadalupe,* p. 62.
14. The question of whether the Spaniards had the right to conquer Mexico is a difficult one, and the modern secular tendency has been to reject this idea. However, given that Western expansion was inevitable, and the horrendous nature of Aztec society, on balance it seems that the conquest was justified, and indeed that the Spanish had a *duty* to end such an evil system. See Carroll, *Our Lady of Guadalupe,* pp. 22–23.

15. Meyer and Sherman, *The Course of Mexican History*, pp. 130–31.
16. Ibid., pp. 141–42.
17. McAlister, *Spain and Portugal in the New World*, pp. 168, 184–89.
18. Ibid., p. 169.
19. According to Dr Charles Wahlig, Juan Diego was not an Aztec but a member of the *Chichimeca* people, who had arrived in the area before the Aztecs. He was probably one of the middle class and a landowner, although one who voluntarily embraced poverty. See Dr C. Wahlig, "Juan Diego, Ambassador of the Queen of Heaven," in *A Handbook on Guadalupe*, pp. 42–43.
20. Br Francis Mary, "Nican Mopohua: Original Account of Guadalupe," in *A Handbook on Guadalupe*, p. 194.
21. Ibid., pp. 194–96.
22. Johnston, *The Wonder of Guadalupe*, p. 29.
23. D. Demarest and C. Taylor, eds., *The Dark Virgin: the Book of Our Lady of Guadalupe*, (Coley Taylor, New York, 1956), pp. 73–74.
24. Br Francis Mary, "Nican Mopohua: Original Account of Guadalupe," in *A Handbook on Guadalupe*, p. 200.
25. Ibid., p. 201.
26. Meyer and Sherman, *The Course of Mexican History*, p. 186.
27. W. H. Carroll points out that it may be that "Guadalupe" was actually the word used and meant, and that this would indicate a deliberate identification with the Spanish shrine, so as to draw the Aztecs and Spaniards closer together. However, this does not affect the idea that the Aztecs could have understood this in their own way as Coatlaxopeuh, or some such similar word; see Carroll, *Our Lady of Guadalupe*, pp. 104–5. This word or a variant seems to be the most favored choice historically amongst scholars. See Br Francis Mary, "What about the name 'Guadalupe,'" in *A Handbook on Guadalupe*, pp. 179–82.
28. P. Fehlner, "Guadalupe, The Immaculate Conception and the Franciscans" in *A Handbook on Guadalupe*, pp. 159–62.
29. Smith, *The Aztecs*, pp. 213, 216, 219, 264.
30. Carroll, *Our Lady of Guadalupe*, pp. 8–9.
31. C. Wahlig, "Juan Diego, Ambassador of the Queen of Heaven," in *A Handbook on Guadalupe*, pp. 46–47.
32. St Justin Martyr, "Dialogue with Trypho, ch. 100," in *The Fathers of the Church*, vol. 6, trans. T. B. Falls, (Catholic University of America Press, 1977), pp. 304–305.
33. St Cyril of Jerusalem, "The Works of St Cyril of Jerusalem, vol. 1," in *The Fathers of the Church*, vol. 61, trans. L. P. McCauley and A. A. Stephenson, (Catholic University of America Press, 1977), XII, 15, pp. 234–35.
34. Bertrand Buby, SM, *Mary of Galilee*, Vol. 3, *The Marian Legacy of the Early Church*, (Alba House, New York, 1997), p. 107, (*De virginitate, MU* 71, 212–219), from S. E. Campos, *Corpus Marianum Patristicum*, pars. II, (Burgos: Ediciones Aldecoa, S.A., 1970), p. 60 (#548).

35. Ibid., p. 188, (Sermon. 28, *In Nat. Dom.* xx, xxi, xxvi).
36. Ibid., p. 165, from *A Select Library of Nicene and Post-Nicene Fathers of the Christian Church,* trans. Philip Schaff and Henry Wace, vol. 6 (New York: Christian Literature, 1893), p. 30, par. 21.
37. Stefano M. Manelli, FFI, *All Generations Shall Call Me Blessed: Biblical Mariology,* trans. Peter Damian Fehlner, FFI, (Academy of the Immaculate, New Bedford, 1995), pp. 21–26.
38. Demarest and Taylor, *The Dark Virgin,* p. 30.
39. Br Francis Mary, "Nican Mopohua: Original Account of Guadalupe," in *A Handbook on Guadalupe,* pp. 193–94.
40. Demarest and Taylor, *The Dark Virgin,* p. 109.
41. Henry Bettenson, ed. and trans., *The Early Christian Fathers,* (Oxford University Press, Oxford, 1983), pp. 82–83, (*Adversus Haereses,* III. xxi. 10).
42. Luigi Gambero, SM, *Mary and the Fathers of the Church,* trans. T. Buffer, (Ignatius Press, San Francisco, 1999), p. 178.
43. Kathleen E. McVey, trans., *Ephrem the Syrian, Hymns,* (Paulist Press, New York, 1989), p. 65, (Hymns on the Nativity, 1.16).
44. Gambero, *Mary and the Fathers of the Church,* p. 269.
45. For information about the historical reality of Genesis as opposed to modern evolutionary theories, and problems with evolution generally, see the section *Further Reading.*
46. Johnston, *The Wonder of Guadalupe,* pp. 62–64.
47. Demarest and Taylor, *The Dark Virgin,* pp. 5–7.
48. Jody Brant Smith, *The Image of Guadalupe,* (Mercer University Press, Macon, 1994), pp. 18–19; Carroll, *Our Lady of Guadalupe,* pp. 98–99.
49. Br Francis Mary, "What the Church . . . Has to say about Guadalupe," in *A Handbook on Guadalupe,* pp. 172–73.
50. Smith, *The Image of Guadalupe,* pp. 13–17; C. Wahlig, ". . .The Battle of Lepanto," in *A Handbook on Guadalupe,* p. 102.
51. Demarest and Taylor, *The Dark Virgin,* pp. 111–12.
52. Ibid., pp. 165–67.
53. Ibid., pp. 22–23.
54. Ibid., pp. 175–77.
55. H. Leies, *Mother for a New World: Our Lady of Guadalupe,* (Newman Press, Maryland, 1964), pp. 156–57.
56. Ibid., pp. 151–52.
57. Demarest and Taylor, *The Dark Virgin,* p. 10.
58. Smith, *The Image of Guadalupe,* pp. 53–58.
59. Interestingly enough the Image apparently rejects insects and dust, and even maintains normal human body temperature, regardless of atmospheric conditions. See J. Barber, "The Tilma and its Miraculous Image," in *A Handbook on Guadalupe,* p. 62.
60. Smith, *The Image of Guadalupe,* pp. 61–65.
61. One of the many interesting points about the Image itself is that the number of stars on the blue mantle is forty-six, which, as Professor Jody Brant Smith has pointed out, is the number of years it took to

build the Temple in Jerusalem, a Temple which Jesus compared to his body (John 2:19–22). See Smith, *The Image of Guadalupe*, pp. 47–48. In a sense, the time it took for the "construction" of Jesus' body was nine months—the time he spent in the womb of Mary before he was born, and this is significant in that Our Lady of Guadalupe has been adopted as a Pro-life symbol, with some arguing that in the Image she actually seems pregnant. Perhaps even stranger than this is the fact that there are also forty-six chromosomes in the nucleus of each cell of the human body: see Smith, *The Image of Guadalupe*, p. xvii; J. Barber, "Holy Mary of Guadalupe, Prolife Patron," in *A Handbook on Guadalupe*, p. 135. It also seems that the pattern of stars on the *tilma* corresponds to the constellations as they would have been seen in the sky over Mexico City in December 1531. See J. Barber, "The Sacred Image is a Divine Codex," in *A Handbook on Guadalupe*, pp. 69–70.

62. Johnston, *The Wonder of Guadalupe*, p. 133; J. Barber, "The Tilma and its Miraculous Image," in *A Handbook on Guadalupe*, pp. 58–59.
63. Smith, *The Image of Guadalupe*, pp. 67–73.
64. Michael P. Carroll, *The Cult of the Virgin Mary, Psychological Origins*, (Princeton University Press, Princeton, 1986), pp. 185–94. Carroll's analysis of the other major Marian apparitions follows essentially the same psychoanalytical method.
65. Carroll, *Our Lady of Guadalupe*, pp. 80, 107–110.
66. Leies, *Mother for a New World*, pp. 72–73.
67. C. Hawkins, "The Iconography of Guadalupe," in *A Handbook on Guadalupe*, pp. 63–67.
68. Carroll, *Our Lady of Guadalupe*, p. 113.
69. Ibid., pp. 186–89.
70. Demarest and Taylor, *The Dark Virgin*, pp. 2–3.
71. Smith, *The Image of Guadalupe*, p. 52; C. Rengers, "Mother of the Americas" in *A Handbook on Guadalupe*, p. 8.
72. Cf. Hilaire Belloc, *The Crisis of Civilization*, (TAN Books and Publishers, Rockford, 1992), pp. 25–30.
73. J. Daniélou and H. Marrou, *The Christian Centuries*, vol. 1, (Darton, Longman & Todd, London, 1964), pp. 249–53; Warren H. Carroll, *A History of Christendom*, vol. 2, *The Building of Christendom*, (Christendom Press, Front Royal, 1987), pp. 11–12, 92–95; W. Burghardt, "Mary in Patristic Thought," in Juniper Carol, OFM, ed., *Mariology*, vol. 2, (Bruce Publishing Co., Milwaukee, 1957), pp. 116, 125.
74. Daniélou & Marrou, *The Christian Centuries*, Vol. 1, pp. 255–66; Carroll, *A History of Christendom*, Vol. 2, pp. 64–65.
75. Christopher Dawson, *The Dynamics of World History*, (Sheed & Ward, London, 1957), pp. 325, 350–51; Judith Herrin, *The Formation of Christendom*, (Fontana Press, London, 1987), pp. 116–18.
76. Christopher Dawson, *Progress and Religion*, (Sheed & Ward, London, 1938), pp. 172–73; Christopher Dawson, *Religion and the Rise of*

Western Culture, (Image Books, New York, 1958), pp. 57–58.

77. Christopher Dawson, *The Making of Europe*, (Sheed & Ward, London, 1946), pp. 192–94; Dawson, *Progress and Religion*, pp. 173–74; D. Knowles and D. Obolensky, *The Christian Centuries*, vol. 2, *The Middle Ages*, (Darton, Longman & Todd, London, 1969), pp. 4–5, 31–33, 203–4, 292.

78. H. Daniel-Rops, *Cathedral and Crusade*, trans. J. Warrington, (E. P. Dutton & Co, Inc., New York, 1957) p. 371; Knowles and Obolensky, *The Christian Centuries*, vol. 2, pp. 393–94; Warren H. Carroll, *A History of Christendom*, vol. 3, *The Glory of Christendom*, (Christendom Press, Front Royal, 1993), pp. 264–65.

79. Carroll, *A History of Christendom*, vol. 3, pp. 31–32.

80. Knowles and Obolensky, *The Christian Centuries*, vol. 2., pp. 261, 293; Daniel-Rops, *Cathedral and Crusade*, pp. 145–48, 165.

81. Carroll, *A History of Christendom*, vol. 3, pp. 164–69; Daniel-Rops, *Cathedral and Crusade*, pp. 149–58; C. P. Ceroke, O Carm., "The Scapular Devotion," in Juniper Carol, ed., *Mariology*, vol. 3, (Bruce Publishing Co., Milwaukee, 1961), pp. 128–40; G. Shea, "The Dominican Rosary," in *Mariology*, vol. 3, pp. 109–10, 114–18.

82. K. Bihlmeyer and H. Tüchle, *Church History*, vol. 2, *The Middle Ages*, (Newman Press, Westminster, 1963), pp. 265–68, 270–75, 338–40; Dawson, *Religion and the Rise of Western Culture*, p. 217; Belloc, *The Crisis of Civilization*, pp. 64–65, 77–78; Carroll, *A History of Christendom*, vol. 3, pp. 389–96, 491–92, 514–26.

83. Bihlmeyer and Tüchle, *Church History*, vol. 2, pp. 379–88; s.v. "Vincent Ferrer" in Charles Hebermann, et al., eds., *The Catholic Encyclopedia*, vol. 15, (The Encyclopedia Press Inc., New York, 1913), pp. 437–38; A. Pradel, *St Vincent Ferrer*, (Washbourne, London, 1875), pp. 32–33, 38, 252–53.

84. Knowles and Obolensky, *The Christian Centuries*, vol. 2, pp. 430–31, 446–49, 451–56, 460–61; Carroll, *A History of Christendom*, vol. 3, pp. 535–37, 672, 683–86, 708–709; Pierre Janelle, *The Catholic Reformation*, (Collier-Macmillan, London, 1971), pp. 22–23; Dawson, *Progress and Religion*, p. 186.

85. References to countries such as "Germany" or "Italy," prior to their modern reunification in the nineteenth century, although anachronistic, are used to avoid confusion.

86. Bihlmeyer and Tüchle, *Church History*, vol. 2, pp. 502–509; Knowles and Obolensky, *The Christian Centuries*, vol. 2, p. 438.

87. Bihlmeyer and Tüchle, *Church History*, vol. 2, pp. 509–14.

88. Janelle, *The Catholic Reformation*, pp. 8–9.

89. Ibid., pp. 13–14.

90. Christopher Dawson, *The Dividing of Europe*, (Sheed & Ward, New York, 1965), pp. 71–74, (quote); H. Daniel-Rops, *The Protestant Reformation*, trans. A. Butler, (J. M. Dent & Sons Ltd, London, 1970), pp. 290–94.

91. Bihlmeyer and Tüchle, *Church History*, vol. 2, pp. 514–55.

92. Ibid., pp. 515–16; Carroll, *A History of Christendom*, vol. 3, pp. 647–50, 653–54.
93. Dawson, *Progress and Religion*, p. 188; James Hitchcock, *What is Secular Humanism?* (RC Books, Harrison, 1982), p. 30.
94. Daniel-Rops, *The Protestant Reformation*, pp. 284–89.
95. Louis Bouyer, *The Spirit and Forms of Protestantism*, (Collins, London, 1963), pp. 171–75.
96. Daniel-Rops, *The Protestant Reformation*, pp. 298–301; Bernard Reardon, *Religious thought in the Reformation*, (Longman, London, 1981), pp. 22–23.
97. Daniel-Rops, *The Protestant Reformation*, pp. 301–3.
98. Ibid., pp. 304–12.
99. Ibid., pp. 444–49.
100. Salvatore Bonano, CMF, "Marian Shrines and Apparitions," in Juniper Carol, ed., *Mariology*, vol. 3, p. 342.
101. Daniel-Rops, *The Protestant Reformation*, pp. 451–59.
102. Ibid., pp. 312–16, 332–38.
103. Ibid., pp. 345–46.
104. Dawson, *The Dividing of Europe*, pp. 92–99.
105. Ibid., pp. 101–5.
106. Ibid., pp. 69–71.
107. H. Daniel-Rops, *The Catholic Reformation*, trans. J. Warrington, (J. M. Dent & Sons Ltd, London, 1962), p. 2.
108. Daniel-Rops, *The Protestant Reformation*, pp. 454–73.
109. Dawson, *The Dividing of Europe*, pp. 112–16; Daniel-Rops, *The Protestant Reformation*, pp. 473–78.
110. Belloc, *The Crisis of Civilization*, pp. 104–7.
111. Dawson, *The Dividing of Europe*, pp. 107–8; cf. Owen Chadwick, *The Reformation*, (Penguin Books, Middlesex, 1977), pp. 97, 384–85.
112. Cf. *Dei Verbum*, n. 10.
113. Bouyer, *Spirit and Forms of Protestantism*, p. 104; R. H. Tawney, *Religion and the Rise of Capitalism*, (Penguin, Middlesex, 1966), p. 122; Daniel-Rops, *The Protestant Reformation*, pp. 408, 431–35.
114. Daniel-Rops, *The Catholic Reformation*, pp. 2–4; Dawson, The *Dividing of Europe*, pp. 141–43.
115. Daniel-Rops, *The Catholic Reformation*, pp. 5–8, 48–58; Dawson, *The Dividing of Europe*, pp. 152–54.
116. Daniel-Rops, *The Catholic Reformation*, pp. 70–79; cf. Chadwick, *The Reformation*, pp. 266–68.
117. Daniel-Rops, *The Catholic Reformation*, pp. 83–99.
118. S. Bonano, CMF, "Mary's Immunity from Actual Sin," in Juniper Carol, ed., *Mariology*, vol. 1, (Bruce Publishing Co., Milwaukee, 1955), p. 398.
119. Yves Chiron, *Enquête sur les Apparitions de la Vierge*, (Éditions J'ai Lu, Paris, 1995), pp. 81–82.
120. Daniel-Rops, *The Catholic Reformation*, pp. 104–110.
121. *The Catholic Encyclopedia*, vol. 9, s.v. "Lepanto," p. 182.

122. Demarest and Taylor, *The Dark Virgin*, p. 13.
123. Smith, *The Image of Guadalupe*, p. 7.
124. *The Catholic Encyclopedia*, vol. 12, s.v. "Pius V," p. 131.
125. E. Addis and T. Arnold, *A Catholic Dictionary*, (Virtue & Co., London, 1954), p. 541.
126. G. Shea, "The Dominican Rosary," in *Mariology*, vol. 3, pp. 117–18.
127. Dawson, *The Dividing of Europe*, pp. 123–26.
128. Collinson, "The Late Medieval Church and its Reformation," in John McManners, ed., *The Oxford History of Christianity*, (OUP, Oxford, 1993), p. 256.
129. Dawson, *The Dividing of Europe*, pp. 177–84; Belloc, *The Crisis of Civilization*, pp. 98–99.
130. Dawson, *The Dividing of Europe*, p. 195.
131. H. M. Gillett, *Famous Shrines of Our Lady*, vol. 2, (Samuel Walker, London, 1960), pp. 241–44, 247–51.
132. William Christian, *Apparitions in Late Medieval and Renaissance Spain*, (Princeton University Press, Princeton, 1981), pp. 140–44.
133. H. M. Gillett, *Famous Shrines of Our Lady*, vol. 1, (Samuel Walker, London, 1961), pp. 161–68; Gillett, *Famous Shrines of Our Lady*, vol. 2, pp. 121–29.
134. Daniel-Rops, *The Protestant Reformation*, pp. 492–96; cf. Chadwick, *The Reformation*, pp. 104–107, 117–23.
135. Daniel-Rops, *The Protestant Reformation*, pp. 514–20; see also Christopher Dawson, *The Judgement of Nations*, (Sheed & Ward, London, 1943), p. 124; Daniel-Rops, *The Catholic Reformation*, pp. 203–9.
136. Michael Graves, *Burghley*, (Longman, London, 1998), pp. 9–10, 40, 42, 44.
137. Hilaire Belloc, *Characters of the Reformation*, (TAN Books and Publishers, Rockford, 1992), p. 125.
138. Carroll, *A History of Christendom*, vol. 3, p. 698.
139. Dawson, *The Dividing of Europe*, pp. 118–22.
140. Daniel-Rops, *The Catholic Reformation*, pp. 209–13.
141. Tawney, *Religion and the Rise of Capitalism*, p. 273.
142. This is obviously not a criticism of family life, which remains the cornerstone of Christian civilization, but merely the observation that religious ideals were becoming progressively "privatized" and confined to the home, and thus were not able to influence society as a whole so effectively as had previously been the case.
143. Dawson, *The Dynamics of World History*, pp. 163–64; Tawney, *Religion and the Rise of Capitalism*, pp. 198–99.
144. H. Daniel-Rops, *The Church in the Seventeenth Century*, trans. J. Buckingham, (J. M. Dent & Sons Ltd, London, 1963), p. 141.
145. Daniel-Rops, *The Church in the Seventeenth Century*, pp. 149–51; Norman Davies, *Europe: A History*, (Pimlico, London, 1997), p. 568.
146. Dawson, *The Dividing of Europe*, pp. 138–40.
147. Ibid., pp. 8–9, 159–61.

148. Christopher Dawson, *Understanding Europe*, (Sheed & Ward, London, 1952), pp. 207–10.
149. Tawney, *Religion and the Rise of Capitalism*, pp. 106–7, *emphasis added.*
150. Christopher Dawson, *The Historic Reality of Christian Culture*, (Routledge & Kegan Paul, London, 1960), pp. 66, 75; Hitchcock, *What is Secular Humanism?* pp. 30–31. Clearly, optimism is not the same as the Christian virtue of hope, but it nevertheless involves looking at the world and its problems in a positive way, and thus it can provide a basis for hope.
151. Dawson, *The Judgement of the Nations*, p. 94 (quote); cf. Dietrich von Hildebrand, *Trojan Horse in the City of God*, pp. 69–72, 183.
152. Tawney, *Religion and the Rise of Capitalism*, pp. 123–24.
153. Lawrence Burke, OFM, "Our Lady in Art," in *Mariology*, vol. 3, p. 418; Dawson, *The Historic Reality of Christian Culture*, p. 67.
154. Bouyer, *Spirit and Forms of Protestantism*, p. 136; see also Einar Molland, *Christendom*, (A.R. Mowbray & Co. Limited, London, 1961), p. 265.
155. Dawson, *The Dividing of Europe*, pp. 209–11; see also J. Randall, *The Making of the Modern Mind*, (Columbia University Press, New York, 1976), pp. 160–61; Molland, *Christendom*, p. 265.
156. Tawney, *Religion and the Rise of Capitalism*, pp. 111–17.
157. Ibid., pp. 119–21.
158. Belloc, *The Crisis of Civilization*, pp. 149–50.
159. Amintore Fanfani, *Catholicism, Protestantism and Capitalism*, (Sheed & Ward, London, 1935), pp. 210–15.
160. Daniel-Rops, *The Church in the Seventeenth Century*, pp. 303–5.
161. Paul Hazard, *The European Mind (1680–1715)*, (Hollis & Carter, London, 1953), pp. 83–84.
162. Christopher Dawson, *The Gods of Revolution*, (Sidgwick & Jackson, London, 1972), pp. 16–18; Dawson, *The Dividing of Europe*, pp. 260–62; Hazard, *The European Mind (1680–1715)*, pp. 275–76; Hitchcock, *What is Secular Humanism?* p. 35.
163. C. R. Kesler, "The Different Enlightenments," in W. Rusher, ed., *The Ambiguous Legacy of the Enlightenment*, (University Press of America, Lanham, 1995), pp. 104–5.
164. Daniel-Rops, *The Church in the Seventeenth Century*, pp. 307–8.
165. Fanfani, *Catholicism, Protestantism and Capitalism*, pp. 140–41.
166. Ibid., pp. 175–79; Belloc, *The Crisis of Civilization*, pp. 115–16.
167. Fanfani, *Catholicism, Protestantism and Capitalism*, pp. 87–90.
168. Dawson, *The Dividing of Europe*, pp. 9–12; Hitchcock, *What is Secular Humanism?* p. 34.
169. Tawney, *Religion and the Rise of Capitalism*, pp. 109–10; see also Randall, *The Making of the Modern Mind*, pp. 137–38.
170. Fanfani, *Catholicism, Protestantism and Capitalism*, pp. 190–97; Belloc, *The Crisis of Civilization*, p. 126; but cf. Owen Chadwick, *The Secularization of the European Mind in the Nineteenth Century*, (Cambridge University Press, Cambridge, 1975), pp. 7–8.

171. Hazard, *The European Mind (1680–1715)*, pp. 73–76, 91–92; see also Dawson, *Understanding Europe*, pp. 137–41.

172. Fanfani, *Catholicism, Protestantism and Capitalism*, pp. 207–9. Modern criticism of this approach has been based on a critique of the ideas of the sociologist Max Weber (1864–1920), especially his book *The Protestant Ethic and the Spirit of Capitalism*. Although he agrees with Fanfani on a number of points Weber has a different emphasis. It is probably fair to say that Weber was more concerned with what was *intrinsic* to Protestantism that made it favorable to the rise of capitalism, whereas Fanfani saw the *removal* of medieval Catholicism itself as the decisive point, a subtle but important difference. As is the case of a number of Catholic writers, there has been a tendency to ignore Fanfani's work. See Dirk Käsler, *Max Weber, An introduction to his life and work*, trans. P. Hurd, (Polity Press, Cambridge, 1988), pp. 74–94.

173. Dawson, *The Dividing of Europe*, pp. 196–99.

174. Dawson, *The Gods of Revolution*, pp. 6–9.

175. Dawson, *The Dividing of Europe*, pp. 211–12; Burke, "Our Lady in Art," in *Mariology*, vol. 3, p. 419.

176. Bouyer, *Spirit and Forms of Protestantism*, pp. 209–11.

177. H. Daniel-Rops, *The Church in the Eighteenth Century*, trans. J. Warrington, (J. M. Dent & Sons Ltd, London, 1964), pp. 1–4.

178. Daniel-Rops, *The Church in the Eighteenth Century*, pp. 10–13. See also Pope John Paul II, *Crossing the Threshold of Hope*, ed. Vittorio Messori, tr. J. and M. McPhee, (Jonathan Cape, London, 1994), pp. 37–38.

179. Joseph de Torre, *Christian Philosophy*, (Vera-Reyes, Inc., Manilla, 1981), p. 296.

180. Dawson, *Progress and Religion*, p. 11; Hazard, *The European Mind (1680–1715)*, pp. 130–33; Margaret C. Jacob, *The Radical Enlightenment: Pantheists, Freemasons and Republicans*, (George Allen & Unwin, London, 1981), pp. 43, 44–45.

181. Dawson, *The Dynamics of World History*, pp. 123–44; Randall, *The Making of the Modern Mind*, pp. 143–45, 282–83; R. H. Kennington, "Blumenberg and the Legitimacy of the Modern Age," in *The Ambiguous Legacy of the Enlightenment*, pp. 27–29. See also John Paul II, *Crossing the Threshold of Hope*, pp. 52–53.

182. Dawson, *The Dividing of Europe*, pp. 253–55.

183. E.E.Y. Hales, *The Catholic Church in the Modern World*, (Eyre & Spottiswoode, London, 1958), pp. 19–23.

184. Dawson, *The Dividing of Europe*, pp. 221–30.

185. Daniel-Rops, *The Church in the Seventeenth Century*, pp. 226–27.

186. Ibid., pp. 311–18.

187. Daniel-Rops, *The Church in the Eighteenth Century*, pp. 145–49; Hazard, *The European Mind (1680–1715)*, pp. 58–62; cf. G. R. Cragg, *The Church and the Age of Reason, 1648–1789*, (Penguin Books, Middlesex, 1966), pp. 95–97.

188. *The Catholic Encyclopedia*, vol. 7, s.v. "Heart of Jesus," pp. 165–66.

189. Fr Arthur B. Calkins, *Totus Tuus: John Paul II's Program of Marian*

Consecration and Entrustment, (Academy of the Immaculate, New Bedford, 1992), pp. 60–61; see also Chiron, *Enquête sur les Apparitions de la Vierge*, pp. 139–42.

190. L. Verheylezoon, *Devotion to the Sacred Heart*, (TAN Books and Publishers, Rockford, 1978), pp. xxiii–xxviii.

191. Ibid., p. 235.

192. The Brown Scapular is a sacramental approved over the centuries by many popes. In Church tradition those who wear the scapular, say the Little Office of Our Lady, (or the rosary for those with a dispensation), and observe chastity, according to their state of life, will not go to hell. The *sabbatine privilege* refers to the belief that those fulfilling the above stipulations will be delivered from purgatory on the first Saturday after their death.

193. Verheylezoon, *Devotion to the Sacred Heart*, pp. 237–39.

194. Ibid., pp. xxviii–xxx.

195. *The Catholic Encyclopedia vol. VII*, s.v. "Heart of Mary," pp. 168–69.

196. John F. Murphy, "The Immaculate Heart," in *Mariology*, vol. 3, pp. 168–178.

197. Patrick J. Gaffney, SMM, "The Holy Slavery of Love," in *Mariology*, vol. 3, pp. 143–49.

198. Fr Reginald Garrigou-Lagrange, OP, trans. Fr B. Kelly, *The Mother of the Saviour*, (TAN Books and Publishers, Rockford, 1993), p. 256, n. 19.

199. St Louis de Montfort, *True Devotion to the Blessed Virgin*, (Montfort Press, Liverpool, 1976), p. 1.

200. Gaffney, "The Holy Slavery of Love," in *Mariology*, vol. 3, pp. 150–161.

201. De Montfort, *True Devotion to the Blessed Virgin*, pp. 4–6.

202. Ibid., pp. 18–26.

203. Daniel-Rops, *The Church in the Seventeenth Century*, pp. 251–52; cf. Cragg, *The Church and the Age of Reason*, pp. 199–207.

204. Daniel-Rops, *The Church in the Seventeenth Century*, p. 325.

205. Daniel-Rops, *The Church in the Eighteenth Century*, pp. 22–23.

206. Hazard, *The European Mind (1680–1715)*, pp. 307–18; Hitchcock, *What is Secular Humanism?* p. 37.

207. Hazard, *The European Mind (1680–1715)*, pp. 442–47.

208. From an orthodox Christian point of view, though, this position is not correct, because even China would have received the "primitive revelation" which all ancient peoples have apparently received, particularly belief in one supreme deity, and thus this would have influenced subsequent beliefs.

209. Hazard, *The European Mind (1680–1715)*, pp. 8–28, 85–90.

210. Ibid., pp. 92–98, 109–14; 284–88; cf. Cragg, *The Church and the Age of Reason*, pp. 48–49.

211. De Torre, *Christian Philosophy*, pp. 294, 299.

212. Daniel-Rops, *The Church in the Eighteenth Century*, pp. 36–41; cf. Cragg, *The Church and the Age of Reason*, pp. 234–37, 242–45.

213. Daniel-Rops, *The Church in the Eighteenth Century*, pp. 41–44.
214. Ibid., pp. 45–48; Cragg, *The Church and the Age of Reason*, pp. 239–41; cf. Jacob, *The Radical Enlightenment*, pp. 101–102.
215. Daniel-Rops, *The Church in the Eighteenth Century*, pp. 51–54; Cragg, *The Church and the Age of Reason*, pp. 238–39.
216. Dawson, *The Gods of Revolution*, pp. 34–36; Randall, *The Making of the Modern Mind*, pp. 315–16, 349–54.
217. J. M. Roberts, *The Triumph of the West*, (British Broadcasting Corporation, London, 1985), p. 253.
218. Dawson, *The Dividing of Europe*, pp. 263–67.
219. Hazard, *The European Mind (1680–1715)*, pp. 432–33; Hitchcock, *What is Secular Humanism?* p. 37.
220. Fr E. Cahill, *Freemasonry and the Anti-Christian Movement*, (Gill, Dublin, 1959), pp. 10–13; see also Rev. Robert Bradley, SJ, *The Masonic Movement and the Fatima Message*, (AMI Press, Washington, 1990), pp. 2–4.
221. Daniel-Rops, *The Church in the Eighteenth Century*, pp. 60–65; Cahill, *Freemasonry and the Anti-Christian Movement*, pp. 1–6, 252; Cragg, *The Church and the Age of Reason*, p. 207; cf. Jacob, *The Radical Enlightenment*, pp. 23–24, 27, 38–39, 87–88, 109–11, 121–22.
222. Cahill, *Freemasonry and the Anti-Christian Movement*, pp. 13, 30–31, 65–66; *The Catholic Encyclopedia*, vol. 9, s.v. "Masonry" p. 780.
223. Cf. John Cavanaugh-O'Keefe, *Introduction to Genetics*, (American Life League, Stafford, 1995), p. 20. John Cavanaugh-O'Keefe makes this distinction concerning Genetics; but it seems to apply equally to Freemasonry and indeed to many of the other major ideological movements of modern times.
224. Cahill, *Freemasonry and the Anti-Christian Movement*, pp. 49–50, 54–55, 118–23, 133–34; cf. Jacob, *The Radical Enlightenment*, pp. 112–13, and *The Catholic Encyclopedia*, vol. 9, s.v. "Masonry," pp. 777, 779.
225. Dawson, *Progress and Religion*, p. 5.
226. Cf. E. Braun, "The Roots of the Enlightenment," pp. 4, 6–7, 15, and E. van den Haag, "The Desolation of Reality," pp. 76–78, in *The Ambiguous Legacy of the Enlightenment*. See also von Hildebrand, *Trojan Horse in the City of God*, p. 120.
227. Daniel-Rops, *The Church in the Eighteenth Century*, pp. 173–78; Molland, *Christendom*, 272–74, 283, 292.
228. Bouyer, *Spirit and Forms of Protestantism*, pp. 220–21.
229. Dawson, *The Dividing of Europe*, p. 87; Randall, *The Making of the Modern Mind*, p. 536.
230. Daniel-Rops, *The Church in the Eighteenth Century*, pp. 188–91.
231. Tawney, *Religion and the Rise of Capitalism*, pp. 21–23.
232. Daniel-Rops, *The Church in the Eighteenth Century*, pp. 214–18.
233. Ibid., pp. 236–44.
234. Dawson, *Understanding Europe*, pp. 229–30.
235. Daniel-Rops, *The Church in the Eighteenth Century*, pp. 245–53.
236. Ibid., pp. 258–68; cf. Alec Vidler, *The Church in an Age of Revolution*,

(Penguin, Middlesex, 1971), pp. 11–14.

237. Dawson, *The Dividing of Europe*, pp. 189–91.

238. Dawson, *The Gods of Revolution*, p. 32.

239. Dawson, *The Dividing of Europe*, pp. 269–70; Hitchcock, *What is Secular Humanism?* pp. 49–54.

240. Dawson, *The Gods of Revolution*, pp. 39–46.

241. Roberts, *The Triumph of the West*, pp. 280–81.

242. Dawson, *The Dividing of Europe*, p. 268; Randall, *The Making of the Modern Mind*, pp. 381–82, 383.

243. Dawson, *The Dynamics of World History*, pp. 282–83.

244. Dawson, *The Gods of Revolution*, pp. 51–55.

245. Ibid., pp. 59–60; see also Cahill, *Freemasonry and the Anti-Christian Movement*, pp. 13–14, 98; *The Catholic Encyclopedia*, vol. 9, s.v. "Masonry," p. 781 (quote); but see also Jacob, *The Radical Enlightenment*, pp. 106, 113–14, for a different point of view.

246. *The Catholic Encyclopedia*, vol. 2, "Barruel," p. 310, and vol. 9, s.v. "Masonry," p. 776; cf. Dorinda Outram, *The Enlightenment*, (Cambridge University Press, Cambridge, 1995), pp. 114–16. Outram argues against the idea that there was a conspiracy.

247. Warren H. Carroll, *The Guillotine and the Cross*, (Christendom Press, Front Royal, 1991), pp. 25–27.

248. H. Daniel-Rops, *The Church in an Age of Revolution*, trans. J. Warrington, (J. M. Dent & Sons Ltd, London, 1965), pp. 1–5; Vidler, *The Church in an Age of Revolution*, pp. 14–15.

249. Dawson, *The Gods of Revolution*, p. 69.

250. Daniel-Rops, *The Church in an Age of Revolution*, pp. 6–13.

251. Dawson, *The Gods of Revolution*, pp. 72–75.

252. Ibid., p. 68.

253. Daniel-Rops, *The Church in an Age of Revolution*, pp. 14–21.

254. Carroll, *The Guillotine and the Cross*, p. 44.

255. Ibid., pp. 62–83.

256. Dawson, *The Gods of Revolution*, pp. 103–6.

257. Daniel-Rops, *The Church in an Age of Revolution*, pp. 21–25; Carroll, *The Guillotine and the Cross*, pp. 113–19.

258. Dawson, *The Gods of Revolution*, pp. 92–95; see also Davies, *Europe: A History*, p. 709.

259. Daniel-Rops, *The Church in an Age of Revolution*, pp. 25–34.

260. Carroll, *The Guillotine and the Cross*, p. 183.

261. Ibid., pp. 102–3.

262. Daniel-Rops, *The Church in an Age of Revolution*, pp. 40–45.

263. Dawson, *The Gods of Revolution*, pp. 116–25; see also Davies, *Europe: A History*, pp. 703–4.

264. Dawson, *The Dynamics of World History*, pp. 227–28; Dawson, *The Dividing of Europe*, pp. 275–81.

265. Daniel-Rops, *The Church in an Age of Revolution*, pp. 50–62.

266. Hales, *The Catholic Church in the Modern World*, pp. 58–59; Vidler, *The Church in an Age of Revolution*, pp. 18–20.

267. Daniel-Rops, *The Church in an Age of Revolution*, pp. 75–81, 92–99, 103–6.
268. Dawson, *The Gods of Revolution*, pp. 150–54.
269. Carroll, *The Guillotine and the Cross*, pp. 198–200.
270. Dawson, *The Dividing of Europe*, p. 287.
271. Daniel-Rops, *The Church in an Age of Revolution*, pp. 128, 141–45.
272. Daniel-Rops, *The Church in an Age of Revolution*, pp. 119–20; Dawson, *The Judgement of the Nations*, p. 61.
273. Hales, *The Catholic Church in the Modern World*, pp. 76–81; Harry Hearder, *Europe in the Nineteenth Century, 1830–1880*, (Longman, London, 1988), pp. 32–33.
274. Dawson, *The Dividing of Europe*, pp. 191–92.
275. Dawson, *The Gods of Revolution*, pp. 129–38; see also Aidan Nichols, OP, *Catholic Thought since the Enlightenment, A Survey*, (Unisa Press, Pretoria, 1988), pp. 36–38.
276. Dawson, *The Dividing of Europe*, pp. 268–69.
277. Daniel-Rops, *The Church in an Age of Revolution*, pp. 157–62; Peter Gay and R. K. Webb, *Modern Europe Since 1815*, (Harper & Row, New York, 1973), p. 680.
278. Randall, *The Making of the Modern Mind*, pp. 421–22, 458–59; Outram, *The Enlightenment*, pp. 58–60.
279. Rev. Michael Walsh, *The Apparition at Knock*, (St Jarlath's College, Tuam, 1959), p. 69; see also R. Garrigou-Lagrange, *The Three Ages of the Interior Life*, vol. 2, trans. M. Timothea Doyle, (B. Herder Book Co., St Louis, 1948), pp. 586–88.
280. Walsh, *The Apparition at Knock*, p. 12; see also A. Tanquery, *The Spiritual Life, A Treatise on Ascetical and Mystical Theology*, (Desclée, Belgium, 1950), pp. 704–705, and A. Poulain, *The Graces of Interior Prayer*, (Kegan Paul, London, 1912), p. 302.
281. This last point parallels the attitude taken in the episcopal investigation of the apparitions at Beauraing. See Mgsr Edouard Ranwez, "The Value of the Episcopal Declarations concerning the events at Beauraing," in *Marian Library Studies*, no. 96, (Marian Library, Dayton, 1963), pp. 2–3. Similarly, the term "visionary," at least in English, seems to have acquired a negative sense, that is a description of a false "seer," and so has not been used here in discussing the approved Marian apparitions.
282. Fr Frederick M. Jelly OP, "Discerning the Miraculous: Norms for Judging Apparitions and Private Revelations," in *Marian Studies* 44, (1993), p. 44.
283. Fr Karl Rahner, SJ, *Visions and Prophecies*, (Burns & Oates, London, 1963), pp. 31–39, n. 37, 51, n. 47.
284. Hilda Graef, *Mary: A History Of Doctrine and Devotion*, pt 2, (Sheed & Ward, London, 1994), pp. 144–45.
285. Walsh, *The Apparition at Knock*, pp. 68–69; see also Poulain, *The Graces of Interior Prayer*, pp. 351–61, 382.
286. Cf. John Beevers, *The Golden Heart: the Story of Beauraing*, (Browne &

Nolan, Dublin, 1956), pp. 57–59.

287. Poulain, *The Graces of Interior Prayer*, pp. 349–50.

288. Kevin Orlin Johnson, *Apparitions: Mystic Phenomena and what they mean*, (Panagaeus Press, Dallas, 1998), pp. 286–88; Walsh, *The Apparition at Knock*, p. 10. See also Jordan Aumann, OP, *Spiritual Theology*, (Our Sunday Visitor, Huntington, 1980), pp. 428–29. On this point Fr Jelly says: "According to Vatican II's *Dei Verbum*, the magisterium of the Church has the charism of infallibility only when Scripture and Tradition, in mutual interdependence, form the foundation for a dogma—whether solemnly defined by an ecumenical council, by an *ex cathedra* pronouncement of the Pope, or by the universal ordinary magisterium, that is the constant preaching and teaching (*sensus fidelium*) of the Church as a whole. The certitude that can be reached as a result of investigating apparitions and private revelations can never be the certitude of divine faith ..." Jelly, "Discerning the Miraculous: Norms for Judging Apparitions and Private Revelations," in *Marian Studies* 44, (1993), p. 44.

289. Walsh, *The Apparition at Knock*, pp. 12–13.

290. William G. Most, *Mary in our Life*, (The Mercier Press, Cork, 1955), p. 217.

291. Cf. Joseph de Sainte-Marie, OCD, *Reflections on the Act of Consecration at Fatima of Pope John Paul II on 13th May 1982*, trans. W. Lawson, (Augustine Publishing Company, Devon, 1983), pp. 23–24; and Ranwez, "The Value of the Episcopal Declarations concerning the events at Beauraing," in *Marian Library Studies*, 96, pp. 3–4.

292. Louis Lochet, *Apparitions of Our Lady, Their Place in the life of the Church* (Herder, Freiburg, 1960), pp. 46–48, 68, 72, 81–86.

293. Walsh, *The Apparition at Knock*, pp. 13–14; Lochet, *Apparitions of Our Lady*, pp. 34–35.

294. See Manelli, *All Generations Shall Call Me Blessed*, pp. 50–58.

295. Boniface Ramsey OP, *Beginning to Read the Fathers*, (Darton, Longman & Todd, London, 1986), pp. 16, 22, 25, 27–31; see also G. W. H. Lampe, *Essays on Typology*, pt 1," The Reasonableness of Typology," (SCM Press, London, 1957), pp. 29–31.

296. Jean Daniélou, SJ, *From Shadows to Reality: Studies in the Biblical Typology of the Fathers*, trans. W. Hibberd, (Burns & Oates, London, 1960), pp. 149, 157. St John Chrysostom also saw such a link: "Prophecy in type is that which takes place in deeds or in historical realities; the other prophecy is one in words. For God has persuaded some by highly insightful words, while he has bolstered the certitude of others, the less sophisticated, through the vision of events." St John Chrysostom, *Sixth Sermon on Penance, n. 4*, PG 49:320, quoted in Bertrand de Margerie, SJ, *An Introduction to the History of Exegesis*, 1, *The Greek Fathers*, trans. L. Maluf, (Saint Bede's Publications, Petersham, 1993), p. 169.

297. Manelli, *All Generations Shall Call Me Blessed*, pp. 50, n. 1, 82–83, n. 1, 84–89.

298. Ibid., pp. 58–64.
299. The official position of the Church regarding typology in its main Christological sense is set out in the *Catechism* as follows: "The Church, as early as apostolic times, and then constantly in her Tradition, has illuminated the unity of the divine plan in the two Testaments through *typology*, which discerns in God's works of the Old Covenant prefigurations of what he accomplished in the fullness of time in the person of his incarnate Son," no. 128. See also 129 and 130.
300. Henri de Lubac, *Medieval Exegesis*, vol. 1, *The Four Senses of Scripture*, (T & T Clark, Edinburgh, 1998), pp. 259, 452, n. 86; see also Woollcombe, *Essays on Typology*, pt 2, "The Biblical Origins and Patristic Development of Typology," pp. 39–40, n. 1.
301. André Feuillet, *Jesus and His Mother*, trans. L. Maluf, (St Bede's Publications, Massachusetts, 1984), pp. 12–14; see also John Saward, *Redeemer in the Womb*, (Ignatius Press, San Francisco, 1993), pp. 27–28. St Luke's approach here does not correspond to *midrash*, a Jewish way of reflecting on Scripture so as to bring out its significance. This was more concerned with providing a commentary or explanation with a homiletic purpose, than in a literal interpretation of the text.
302. Joseph Dirvin, CM, *Saint Catherine Labouré of the Miraculous Medal*, (TAN Books and Publishers, Rockford, 1984), pp. 15–17, 21–22, 25–26.
303. Ibid., pp. 36, 59–67, 75–78.
304. Rev. Réne Laurentin, *The Life of Catherine Labouré*, trans. P. Inwood, (Collins, London, 1983), pp. 71–73.
305. Ibid., pp. 73–76.
306. Dirvin, *Saint Catherine Labouré*, pp. 86–87.
307. Daniel-Rops, *The Church in an Age of Revolution*, pp. 182–85; Dirvin, *Saint Catherine Labouré*, pp. 88–90.
308. Daniel-Rops, *The Church in an Age of Revolution*, pp. 176–82.
309. Laurentin, *The Life of Catherine Labouré*, p. 79.
310. Dirvin, *Saint Catherine Labouré*, pp. 92–93.
311. See Jaroslav Pelikan, *Mary Through the Centuries: Her Place in the History of Culture*, (Yale University Press, New Haven, 1996), pp. 130–33.
312. Fr H. M. Manteau-Bonamy, OP, *Immaculate Conception and the Holy Spirit: The Marian Teachings of Father Kolbe*, (Prow Books/Franciscan Marytown Press, Libertyville, 1977), pp. 92, 98.
313. Laurentin, *The Life of Catherine Labouré*, p. 80.
314. Dirvin, *Saint Catherine Labouré*, pp. 94–105.
315. Laurentin, *The Life of Catherine Labouré*, pp. 92–93, 109–11.
316. Ibid., pp. 102, 280.
317. Dirvin, *Saint Catherine Labouré*, pp. 113–20.
318. Laurentin, *The Life of Catherine Labouré*, p. 97.
319. Dirvin, *Saint Catherine Labouré*, pp. 156–63.

320. Gambero, *Mary and the Fathers of the Church*, p. 405, *Homily 1 on the Dormition* 8; PG 96: 713A.

321. Ibid., p. 403, *Homily on the Nativity* 3; PG 96:665 A.

322. *Theotokos: A Theological Encyclopedia of the Blessed Virgin Mary*, 2d ed., s.v. "Mediation, Mary Mediatress," p. 240, (*Serm. II in Annunt. S. Mariae*, in PG 89:1389); pp. 8, 338.

323. There is an oblique reference to Jacob's ladder in St John's Gospel, on the occasion when Nathanael confessed his belief in Jesus as the Messiah. This happened just after Jesus had revealed some mysterious knowledge he had of Nathanael, telling him that he would see great things including, "heaven opened, and the angels of God ascending and descending upon the Son of Man" (John 1:47–51). This text implies that we are meant to take the account of Jacob's ladder seriously.

324. Laurentin, *The Life of Catherine Labouré*, p. 74.

325. Ibid., p. 75.

326. Louis Bouyer, *Woman and Man with God*, (Darton, Longman & Todd, London, 1960), pp. 39–40; Manelli, *All Generations Shall Call Me Blessed*, pp. 351–62.

327. Don Sharkey, *The Woman Shall Conquer*, (The Bruce Publishing Company, Milwaukee, 1952), p. 25.

328. Dirvin, *Saint Catherine Labouré*, pp. 121–22.

329. Ibid., p. 122.

330. Calkins, *Totus Tuus*, p. 67.

331. Dirvin, *Saint Catherine Labouré*, pp. 164–66. Another French Sister of Charity, Appolline Andreveux, living in Troyes, was privileged with several apparitions during 1845, this time of Christ suffering his Passion. In July 1846 he again appeared to her holding in his hand a red scapular, one part of which had a picture of Christ on the cross with the instruments used for his Crucifixion, and the words, "Holy Passion of Our Lord Jesus Christ, save us." The other part had an image of the Hearts of Jesus and Mary under a cross and the words, "Sacred Hearts of Jesus and Mary, protect us." She was more fortunate than her two predecessors, and this scapular was approved by Pius IX in 1847.

332. Ibid., pp. 166–68.

333. Ibid., pp. 168–70.

334. Christopher Hollis, The *Breakdown of Money*, (Sheed & Ward, London, 1934), pp. 12–18; Belloc, *The Crisis of Civilization*, pp. 133–37.

335. Daniel-Rops, *The Church in an Age of Revolution*, pp. 316–19; Randall, *The Making of the Modern Mind*, pp. 358–63, 444–45, 579–80, 603–604; Hearder, *Europe in the Nineteenth Century, 1830–1880*, pp. 51–52; Dawson, *Understanding Europe*, pp. 247–48.

336. Randall, *The Making of the Modern Mind*, pp. 328–29.

337. Hollis, *The Breakdown of Money*, p. 6; Randall, *The Making of the Modern Mind*, pp. 329–31.

338. Hollis, *The Breakdown of Money*, pp. 1–12; Hearder, *Europe in the*

Nineteenth Century, 1830–1880, pp. 130–39; cf. Vidler, *The Church in an Age of Revolution,* pp. 91–94.

339. Hollis, *The Breakdown of Money,* pp. xix–xx; see also Gay and Webb, *Modern Europe Since 1815,* p. 599; Hearder, *Europe in the Nineteenth Century, 1830–1880,* pp. 88–89.

340. Vidler, *The Church in an Age of Revolution,* pp. 68–73.

341. Daniel-Rops, *The Church in an Age of Revolution,* pp. 232–34.

342. Ibid., pp. 237–42.

343. John Beevers, *The Sun Her Mantle,* (Browne & Nolan Ltd, Dublin, 1954), pp. 23–24.

344. Fr Jean Jaouen, *A Grace called La Salette,* trans. N. Théroux, (La Salette Publications, Attleboro, 1991), pp. 37–40; Beevers, *The Sun Her Mantle,* p. 26.

345. Archbishop William Ullathorne, *The Holy Mountain of La Salette,* (Preserving Christian Publications, Albany, 1996), p. 33.

346. Jaouen, *A Grace called La Salette,* pp. 40–42, 49–50; Beevers, *The Sun Her Mantle,* pp. 26–28.

347. Jaouen, *A Grace called La Salette,* p. 42; Beevers, *The Sun Her Mantle,* pp. 29–30.

348. Jaouen, *A Grace called La Salette,* pp. 42–44; Beevers, *The Sun Her Mantle,* pp. 30–31.

349. Jaouen, *A Grace called La Salette,* pp. 44–52; Beevers, *The Sun Her Mantle,* pp. 31–33.

350. Jaouen, *A Grace called La Salette,* pp. 3–5, 52; Beevers, *The Sun Her Mantle,* pp. 35–36.

351. Jaouen, *A Grace called La Salette,* pp. 9–14; Beevers, *The Sun Her Mantle,* pp. 36–41.

352. Jaouen, *A Grace called La Salette,* pp. 55–56, 63, 66–69, 84–85, 150–51; Beevers, *The Sun Her Mantle,* pp. 41–43.

353. Ullathorne, *The Holy Mountain of La Salette,* pp. 78–81, 85; see also Jaouen, *A Grace called La Salette,* pp. 160–164.

354. Beevers, *The Sun Her Mantle,* pp. 44–50.

355. Ibid., pp. 50–51.

356. Francis Trochu, *The Curé d'Ars,* (Burns, Oates & Washbourne, London, 1949), p. 281.

357. Jaouen, *A Grace called La Salette,* pp. 71; Beevers, *The Sun Her Mantle,* pp. 56–60.

358. Jaouen, *A Grace called La Salette,* pp. 188–224; Beevers, *The Sun Her Mantle,* pp. 62–66.

359. Trochu, *The Curé d'Ars,* pp. 510–11.

360. Ullathorne, *The Holy Mountain of La Salette,* pp. 93–99.

361. Jaouen, *A Grace called La Salette,* pp. 74–78; Beevers, *The Sun Her Mantle,* pp. 67–71. In opposition to this view of the secrets, however, we have the testimony of Fr Giraud, one of the first Missionaries of Our Lady of La Salette. He had an audience with Pius IX during which he was told by the Pope that the secrets were very vague and quite commonplace. He apparently told Fr Giraud that Fathers

Rousselot and Gerin had been in quite an emotional state during their audience. Thus they may have misinterpreted Pius IX's reaction to the secrets. It is certainly possible that the expressions attributed above to the Pope can be interpreted in an "ordinary" way, without assuming that the secrets have a particularly dreadful content. These points were made by Fr Louis de Pontbriand, Rector of the shrine at La Salette, and Fr Jean Stern, in private correspondence with the author. See also Stern, *La Salette, Documents authentiques,* vol. 3, (La Salette, 1991), p. 48.

362. Jaouen, *A Grace called La Salette,* pp. 79–82, 87–89, 177–79, 225–55; Beevers, *The Sun Her Mantle,* pp. 72–80.

363. Jaouen, *A Grace called La Salette,* pp. 257–62, 267–72; Beevers, *The Sun Her Mantle,* pp. 80–104. Other writers view Mélanie differently, almost as a saint. See, for example, Mary Alice Dennis, *Melanie,* (TAN Books and Publishers, Rockford, 1995).

364. Graef, *Mary: A History Of Doctrine and Devotion,* pt 2, p. 101, n. 1. Graef further points to alleged similarities between the discourse of Mary to the two children and a document called the *Letter fallen from heaven,* a poorly-written work concerned with a lack of Sunday observance in circulation at the time. However, Jean Jaouen, author of an authoritative work on La Salette, *A Grace called La Salette,* argues that as regards religious content, style, order, and emphasis, the *Letter fallen from heaven* and Mary's message are as different as night and day, even if there are some purely accidental verbal similarities between some of their expressions. Graef, *Mary: A History Of Doctrine and Devotion,* pt 2, p. 103; see also Jaouen, *A Grace called La Salette,* p. 175, and Joachim Bouflet and Philippe Boutry, *Un signe dans le ciel: Les apparitions de la Vierge,* (Bernard Grasset, Paris, 1997), pp. 129–33.

365. Graef, *Mary: A History Of Doctrine and Devotion,* pt 2, p. 103; but cf. Jaouen, *A Grace called La Salette,* pp. 152–54.

366. Verses 17–26 in other versions.

367. Beevers, *The Sun Her Mantle,* p. 30, 32.

368. Daniel-Rops, *The Church in an Age of Revolution,* pp. 242–43; Gay and Webb, *Modern Europe Since 1815,* pp. 714–15; Hearder, *Europe in the Nineteenth Century, 1830–1880,* pp. 62–63, 125–27, 162.

369. Daniel-Rops, *The Church in an Age of Revolution,* pp. 247–50; cf. Vidler, *The Church in an Age of Revolution,* pp. 74–75.

370. Daniel-Rops, *The Church in an Age of Revolution,* pp. 322–25.

371. Fanfani, *Catholicism, Protestantism and Capitalism,* pp. 60–61.

372. Daniel-Rops, *The Church in an Age of Revolution,* pp. 326–35.

373. Ibid., pp. 252–55.

374. Ibid., pp. 255–56.

375. See, for example, Ignace de la Potterie, SJ, *Mary in the Mystery of the Covenant,* trans. B. Buby, (Alba House, New York, 1992), pp. 7–13.

376. Paul F. Palmer, SJ, *Mary in the Documents of the Church,* (Burns Oates, London, 1953), p. 53; see also *Theotokos: A Theological Encyclopedia of*

the Blessed Virgin Mary, 2d ed., s.v. "Proclus of Constantinople," p. 296.

377. Daniel-Rops, *The Church in an Age of Revolution*, pp. 257–61; cf. Vidler, *The Church in an Age of Revolution*, pp. 249–50.

378. O. Chadwick, "Great Britain and Europe," in *The Oxford History of Christianity*, pp. 368–69; see also Gay and Webb, *Modern Europe Since 1815*, pp. 781, 786.

379. Daniel-Rops, *The Church in an Age of Revolution*, pp. 265–69; Hales, *The Catholic Church in the Modern World*, p. 126.

380. Mgr Joseph Deery, *Our Lady of Lourdes*, (Browne & Nolan, Dublin, 1958), pp. 9–15.

381. Ibid., pp. 16–20, 25.

382. Réne Laurentin, *Bernadette of Lourdes*, trans. J. Drury, (Darton, Longman & Todd, London, 1980), pp. 34–38.

383. Michel de Saint-Pierre, *Bernadette and Lourdes*, (Hutchinson, London, 1954), pp. 40–41; Laurentin, *Bernadette of Lourdes*, pp. 40–41.

384. Laurentin, *Bernadette of Lourdes*, pp. 42–44; see also Deery, *Our Lady of Lourdes*, p. 23.

385. This was the day that Bernadette was reported to have heard "diabolical voices," but according to Réne Laurentin, the French Mariologist, there are good reasons for discounting this report since it was based only on indirect and somewhat suspect evidence. See Réne Laurentin, *Les Apparitions de Lourdes*, (P. Lethielleux, Paris, 1987), p. 71.

386. Laurentin, *Bernadette of Lourdes*, p. 45; de Saint-Pierre, *Bernadette and Lourdes*, pp. 50–51, 55–56.

387. Deery, *Our Lady of Lourdes*, p. 24.

388. Laurentin, *Bernadette of Lourdes*, pp. 45–51; Deery, *Our Lady of Lourdes*, pp. 27–29.

389. Laurentin, *Bernadette of Lourdes*, pp. 55–57, 94.

390. Ibid., pp. 58–63; Laurentin, *Les Apparitions de Lourdes*, p. 123.

391. Deery, *Our Lady of Lourdes*, pp. 31–32.

392. Ibid., pp. 33–34, 44–46.

393. De Saint-Pierre, *Bernadette and Lourdes*, pp. 79–80.

394. Deery, *Our Lady of Lourdes*, pp. 143–45.

395. Kselman, *Miracles and Prophecies in Nineteenth-Century France*, p. 197.

396. Theodore Mangiapan, *Lourdes: Miraculous Cures*, (Lourdes, 1987), pp. 26–27.

397. Deery, *Our Lady of Lourdes*, pp. 35–36.

398. Sandra Zimdars-Swartz argues that the presence of a copy of a broadsheet related to La Salette at this shrine, "suggests that the messages and miracles of La Salette played an important part in shaping people's expectations and experiences of Lourdes." Obviously there is a degree of truth in this, but at the same time, there must have been *really* miraculous events happening at Lourdes, otherwise such expectations would very quickly have been

dashed. See Sandra Zimdars-Swartz, *Encountering Mary: From La Salette to Medjugorje*, (Princeton University Press, Princeton, 1991), p. 58.

399. Laurentin, *Bernadette of Lourdes*, pp. 81–82.
400. Ibid., pp. 25, 183, (quote), *emphasis added.*
401. Deery, *Our Lady of Lourdes*, pp. 37–38.
402. Laurentin, *Bernadette of Lourdes*, p. 83.
403. Deery, *Our Lady of Lourdes*, pp. 46–48.
404. Ibid., pp. 48–49.
405. Laurentin, *Bernadette of Lourdes*, pp. 86–90.
406. Ibid., pp. 111–13.
407. Deery, *Our Lady of Lourdes*, pp. 50–52.
408. Laurentin, *Bernadette of Lourdes*, pp. 225–36.
409. Deery, *Our Lady of Lourdes*, pp. 85–87.
410. *Theotokos: A Theological Encyclopedia of the Blessed Virgin Mary*, 2d ed., pp. 101, 113, 170, 296; Gambero, *Mary and the Fathers of the Church*, p. 235.
411. Ibid., s.v. "Severus of Antioch," p. 325, (*Critique du Tome de Julien d'Halicarnasse*, 111).
412. Buby, *Mary of Galilee*, vol. 3, pp. 245–46, (*In Natalitia Domini*, PG 46: 1133).
413. Ronald Knox, *Occasional Sermons*, ed. Philip Caraman, (Burns & Oates, London, 1960), pp. 85–87.
414. Ibid., pp. 85, 89.
415. Manteau-Bonamy, *Immaculate Conception and the Holy Spirit*, pp. 5, 7, 47, 49, 72, 74, 123,132.
416. Ibid., p. 7.
417. Kselman, *Miracles and Prophecies in Nineteenth-Century France*, pp. 4–8.
418. Ibid., p. 37.
419. Ibid., p. 110.
420. Ibid., pp. 40–41, 46–47.
421. Ibid., pp. 55–56.
422. Ibid., pp. 144–45.
423. Ibid., pp. 147–60. Between 1928 and 1971 one writer compiled a list of over two hundred alleged Marian apparitions, of which only two, Beauraing and Banneux in Belgium, were accepted by the Church. See Michael O'Carroll, CSSp, *Medjugorje: Facts, Documents, Theology*, (Veritas, Dublin, 1986), p. 7. Some of the major nineteenth-century apparitions, such as Lourdes, were followed by reports of further false apparitions.
424. See Rev. Robert Bradley, SJ, *Fatima and Modernism*, (AMI Press, Washington, 1991), p. 10.
425. Randall, *The Making of the Modern Mind*, pp. 461–63, 554–55.
426. De Torre, *Christian Philosophy*, pp. 307–8; Daniel-Rops, *The Church in an Age of Revolution*, pp. 311–14; Randall, *The Making of the Modern Mind*, pp. 485–88; Hearder, *Europe in the Nineteenth Century, 1830–1880*, pp. 397–99.

427. Hearder, *Europe in the Nineteenth Century, 1830–1880*, pp. 399–400.

428. Dawson, *Progress and Religion*, p. 21; Randall, *The Making of the Modern Mind*, pp. 489–90; G. Niemeyer, "Enlightenment to Ideology: the Apotheosis of the Human Mind," in *The Ambiguous Legacy of the Enlightenment*, pp. 57–60.

429. For more information on the Church and Creation/Evolution see Gerard J. Keane's *Creation Rediscovered: Evolution and the Importance of the Origins Debate*, (TAN Books and Publishers, Rockford, 1999).

430. Randall, *The Making of the Modern Mind*, pp. 506–7; cf. Belloc, *The Crisis of Civilization*, pp. 155–58; Paul Johnson, *Modern Times: The World from the Twenties to the Eighties*, (Harper & Row, New York, 1983), pp. 5, 117–18; cf. Chadwick, *Secularization of the European Mind in the Nineteenth Century*, pp. 180–81, 241. For evidence about Freud's cocaine addiction and the effect this had on the development of his psychoanalytic theories, see E. M. Thornton, *The Freudian Fallacy, Freud and Cocaine*, (Paladin, London, 1986). For evidence about his possible sexual deviancy and other aberrations, see E. Michael Jones, *Degenerate Moderns*, (Ignatius Press, San Francisco, 1993), pp. 153–233. For details of the flawed nature of both Darwin and evolution itself see M. Bowden, *The Rise of the Evolution Fraud*, (Sovereign Publications, Bromley, 1982).

431. De Torre, *Christian Philosophy*, p. 306.

432. H. Daniel-Rops, *A Fight for God*, trans. J. Warrington, (J. M. Dent & Sons Ltd, London, 1966), pp. 24–25; see also Hearder, *Europe in the Nineteenth Century, 1830–1880*, pp. 62–66. It is possible that Marx was a Satanist, and certainly he seems to have been motivated by a hatred for humanity. See Fr Robert Fox, *Fatima Today*, (Christendom, Front Royal, 1983), pp. 205–12.

433. Dawson, *The Dynamics of World History*, pp. 356–58.

434. Daniel-Rops, *A Fight for God*, pp. 25–27; Belloc, *The Crisis of Civilization*, pp. 139–41.

435. Dawson, *Progress and Religion*, pp. 27–32, (quote); Vidler, *The Church in an Age of Revolution*, pp. 28–29.

436. Dawson, *Understanding Europe*, pp. 188 (quote), 190–91, 195.

437. Daniel-Rops, *The Church in an Age of Revolution*, pp. 267–68; Hitchcock, *What is Secular Humanism?* p. 48.

438. Daniel-Rops, *The Church in an Age of Revolution*, pp. 268–75, 278–83.

439. Gay and Webb, *Modern Europe Since 1815*, pp. 760–66, 804–6; Hearder, *Europe in the Nineteenth Century, 1830–1880*, pp. 114–15.

440. Daniel-Rops, *The Church in an Age of Revolution*, pp. 283–85; Nichols, *Catholic Thought since the Enlightenment, A Survey*, pp. 65–66.

441. *The Catholic Encyclopedia*, vol. 2, s.v. "Bosco," pp. 689 ff.

442. See E. M. Brown, ed., *Dreams, Visions and Prophecies of Don Bosco*, (Don Bosco Publications, New Rochelle, 1986), pp. 105–8, for details of this dream.

443. Daniel-Rops, *The Church in an Age of Revolution*, pp. 286–89.

444. Ibid., pp. 289–98; see also Randall, *The Making of the Modern Mind*, pp. 544–45.
445. Daniel-Rops, *The Church in an Age of Revolution*, pp. 299–302; Hearder, *Europe in the Nineteenth Century, 1830–1880*, p. 170.
446. Cahill, *Freemasonry and the Anti-Christian Movement*, pp. 123–26.
447. Gay and Webb, *Modern Europe Since 1815*, p. 803; *The Catholic Encyclopedia*, vol. 9, s.v. "Masonry," p. 781.
448. Cahill, *Freemasonry and the Anti-Christian Movement*, pp. 126–30.
449. *The Catholic Encyclopedia*, vol. 9, s.v. "Masonry," p. 781.
450. Daniel-Rops, *The Church in an Age of Revolution*, pp. 307–9.
451. W. R. Farmer, "State Interesse and Marcan Priority," in *The Four Gospels: 1992*, vol. 3, ed. F. van Segbroeck et al., (Leuven University Press, 1992), pp. 2478, 2483–84, 2490–96.
452. Hales, *The Catholic Church in the Modern World*, pp. 229–31; Daniel-Rops, *A Fight for God*, pp. 85–97; Gay and Webb, *Modern Europe Since 1815*, pp. 794, 801, 917.
453. Beevers, *The Sun Her Mantle*, pp. 120–22.
454. R. Laurentin and A. Durand, *Pontmain Histoire Authentique, Un Signe dans le Ciel*, (Apostolat des Editions & P. Lethielleux, Paris, 1971), pp. 28–30; Beevers, *The Sun Her Mantle*, pp. 122–24.
455. Laurentin and Durand, *Pontmain Histoire Authentique*, p. 34.
456. Beevers, *The Sun Her Mantle*, pp. 124–25.
457. Ibid., pp. 125–27. Earlier that evening, at the Reuilly house of Catherine Labouré, the sisters observed the remarkable color of the western sky, which some felt was an omen. Catherine looked but said nothing, although later, when the events of Pontmain became known, it was suspected that she had some inkling of what had happened. It appears that she certainly believed that Mary appeared there, since she said as much to a fellow nun in 1872, telling her to send her prayer intentions to the village, because, "the Blessed Virgin revealed herself there ..." Laurentin, *The Life of Catherine Labouré*, pp. 169, 196.
458. Beevers, *The Sun Her Mantle*, pp. 127–28.
459. Laurentin and Durand, *Pontmain Histoire Authentique*, pp. 75–95.
460. Fr M. Richard, *What Happened at Pontmain*, (Ave Maria Institute, Washington, 1971), pp. 20–21.
461. Carroll, *The Cult of the Virgin Mary*, p. 199; see also Laurentin and Durand, *Pontmain Histoire Authentique*, p. 23.
462. Richard, *What Happened at Pontmain*, pp. 29–30; Laurentin and Durand, *Pontmain Histoire Authentique*, pp. 28–30.
463. Chiron, *Enquête sur les Apparitions de la Vierge*, p. 224. Michael Carroll then goes on to imply that the additional details reported by the children, as the apparition progressed, were deliberately made up by them. He adds that the children were probably "unconsciously" prompted to report certain things, such as the message "But pray my children," by the commotion caused by a man entering the village, seeing the crowd, hearing the prayers and hymns and saying, "You

have only to pray! The Prussians are at Laval." Again, however, this a purely gratuitous suggestion, and implies that the children were deluded or frauds. Carroll, *The Cult of the Virgin Mary*, p. 201.

464. Richard, *What Happened at Pontmain*, pp. 40–41, n. 21.

465. McVey, *Ephrem the Syrian, Hymns*, p. 373, (Hymns on Virginity, 25.11).

466. Ibid., pp. 151–52, nn. 371, 372, (Hymns on the Nativity, 16.16–17).

467. Gambero, *Mary and the Fathers of the Church*, p. 351.

468. Ibid., p. 409, *Homily 1 on the Dormition* 12–13; PG 96:717 D–720 C.

469. Richard, *What Happened at Pontmain*, p. 76, n. 4.

470. Ibid., p. 32.

471. Ibid., p. 36, also n. 14.

472. Ibid., p. 36.

473. Laurentin and Durand, *Pontmain Histoire Authentique*, pp. 154–55.

474. This connection between Mary at Pontmain and the Jewish high priest might give rise to the idea that perhaps Mary could be identified with the idea of priesthood generally, and thus that such an identification might give indirect support to the idea of women priests within the Catholic Church. But the adoption of such an attitude would be to misunderstand the typology of this apparition. It is not concerned with the *person* of the high priest as such, but rather with his significance as a Marian type, and in particular with the idea that he acted as an intercessor for the people.

475. *Theotokos: A Theological Encyclopedia of the Blessed Virgin Mary*, 2d ed., s.v. "Ambrose," p. 19, (*Exhort. Virg. V. 31*, PL 16:345).

476. McVey, *Ephrem the Syrian, Hymns*, p. 65, (Hymns on the Nativity 1.17).

477. Gambero, *Mary and the Fathers of the Church*, p. 368, *In Ezechielem* 2, 8, 9; PL 76: 1033–34.

478. Laurentin, *The Life of Catherine Labouré*, p. 187; see also Gay and Webb, *Modern Europe Since 1815*, pp. 813–14.

479. Dirvin, *Saint Catherine Labouré*, pp. 197–208.

480. Daniel-Rops, *A Fight for God*, pp. 82–84.

481. Laurentin, *The Life of Catherine Labouré*, pp. 96, 212, 238.

482. Dirvin, *Saint Catherine Labouré*, pp. 208–24.

483. Dirvin, *Saint Catherine Labouré*, pp. 225–30; Laurentin, *The Life of Catherine Labouré*, p. 263.

484. Gillett, *Famous Shrines of Our Lady*, vol. 1, pp. 175–76.

485. Ibid., pp. 176–78.

486. Ibid., pp. 178–80.

487. Sharkey, *The Woman Shall Conquer*, pp. 89–90.

488. Gillett, *Famous Shrines of Our Lady*, vol. 1, p. 180; Sharkey, *The Woman Shall Conquer*, pp. 90–91.

489. Br Francis Mary, *Marian Shrines of Italy*, (Academy of the Immaculate, New Bedford, 2000), p. 146.

490. There were a number of other Marian apparitions during this general period, including Philippsdorf (1866) in Bohemia,

Pellevoisin (1876) in France, and Gietrzwalde (1877) in Poland, but none of these has assumed any sort of "international" status. See also Chiron, *Enquête sur les Apparitions de la Vierge*, pp. 220–24, 241–55, 255–59.

491. Catherine Rynne, *Knock 1879–1979*, (Veritas, Dublin, 1979), pp. 1–4; Gay and Webb, *Modern Europe Since 1815*, p. 819; Hearder, *Europe in the Nineteenth Century, 1830–1880*, pp. 94–95, 119–20.

492. Walsh, *The Apparition at Knock*, p. 113.

493. Rynne, *Knock 1879–1979*, p. 9.

494. Mary Purcell, "Our Lady of Silence," in J. Delaney, ed., *A Woman clothed with the Sun*, (Doubleday, New York, 1961), pp. 147–50.

495. Rynne, *Knock 1879–1979*, p. 10.

496. Walsh, *The Apparition at Knock*, p. 22.

497. Purcell, "Our Lady of Silence," in *A Woman clothed with the Sun*, pp. 150–53.

498. Ibid., pp. 153–54; Rynne, *Knock 1879–1979*, pp. 15–16.

499. Purcell, "Our Lady of Silence," in *A Woman clothed with the Sun*, pp. 154–56.

500. Walsh, *The Apparition at Knock*, p. 20.

501. Purcell, "Our Lady of Silence," in *A Woman clothed with the Sun*, pp. 156–58.

502. Walsh, *The Apparition at Knock*, pp. 25–26.

503. Ibid., pp. 36, 43–44.

504. Ibid., pp. 72, 74–78.

505. Ibid., pp. 78–81.

506. Ibid., pp. 15–18.

507. Rynne, *Knock 1879–1979*, pp. 63–66.

508. Ibid., pp. 52–53.

509. Walsh, *The Apparition at Knock*, p. 20.

510. Purcell, "Our Lady of Silence," in *A Woman clothed with the Sun*, pp. 161–63.

511. Rynne, *Knock 1879–1979*, pp. 123–30.

512. Ibid., pp. 4–6.

513. Ibid., pp. 96–97.

514. Purcell, "Our Lady of Silence," in *A Woman clothed with the Sun*, pp. 163–68.

515. Ibid., pp. 166–68.

516. Rynne, *Knock 1879–1979*, pp. 106–107, 132–33, 155–56.

517. *Theotokos: A Theological Encyclopedia of the Blessed Virgin Mary*, 2nd ed., s.v. "Ark," p. 50, *In Ps.*, 23(22), *apud* Theodoret. "Dial I," in GCS, 1, 2, 147.

518. Buby, *Mary of Galilee*, vol. 3, p. 107, from Campos, *Corpus Marianum Partisticum*, pars. II, p. 63 (#556). Fr Michael O'Carroll comments that if this passage is not by St Athanasius then it is still probably from a fourth-century writer. *Theotokos: A Theological Encyclopedia of the Blessed Virgin Mary*, 2d ed., pp. 50, 62.

519. *Theotokos: A Theological Encyclopedia of the Blessed Virgin Mary*, 2d ed., s.v. "Ark," p. 50, (*In S. Mariam Deip.*, in PO 19:338).

520. Ibid., pp. 25, 50, 200, 325.
521. Gambero, *Mary and the Fathers of the Church*, p. 256.
522. Rynne, *Knock 1879–1979*, p. 27.
523. Walsh, *The Apparition at Knock*, p. 21.
524. Ibid., p. 33.
525. Ibid., pp. 29–30.
526. See Dietrich von Hildebrand, *The Devastated Vineyard*, (Roman Catholic Books, Harrison, 1985), pp. 31ff.
527. Dawson, *The Gods of Revolution*, pp. 155–60; see also Roberts, *Europe: 1880–1945*, pp. 228–30.
528. Roberts, *Europe: 1880–1945*, pp. 215–18; Dawson, *Understanding Europe*, pp. 81–82.
529. Daniel-Rops, *A Fight for God*, pp. 20–24; Hitchcock, *What is Secular Humanism?* p. 46; Randall, *The Making of the Modern Mind*, pp. 607–11.
530. Johnson, *Modern Times*, pp. 11–12, 48.
531. Daniel-Rops, *A Fight for God*, pp. 6–15.
532. Ibid., pp. 43–48, 98–103.
533. Ibid., pp. 128–30; Roberts, *Europe: 1880–1945*, p. 242; Nichols, *Catholic Thought since the Enlightenment, A Survey*, p. 91.
534. Gay and Webb, *Modern Europe Since 1815*, pp. 860–61.
535. Daniel-Rops, *A Fight for God*, pp. 144–49.
536. Gay and Webb, *Modern Europe Since 1815*, pp. 806–8, 855, 924.
537. Chadwick, "Great Britain and Europe," in *The Oxford History of Christianity*, pp. 369–70; Gay and Webb, *Modern Europe Since 1815*, p. 818.
538. *The Catholic Encyclopedia*, vol. 9, s.v. "Masonry," pp. 781–83.
539. Daniel-Rops, *A Fight for God*, pp. 168–76.
540. Hales, *The Catholic Church in the Modern World*, pp. 254–55.
541. See Davies, *Europe: A History*, p. 803.
542. Calkins, *Totus Tuus*, pp. 81–91.
543. Hearder, *Europe in the Nineteenth Century, 1830–1880*, pp. 37, 153–54, 185–86.
544. Hales, *The Catholic Church in the Modern World*, pp. 227–28.
545. Ibid., pp. 155–58; Hollis, *The Breakdown of Money*, pp. 92–94; Gay and Webb, *Modern Europe Since 1815*, pp. 839, 841, 848–49, 867–68.
546. Hales, *The Catholic Church in the Modern World*, p. 265; Daniel-Rops, *A Fight for God*, pp. 179–81.
547. Daniel-Rops, *A Fight for God*, pp. 203–8; see also Nichols, *Catholic Thought since the Enlightenment, A Survey*, pp. 83–84.
548. Daniel-Rops, *A Fight for God*, pp. 226–30; but cf. Nichols, *Catholic Thought since the Enlightenment, A Survey*, pp. 87–88.
549. Bradley, *Fatima and Modernism*, pp. 5–6.
550. See Fox, *Fatima Today*, p. 143.
551. Daniel-Rops, *A Fight for God*, pp. 241–46.
552. Warren H. Carroll, *1917: Red Banners, White Mantle*, (Christendom Press, Front Royal, 1984), pp. 1–7.

553. Gay and Webb, *Modern Europe Since 1815*, pp. 939–40, 964; see also Roberts, *Europe: 1880–1945*, p. 330.
554. Carroll, *1917: Red Banners, White Mantle*, pp. 8–11; Johnson, *Modern Times*, p. 107.
555. Carroll, *1917: Red Banners, White Mantle*, pp. 11–24, 29–36.
556. Ibid., pp. 45–52.
557. Ibid., pp. 36–43; see also Roberts, *Europe: 1880–1945*, pp. 301–2.
558. Carroll, *1917: Red Banners, White Mantle*, pp. 57–63; cf. Gay and Webb, *Modern Europe Since 1815*, pp. 954–55.
559. Carroll, *1917: Red Banners, White Mantle*, pp. 63–66, quote p. 64 from R. Payne, *The Life and Death of Lenin*, (New York, 1964), pp. 311–12.
560. Carroll, *1917: Red Banners, White Mantle*, pp. 74–75.
561. Ibid., pp. 69–72, quote p. 72 from W. Walsh, *Our Lady of Fatima*, (New York, 1958), pp. 50–51; Fr A. M. Martins, SJ and Fr Robert Fox, *Documents on Fatima and The Memoirs of Sister Lucia*, (Fatima Family Apostolate, Alexandria, 1992), trans. of *Novos Documentos de Fatima*, (Porto, 1984), p. 95. "Iria" comes from the Greek word *eirene* meaning peace.
562. Carroll, *1917: Red Banners, White Mantle*, pp. 78–80, 83–91; Johnson, *Modern Times*, p. 107.
563. Carroll, *1917: Red Banners, White Mantle*, pp. 93–99.
564. Ibid., pp. 104–106; cf. Gay and Webb, *Modern Europe Since 1815*, p. 948.
565. Carroll, *1917: Red Banners, White Mantle*, pp. 109–18.
566. Warren H. Carroll, *The Rise and Fall of the Communist Revolution*, (Christendom Press, Front Royal, 1995), p. 100; see also Johnson, *Modern Times*, pp. 66–70.
567. Dawson, *The Judgement of Nations*, p. 25.
568. Carroll, *Rise and Fall of the Communist Revolution*, pp. 71, 129, quote from Martin Gilbert, *Winston S. Churchill*, vol. 4: "The Stricken World, 1916–1922," (Boston, 1975), pp. 235, 246.
569. Carroll, *Rise and Fall of the Communist Revolution*, pp. 129, 134–36.
570. Carroll, *1917: Red Banners, White Mantle*, pp. 122–25.
571. Carroll, *Rise and Fall of the Communist Revolution*, pp. 108–9, 142.
572. Francis Johnston, *Fatima: the Great Sign*, (Augustine Publishing Company, Devon, 1980), p. 23.
573. Martins and Fox, *Documents on Fatima*, pp. 299–300, 395–96; John de Marchi, *Fatima from the beginning*, trans. I. M. Kingsbury, (Missões Consolata, Fatima, 1983), p. 45.
574. Fr Louis Kondor, ed., *Fatima in Lucia's own words*, (Postulation Centre, Fatima, 1976), pp. 150–51. This volume contains Sr Lucia's four memoirs and is her own work, although edited by Fr Kondor. The details given here are thus drawn from the most important eyewitness account of the apparitions; see also De Marchi, *Fatima from the beginning*, p. 46, and Martins and Fox, *Documents on Fatima*, pp. 300–1, 396.
575. Kondor, *Fatima in Lucia's own words*, pp. 151–52; see also De Marchi,

Fatima from the beginning, p. 47, and Martins and Fox, *Documents on Fatima*, pp. 301, 396.

576. Kondor, *Fatima in Lucia's own words*, p. 152; see also Martins and Fox, *Documents on Fatima*, p. 397.

577. Kondor, *Fatima in Lucia's own words*, p. 152; see also Martins and Fox, *Documents on Fatima*, p. 397.

578. Kondor, *Fatima in Lucia's own words*, pp. 152–54; see also Martins and Fox, *Documents on Fatima*, p. 397.

579. Kondor, *Fatima in Lucia's own words*, p. 49; Beevers, *The Sun Her Mantle*, p. 150; cf. Graef, *Mary: A History Of Doctrine and Devotion*, pt 2, p. 136.

580. Martins and Fox, *Documents on Fatima*, p. 395.

581. De Marchi, *Fatima from the beginning*, pp. 50–51; see also Martins and Fox, *Documents on Fatima*, p. 398. Lucia also reported seeing a "star" near the bottom of Our Lady's tunic (see Thomas McGlynn, *Vision of Fatima*, Skeffington & Son, London, 1951, p. 53). Some commentators have linked this with the Old Testament story of Queen Esther, whose name means "star." She is reported as intervening to save the Jewish people on the thirteenth of the month, just as Mary appeared at Fatima on the thirteenth of six successive months. See, for example, Johnston, *Fatima: the Great Sign*, p. 9.

582. De Marchi, *Fatima from the beginning*, pp. 51–53. Hilda Graef criticizes this point about Amelia being in purgatory until the end of the world, as "an unbelievable fate for a small child," and suggests that this information was subsequently "suppressed." But she is mistaken because Amelia was a young woman who was "about 18 or 20 years old when she died," according to Lucia's fourth memoir; as such she was quite capable of committing sins which would have entailed a long period of purification in purgatory after death. See Graef, *Mary: A History Of Doctrine and Devotion*, pt 2, p. 137, and Martins and Fox, *Documents on Fatima*, p. 398–99.

583. Kondor, *Fatima in Lucia's own words*, p. 158; see also De Marchi, *Fatima from the beginning*, pp. 51–53, and Martins and Fox, *Documents on Fatima*, pp. 399–400.

584. Kondor, *Fatima in Lucia's own words*, p. 29; see also De Marchi, *Fatima from the beginning*, pp. 53–54, and Martins and Fox, *Documents on Fatima*, p. 400.

585. De Marchi, *Fatima from the beginning*, pp. 55–60.

586. Ibid., pp. 60–66.

587. Kondor, *Fatima in Lucia's own words*, pp. 160–61. This last sentence is found in a letter written in 1927 by Sr Lucia to her confessor, cited in Martins and Fox, *Documents on Fatima*, p. 241.

588. Kondor, *Fatima in Lucia's own words*, pp. 160–61; see also Martins and Fox, *Documents on Fatima*, pp. 400–1.

589. De Marchi, *Fatima from the beginning*, p. 68.

590. Ibid., pp. 69–73.

591. Ibid., pp. 74–76.

592. Kondor, *Fatima in Lucia's own words*, p. 161; see also Martins and Fox, *Documents on Fatima*, p. 401.

593. Kondor, *Fatima in Lucia's own words*, pp. 161–62; see also Martins and Fox, *Documents on Fatima*, pp. 401–2.

594. De Marchi, *Fatima from the beginning*, p. 78.

595. The report that Mary told the children to pray for the souls in hell, a theological impossibility since they are beyond prayer and repentance, is clearly false. Rather she was encouraging prayer and sacrifice to *prevent* people ending up in hell. See Fr Benedict Groeschel, CFR, *A Still Small Voice: A Practical Guide on Reported Revelations*, (Ignatius Press, San Francisco, 1993), p. 66.

596. Kondor, *Fatima in Lucia's own words*, p. 162; see also Martins and Fox, *Documents on Fatima*, p. 402.

597. Kondor, *Fatima in Lucia's own words*, p. 101.

598. Ibid., pp. 162–66; see also Martins and Fox, *Documents on Fatima*, p. 402.

599. De Marchi, *Fatima from the beginning*, pp. 79–80.

600. Rev. Frederick L. Miller, *The Significance of Fatima*, (AMI Press, Washington, 1993), p. 34.

601. De Marchi, *Fatima from the beginning*, pp. 85–94.

602. Ibid., pp. 95–99.

603. Kondor, *Fatima in Lucia's own words*, p. 167; see also De Marchi, *Fatima from the beginning*, pp. 103–7, and Martins and Fox, *Documents on Fatima*, pp. 185, 402–3.

604. De Marchi, *Fatima from the beginning*, pp. 108–10.

605. Ibid., pp. 110–13.

606. Kondor, *Fatima in Lucia's own words*, pp. 167–68; Fox, *Fatima Today*, pp. 60, 153.

607. Kondor, *Fatima in Lucia's own words*, pp. 167–68; see also Martins and Fox, *Documents on Fatima*, pp. 403–4.

608. De Marchi, *Fatima from the beginning*, pp. 112–13.

609. Ibid., pp. 115–27.

610. Martins and Fox, *Documents on Fatima*, pp. 194–99, 212–13.

611. De Marchi, *Fatima from the beginning*, pp. 127–32.

612. Kondor, *Fatima in Lucia's own words*, pp. 168–70; see also Martins and Fox, *Documents on Fatima*, pp. 404–5.

613. De Marchi, *Fatima from the beginning*, pp. 135–36.

614. Ibid., pp. 136–37; see also Martins and Fox, *Documents on Fatima*, pp. 170–171.

615. De Marchi, *Fatima from the beginning*, pp. 137–39; see also Martins and Fox, (*Documents on Fatima*, pp. 178–79. and Fr Stanley L. Jaki, *God and the Sun at Fatima*, (Real View Books, Royal Oak, 1999), pp. 128–37. Fr Jaki points out that there has been some confusion between the above Dr Garrett, a lawyer, and his father, Prof. Garrett, a scientist, in Fatima literature. However, this does not seem to have affected the reliability of the testimony gained, and is due to a simple mix-up on the part of later writers (see p. 220).

616. De Marchi, *Fatima from the beginning*, p. 136.
617. Mabel Norton, *Eye Witness at Fatima*, (Macmillan & Co., Limited, London, 1950), pp. 11–14; 88–89.
618. De Marchi, *Fatima from the beginning*, pp. 140–141.
619. John M. Haffert, *Meet the Witnesses*, (AMI International Press, Fatima, 1961), pp. 37–38.
620. De Marchi, *Fatima from the beginning*, p. 141.
621. See ibid., pp. 142–57. This point is dealt with extensively by Fr Antonio Martins. He supports the point about the tiredness of the children, and also describes the confusion just after the miracle of the sun, when the children were bombarded with questions. He produces evidence to show that it is possible that there was a mix-up and that some of the crowd mistakenly believed that Lucia had said that the war would end that day. This report was then spread through the crowd, despite Lucia's attempts to correct it. See Fr Antonio Martins, SJ, *Fatima, Way of Peace*, (Augustine Publishing Company, Devon, 1989), pp. 27–52.
622. De Marchi, *Fatima from the beginning*, pp. 178–86.
623. Ibid., pp. 186–201.
624. Ibid., pp. 201–3.
625. Fox, *Fatima Today*, p. 65. This congregation was fully approved by the Church in 1940.
626. De Marchi, *Fatima from the beginning*, pp. 225–27; see also Martins and Fox, *Documents on Fatima*, pp. 247–53.
627. De Marchi, *Fatima from the beginning*, p. 93.
628. *Theotokos: A Theological Encyclopedia of the Blessed Virgin Mary*, 2d ed., s.v. "Jerome," p. 196, (*In Is. 4, 11, 1–3*, in CSEL 73, 102–105) and p. 296.
629. Gambero, *Mary and the Fathers of the Church*, p. 211, *Tractatus de Psalmo* 77, 14; CCL 78, 72.
630. *Theotokos: A Theological Encyclopedia of the Blessed Virgin Mary*, 2d ed., s.v. "Ambrose," p. 18, (*In Ps., 118, V, 3*, PL 15:1251–1252).
631. Palmer, *Mary in the Documents of the Church*, p. 27, *The Instruction of a Virgin*, 13, 81–86 (PL 16:325–26).
632. The Carmelite scholar, Joseph de Sainte Marie, OCD, makes a similar comparison between Elijah's calling on God to send down fire from heaven and the Miracle of the Sun at Fatima, in his *La Vierge du Mont-Carmel, Mystère Prophètie: Élie, Thérèse d'Avila, Fatima*, (Éditions P. Lethielleux, Paris, 1985), p. 268.
633. See Peter Slattery, *The Springs of Carmel: An Introduction to Carmelite Spirituality*, (St Paul Publications, Homebush, 1990), pp. 51–56, and Gambero, *Mary and the Fathers of the Church*, pp. 354–57.
634. Kondor, *Fatima in Lucia's own words*, p. 170; De Marchi, *Fatima from the Beginning*, p. 143.
635. Jaki, *God and the Sun at Fatima*, pp. 37, 58, 149, 275, 370.
636. Ibid., pp. 109, 115–16, 118–19, 124, 178, 191, 193, 210–11, 261.
637. Ibid., pp. 256, 337–38 (quote p. 338).
638. Ibid., pp. 343–46 (quote p. 346).

639. Ibid., p. 347.
640. Ibid., pp. 348–50.
641. Martins and Fox, *Documents on Fatima*, p. 250.
642. Graef, *Mary: A History Of Doctrine and Devotion*, pt 2, pp. 139–40.
643. Zimdars-Swartz, *Encountering Mary*, pp. 67–68.
644. Ibid., pp. 68–77, 80–83.
645. Ibid., p. 248.
646. Ibid., pp. 11, 248–49.
647. Elliot Miller and Kenneth R. Samples, *The Cult of the Virgin: Catholic Mariology and the Apparitions of Mary*, (Baker Book House Company, Grand Rapids, 1994), pp. 88–116. The major approved apparitions, and those at Bayside, which have been condemned, are dealt with in only 12 pages of text.
648. Ibid., pp. 126–27.
649. Ibid., pp. 128–29.
650. Ibid., pp. 129–30. Samples then goes on to mention a number of scriptural passages which show the possibility of satanically-produced miracles and signs; but clearly all this has to be understood in the right context, that of "testing the spirits" to see if they come from God (cf. 2 Cor. 11:14–15; 2 Thess. 2:9–10).
651. Ibid., pp. 133–34.
652. Ibid., p. 134.
653. Roberts, *Europe: 1880–1945*, pp. 319–21, 395–96, 439–40.
654. Daniel-Rops, *A Fight for God*, pp. 247–50.
655. Ibid., pp. 256–60; Johnson, *Modern Times*, pp. 108–9; see also Gay and Webb, *Modern Europe Since 1815*, pp. 963–64, 1000; Roberts, *Europe: 1880–1945*, p. 462.
656. Carroll, *Rise and Fall of the Communist Revolution*, pp. 144–47; Davies, *Europe: A History*, pp. 935–37.
657. Carroll, *1917: Red Banners, White Mantle*, pp. 122–30; Johnson, *Modern Times*, p. 93.
658. Gay and Webb, *Modern Europe Since 1815*, pp. 976–77; see also Roberts, *Europe: 1880–1945*, pp. 343–45.
659. Daniel-Rops, *A Fight for God*, pp. 73–78, 281–85.
660. Fox, *Fatima Today*, p. 217; see also Martins and Fox, *Documents on Fatima*, pp. 241–42.
661. Martins and Fox, *Documents on Fatima*, pp. 235–37, 242.
662. The setting aside of the first Saturday of the month as a special day of reparation to Mary did not originate at Fatima, but had been practiced since the time of St John Eudes in the seventeenth century. The practice was given a further boost by an Italian nun, Sr Dolores Inglese, in the late nineteenth century, and was indulgenced by both popes St Pius X and Benedict XV. It was the message of Fatima, however, which gave it its present form. In return for complying with this request concerning the Five First Saturdays devotion, Mary promised "all the graces necessary for salvation." See Francis D. Costa, SSS, "Mary's Day and Mary's Months," in *Mariology*, vol. 3, p. 57.

663. Fox, *Fatima Today*, pp. 217–18; see also Martins and Fox, *Documents on Fatima*, p. 246.

664. Fox, *Fatima Today*, pp. 221–22; see also Martins and Fox, *Documents on Fatima*, pp. 355–56.

665. Carroll, *Rise and Fall of the Communist Revolution*, pp. 232–33.

666. See Brother Michel de la Sainte Trinité, *Fatima Revealed ... And Discarded*, trans. Timothy Tindal-Robertson, (Augustine Publishing Company, Devon, 1988), pp. 74–79.

667. Martins and Fox, *Documents on Fatima*, p. 246.

668. Ibid., pp. 243, 261–62.

669. Daniel-Rops, *A Fight for God*, pp. 32–35.

670. Roberts, *Europe: 1880–1945*, pp. 483, 491.

671. Hollis, *The Breakdown of Money*, pp. 159–68; see also Johnson, *Modern Times*, pp. 134–36.

672. Johnson, *Modern Times*, pp. 138–44.

673. Ibid., pp. 267–70; Carroll, *Rise and Fall of the Communist Revolution*, pp. 226–30.

674. Johnson, *Modern Times*, pp. 271–75, 300–1; see also Gay and Webb, *Modern Europe Since 1815*, pp. 983–94; Carroll, *Rise and Fall of the Communist Revolution*, pp. 224–25, 243–50, 254–60, 293–94.

675. Johnson, *Modern Times*, pp. 275–77, 305–8; see also Carroll, *Rise and Fall of the Communist Revolution*, p. 233, 242, and Davies, *Europe: A History*, p. 952.

676. Johnson, *Modern Times*, pp. 346–49, 354.

677. Daniel-Rops, *A Fight for God*, pp. 293–95.

678. Don Sharkey, "The Virgin with the Golden Heart," in *A Woman clothed with the Sun*, pp. 215–18.

679. Beevers, *The Golden Heart: the Story of Beauraing*, pp. 14–15; Sharkey, "The Virgin with the Golden Heart," in *A Woman clothed with the Sun*, pp. 218–20.

680. D. Sharkey and J. Debergh, *Our Lady of Beauraing*, (Abbey Press, Indiana, 1973), p. 19.

681. Sharkey, "The Virgin with the Golden Heart," in *A Woman clothed with the Sun*, pp. 220–22.

682. Beevers, *The Golden Heart*, pp. 17–25 ; Sharkey and Debergh, *Our Lady of Beauraing*, pp. 42–46.

683. Beevers, *The Golden Heart*, pp. 25–27; Sharkey, "The Virgin with the Golden Heart," in *A Woman clothed with the Sun*, pp. 222–24.

684. Beevers, *The Golden Heart*, pp. 29–30; Beevers, *The Sun Her Mantle*, pp. 184–85.

685. Sharkey and Debergh, *Our Lady of Beauraing*, pp. 51, 61.

686. Ibid., pp. 68–72, 92–96.

687. Ibid., pp. 80–83.

688. Ibid., pp. 83–106; F. Toussaint and C. Joset, *Beauraing, Les apparitions*, (Desclée De Brouwer, 1981), pp. 69–74.

689. Sharkey, "The Virgin with the Golden Heart," in *A Woman clothed with the Sun*, pp. 224–26; Sharkey and Debergh, *Our Lady of*

Beauraing, pp. 120–21.

690. Sharkey, "The Virgin with the Golden Heart," in *A Woman clothed with the Sun*, pp. 226–28. It is worth noting that there is a similarity here to the events that preceded the apparitions of Mary at Fatima; that is, a sound like a clap of thunder and a flash of lightning, which likewise were seen and heard by many people apart from the seers.

691. Herbert Thurston, *Beauraing and other Apparitions*, (Burns, Oates & Washbourne, London, 1934), pp. 15–16.

692. Sharkey and Debergh, *Our Lady of Beauraing*, p. 132; see also Toussaint and Joset, *Beauraing, Les apparitions*, pp. 86, 195.

693. Carroll, *The Cult of the Virgin Mary*, pp. 128–29.

694. Ibid., pp. 117–18.

695. Ibid., pp. 125–26.

696. *Theotokos: A Theological Encyclopedia of the Blessed Virgin Mary*, 2d ed., pp. 23, 101, 113, 324.

697. Buby, *Mary of Galilee*, vol. 3, p. 123, quote from C. W. Neumann, *The Blessed Virgin in the Works of Saint Ambrose*, (Fribourg, Switzerland: U. Press, 1962), pp. 268–69, (*De inst. virg.* 8:51–57).

698. Ibid., pp. 159–60, quote from Schaff and Wace, op. cit. vol. 6, pp. 78–79, par. 21.

699. For instance Ps 5:7; 18:6; 27:4; 48:9; 138:2.

700. Sharkey and Debergh, *Our Lady of Beauraing*, pp. 160–63.

701. Ibid., pp. 155–56.

702. Ibid., p. 74.

703. In the same year the French writer Jean Hellé published a book entitled *Les Miracles*, which related the facts on Beauraing according to the faulty study produced by the French Carmelites in 1933. Mgr Charue protested at this and Hellé went to Beauraing where he met a member of the doctrinal commission, with the result that in the Dutch translation of his work he suppressed the chapter on Beauraing. This fact does not instill much confidence in his remarks on the other Marian apparitions in the book. When it was translated into English and published as *Miracles* in 1952, the offending chapter was included, and to make matters worse, Hellé implied that the Church had condemned the apparitions at Beauraing, even though they were approved three years earlier. See Toussaint and Joset, *Beauraing, Les apparitions*, pp. 170–71; Sharkey and Debergh, *Our Lady of Beauraing*, p. 146.

704. Sharkey and Debergh, *Our Lady of Beauraing*, pp. 173–75.

705. Sharkey, "The Virgin with the Golden Heart," in *A Woman clothed with the Sun*, pp. 232–34.

706. Robert M. Maloy, SM, "The Virgin of the Poor," in *A Woman clothed with the Sun*, pp. 241–47; L. Wuillaume, SJ, *Banneux: a message for our time*, (Banneux Shrine, Banneux, 1995), pp. 3–6.

707. Maloy, "The Virgin of the Poor," in *A Woman clothed with the Sun*, pp. 247–49; Wuillaume, *Banneux: a message for our time*, pp. 6–9.

708. Maloy, "The Virgin of the Poor," in *A Woman clothed with the Sun*, pp.

249–50; Wuillaume, *Banneux: a message for our time*, pp. 9–10. The words used by Mariette to convey Mary's words in this and the following apparitions follow the meaning and order set out in *Histoire critique des apparitions de Banneux*, (Movement Eucharistique et Missionaire, Namur, 1985), by R. Rutten, pp. 57–58, and passim.

709. Maloy, "The Virgin of the Poor," in *A Woman clothed with the Sun*, pp. 250–51. Maloy writes of Mariette falling to the ground and kneeling *three* times before finally kneeling a *fourth* time at the spring. But other sources indicate only *two* falls on the way to the spring, e.g. Wuillaume, *Banneux: a message for our time*, p. 12 (quote), and Damien Walne and Joan Flory, *The Virgin of the Poor*, (CTS, London, 1983), p. 6. The importance of this point will become clear further on.

710. Maloy, "The Virgin of the Poor," in *A Woman clothed with the Sun*, pp. 251–52; Wuillaume, *Banneux: a message for our time*, p. 14.

711. Maloy, "The Virgin of the Poor," in *A Woman clothed with the Sun*, pp. 252–55; Wuillaume, *Banneux: a message for our time*, pp. 16–18.

712. Maloy, "The Virgin of the Poor," in *A Woman clothed with the Sun*, pp. 256–60; Wuillaume, *Banneux: a message for our time*, pp. 24–29.

713. Maloy, "The Virgin of the Poor," in *A Woman clothed with the Sun*, pp. 260–62; Wuillaume, *Banneux: a message for our time*, pp. 30–34.

714. Wuillaume, *Banneux: a message for our time*, p. 53.

715. Buby, *Mary of Galilee*, vol. 3, p. 219; emphasis added.

716. Maloy, "The Virgin of the Poor," in *A Woman clothed with the Sun*, pp. 264–65.

717. Roberts, *Europe: 1880–1945*, pp. 468–69.

718. This point and the general connection between the apparitions in Belgium and the rise of Nazism is made in *The Apparitions of Our Lady in their Historical Context*, pp. 18–19. This is a booklet published by the "Church in History Information Centre," Birkenhead, England.

719. Daniel-Rops, *A Fight for God*, pp. 315–16. Dietrich von Hildebrand, (*Trojan Horse in the City of God*, pp. 62–63), sees the failure of the German bishops, in 1933, to condemn National Socialism, as a tragic mistake. He argues that they could and should have provided much needed leadership through such a condemnation.

720. Hales, *The Catholic Church in the Modern World*, pp. 292–95; Johnson, *Modern Times*, pp. 280–87, 295, 342, 343–44; Roberts, *Europe: 1880–1945*, pp. 466–68, 470–71.

721. Johnson, *Modern Times*, p. 311.

722. Daniel-Rops, *A Fight for God*, pp. 303–8.

723. Dawson, *The Judgement of Nations*, p. 26; Roberts, *Europe: 1880–1945*, p. 474.

724. Dawson, *The Judgement of Nations*, pp. 27–30.

725. Dawson, *Understanding Europe*, pp. 78–79; see also Davies, *Europe: A History*, p. 854.

726. Dawson, *The Gods of Revolution*, pp. 162–63.

727. Gay and Webb, *Modern Europe Since 1815*, p. 1072; Hearder, *Europe in the Nineteenth Century, 1830–1880*, p. 268.

728. Daniel-Rops, *A Fight for God*, pp. 318–19; Johnson, *Modern Times*, pp. 342–43; see also Roberts, *Europe: 1880–1945*, pp. 69–72.
729. Daniel-Rops, *A Fight for God*, pp. 28–30, 31; Johnson, *Modern Times*, pp. 129–30; but cf. Chadwick, *Secularization of the European Mind in the Nineteenth Century*, pp. 132–33.
730. Cavanaugh-O'Keefe, *Introduction to Genetics*, pp. 1, 5–7.
731. Ibid., pp. 8–9.
732. Richard Pipes, *Russia under the Bolshevik Regime*, (New York, 1993), p. 259, cited in Carroll, *Rise and Fall of the Communist Revolution*, pp. 120–21; Johnson, *Modern Times*, pp. 102, 133–34, 277–79, 293, 296; see also Roberts, *Europe: 1880–1945*, pp. 472–73.
733. Daniel-Rops, *A Fight for God*, pp. 260–64.
734. Hales, *The Catholic Church in the Modern World*, pp. 290–91; Johnson, *Modern Times*, pp. 326–27, 330; Carroll, *Rise and Fall of the Communist Revolution*, pp. 285–92. This victory also had important repercussions for the rest of Europe, since it prevented Communism gaining a foothold in the West. In the case of Spain, and later too with Chile in the seventies, criticisms have been made about the "right-wing" nature of the governments under Franco and Pinochet respectively. It is true that both were harsh and allowed little freedom, but this only further underlines the awful nature of Communism: even where it fails, its effects are so terrible that it induces a reaction which goes beyond what is strictly necessary. Having said that, if Communism had gained power in either country, it would have represented a grave threat to democracy in Europe or South America. And judging from Communism's past record, many more people would have died than under either Franco or Pinochet.
735. Hales, *The Catholic Church in the Modern World*, pp. 295–97.
736. Daniel-Rops, *A Fight for God*, pp. 335–36.
737. Martins and Fox, *Documents on Fatima*, pp. 263–64.
738. Fox, *Fatima Today*, p. 224.
739. Martins and Fox, *Documents on Fatima*, pp. 286–87, 288.
740. Ibid., pp. 291–92.
741. Ibid., p. 328.
742. See De Marchi, *Fatima from the beginning*, p. 250; see also Joseph de Sainte-Marie, *Reflections on the Act of Consecration*, p. 13.
743. Fox, *Fatima Today*, pp. 157–58.
744. Kondor, *Fatima in Lucia's own words*, p. 104. Writers such as Hilda Graef have criticized this point about the consecration of Russia leading to its conversion. But as events have shown, the years following the consecration made by Pope John Paul II in 1984 have led to remarkable changes in many parts of the formerly Communist world, and not just Russia. Cf. Graef, *Mary: A History Of Doctrine and Devotion*, pt 2, p. 140.
745. Timothy Tindal-Robertson, *Message of Fatima*, (Catholic Truth Society, London, 1998), p. 42.
746. Martins and Fox, *Documents on Fatima*, p. 370.

747. Martins, *Fatima, Way of Peace,* pp. 12–13.
748. Sr Sophia Michalenko, CMGT, *Mercy my Mission,* (Divine Mercy Publications, Dublin, 1987), pp. vi, 31–32, 57.
749. Ibid., pp. 91–92.
750. Decree Prot. N. 1002/00/L in *L'Osservatore Romano,* n. 22, (31 May 2000), p. 2.
751. Ibid., pp. 113–14, 157.
752. Ibid., pp. 237, 245, 253.
753. Johnson, *Modern Times,* pp. 352–57.
754. Hales, *The Catholic Church in the Modern World,* pp. 300–2; Johnson, *Modern Times,* pp. 358–61.
755. Johnson, *Modern Times,* pp. 361–62.
756. Ibid., pp. 364–70.
757. Davies, *Europe: A History,* p. 1008.
758. Martins and Fox, *Documents on Fatima,* p. 335.
759. Ibid., pp. 347–48.
760. Francis Johnston, *Alexandrina, The Agony and The Glory,* (TAN Books and Publishers, Rockford, 1982), pp. 40–44, 100, and passim.
761. Martins and Fox, *Documents on Fatima,* p. 348.
762. Martins, *Fatima, Way of Peace,* pp. 71–76.
763. The idea present here of war being a punishment for sin does not accord well with the modern mentality which denies sin altogether. However, the Bible is clear that there is an intrinsic connection between sin and distress, beginning with the original sin in the book of Genesis. See, for example, Judg. 2:11–15; 2 Sam. 24; 1 Kings 17:11; 2 Kings 21. The prophets too were convinced of a connection between sin and an inevitable punishment, e.g., Hos. 13:1–15; Amos 2:1–16, 3:9–11, 6; Mic. 3:1–12. In short, within biblical and Christian teaching generally there is an intimate connection between sin and punishment; and so this part of the secret of Fatima, which links mankind's wrongdoing with war, sadly fits in all too well with an ancient pattern. Martins, *Fatima, Way of Peace,* pp. 16–22.
764. Martins and Fox, *Documents on Fatima,* p. 373.
765. Calkins, *Totus Tuus,* pp. 98–102.
766. Martins and Fox, *Documents on Fatima,* p. 417.
767. Johnston, *Fatima: the Great Sign,* p. 88, n. 5. See *The Second World War* by Sir Winston Churchill, vol. 4, 33.
768. Johnson, *Modern Times,* pp. 372–88.
769. Ibid., pp. 399–400, 406–9, 413–22.
770. Ibid., pp. 429, 432–37; Carroll, *Rise and Fall of the Communist Revolution,* pp. 328–29, 332, 338–39, 342–44, 346–49.
771. Johnson, *Modern Times,* pp. 438–43, 450–52; Carroll, *Rise and Fall of the Communist Revolution,* pp. 354–55, 379–80.
772. Johnson, *Modern Times,* pp. 451, 452–53, 546, 549–51; Carroll, *Rise and Fall of the Communist Revolution,* p. 469–71, 475–80.
773. Hales, *The Catholic Church in the Modern World,* pp. 299–300, 309–10;

Johnson, *Modern Times,* pp. 577–82, 586–87; cf. Gay and Webb, *Modern Europe Since 1815,* pp. 1090–92.

774. Dietrich von Hildebrand, (*Trojan Horse in the City of God,* p. 142), claims that Heidegger's philosophy has had a very negative effect on more recent theological thinking, particularly through his influence on writers such as Bultmann, the champion of "demythologization," that is, the removal of anything supernatural from the Gospels.

775. Johnson, *Modern Times,* pp. 575–77, 588–95, 612; Davies, *Europe: A History,* pp. 1062–64; cf. Gay and Webb, *Modern Europe Since 1815,* pp. 1093–96, 1111–12.

776. Hales, *The Catholic Church in the Modern World,* pp. 311–12.

777. Kyra Audley-Charles, "Our Lady of Revelation," *The Crusader of Mary Immaculate Magazine,* March 2000, pp. 5, 11; Br Francis Mary, *Marian Shrines of Italy,* p. 33.

778. Audley-Charles, "Our Lady of Revelation," *The Crusader of Mary Immaculate Magazine,* April 2000, p. 4; Br Francis Mary, *Marian Shrines of Italy,* pp. 33–35.

779. Audley-Charles, "Our Lady of Revelation," *The Crusader of Mary Immaculate Magazine,* May 2000, pp. 5–6; Br Francis Mary, *Marian Shrines of Italy,* pp. 34–37.

780. In *Tutti le Apparizioni della Madonna in 2,000 anni di Storia,* p. 294, by Gottfried Hierzenberger and Otto Nedomansky, published by Piemme in 1996. (Cited by Audley-Charles in the above article).

781. Audley-Charles, "Our Lady of Revelation," *The Crusader of Mary Immaculate Magazine,* June 2000, pp. 12, 14; Br Francis Mary, *Marian Shrines of Italy,* p. 38.

782. Christopher Duggan, *A Concise History of Italy,* (Cambridge University Press, Cambridge, 1994), pp. 250–55; Johnson, *Modern Times,* p. 579.

783. Johnson, *Modern Times,* pp. 588–89.

784. This section on L'Ile Bouchard is based on an unpublished manuscript by Paul Rhoads, called "The Marian Apparitions at the Church of St Gilles, in L'Ile Bouchard, France, from 8 to 14 December, 1947." This work is a collation of several accounts published in French, as well as interviews with people close to the events, including Jacqueline Aubry.

785. Chiron, *Enquête sur les Apparitions de la Vierge,* pp. 296–97; Philippe Anthonioz, *Marie Apparaît à L'Ile Bouchard,* (O.E.I.L., Paris, 1989), pp. 22–24.

786. Rev. Raymond Peyret, *Marthe Robin, The Cross and the Joy,* trans. Clare Will Faulhaber, (Alba House, New York, 1983), pp. 49–55.

787. Bernard Peyrous, *Les Evénements de L'Ile Bouchard,* (Éditions de l'Emmanuel, Paris, 1997), p. 35. See also Anthonioz, *Marie Apparaît à L'Ile Bouchard,* pp. 47–49.

788. *Maman du Ciel* literally means "Heavenly Mum/Mummy," or "Heavenly Mom/Mommy," all of which sound somewhat sugary. Thus it seems better to use "Heavenly Mother" in English.

789. Chiron, *Enquête sur les Apparitions de la Vierge,* p. 299.

790. *L'Ile Bouchard: La Vierge et ses apparitions,* (Tequi, Paris, 1992).

791. See *A Catholic Commentary on Holy Scripture,* Dom Bernard Orchard, et al., (Thomas Nelson & Sons, London, 1960), Sections 494g, m–o, 495k, 573d.

792. Ibid., 574d, e.

793. See, for example, *Lumen Gentium,* 63, where St Ambrose's description of Mary as a type of the Church is quoted with approval.

794. See Orchard, et al., *A Catholic Commentary on Holy Scripture,* 509c.

795. John Steinmueller and Kathryn Sullivan, *Catholic Biblical Encyclopedia, Old Testament,* (Wagner, New York, 1959), s.v. "Beryl."

796. Buby, *Mary of Galilee,* vol. 3, p. 165. (*Letter* 22).

797. Ibid., p. 312.

798. Gambero, *Mary and the Fathers of the Church,* p. 314. *Homily 67,* PO 8: 354–55.

799. Buby, *Mary of Galilee,* vol. 3, p. 293.

800. Br Francis Mary, *Marian Shrines of Italy,* p. 37.

801. Joachim Bouflet, *Les Faussaires de Dieu,* (Presses de la Renaissance, Paris, 2000), pp. 70, 98; René Laurentin, *The Apparitions of the Blessed Virgin Today,* (Veritas Publications, Dublin, 1991), p. 40.

802. Bouflet, *Les Faussaires de Dieu,* pp. 584–85.

803. Chiron, *Enquête sur les Apparitions de la Vierge,* pp. 301, 431, n. 3.

804. Laurentin, *The Apparitions of the Blessed Virgin Today,* pp. 153–54.

805. C. Freithoff, *Complete Mariology,* (Blackfriars, London, 1958), pp. 155–59; Garrigou-Lagrange, *The Mother of the Saviour,* pp. 144–48.

806. The apparition at Knock points to the possibility of both Saints Joseph and John also being assumed into heaven. In neither case has any cult arisen around their bodily relics.

807. Lawrence P. Everett, CSSR, "Mary's Death and Bodily Assumption," in Juniper Carol, ed., *Mariology,* vol. 2, (Bruce Publishing Co., Milwaukee, 1957), p. 483.

808. Ibid., pp. 488–92.

809. Freithoff, *Complete Mariology,* pp. 143–46.

810. Martins, *Fatima, Way of Peace,* pp. 24–25.

811. Evelyn M. Raabe, "Weeping Madonna of Syracuse, Sicily," in Br Francis Mary, *Marian Shrines of Italy,* pp. 157–58; Michel de la Sainte Trinité, *The Whole Truth about Fatima,* vol. 3, *The Third Secret,* (Immaculate Heart Publications, Buffalo, 1990), pp. 341–43.

812. Raabe, "Weeping Madonna of Syracuse, Sicily," in Br Francis Mary, *Marian Shrines of Italy,* pp. 158–60; De la Sainte Trinité, *The Whole Truth about Fatima,* Vol. 3, pp. 343–45.

813. Raabe, "Weeping Madonna of Syracuse, Sicily," in Br Francis Mary, *Marian Shrines of Italy,* pp. 160–61; De la Sainte Trinité, *The Whole Truth about Fatima,* vol. 3, pp. 345–49.

814. Martins and Fox, *Documents on Fatima,* pp. 110–13; Fox, *Rediscovering Fatima,* p. 107; George Weigel, *Witness to Hope: The Biography of Pope John Paul II,* (Cliff Street Books, New York, 1999), pp. 228–29.

815. Kondor, *Fatima in Lucia's own words*, pp. 104–5, 149, 161–62. see also Martins and Fox, *Documents on Fatima*, pp. 395, 402.

816. See Fr Robert Fox, *Rediscovering Fatima*, (Our Sunday Visitor, Inc., Huntington, 1982), p. 107, and Zimdars-Swartz, *Encountering Mary*, pp. 167–68.

817. Rahner, *Visions and Prophecies*, pp. 11–12, 16 (quote), 29–30.

818. Garrigou-Lagrange, *The Three Ages of the Interior Life*, vol. 2, p. 589, *emphasis added.*

819. Ibid., p. 591. There is a possibility of deception, however, because the individual may confuse what is happening in the intellect with the devil's effects on the imagination. Obviously, too, all these phenomena are subject to a proper process of spiritual discernment.

820. Martins and Fox, *Documents on Fatima*, p. 114; see also Martins, *Fatima, Way of Peace*, pp. 5–6.

821. Martins and Fox, *Documents on Fatima*, pp. 334–35, 344.

822. Tindal-Robertson, *Message of Fatima*, pp. 74–75.

823. Carroll, *Rise and Fall of the Communist Revolution*, pp. 685–89; see also Weigel, *Witness to Hope*, pp. 422–25.

824. Tindal-Robertson, *Fatima, Russia and Pope John Paul II*, pp. 7–11, 13, 18, 23.

825. Joseph de Sainte-Marie, *Reflections on the Act of Consecration*, pp. 1–4, 8.

826. Tindal-Robertson, *Fatima, Russia and Pope John Paul II*, p. 243.

827. Ibid., p. 248.

828. Ibid., pp. 23–27, 39, 253–56.

829. Fr Robert Fox, *The Collegial Consecration of Russia is Accomplished*, (Augustine Publishing Company, Devon, 1990), pp. 3–6.

830. Miller, *Exploring Fatima*, pp. 100–101.

831. Tindal-Robertson, *Fatima, Russia and Pope John Paul II*, pp. 59–60.

832. Martins and Fox, *Documents on Fatima*, pp. 84–85.

833. Martins and Fox, *Documents on Fatima*, p. 86. Sr Lucia also wrote three letters to the journal *30 Days* in which she confirmed that the collegial consecration had been accomplished, see also Tindal-Robertson, *Fatima, Russia and Pope John Paul II*, p. 27.

834. Vatican, 20 Dec 2001, CWNews.com and VIS. She also made it clear that the third part of the secret had been revealed in its entirety, again to counter rumors to the contrary.

835. Fox, *The Collegial Consecration of Russia is Accomplished*, pp. 13–15.

836. See Fr Ralph Wiltgen, SVD, *The Rhine flows into the Tiber: A History of Vatican II*, (TAN Books and Publishers, Rockford, 1985), p. 241.

837. See Calkins, *Totus Tuus*, pp. 147–48, 277–78.

838. Ibid., pp. 164–65.

839. Ibid., pp. 189–205.

840. Ibid., pp. 260–64.

841. Johnson, *Modern Times*, pp. 654–57; Carroll, *Rise and Fall of the Communist Revolution*, pp. 562–63, 572–73, 575–79, 582, 597–99, 606–13.

842. Johnson, *Modern Times,* pp. 674, 683–85, 687, 688–89, 694–96, 709; Carroll, *Rise and Fall of the Communist Revolution,* pp. 628–30, 684–85.
843. Carroll, *Rise and Fall of the Communist Revolution,* pp. 628–34, 639–47.
844. Johnson, *Modern Times,* pp. 675–83, 712–14, 728; Carroll, *Rise and Fall of the Communist Revolution,* pp. 447–48, 450–54, 650.
845. See Weigel, *Witness to Hope,* pp. 280–81.
846. Carroll, *Rise and Fall of the Communist Revolution,* pp. 648–51, 705 (quote).
847. Ibid., pp. 652–53, 683–84, 734–35; Johnson, *Modern Times,* pp. 699–700, 722–23.
848. Tindal-Robertson, *Fatima, Russia and Pope John Paul II,* p. 229.
849. Ibid., pp. 42–45, 46–50; Carroll, *Rise and Fall of the Communist Revolution,* pp. 700–701, 703–704, 708, 714, 734, 743–44; see also Weigel, *Witness to Hope,* pp. 585–88, 601–605.
850. Tindal-Robertson, *Message of Fatima,* pp. 63–64.
851. Martins and Fox, *Documents on Fatima,* pp. 87–88; see also Weigel, *Witness to Hope,* pp. 617–18.
852. Tindal-Robertson, *Fatima, Russia and Pope John Paul II,* pp. 83–90; Carroll, *Rise and Fall of the Communist Revolution,* pp. 753–56; 769–78.
853. Carroll, *Rise and Fall of the Communist Revolution,* pp. 779–80; Warren H. Carroll, *A History of Christendom,* vol. 1, *The Founding of Christendom,* (Christendom Press, Front Royal, 1993), pp. 527–29.
854. Soul Magazine, July–August 2000, pp. 12–15.
855. Ibid., pp. 21–22.
856. Soul Magazine, September–October 2000, p. 10.
857. Ibid., p. 20.
858. Miller, "Mary: Catechist at Fatima," in *Exploring Fatima,* pp. 48–50.
859. Joseph de Sainte-Marie, *Reflections on the Act of Consecration,* pp. 11, 22.
860. Weigel, *Witness to Hope,* pp. 858–61.
861. Kondor, *Fatima in Lucia's own words,* pp. 108–9.
862. See Weigel, *Witness to Hope,* pp. 855–56.
863. See *Christendom Awake,* by Fr Aidan Nichols OP, (T & T Clark, Edinburgh, 1999), for more details as to how Christendom can be revitalized.
864. Cited in Weigel, *Witness to Hope,* p. 262.
865. Ibid., p. 776.

Select Bibliography

Beevers, John, *The Sun Her Mantle* (Browne & Nolan Ltd, Dublin, 1954).

———, *The Golden Heart: the Story of Beauraing* (Browne & Nolan, Dublin, 1956).

Belloc, Hilaire, *The Crisis of Civilization* (TAN Books and Publishers, Rockford, 1992).

———, *Characters of the Reformation* (TAN Books and Publishers, Rockford, 1992).

Bihlmeyer K., and H. Tüchle, *Church History,* vol. 2, *The Middle Ages* (Newman Press, Westminster, 1963).

Bouflet, Joachim, *Les Faussaires de Dieu* (Presses de la Renaissance, Paris, 2000).

Bouflet, Joachim, and Philippe Boutry, *Un Signe dans le Ciel: Les apparitions de la Vierge* (Bernard Grasset, Paris, 1997).

Bouyer, Louis, *Woman and Man with God* (Darton, Longman & Todd, London, 1960).

———, *The Spirit and Forms of Protestantism* (Collins, London, 1963).

Brown, E. M., ed., *Dreams, Visions and Prophecies of Don Bosco* (Don Bosco Publications, New Rochelle, 1986).

Buby, Bertrand, SM, *Mary of Galilee,* vol. 3, *The Marian Legacy of the Early Church* (Alba House, New York, 1997).

Cahill, E., Fr, *Freemasonry and the Anti-Christian Movement* (Gill, Dublin, 1959).

Calkins, Fr Arthur B., *Totus Tuus: John Paul II's Program of Marian Consecration and Entrustment* (Academy of the Immaculate, New Bedford, 1992).

Carol, Juniper, OFM, ed., *Mariology,* 3 vols. (Bruce Publishing Co., Milwaukee, 1955–61).

Carroll, Michael P., *The Cult of the Virgin Mary, Psychological Origins,* (Princeton University Press, Princeton, 1986).

Carroll, Warren H., *Our Lady of Guadalupe and the Conquest of Darkness,* (Christendom Press, Front Royal, 1983).

————, *1917: Red Banners, White Mantle* (Christendom Press, Front Royal, 1984).

————, *The Guillotine and the Cross* (Christendom Press, Front Royal, 1991).

————, *A History of Christendom,* vol. 1, *The Founding of Christendom* (Christendom Press, Front Royal, 1993).

————, *A History of Christendom,* vol. 2, *The Building of Christendom* (Christendom Press, Front Royal, 1987).

————, *A History of Christendom,* vol. 3, *The Glory of Christendom* (Christendom Press, Front Royal, 1993).

————, *The Rise and Fall of the Communist Revolution* (Christendom Press, Front Royal, 1995).

Cavanaugh-O'Keefe, John, *Introduction to Genetics* (American Life League, Stafford, 1995).

Chadwick, Owen, *The Reformation* (Penguin Books, Middlesex, 1977).

————, *The Secularization of the European Mind in the Nineteenth Century* (Cambridge University Press, Cambridge, 1975).

Chiron, Yves, *Enquête sur les Apparitions de la Vierge* (Éditions J'ai Lu, Paris, 1995).

Cragg, G. R., *The Church and the Age of Reason, 1648–1789* (Penguin Books, Middlesex, 1966).

Daniel-Rops, H., *Cathedral and Crusade,* trans. J. Warrington (E. P. Dutton & Co, Inc., New York, 1957).

————, *The Protestant Reformation,* trans. A. Butler (J. M. Dent & Sons Ltd., London, 1970).

————, *The Catholic Reformation,* trans. J. Warrington (J. M. Dent & Sons Ltd, London, 1962).

————, *The Church in the Seventeenth Century,* trans. J. Buckingham (J. M. Dent & Sons Ltd, London, 1963).

————, *The Church in the Eighteenth Century,* trans. J. Warrington (J. M. Dent & Sons Ltd, London, 1964).

————, *The Church in an Age of Revolution,* trans. J. Warrington (J. M. Dent & Sons Ltd, London, 1965).

————, *A Fight for God,* trans. J. Warrington (J. M. Dent & Sons Ltd, London, 1966).

Daniélou, Jean, SJ, *From Shadows to Reality: Studies in the Biblical Typology of the Fathers,* trans. W. Hibberd (Burns & Oates, London, 1960).

Daniélou, J., and H. Marrou, *The Christian Centuries,* vol. 1, (Darton, Longman & Todd, London, 1964).

Davies, Norman, *Europe: A History* (Pimlico, London, 1997).

Dawson, Christopher, *Progress and Religion* (Sheed & Ward, London, 1938).

————, *The Judgement of the Nations* (Sheed & Ward, London, 1943).

————, *The Making of Europe* (Sheed & Ward, London, 1946).

————, *Understanding Europe* (Sheed & Ward, London, 1952).

————, *The Dynamics of World History* (Sheed & Ward, London, 1957).

————, *Religion and the Rise of Western Culture* (Image Books, New York, 1958).

————, *The Historic Reality of Christian Culture* (Routledge & Kegan Paul, London, 1960).

————, *The Dividing of Europe* (Sheed & Ward, New York, 1965).

————, *The Gods of Revolution* (Sidgwick & Jackson, London, 1972).

De la Sainte Trinité, Frère Michel, *The Whole Truth about Fatima*, vol. 3, *The Third Secret* (Immaculate Heart Publications, Buffalo, 1990).

De Lubac, Henri, SJ, *Medieval Exegesis*, vol. 1, *The Four Senses of Scripture* (T & T Clark, Edinburgh, 1998).

De Marchi, John, IMC, *Fatima from the beginning*, trans. I. M. Kingsbury (Missões Consolata, Fatima, 1983).

De Montfort, St Louis, *True Devotion to the Blessed Virgin* (Montfort Press, Liverpool, 1976).

De Saint-Pierre, Michel, *Bernadette and Lourdes* (Hutchinson, London, 1954).

De Torre, Joseph, *Christian Philosophy* (Vera-Reyes, Inc., Manilla, 1981).

Deery, Mgr Joseph, *Our Lady of Lourdes* (Browne & Nolan, Dublin, 1958).

Delaney, John, ed., *A Woman clothed with the Sun* (Doubleday, New York, 1961).

Demarest, D., and C. Taylor, eds, *The Dark Virgin: the Book of Our Lady of Guadalupe* (Coley Taylor, New York, 1956).

Dirvin, Joseph, CM, *Saint Catherine Labouré of the Miraculous Medal* (TAN Books and Publishers, Rockford, 1984).

Fanfani, Amintore, *Catholicism, Protestantism and Capitalism* (Sheed & Ward, London, 1935).

Farmer, W. R., "State Interesse and Marcan Priority," in *The Four Gospels: 1992*, vol. 3, ed. F. van Segbroeck et al. (Leuven University Press, 1992).

Fox, Fr Robert, *Rediscovering Fatima* (Our Sunday Visitor, Inc., Huntington, 1982).

————, *Fatima Today* (Christendom, Front Royal, 1983).

————, *The Collegial Consecration of Russia is Accomplished* (Augustine Publishing Company, Devon, 1990).

Freithoff, C., *Complete Mariology* (Blackfriars, London, 1958).

Gambero, Luigi, SM, *Mary and the Fathers of the Church,* trans. T. Buffer (Ignatius Press, San Francisco, 1999).

Garrigou-Lagrange, Reginald, OP, *The Three Ages of the Interior Life,* 2 vols, trans. Sr M. Timothea Doyle (B. Herder Book Co., St. Louis, 1948).

————, *The Mother of the Saviour,* trans. Fr B. Kelly (TAN Books and Publishers, Rockford, 1993).

Gay, Peter, and R. K. Webb, *Modern Europe Since 1815* (Harper & Row, New York, 1973).

Gillett, H. M., *Famous Shrines of Our Lady,* vol. 1 (Samuel Walker, London, 1961).

————, *Famous Shrines of Our Lady,* vol. 2, (Samuel Walker, London, 1960).

Graef, Hilda, *Mary: A History of Doctrine and Devotion* (Sheed & Ward, London, 1994).

Haffert, John M., *Meet the Witnesses* (AMI International Press, Fatima, 1961).

Hales, E.E.Y., *The Catholic Church in the Modern World* (Eyre & Spottiswoode, London, 1958).

Hazard, Paul, *The European Mind (1680–1715)* (Hollis & Carter, London, 1953).

Hearder, Harry, *Europe in the Nineteenth Century, 1830–1880* (Longman, London, 1988).

Hebermann, Charles, et al., eds, *The Catholic Encyclopedia,* 15 vols., (The Encyclopedia Press Inc., New York, 1913).

Hitchcock, James, *What is Secular Humanism?* (RC Books, Harrison, 1982).

Hollis, Christopher, The *Breakdown of Money* (Sheed & Ward, London, 1934).

Jacob, Margaret C., *The Radical Enlightenment: Pantheists, Freemasons and Republicans* (George Allen & Unwin, London, 1981).

Jaki, Fr Stanley L., *God and the Sun at Fatima* (Real View Books, Royal Oak, 1999).

Janelle, Pierre, *The Catholic Reformation* (Collier–Macmillan, London, 1971).

Jaouen, Fr Jean, *A Grace called La Salette,* trans. N. Théroux (La Salette Publications, Attleboro, 1991).

Jelly, Fr Frederick M., OP, "Discerning the Miraculous: Norms for Judging Apparitions and Private Revelations," *Marian Studies* 44 (1993).

John Paul II, Pope, *Crossing the Threshold of Hope,* ed. Vittorio Messori, trans. J. and M. McPhee, (Jonathan Cape, London, 1994).

Johnson, Kevin Orlin, *Apparitions: Mystic Phenomena and what they mean* (Panagaeus Press, Dallas, 1998).

Johnson, Paul, *Modern Times: The World from the Twenties to the Eighties* (Harper & Row, New York, 1983).

Johnston, Francis, *Fatima: the Great Sign* (Augustine Publishing Company, Devon, 1980).

———, *Alexandrina, The Agony and the Glory* (TAN Books and Publishers, Rockford, 1982).

———, *The Wonder of Guadalupe* (Augustine Publishing Company, Devon, 1981).

Joseph de Sainte-Marie, OCD, *Reflections on the Act of Consecration at Fatima of Pope John Paul II on 13th May 1982,* trans. W. Lawson (Augustine Publishing Company, Devon, 1983).

Kavelage, Francis Mary, Br, *A Handbook on Guadalupe* (Academy of the Immaculate, New Bedford, 1997).

———, *Marian Shrines of Italy* (Academy of the Immaculate, New Bedford, 2000).

Knowles, D., and D. Obolensky, *The Christian Centuries,* vol. 2, *The Middle Ages* (Darton, Longman & Todd, London, 1969).

Knox, Ronald, Mgr, *Occasional Sermons,* ed. Philip Caraman (Burns & Oates, London, 1960).

Kondor, Fr Louis, ed., *Fatima in Lucia's own words* (Postulation Centre, Fatima, 1976).

Kselman, Thomas, *Miracles and Prophecies in Nineteenth-Century France* (Rutgers University Press, New Brunswick, 1983).

Lampe, G.W.H., and K.J. Woollcombe, *Essays on Typology,* Part 1," The Reasonableness of Typology," G.W.H. Lampe; Part 2, "The Biblical Origins and Patristic Development of Typology," K.J. Woollcombe (SCM Press, London, 1957).

Laurentin, Réne, *Bernadette of Lourdes,* trans. J. Drury (Darton, Longman & Todd, London, 1980).

———, *The Life of Catherine Labouré,* trans. P. Inwood (Collins, London, 1983).

———, *The Apparitions of the Blessed Virgin Today* (Veritas Publications, Dublin, 1991).

Laurentin, R., and A. Durand, *Pontmain Histoire Authentique, Un Signe dans le Ciel* (Apostolat des Editions & P. Lethielleux, Paris, 1971).

Leies, H., *Mother for a New World: Our Lady of Guadalupe* (Newman Press, Maryland, 1964).

Lochet, Louis, *Apparitions of Our Lady, Their Place in the life of the Church* (Herder, Freiburg, 1960).

Manelli, Stefano M., FFI, *All Generations Shall Call Me Blessed: Biblical Mariology*, trans. Peter Damian Fehlner, FFI, (Academy of the Immaculate, New Bedford, 1995).

Mangiapan, Thomas, *Lourdes: Miraculous Cures* (Lourdes, 1987).

Manteau-Bonamy, Fr H. M., OP, *Immaculate Conception and the Holy Spirit: The Marian Teachings of Father Kolbe* (Prow Books/Franciscan Marytown Press, Libertyville, 1977).

Martins, Fr Antonio, SJ, *Fatima, Way of Peace*, (Augustine Publishing Company, Devon, 1989).

Martins, Fr A.M., SJ, and Fr Robert Fox, *Documents on Fatima and The Memoirs of Sister Lucia* (Fatima Family Apostolate, Alexandria, 1992), trans. of *Novos Documentos de Fatima*, (Porto, 1984).

McAlister, L., *Spain and Portugal in the New World, 1492–1700* (University of Minnesota Press, Minneapolis, 1984).

McVey, Kathleen E., trans. *Ephrem the Syrian, Hymns* (Paulist Press, New York, 1989).

Meyer M., and W. Sherman, *The Course of Mexican History* (Oxford University Press, New York, 1983).

Michalenko, Sr Sophia, *Mercy my Mission* (Divine Mercy Publications, Dublin, 1987).

Miller, Elliot and Kenneth R. Samples, *The Cult of the Virgin: Catholic Mariology and the Apparitions of Mary* (Baker Book House Company, Grand Rapids, 1994).

Miller, Rev. Frederick, ed., *Exploring Fatima* (AMI Press, New Jersey, 1989).

——, *The Significance of Fatima* (AMI Press, Washington, 1993).

Molland, Einar, *Christendom* (A.R. Mowbray & Co. Limited, London, 1961).

Most, William G., *Mary in our Life* (The Mercier Press, Cork, 1955).

Nichols, Aidan, OP, *Catholic Thought since the Enlightenment, A Survey* (Unisa Press, Pretoria, 1988).

Norton, Mabel, *Eye Witness at Fatima* (Macmillan & Co., Limited, London, 1950).

O'Carroll, Michael, CSSp, *Theotokos: A Theological Encyclopedia of the Blessed Virgin Mary* (The Liturgical Press, Collegeville, 1990).

Orchard, Dom Bernard, et al., *A Catholic Commentary on Holy Scripture* (Thomas Nelson & Sons, London, 1960).

Outram, Dorinda, *The Enlightenment* (Cambridge University Press, Cambridge, 1995).

Palmer, Paul F., SJ, *Mary in the Documents of the Church* (Burns Oates, London, 1953).

Peyret, Rev. Raymond, *Marthe Robin, The Cross and the Joy*, trans. Clare Will Faulhaber (Alba House, New York, 1983).

Poulain, A., *The Graces of Interior Prayer* (Kegan Paul, London, 1912).

Rahner, Fr Karl, SJ, *Visions and Prophecies*, trans. C. Henkey and R. Strachan (Burns & Oates, London, 1963).

Ramsey, Boniface, OP, *Beginning to Read the Fathers* (Darton, Longman & Todd, London, 1986).

Randall, J., *The Making of the Modern Mind* (Columbia University Press, New York, 1976).

Ranwez, Mgsr Edouard, "The Value of the Episcopal Declarations concerning the events at Beauraing," in *Marian Library Studies*, No. 96 (Marian Library, Dayton, 1963).

Richard, Fr M., *What Happened at Pontmain* (Ave Maria Institute, Washington, 1971).

Roberts, J. M., *The Triumph of the West* (British Broadcasting Corporation, London, 1985).

———, *Europe: 1880–1945* (Longman, London, 1989).

Rusher, W., ed., *The Ambiguous Legacy of the Enlightenment* (University Press of America, Lanham, 1995).

Rynne, Catherine, *Knock 1879–1979* (Veritas, Dublin, 1979).

Sharkey, Don, *The Woman Shall Conquer* (The Bruce Publishing Company, Milwaukee, 1952).

Sharkey, D., and J. Debergh, *Our Lady of Beauraing* (Abbey Press, Indiana, 1973).

Smith, Jody Brant, *The Image of Guadalupe* (Mercer University Press, Macon, 1994).

Steinmueller, John, and Kathryn Sullivan, *Catholic Biblical Encyclopedia, Old Testament* (Wagner, New York, 1959).

Tanquery, A., *The Spiritual Life, A Treatise on Ascetical and Mystical Theology* (Desclée, Belgium, 1950).

Tawney, R. H., *Religion and the Rise of Capitalism* (Penguin, Middlesex, 1966).

Tindal-Robertson, Timothy, *Fatima, Russia and Pope John Paul II*, Revised Edition (Gracewing, Leominster, 1998).

———, *Message of Fatima* (Catholic Truth Society, London, 1998).

Toussaint, F., and C. Joset, *Beauraing, Les apparitions*, (Desclée De Brouwer, 1981).

Trochu, Francis, *The Curé d'Ars* (Burns, Oates & Washbourne, London, 1949).

Ullathorne, Archbishop William, *The Holy Mountain of La Salette* (Preserving Christian Publications, Albany, 1996).

Verheylezoon, Fr Louis, SJ, *Devotion to the Sacred Heart* (TAN Books and Publishers, Rockford, 1978).

Vidler, Alec, *The Church in an Age of Revolution* (Penguin, Middlesex, 1971).

von Hildebrand, Dietrich, *Trojan Horse in the City of God* (Sands & Co. Ltd., London, 1969).

Walsh, Rev. Michael, *The Apparition at Knock* (St Jarlath's College, Tuam, 1959).

Walsh, William Thomas, *Our Lady of Fatima* (The Macmillan Company, New York, 1948).

Weigel, George, *Witness to Hope: The Biography of Pope John Paul II* (Cliff Street Books, New York, 1999).

Wuillaume, L., SJ, *Banneux: a message for our time* (Banneux Shrine, Banneux, 1995).

Zimdars-Swartz, Sandra, *Encountering Mary: From La Salette to Medjugorje* (Princeton University Press, Princeton, 1991).

Index